Charles Tennant Couper

Report of the trial of the dynamitards, Terence M'Dermott : before the High Court of Justiciary, at Edinburgh December 17th 21st, 1883, for treason-felony

Charles Tennant Couper

Report of the trial of the dynamitards, Terence M'Dermott : before the High Court of Justiciary, at Edinburgh December 17th 21st, 1883, for treason-felony

ISBN/EAN: 9783337156893

Printed in Europe, USA, Canada, Australia, Japan

Cover: Foto ©Suzi / pixelio.de

More available books at **www.hansebooks.com**

REPORT

OF THE

OF THE DYNAMITAR

REPORT

OF THE

TRIAL OF THE DYNAMITARDS,

TERENCE M'DERMOTT, THOMAS DEVANY,
PETER CALLAGHAN OR KELLOCHAN, HENRY M'CANN,
JAMES M'CULLAGH OR M'CULLOCH,
JAMES DONNELLY, JAMES KELLY, PATRICK M'CABE,
PATRICK DRUM, DENIS CASEY,

BEFORE THE

HIGH COURT OF JUSTICIARY, AT EDINBURGH,

DECEMBER 17TH, 18TH, 19TH, 20TH, AND 21ST, 1883,

For Treason-Felony, under the Statute 11 *Vict. Cap.* 12, *Section* 3,
*or otherwise Conspiracy to effect an Alteration of the Laws
and Constitution of the Realm by Force*

BY

CHARLES TENNANT COUPER,
ADVOCATE.

EDINBURGH:
WILLIAM GREEN,
Law Publisher.

1884.

NOTE BY THE EDITOR.

In the following pages the Reporter has endeavoured to lay before the public and the profession a full and accurate report of the trial of the ten Dynamitards, which took place before the High Court of Justiciary at Edinburgh upon the 17th, 18th, 19th, 20th, and 21st December 1883.

The case presents a new phase of crime, and the charge is the second only that has in Scotland been brought under the Treason Felony Act, the first being that against the Chartists, James Cumming and others, before the High Court of Justiciary on 7th November 1848, reported in the Justiciary Reports by Mr. John Shaw at page 17.

The trial is also the third only that has taken place in Great Britain upon a charge involving the illegal use of dynamite, the other two being that of Thomas Gallachar, Alfred Whitehead, and others, before the Central Criminal Court at London on 11th, 12th, 13th, and 14th June 1883, and the trial of Timothy Featherstone and others before the Assizes at Liverpool on 7th, 8th, and 9th August in the same year. Much of the evidence adduced at the latter, from having been readduced at the present trial, will be found reported in these pages, with the addition of some very able and interesting scientific evidence, the result of previous experience and of investigations and experiments made with reference to this trial.

The Reporter desires here to acknowledge the facilities afforded to him by the Bench and the Counsel engaged on both sides of the Bar.

The Lord Justice-Clerk has favoured him by revising his Charge to the Jury, and the Lord Advocate and the other Counsel engaged at the trial have done him the favour of revising their speeches.

EDINBURGH, 3 CHARLOTTE SQUARE,
23rd May 1884.

CONTENTS.

	PAGE
Indictment,	2
Inventory of Productions,	12
List of Witnesses,	18
List of Jurymen,	24

EVIDENCE FOR THE CROWN.

		PAGE
1.	J. M. Gibson,	25
2.	Wm. Key,	28
3.	Thos. Butler,	29
4.	Gavin Laurie,	30
5.	G. Longmuir,	31
6.	R. Aitken,	31
7.	Mrs. M'Kersie,	33
8.	Jessie M'Kersie,	33
9.	Margaret Smith,	34
10.	J. Davidson,	35
11.	Jas. M'Murray,	35
12.	C. Simpson,	35
13.	Adam Barr,	35
14.	Arch. Barr,	37
15.	J. Anderson,	37
16.	Thos. Frater,	38
17.	D. Ferguson,	38
18.	G. Murray,	38
19.	Thos. Smith,	39
20.	Jas. Long,	40
21.	John Lambie,	41
22.	John Boyd,	43
23.	Colonel Majendie,	43
24.	John Horan,	54
25.	Geo. Hughes,	56
26.	William Porter,	69

CONTENTS.

	PAGE
27. Thomas M'Ginnes,	71
28. John Niven,	71
29. W. M'Elhinny,	72
30. Mrs. Mitchell,	72
31. John Mitchell,	73
32. J. B. Guthrie,	74
33. J. Ballingall,	75
34. James Montgomery,	75
35. Alexander Reid,	77
36. John Inglis,	77
37. James Johnston,	77
38. James Armstrong,	78
39. James Steel,	80
40. James Haire,	80
41. Levi Barrow,	80
42. Thomas Sutherland,	81
43. C. Johnston,	81
44. Mrs. M'Lachlan,	81
45. Christina Colquhoun,	83
46. Mrs. Bain,	83
47. R. Munro,	83
48. M. M'Cullough,	84
49. M. Buchanan,	85
50. John Getty,	86
51. James Gillick,	87
52. George Steed,	88
53. A. Campbell,	88
54. Archibald Carmichael,	89, 109
55. William Dreghorn,	90
56. C. J. Danchert,	91
57. F. Scannel,	92
58. R. F. Starkie,	92
59. Thomas Shannon,	94
60. George Marsh,	95, 98
61. George Williams,	96
62. R. Carleton,	96
63. J. S. Peake,	97
64. J. Schonman,	98
65. J. G. Littlechild,	99
66. Ebenezer Mears,	101
67. Fred. Lawley,	101
68. Alfred L. Foster,	101
69. J. C. Brown,	101
70. August Dupré,	106
71. D. Sutherland,	110
72. John Neil,	111
73. John Elliott,	111
74. James Chesney,	111
75. P. Murphy,	111
76. G. H. Chapman,	112
77. William Lamie,	112

DECLARATIONS.

		PAGE
Terence M'Dermott's Declaration,	. .	116
Thomas Devany's ,,	. .	117
Peter Callaghan's ,,	. .	118
Henry M'Cann's ,,	. .	119
James M'Cullagh's ,, (First)	.	120
,, ,, ,, (Second)	.	122
James Donnelly's ,,	.	123
James Kelly's ,,	.	124
Patrick M'Cabe's ,,	.	125
Patrick Drum's ,,	.	126
Denis Casey's ,,	.	126

EVIDENCE FOR TERENCE M'DERMOTT.

1. John Hesson, ... 127
2. Andrew Logan, ... 127
3. James Campbell, ... 128
4. M. M'Dermott, ... 128
5. Mrs. Elizabeth M'Dermott, . 129
6. P. M'Dermott, . . . 130

EVIDENCE FOR PETER CALLAGHAN.

7. Ann Callaghan, . . 130
8. P. Callaghan, . . 131
9. M. Callaghan, . . 131

EVIDENCE FOR JAMES DONNELLY.

10. P. M'Kenna, . . . 131

EVIDENCE FOR PATRICK M'CABE.

11. M. M'Cabe, . 132
12. C. M'Cabe, . 132
13. Mrs. Freeman, . 132
14. James Freeman, 133

EVIDENCE FOR DENIS CASEY.

15. Rose Casey, 133

EVIDENCE FOR HENRY M'CANN.

16. John M'Cann, . . 133
17. Mrs. M'Cann, . 134
18. Mrs. Barclay, . 134
19. Rev. M. M'Ginn, 135

CONTENTS.

EVIDENCE FOR PATRICK DRUM.

	PAGE
20. Mrs. O'Brien,	136
21. Henry O'Brien,	137
22. Mrs. Stewart,	138
23. Francis Canning,	138
24. Dr. Sutherland,	138

GENERAL EVIDENCE IN DEFENCE.

25. James Cogans,	138
26. Patrick M'Kenna,	139
27. John Ward,	140
Address by the Lord Advocate,	141
,, by Mr. Rhind,	193
,, ,, Mr. Kennedy,	205
,, ,, Mr. Orr,	223
,, ,, Mr. Guthrie,	229
Charge to the Jury by the Lord Justice-Clerk,	232
Verdict,	253
Sentence	254

THE TRIAL.

HIGH COURT OF JUSTICIARY
AT EDINBURGH.

DECEMBER 17, 18, 19, 20, AND 21, 1883.

Judges Present—

THE RIGHT HONOURABLE THE LORD JUSTICE-CLERK.
THE HONOURABLE LORD MURE.
THE HONOURABLE LORD CRAIGHILL.

TRIAL
AT THE INSTANCE OF

HER MAJESTY'S ADVOCATE as Public Prosecutor.

Counsel: *The Lord Advocate (The Right Honourable John Blair Balfour); David Brand, Advocate-Depute; Æneas J. G. Mackay, Advocate-Depute.*
Crown Agent: *Charles B. Logan, W.S.*

Against—

TERENCE M'DERMOTT.—Counsel: *John Rhind, J. R. Baxter,* and *J. F. Maclennan.*
THOMAS DEVANY.—Counsel: *John Rhind, J. R. Baxter,* and *J. F. Maclennan.*
PETER CALLAGHAN or KELLOCHAN.—Counsel: *John Rhind, J. R. Baxter,* and *J. F. Maclennan.*
HENRY M'CANN.—Counsel: *N. J. D. Kennedy.*
JAMES M'CULLAGH or M'CULLOCH.—Counsel: *R. L. Orr.*
JAMES DONNELLY.—Counsel: *John Rhind, J. R. Baxter,* and *J. F. Maclennan.*
JAMES KELLY.—Counsel: *John Rhind, J. R. Baxter,* and *J. F. Maclennan.*
PATRICK M'CABE.—Counsel: *John Rhind, J. R. Baxter,* and *J. F. Maclennan.*
PATRICK DRUM.—Counsel: *C. J. Guthrie* and *W. D. Lyell.*
DENIS CASEY.—Counsel: *John Rhind, J. R. Baxter,* and *J. F. Maclennan.*

Agents for M'DERMOTT, DEVANY, CALLAGHAN, DONNELLY, KELLY, M'CABE, and CASEY: *William Officer, S.S.C., Edinburgh,* and *Joseph Shaughnessy, Writer, Glasgow.*
Agents for M'CANN, M'CULLAGH, and DRUM: *A. S. & J. Drummond, Writers, Glasgow.*

The following indictment was duly served upon each of the accused:—

TERENCE M'DERMOTT, now or lately hammerman or chemical worker, and lately residing in or near Doblie's Loan, Glasgow, THOMAS DEVANY, now or lately quay labourer, and lately residing in or near Portugal Lane, South Side, Glasgow, PETER CALLAGHAN or KELLOCHAN, now or lately labourer, and lately residing in or near Rose Street, South Side, Glasgow, HENRY M'CANN, now or lately boot and shoe maker, and lately residing in or near Stirling Street, Glasgow, JAMES M'CULLAGH or M'CULLOCH, now or lately chemical worker, formerly residing in Glasgow, and lately residing in or near Cuthbert Street, Hebburn-on-Tyne, JAMES DONNELLY, now or lately labourer or chemical worker, and lately residing in or near Villiers Street, Glasgow, JAMES KELLY, now or lately hammerman, and lately residing in or near Kirk Street, Calton, Glasgow, PATRICK M'CABE, now or lately general dealer, and lately residing in or near Rose Street, South Side, Glasgow, PATRICK DRUM, now or lately hawker, and lately residing in or near Rose Street, South Side, Glasgow, and DENIS CASEY, now or lately scavenger, and lately residing in or near Kirk Street, Calton, Glasgow, all now or lately prisoners in the Duke Street Prison of Glasgow, you are indicted and accused, at the instance of The Right Honourable John Blair Balfour, Her Majesty's Advocate for Her Majesty's interest: THAT ALBEIT, by an Act passed in the eleventh year of the reign of Her Majesty Queen Victoria, Chapter twelve, entituled "An Act for the Better Security of the Crown and Government of the United Kingdom," it is by section third of the said Act enacted "That if any person whatsoever, after the passing of this Act, shall, within the United Kingdom or without, compass, imagine, invent, devise, or intend to deprive or depose Our Most Gracious Lady the Queen, Her heirs or successors, from the style, honour, or Royal name of the Imperial Crown of the United Kingdom, or of any other of Her Majesty's dominions and countries, or to levy war against Her Majesty, Her heirs or successors, within any part of the United Kingdom, in order, by force or constraint, to compel Her or them to change Her or their measures or counsels, or in order to put any force or constraint upon, or in order to intimidate or overawe, both Houses, or either House of Parliament, or to move or stir any foreigner or stranger with force to invade the United Kingdom, or any other Her Majesty's dominions or countries under the obeisance of Her Majesty, Her heirs or successors, and such compassings, imaginations, inventions, devices, or intentions, or any of them, shall express, utter, or declare by publishing any printing or writing, or by open and advised speaking, or by any overt act or deed, every person so offending shall be guilty of felony, and being convicted thereof, shall be liable at the discretion of the Court to be transported beyond the seas for the term of his or her natural life, or for any term not less than seven years, or to be imprisoned for any term not exceeding two years, with or without hard labour, as the Court shall direct:" AND ALBEIT, by the laws of this, and of every other well-governed realm, the wickedly and feloniously conspiring to effect an alteration of the laws and constitution of the realm, by force and violence, is a crime of an heinous nature, and severely punishable: YET TRUE IT IS AND OF VERITY, that you the said Terence M'Dermott, Thomas Devany, Peter Callaghan or Kellochan, Henry M'Cann, James M'Cullagh or M'Culloch, James Donnelly, James Kelly, Patrick M'Cabe, Patrick Drum, and Denis Casey are, all and each or one or more of you, guilty of the statutory crime and felony above libelled, or of the crime of conspiracy at common law above libelled, actors or actor, or art and part: IN SO FAR AS, you being, all and each or one or more of you, members of a secret ribbon society, or other secret society or combination in Glasgow, having for or amongst its objects and purposes the unlawful and criminal objects and purposes of subverting and overthrowing by force and violence, the power and authority of Her Majesty the Queen in that part of the United Kingdom called Ireland, and of compelling or constraining, by force and violence, Her said Majesty to change Her measures or counsels relating to the constitution or government of that part of the United Kingdom called Ireland, and of compelling or constraining by force and violence both Houses or either House of Parliament with regard to their or its measures or legislation relating to that part of the United Kingdom called Ireland, and acting in concert with Edmond O'Brien Kennedy otherwise called Timothy Featherstone, now or lately prisoner in the convict prison at Chatham, who in furtherance of the unlawful and criminal objects and purposes foresaid, in the course of the years 1882 and 1883, at Cork, and other places to the prosecutor unknown in Ireland or England, gave to divers persons, having the same objects and purposes, instructions or aid in the manufacture and use of dynamite and other explosive substances, and as to the mode of exploding the same at or near public or other buildings in Liverpool, London, and other cities in the United Kingdom, and who was in Glasgow during the period between the month of June 1882 and the month of February 1883, or part thereof, and there and then gave instructions or aid to all and each or one or more of you in the manufacture and use of dynamite and other explosive substances, and as to the mode of exploding the same, and also acting in concert with John Henry O'Connor otherwise called Henry Dalton, now or lately prisoner in the convict prison at Chatham, who in furtherance of the unlawful and criminal objects and purposes foresaid, during the months of March and April 1883, in London and other places in England to the prosecutor unknown, gave to divers persons, having the same objects and purposes, instructions or aid in the manufacture and use of dynamite and other explosive substances, and as to the mode of exploding the same at or near public or other buildings in Liverpool, London, and other cities in the United Kingdom, and who was in Glasgow during the said month of March 1883, or part thereof, and gave instructions and aid to all and each or one or more of you in the manufacture and use of dynamite and other explosive substances, and as to the mode of exploding the same; and aided and abetted by John Francis Kearney, formerly signalman at or near the Buchanan Street Station at Glasgow of the Caledonian Railway Company, who has absconded and fled from justice, and whose present address is to the prosecutor unknown, and by divers other persons to the prosecutor unknown, you the said Terence M'Dermott, Thomas Devany, Peter Callaghan or Kellochan, Henry M'Cann, James M'Cullagh or M'Culloch, James Donnelly, James Kelly, Patrick M'Cabe, Patrick Drum, and Denis Casey did, all and each or one or more of you,

> During the period between the month of July 1882 and the month of March 1883, both inclusive, the time or times being to the prosecutor more particularly unknown, and as regards the several overt acts or deeds hereinafter libelled during the period or on or about the dates hereinafter severally specified,

in or near Jail Square, and in or near Saltmarket, Glasgow, and in or near the public green of Glasgow called Glasgow Green, and in or near the public house then and now or lately kept by James Lennox, publican, in or near Saltmarket, Glasgow, and in or near the public house then and now or lately kept by Thomas M'Ginn, in or near Bridgegate, Glasgow, and in or near the stables or other premises in or near Market Street, City, Glasgow, then and now or lately occupied by George Hughes, fruit merchant, now or lately residing in or near Thistle Street, Hutchesontown, Glasgow, and in or near the hall commonly called the Democratic Hall, in or near Nelson Street, City, Glasgow, and in or near Garngad Road, Glasgow, or in one or more of said places, or in some other place or places in or near Glasgow to the prosecutor unknown, wickedly and feloniously, compass, imagine, invent, devise, or intend to levy war against Her Majesty, Her heirs or successors, within that part of the United Kingdom called Scotland, in order by force or constraint to compel Her to change Her measures or counsels, or in order to intimidate or overawe both Houses or either House of Parliament; and such compassings, imaginations, inventions, devices, or intentions, you the said Terence M'Dermott, Thomas Devany, Peter Callaghan or Kellochan, Henry M'Cann, James M'Cullagh or M'Culloch, James Donnelly, James Kelly, Patrick M'Cabe, Patrick Drum, and Denis Casey, all and each or one or more of you, did express, utter, or declare by the following overt acts or deeds, or one or more of them, that is to say—(First), by wickedly and feloniously meeting and conspiring together on numerous occasions with each other, and with the said Edmund O'Brien Kennedy otherwise called Timothy Featherstone, the said John Henry O'Connor otherwise called Henry Dalton, and the said John Francis Kearney, or one or more of them, and other persons to the prosecutor unknown,

During the period between the month of July 1882 and the month of March 1883, both inclusive,

in or near the places specially above libelled, or one or more of them, or at some other place or places in or near Glasgow to the prosecutor unknown, the time or times and the place or places being to the prosecutor more particularly unknown in respect of the secret character and objects of such conspiracy, for and concerning the secret purchasing or procuring of chemical or other materials to be used in the preparation or manufacture of dynamite, lignin-dynamite, or other explosive substance or substances, and the secret preparation or manufacture of dynamite, lignin-dynamite, or other explosive substance or substances, and for and concerning the clandestine laying or placing and exploding by you, or one or more of you, or by your agents and abettors to the prosecutor unknown, of the said dynamite, lignin-dynamite, or other explosive substance or substances, at or near public buildings or buildings used for the service of the public, or other buildings or works in or near Glasgow, with the wicked and felonious intent and design of destroying or seriously injuring the said buildings or works and of endangering the lives, persons, and property of the lieges, and with the further wicked and felonious intent and design, by means of such explosions and the terror and alarm to be thereby created in the minds of Her said Majesty and Her lieges, of compelling Her said Majesty to change Her measures or counsels, or of intimidating or overawing both Houses or either House of Parliament, and that more particularly with regard to Her, their, or its measures or counsels or legislation relating to the Constitution or Government of that part of the United Kingdom called Ireland: (Second), by you, or one or more of you, wickedly and feloniously laying or placing and exploding, or causing to be laid or placed and exploded, by some person or persons to the prosecutor unknown acting upon your instructions, or the instructions of one or more of you,

On or about the 20th day of January 1883 (Sunday),

a quantity of dynamite, lignin-dynamite, or other explosive substance or substances to the prosecutor unknown, and with an apparatus adapted and prepared for exploding the same, beside or near an iron or other metal building, being a gasometer or gas-holder, and then containing 350,000 or thereby cubic feet of gas, situated at or near Lilybank Road, in or near Glasgow, the property of the Lord Provost, Magistrates, and Council of the City of Glasgow, by means of which explosion the said gasometer or gas-holder was rent and broken in several or one or more places, and the gas therein was ignited, and the flames of the said ignited gas having spread to the house in or near Muirhouse Lane, then and now or lately occupied by Thomas Butler, carter, as well as other houses in or near the said Lane, and in the vicinity of the said gasometer or gasholder, the said Thomas Butler, Mrs. Mary M'Nickle or Butler, his wife, and Edward Hughes, dealer, residing in Muirhouse Lane aforesaid, who were all at the time of the said explosion in or near the house of the said Thomas Butler, were scorched and burnt, or otherwise seriously injured; and by the shock and violence of the said explosion, the windows of several of the said houses were broken, the locked or otherwise closed doors of one or more of the said houses were violently forced inwards or broken, and various moveable articles in one or more of the said houses were thrown down and broken: (Third), by you, or one or more of you, wickedly and feloniously laying or placing and exploding, or causing to be laid or placed and exploded, by some person or persons to the prosecutor unknown acting upon your instructions, or the instructions of one or more of you,

On or about the 20th and 21st days of January 1883 (Saturday and Sunday), or one or other of said days,

an oval-shaped tin or other box or machine, containing dynamite, lignin-dynamite, or other explosive substance, and an apparatus adapted and prepared for exploding the same, on or near the bridge or aqueduct by which the Forth and Clyde Canal passes over the Possil Road, in or near Glasgow, with the wicked and felonious design and intent that the said box or machine and explosive substance therein, when exploded, should blow down or make breaches in or otherwise damage the walls or supports of said bridge or aqueduct, so as to allow the water of the said canal to escape and flood the streets, houses, buildings, and works in the vicinity of the said bridge or aqueduct, to their destruction or serious injury, which box or machine having been, on or about the times lastly before libelled, lifted by Adam Barr, gunner in the Royal Horse Artillery, then residing in or near Springburn Road, Glasgow, and now or lately stationed at or near Coventry, from the said bridge or aqueduct, where it had been placed by you, or one or more of you, or by some person or persons acting upon your instructions, or the instructions of one or more of you as aforesaid, with the design and intent above libelled, the explosive substance therein, or part thereof, ignited and exploded, whereby the said Adam Barr, Matthew Barr, iron-planer, then and now or lately residing in Springburn Road aforesaid, Janet Richardson or Gee, wife of George Gee, bottle-blower, and residing with him in or near Kerr Street, off Hopehill Road, Glasgow, the said George Gee and Janet Watson, pocketbook maker, then and now or lately residing in or near Balgray Brae, Springburn, in or near Glasgow, who were on or near said bridge or aqueduct at the time of the explosion foresaid, were burnt or otherwise injured in their persons: and (Fourth), by wickedly and feloniously laying or placing and exploding, or causing to be laid or placed and exploded, by the said John Francis Kearney, then signalman in the employment of the Caledonian Railway Company at or near the Buchanan Street Station in Glasgow of the said Railway, or by some person or persons to the prosecutor unknown acting upon your instructions, or the instructions of one or more of you,

On or about the 20th and 21st day of January 1883 (Saturday and Sunday), or one or other of said days,

a quantity of dynamite, lignin-dynamite, or other explosive substance, with an apparatus adapted and prepared for exploding the same, within or near to a brick or other building or shed, measuring about 29 feet in length and 15 feet in breadth, and forming part of the works or premises of the said Railway Company at or near the Buchanan Street Station foresaid, whereby the walls of said building or shed were thrown down and the materials thereof and of the roof of said building or shed were suddenly and forcibly projected in various directions; and the said several overt acts or deeds above libelled, or one or more of them, were designed and intended by you the said Terence M'Dermott, Thomas Devany, Peter Callaghan or Kellochan, Henry M'Cann, James M'Cullagh or M'Culloch, James Donnelly, James Kelly, Patrick M'Cabe, Patrick Drum, and Denis Casey, to promote or to carry out the said compassings, imaginations, inventions, devices, or intentions above libelled: OR OTHERWISE, and as alternative to the statutory charge before libelled, you the said Terence M'Dermott, Thomas Devany, Peter Callaghan or Kellochan, Henry M'Cann, James M'Cullagh or M'Culloch, James Donnelly, James Kelly, Patrick M'Cabe, Patrick Drum, and Denis Casey did, all and each or one or more of you, acting in concert with the said Edmond O'Brien Kennedy otherwise called Timothy Featherstone, the said John Henry O'Connor otherwise called Henry Dalton, and the said John Francis Kearney, or one or more of them, and divers other persons to the prosecutor unknown, wickedly and feloniously conspire to effect an alteration of the laws and constitution of the realm by force and violence,

During the period between the month of July 1882 and the month of March 1883, both inclusive, and at or near the places above libelled, or one or more of them, or at some other place or places in or near Glasgow to the prosecutor unknown,

the time or times and the place or places being to the prosecutor more particularly unknown, in respect of the secret character and objects of such conspiracy, and more particularly (First), you did, all and each or one or more of you, during the said period between the month of July 1882 and the month of March 1883, both inclusive, and at the places above libelled, or one or more of them, the time or times and the place or places being to the prosecutor more particularly unknown, enter into and carry on a conspiracy to effect an alteration of the laws and constitution of the realm, and especially of that part thereof called Ireland, and did frequently meet and consult, and did, wickedly and feloniously, conspire together with each other and the said Edmond O'Brien Kennedy otherwise called Timothy Featherstone, the said John Henry O'Connor otherwise called Henry Dalton, and the said John Francis Kearney, or one or more of them, and divers other persons to the prosecutor unknown, for and concerning the designs and purposes of the said conspiracy, and especially for and concerning the secret purchase or procuring of chemical or other materials to be used in the preparation and manufacture of dynamite, lignin-dynamite, or other explosive substance or substances, and the secret preparation or manufacture of dynamite, lignin-dynamite, or other explosive substance or substances, and for and concerning the clandestine laying or placing and exploding by you, or one or more of you, or by your agents and abettors to the prosecutor unknown, of the said dynamite, lignin-dynamite, or other explosive substance or substances, at or near public buildings, or buildings used for the service of the public, or other buildings or works in or near Glasgow, with the wicked and felonious intent and design of destroying or seriously injuring such buildings or works, and of endangering the lives, persons, and property of the lieges, and with the further wicked and felonious intent and design, by means of such explosions, and the terror and alarm to be thereby created in the minds of Her said Majesty and Her lieges, to effect an alteration of the laws and constitution of the realm, and more especially of that part thereof called Ireland, by force and violence : (Second), You did, in furtherance of the purposes of the said conspiracy, all and each or one or more of you,

On or about the 20th day of January 1883 (Saturday),

lay or place and explode, or cause to be laid or placed and exploded, by some person or persons to the prosecutor unknown acting upon your instructions, or the instructions of one or more of you, a quantity of dynamite, lignin-dynamite, or other explosive substance to the prosecutor unknown, with an apparatus adapted and prepared for exploding the same beside or near an iron or other metal building, being a gasometer or gasholder, and then containing 350,000 or thereby cubic feet of gas, situated at or near Lilybank Road, in or near Glasgow, the property of the Lord Provost, Magistrates, and Council of the City of Glasgow, by means of which explosion the said gasometer or gasholder was rent and broken in several or one or more places, and the gas therein was ignited, and the flames of the said ignited gas having spread to the house in or near Muirhouse Lane occupied by Thomas Butler, carter, as well as other houses in or near the said Lane and in the vicinity of the said gasometer or gasholder, the said Thomas Butler, Mrs. Mary M'Nickle or Butler his wife, and Edward Hughes, dealer, residing in Muirhouse Lane, who were all at the time of the said explosion in or near the house of the said Thomas Butler, were scorched and burnt, or otherwise severely injured; and by the shock and violence of the said explosion the windows of several of the said houses were broken, the locked or otherwise closed doors of one or more of the said houses were violently forced inwards or broken, and various moveable articles in one or more of the said houses were thrown down and broken: (Third), You did, in furtherance of the purposes of said conspiracy, all and each or one or more of you,

On or about the 20th and 21st day of January 1883 (Saturday or Sunday),

or on one or other of said days, wickedly and feloniously, lay or place and explode, or cause to be laid or placed and exploded, by some person or persons to the prosecutor unknown acting upon your instructions, or the instructions of one or more of you, an oval-shaped tin or other box, or machine containing dynamite, lignin-dynamite, or other explosive substance, and an apparatus adapted and prepared for exploding the same, on or near the bridge or aqueduct by which the Forth and Clyde Canal passes over the Possil Road, in or near Glasgow, with the wicked and felonious design and intent that the said tin box and explosive substance therein, when exploded, should blow down or make breaches in or otherwise damage the walls or supports of said bridge or aqueduct so as to allow the water of the said canal to escape, and flood the streets, houses, buildings, and works in the vicinity of the said bridge or aqueduct, to their destruction or serious injury, which box or machine having been, on or about the time lastly before libelled, lifted by Adam Barr, gunner in the Royal Horse Artillery, then residing in or near Springburn Road, Glasgow, and now or lately stationed at Coventry, from the said bridge or aqueduct, where it had been placed by you as aforesaid, and with the design and intent above libelled, the explosive substance therein, or part thereof, ignited and exploded, whereby the said Adam Barr, Matthew Barr, iron-planer, then and now or lately residing in Springburn Road aforesaid, Janet Richardson or Gee, now wife of George Gee, bottle-blower, and residing with him in or near Kerr Street, off City Road, Glasgow, the said George Gee, and Janet Watson, pocketbook maker, then and now or lately residing in or near Balgray Brae, Springburn, Glasgow, who were on or near said bridge or aqueduct at the time of the explosion foresaid, were burnt or otherwise injured in their persons; and (Fourth), you did, in furtherance of the purposes of said conspiracy, all and each or one or more of you,

On or about the 20th and 21st day of January 1883
(Saturday and Sunday),

or on one or other of said days, wickedly and feloniously lay or place and explode, or cause to be laid or placed and exploded by the said John Francis Kearney, then a signalman in the employment of the Caledonian Railway Company at or near the Buchanan Street Station of said Company, or by some person or persons to the prosecutor unknown acting upon your instructions or the instructions of one or more of you, a quantity of dynamite, lignin-dynamite, or other explosive substance, and an apparatus adapted and prepared for exploding the same within or near to a brick or other building or shed, measuring about 29 feet in length and 15 feet in breadth, and forming part of the works or premises of the said Caledonian Railway Company at or near the Buchanan Street Station foresaid, whereby the walls of said building or shed were thrown down and the materials thereof and of the roof of said building or shed were suddenly and forcibly projected in various directions: And you the said Terence M'Dermott having been apprehended and taken before Walter Cook Spens, Esquire, advocate, sheriff-substitute of Lanarkshire, did, in his presence, at Glasgow, on the 4th day of September 1883, emit and subscribe a declaration: And you the said Thomas Devany having been apprehended and taken before the said Walter Cook Spens, did, in his presence at Glasgow, on the 4th day of September 1883, emit a declaration, which was subscribed by him in your presence, you having declared that you could not write: And you the said Peter Callaghan or Kellochan having been apprehended and taken before the said Walter Cook Spens, did, in his presence at Glasgow, on the 4th day of September 1883, emit a declaration which was subscribed by him in your presence, you having declared that you could not write: And you the said Henry M'Cann having been apprehended and taken before the said Walter Cook Spens, did, in his presence at Glasgow, on the 4th day of September 1883, emit and subscribe a declaration: And you the said James M'Cullagh or M'Culloch having been apprehended and taken before the said Walter Cook Spens, did, in his presence at Glasgow, on the 8th and 15th days of October 1883 respectively, emit and subscribe two several declarations: And you the said James Donnelly having been apprehended and taken before the said Walter Cook Spens, did, in his presence at Glasgow, on the 4th day of September 1883, emit and subscribe a declaration: And you the said James Kelly having been apprehended and taken before the said Walter Cook Spens, did, in his presence at Glasgow, on the 4th and 19th days of September 1883 respectively, emit two several declarations, which were subscribed by him in your presence, you having declared that you could not write: And you the said Patrick M'Cabe having been apprehended and taken before the said Walter Cook Spens, did, in his presence at Glasgow, on the 4th day of September 1883, emit and subscribe a declaration: And you the said Patrick Drum having been apprehended and taken before the said Walter Cook Spens, did, in his presence at Glasgow, on the 4th day of September 1883, emit a declaration, which was subscribed by him in your presence, you having declared that you could not write: And you the said Denis Casey having been apprehended and taken before the said Walter Cook Spens, did, in his presence at Glasgow, on the 4th day of September 1883, emit a declaration, which was subscribed by him in your presence, you having declared that you could not write; Which several Declarations, being to be used in evidence against each of you, by whom the same were respectively emitted; As also the articles, books, and documents enumerated in an Inventory thereof hereunto annexed and referred to, being to be used in evidence against all and each or one or more of you, at the trial of you the said Terence M'Dermott, Thomas Devany, Peter Callaghan or Kellochan, Henry M'Cann, James M'Cullagh or M'Culloch, James Donnelly, James Kelly, Patrick M'Cabe, Patrick Drum, and Denis Casey, will, for that purpose, be in due time lodged in the hands of the Clerk of the High Court of Justiciary before which you are to be tried, that you may respectively have an opportunity of seeing the same: ALL WHICH, or part thereof, being found proven by the verdict of an Assize, or admitted by the respective judicial confessions of you the said Terence M'Dermott, Thomas Devany, Peter Callaghan or Kellochan, Henry M'Cann, James M'Cullagh or M'Culloch, James Donnelly, James Kelly, Patrick M'Cabe, Patrick Drum, and Denis Casey, before the Lord Justice-General, Lord Justice-Clerk, and Lords Commissioners of Justiciary, you the said Terence M'Dermott, Thomas Devany, Peter Callaghan or Kellochan, Henry M'Cann, James M'Cullagh or M'Culloch, James Donnelly, James Kelly, Patrick M'Cabe, Patrick Drum, and Denis Casey OUGHT to be punished with the pains of law, to deter others from committing the like crimes in all time coming.

(Signed) Æ. J. G. MACKAY, *A.D.*

INVENTORY OF ARTICLES, BOOKS, AND DOCUMENTS REFERRED TO IN THE FOREGOING INDICTMENT.

1. A Copy of Report to the Right Honourable the Secretary of State for the Home Department on the circumstances attending three Explosions which occurred in Glasgow on the night of Saturday 20th January and the morning of Sunday 21st January 1883, by Colonel V. D. Majendie, C.B., Her Majesty's Chief Inspector of Explosives.
2. Sixty-Six or thereby Pieces of Broken Metal found at or near Tradeston Gasholder, Glasgow, and Two Pieces of Tape, all more particularly described in Appendix A of the aforesaid Report.
3. A Piece of Twisted Wire.
4. A Piece of a Circular Brass Cap or Tube.
5. A Circular Brass Cap or Piece of Brass Tube.
6. A Tin Box.
7. Sample of Dark-Coloured Powdered Sawdust called Lignin-Dynamite.
8. A Brass Tube and a Brass Tap.
9. Sales Book of the firm of Clolus and Company, Ruchill Glycerine Works, Maryhill, commencing "Feby 3 1882," and still current.
10. Sales Book of the said Firm of Clolus and Company, commencing "18 March 1882," and still current.
11. Outward Order Book of Messrs. A. Hope, Junior, and Co., commencing "March 19th 1881," and ending "30th November 1882."
12. Book, entituled on outside "Cash Book A. H. Jr & Co No. 5," or with a similar title, commencing 1st December 1881, and still current.
13. Book, entituled on outside "Sales Book M'G and M'F No $\frac{2}{11}$," commencing 2nd May 1881, and still current.
14. Petty Cash Book of Messrs. M'Geachie & M'Farlane, commencing 1st Sept. 1881, and still current, and a Parcel Delivery Book of Messrs M'Geachie & M'Farlane, commencing 9th March 1880, and still current.
15. Order Book of Messrs. A. Hope, Junior, and Co., commencing "26th July 1882," and still current.
16. Outward Order Book of Messrs. A. Hope, Junior, & Co., commencing 1st December 1882, and still current.
17. Parcel Delivery Book of Messrs. A. Hope, Junior, & Co., commencing June 12, 1880, and still current, and Parcel Delivery Book of

Messrs. A. Hope, Junior, & Co., commencing 24th November 1879, and still current.

18. Book, entituled on outside "Sales Book No. 11 A H Jr & Co," or with a similar title, commencing 2nd May 1880, and ending 28th February 1883.

19. Book, entituled on outside "Day Book No 0·2 J. M & Co," or with a similar title, commencing 1st April 1881, and still current.

20. A Tin Box found at or near the premises of the "Times" newspaper, Playhouse Yard, London, on the occasion of the explosion there on 15th March 1883.

21. Manifest of the Steamer "Ballycotton," from Glasgow to Cork, on 13th December 1882.

22. Manifest of the Steamer "Cedar," from Glasgow to Cork, on 19th February 1883.

23. Manifest of the Steamer "Amsterdam," from Glasgow to Cork, 21st February 1883.

24. Manifest of the Steamer "Copeland," from Glasgow to Cork, on 2nd April 1883.

25. Book called Quay Book of the Clyde Shipping Co.

26. Clyde Shipping Company's Delivery Order, No. 10192, dated "20. 12 1882," addressed to the storekeeper, "Deliver Mr D O'Herlihy One Carboy Acid," or similarly dated and addressed.

27. Clyde Shipping Company's Delivery Order, No. 10979, dated "9. 3. 1883," addressed to the storekeeper, "Deliver Mr D O'Herlihy one carboy," or similarly dated and addressed.

28. Clyde Shipping Company's Delivery Order, No. 10835, dated "24. Feb 1883," addressed the storekeeper, "Deliver Mr D O'Herlihy one carboy Vitriol," or similarly dated and addressed.

29. Requisition Note from D. O'Herlihy to Clyde Shipping Company, dated Friday 23rd March 1883, marked E.

30. Requisition Note from D. O'Herlihy to Clyde Shipping Company, dated Friday 23rd March 1883, marked F.

31. Label on returned Empty Carboy, addressed "J. Montgomerie and Co. Manufacturing Chemists Port Dundas Glasgow," or similarly addressed.

32. Label on returned empty Carboy, addressed "Alexander Hope Jr & Co. Manufacturing Chemists Coatbridge Street Port Dundas Glasgow," or similarly addressed.

33. Requisition for Money Order by D. O'Herlihy, dated "Cork Fe 17 83," payable to "Alexander Hope & Co Glasgow."

34. Requisition for Money Order by D. O'Herlihy, dated "Cork Fe 17 83," payable to "J. Montgomerie & Co Glasgow."

35. Requisition for Money Order by D. O'Herlihy, dated "Cork Mr 29 1883," payable to "Alexander Hope Junr & Co."

36. Envelope, with Glasgow post mark of 19th February 1883, addressed "Mr D. O'Herlihy 10 Great George Street West Cork," or with a similar address.

37. Hotel Bill of the Star Temperance Hotel, Cowcaddens Street, Glasgow, dated "14 Feby 1883," and subscribed "John Mitchell," or with a similar date and subscription.

38. Letter, dated "Feb 17th 1883," addressed to "Alex.

Hope Junior & Co Man. Chem." and subscribed "D. O'Herlihy 10 Gt George St West, Cork," or similarly dated, addressed, and subscribed.

39. Letter, dated "10 Great George St West Cork Mar 29th 1883," addressed to "Alexander Hope Junior & Co," and subscribed "D. O'Herlihy," or similarly dated, addressed, and subscribed.

40. Letter, dated "Cork Feb 17th 83," addressed "J. Montgomerie & Co," and subscribed "D O'Herlihy 10 Great George St West, Cork," or similarly dated, addressed, and subscribed.

41. A Piece of Paper, with address "D O'Herlihy Ink Manufacturer 10 Gt. George St West Cork Ireland."

42. Piece of Paper, with address "Pat Flanagan at Mr Brannans 24 Convent Road Sutton," or a similar address.

43. Letter, commencing "Dear Pat," and signed "Edmond," or similarly commencing and signed.

44. Document, written on piece of paper, containing a receipt for the preparation of explosives, commencing "Dissolve bi-sulphide of carbon," or with a similar commencement.

45. Letter, dated "Cork Mar 29th 83," addressed to "J Montgomerie & Co," and subscribed "D O'Herlihy," or similarly dated, addressed, and subscribed, with Envelope addressed "J Montgomery & Co Manufacturing Chemists Port Dundas Glasgow Scotland."

46. Two Letters, dated "Cork Male Prison," and subscribed "Yours etc. Fetherstone," or similarly dated and subscribed.

47. A Small Book, containing a pencil entry "Acid Nitrick pure 1.420," or a similar entry.

48. A Pocket Book, containing various Chemical Notes and other Entries, commencing with writing on front page, "Baume's Hydrometer for liquids heavier than water."

49. A Card with addresses in pencil, "10 Gt George St West" and "J. F. K. 41 Stanhope St. G."

50. A Pocket Book, containing entries in pencil "L. 6. 3. 83," "G. 8. 3. 83," and "Ln 17. 3. 83," "M'D. 24. 3. 83," or similar entries.

51. A Pocket Book, with address "John H. O'Connor," and containing entry commencing "That where there is a circle interfered with in its working," or similarly commencing.

52. A Letter, dated "New Ireland Office Bolt Court Fleet St. London E.C. July 29th 1872," commencing "My dear O'Connor," and signed "J. P. M'Donnell," or with a similar date, commencement, and subscription.

53. A Letter, dated "London April 18th 1872," commencing "My dear John," and signed "J. P. M'Donnell," or with a similar date, commencement, and subscription.

54. A Letter, dated "Havre France On board the Erin Sunday Morning," commencing "My dear Father & Mother," and subscribed "J. H. O'Connor," or with a similar date, commencement, and subscription.

55. A Letter, dated "251 Bowery Between Stanton and Houston New York January 9th 1873," commencing "My dear Father &

INVENTORY OF PRODUCTIONS. 15

Mother," and subscribed "John H O'Connor," or with a similar date, commencement, and subscription.

56. A Letter, dated "Glasgow Scotland March 13th 1883," commencing "My dear Father & Mother," and signed "J. H. O'Connor," or with a similar date, commencement, and signature, with relative Envelope.

57. A Receipt signed "H. Dalton," or with a similar signature.

58. A Deal Box.

59. Two Tin Boxes.

60. Three Brass Tubes.

61. A Bottle containing Sulphuric Acid.

62. A Packet of Chlorate of Potash.

63. A Packet of Powdered Sugar.

64. A Piece of Red Orpiment.

65. A Sample of Dynamite found in the two Tin Boxes foresaid.

66. A Revolver, a Box of Cartridges, a Tin Canister containing Powdered Sugar and Chlorate of Potash mixed, a Bottle containing Sulphuric Acid, and a False Beard.

67. A Glass Test Tube.

68. A Packet or Parcel of Red Orpiment.

69. A Copy of the Report to the Right Honourable the Secretary of State for the Home Department on the circumstances attending two Explosions which occurred in London on night of the 15th March 1883 at the offices of the Local Government Board in Whitehall and at the "Times" Newspaper office in Playhouse Yard respectively, by Colonel V. D. Majendie, C.B., H.M. Chief Inspector of Explosives.

70. Report, dated "February 9/1883," on sample 945, and signed "A Dupré," or similarly dated and signed.

71. Report, dated "February 9/1883," on sample 946, and signed "A. Dupré," or similarly dated and signed.

72. Report, dated "February 9/1883," on sample 947, and signed "A. Dupré," or similarly dated and signed.

73. Report, dated "February 9/1883," on sample 948, and signed "A. Dupré," or similarly dated and signed.

74. Report, dated "February 9/1883," on sample 949, and signed "A Dupré," or similarly dated and signed.

75. Report, dated "February 12/1883," on sample 950, and signed "A. Dupré," or similarly dated and signed.

76. Report, dated "February 16/1883," on sample 951, and signed "A. Dupré," or similarly dated and signed.

77. Report, dated "March 3/83," on sample 952, and signed 'A. Dupré," or similarly dated and signed.

78. Report, dated "March 3/1883," on sample 953, and signed "A. Dupré," or similarly dated and signed.

79. Report, dated "March 17/1883," on sample 958, and signed "A. Dupré," or similarly dated and signed.

80. Report, without date, on sample 971, and signed "A. Dupré," or similarly signed.

81. Report, dated "March 31/83," on sample 972, and signed "A. Dupré," or similarly dated and signed.

82. Report, dated "March 31/83," on sample 973, and signed "A. Dupré," or similarly dated and signed.

83. Report, dated "March 31/83," on sample 974, and signed "A. Dupré," or similarly dated and signed.

84. Report, dated "March 31/83," on sample 975, and signed "A. Dupré," or similarly dated and signed.

85. A Copy of "The Penny Pictorial News and Family Story Paper" for Saturday September 1, 1883.

86. An Envelope bearing the Glasgow Post Mark of 19th July, and addressed to Mr. John Kearney, 41 Stanhope Street, or with a similar post mark and address.

87. A Membership Card of "Thomas Devany," of "The National Land League of Great Britain," of date "10th day of April 1881."

88. A Printed Letter or Circular, entituled "National Land League of Great Britain," and signed "Yours respectfully The Committee," or with a similar title and signature.

89. A Membership Card No. 33 Mr. Thos. Devaney of the "Irish Home Rule Confederation of Great Britain."

90. A Membership Card of Thomas Devaney 16 Portugal Lane of "The Irish National Land League."

91. A Membership Card No. 32 Mr Thomas Devaney 16 Portugal Lane, of the "Irish Home Rule Confederation of Great Britain."

92. A Book or Pamphlet, entituled "The Land for the People: An Appeal to all who work by brain or hand, by John Ferguson," or with a similar title.

93. A Membership Card of Thomas Devaney of the "National Land League of Great Britain."

94. A Pamphlet or Printed Letter, entituled "National Land League of Great Britain," and dated "London 11 November 1881," and signed "by order of the Executive Frank Byrne Gen. Secretary," or with a similar title, date, and signature.

95. Supplement of the Paper called the "Weekly Examiner and Ulster Weekly News," of date August 26, 1882.

96. Supplement to the Paper called the "Weekly Freeman," of date 7th January 1882.

97. Supplement to the Paper called "United Ireland," of date September 10, 1881.

98. A Piece of Brass Pipe or Tube.

99. A Five-Chambered Revolver, and a Tin Box containing Thirty-Four or thereby Cartridges.

100. A Quantity of Chalk, and a Paper Bag containing a sample thereof.

101. A Book or Pamphlet, entituled "The Castle Government of Ireland, a Lecture by Michael Davitt," or with a similar title.

102. A small Note Book, with Black Covers, and having several leaves torn out.

103. A small Note Book without covers, and having several leaves torn out.

104. A Pass Book with Black Covers, and having part of the first page torn out.

105. A Printed Hand Bill, commencing "A Public Meeting will be held in the Hall 14 East Nile Street," or with a similar commencement.

106. A Printed Hand Bill, entituled "Irish National League of

Great Britain Glasgow Home Government Branch," or with a similar title.

107. A Subscription Sheet for the Paper called the "Irish Democrat."

108. A Letter dated "July 30th 1882," and commencing "Dear Mary," or with a similar date and commencement.

109. A Letter dated "Agu 29," and commencing "My dere Mary," and signed "Your Husbent to Death J Donnelly," or with a similar date, commencement, and signature.

110. A Copy of the Paper called the "United Irishman," of Saturday July 28, 1883.

111. A Supplement of the Paper called the "Cape Times," of Tuesday July 31, 1883.

112. A Supplement of the Paper called the "Weekly Freeman," of June 2, 1883.

113. A Letter, dated "Hebburn October 6," commencing "Dear Wife and Children," and subscribed "Ja M'C," or with a similar date, commencement, and subscription, and an Envelope addressed "Mrs M'Culloch No 302 Garngade road Back land Townhead Glasgow," or similarly addressed.

114. A Portion of the Paper called the "Glasgow Weekly Mail" of 22nd September 1883.

115. A Copy of the Paper called "United Ireland," for Saturday August 19, 1882.

116. An Extract or Certificate of the Conviction of Denis Deasy, Timothy Featherstone otherwise called Edmond O'Brien Kennedy, Patrick Flanagan, and Henry Dalton otherwise called John Henry O'Connor, of having feloniously, wickedly, and unlawfully compassed and conspired together with others to deprive and depose the Queen from the Style of the Imperial Crown of the United Kingdom of Great Britain and Ireland, of inventing, devising, and intending to levy war against the Queen, and of feloniously, wickedly, and unlawfully compassing, inventing, devising, and intending to levy war upon the Queen, within the United Kingdom, in order to put force and constraint upon, and in order to intimidate and overawe, the Houses of Parliament, and, in order to effect that object, of having manufactured in the City of Cork, and of having brought to Liverpool large quantities of a certain dangerous explosive called dynamite, at the Session of Oyer and Terminer and Gaol Delivery, held at Liverpool, in and for the County of Lancaster, on the Thirtieth day of July 1883.

117. A Plan or Map of the City of Glasgow.

118. A Time Sheet of Thomas Sutherland, Plumber, 198 Parliamentary Road, Glasgow, with pencil writing thereon, commencing "185 Duke St. Clening W.C," or with a similar commencement.

119. A Photograph of Tradeston Gasometer after Explosion.

120. Photograph of Timothy Featherstone.

121. Photograph of Henry Dalton.

122. Document, commencing "Captain M'Call you may preper to die," and ending "The Shamrock of Erin," or similarly commencing and ending.

123. Envelope, with Glasgow Post Mark of 17th February 1883, addressed "Capt M'Call Central Police Chambers Glasgow.'

124. Letter, dated "Friday 30th March 83," commencing "Capt M'Call Dear Sir," and signed "Peace," or with similar date, commencement, and signature.

125. Envelope, with Glasgow Post Mark of 31st March 1883, and addressed "Captain M'Call Chief of Police Central Office Albion St City," or similarly addressed.

126. Letter, dated "Glasgow 4 March 1883," commencing "Lord Provost Glasgow Sir," or with similar date and commencement.

127. Envelope with Glasgow Post Mark of 5th March 1883, addressed "Lord Provost Glasgow."

128. Letter, dated "Glasgow 18 March 1883," commencing "The Lord Provost Sir," and ending "The men had a meeting this afternoon," or with a similar commencement and ending.

Æ. J. G. MACKAY, A.D.

LIST OF WITNESSES.

1. Walter Cook Spens, Esquire, advocate, sheriff-substitute of Lanarkshire.
2. James Neil Hart, writer, Glasgow.
3. William Dixon Gray, now or lately clerk in the sheriff clerk's office, Glasgow.
4. James Roden, now or lately sheriff officer, County Buildings, Glasgow.
5. John Montgomerie Gibson, fitter, now or lately residing in or near Crookston Street, South Side, Glasgow.
6. William Key, gas manager, now or lately residing in or near Queen Mary Avenue, Crosshill, near Glasgow.
7. Thomas Butler, carter, now or lately residing in or near Muirhouse Lane, off Lilybank Road, in or near Glasgow.
8. Mary M'Nickle or Butler, wife of, and now or lately residing with, the said Thomas Butler.
9. Margaret M'Bride or Johnston, widow, now or lately residing in or near Muirhouse Lane aforesaid.
10. Edward Hughes, dealer, now or lately residing in or near Brown's Property, New Cathcart, near Glasgow.
11. Gavin Laurie, apprentice designer, and now or lately residing in or near Naburn Street, South Side, Glasgow.
12. Gabriel Longmuir, clerk, now or lately residing in or near Eglinton Street, Glasgow.
13. Robert Aitken, butcher's assistant, now or lately residing in or near Pollok Street, South Side, in or near Glasgow.
14. Jane Stewart or M'Kersie, wife of, and now or lately residing with, John M'Kersie, blacksmith, at or near Shields Road, in or near Glasgow.
15. Jessie M'Kersie, daughter of, and now or lately residing with, the said John M'Kersie.
16. Margaret Smith, now or lately residing in or near Eglinton Street, Glasgow.

LIST OF WITNESSES.

17. Robert Reid, now or lately night constable in the Southern District of the Glasgow Police.
18. James Davidson, now or lately criminal officer in the Southern District of the Glasgow Police.
19. Joseph Shanks, now or lately day inspector in the Southern District of the Glasgow Police.
20. James M'Murray, apprentice patternmaker, now or lately residing in or near Gallowgate, Glasgow.
21. Charles Simpson, patternmaker, now or lately residing in or near Whitevale Street, Glasgow.
22. Andrew Gillespie, gas engineer and contractor, now or lately residing in or near Seton Terrace, Dennistoun, Glasgow.
23. John Gillespie, draughtsman, now or lately residing in or near Seton Terrace aforesaid.
24. William Foulis, gas engineer, now or lately residing in or near Montgomerie Quadrant, Kelvinside, in or near Glasgow.
25. Adam Barr, now or lately gunner in the A Brigade, N Battery, Royal Horse Artillery, at Coventry.
26. Archibald Barr, furnaceman, now or lately residing in or near Springburn Road, in or near Glasgow.
27. Matthew Barr, iron-planer, now or lately residing in or near Springburn Road aforesaid.
28. Janet Richardson or Gee, wife of, and now or lately residing with, George Gee, bottle-blower, in or near Kerr Street, off Hopehill Road, in or near Glasgow.
29. The said George Gee.
30. Janet Watson, pocketbook maker, now or lately residing in or near Balgray Brae, Springburn, in or near Glasgow.
31. Joseph Anderson, lately night constable in the Northern District of the Glasgow Police, and now or lately residing in or near Shamrock Street, off New City Road, Glasgow.
32. Thomas Frater, now or lately night constable in the Northern District of the Glasgow Police.
33. Donald Ferguson, now or lately night inspector in the Northern District of the Glasgow Police.
34. George Murray, moulder, now or lately residing in or near Colliers Row, Hamilton Hill, off Possil Road, in or near Glasgow.
35. Duncan Henderson, bridge keeper, now or lately residing in or near High Craighall Road, in or near Glasgow.
36. William M'Kay, now or lately office inspector in the Camperdown Station of the Northern District of the Glasgow Police.
37. Henry Hogg, now or lately lieutenant in the Northern District of the Glasgow Police.
38. James Kilpatrick, now or lately lieutenant in the Northern District of the Glasgow Police.
39. Alexander M'Leod, now or lately criminal officer in the Northern District of the Glasgow Police.
40. Thomas Smith, engine driver, now or lately residing in or near New Road, Parkhead, in or near Glasgow.
41. Simon M'Stravick, surfaceman, now or lately residing at or near Hogganfield, in the Barony Parish of Glasgow, and shire of Lanark.

42. John Lambie, assistant locomotive superintendent, now or lately residing in or near Westbank Quadrant, Hillhead, Glasgow.
43. James Long, railway porter, now or lately residing in or near Mill Street, Greenock.
44. Murdoch M'Kay, now or lately night inspector in the Northern District of the Glasgow Police.
45. John Boyd, now or lately superintendent in the Central District of the Glasgow Police.
46. George Brander, now or lately writer, Glasgow.
47. William Alexander Brown, Esquire, Advocate, sheriff-substitute of Aberdeenshire, and formerly procurator-fiscal at Glasgow.
48. Vivian Dering Majendie, C.B., now or lately Her Majesty's chief inspector of explosives, Home Office, London.
49. Arthur Ford, now or lately colonel in the Royal Artillery, and one of Her Majesty's inspectors of explosives, Home Office, London.
50. James Campbell Brown, now or lately professor of chemistry in the University College, Liverpool.
51. August Dupré, now or lately professor of chemistry and Fellow of the Royal Society, and chemical adviser of the Explosives Department of the Home Office.
52. Stephen Alley, engineer, now or lately residing in or near Royal Crescent, Crosshill, near Glasgow.
53. George Hughes, fruit merchant, now or lately residing in or near Thistle Street, Hutchesontown, Glasgow.
54. John Horan, gas producer, now or lately residing in or near Garscube Road, Glasgow.
55. William Porter, now or lately day constable in the Central District of the Glasgow Police.
56. John Divers, assistant cashier, now or lately residing in or near Watt Street, off Paisley Road, Glasgow.
57. Thomas M'Ginnes, shopman, now or lately residing in or near Aird's Lane, off Bridgegate, Glasgow.
58. Thomas M'Ginn, shopman, now or lately residing in or near South Shamrock Street, Glasgow.
59. John Ward, fish dealer, now or lately residing in or near Govan Street, Hutchesontown, Glasgow.
60. Donald Sutherland, now or lately criminal officer in the Central District of the Glasgow Police.
61. Archibald Carmichael, sub-inspector of the Detective Department of the Central District of the Glasgow Police.
62. Jane Ronaldson or Mitchell, wife of, and now or lately residing with, William Mitchell, hotel proprietor, in or near Cowcaddens, Glasgow.
63. John Mitchell, son of, and residing with, the said William Mitchell.
64. James Johnston, manufacturing chemist, now or lately residing at or near Sheriff Park, Rutherglen, near Glasgow.
65. William Gordon Johnston, manufacturing chemist, now or lately residing at or near Sheriff Park, Rutherglen, near Glasgow.
66. David Fergus, carter, now or lately residing in or near Kyle Street, Port-Dundas, Glasgow.

LIST OF WITNESSES.   21

67. John Bunting Guthrie, manufacturing chemist, now or lately residing in or near Regent Park Square, Strathbungo, near Glasgow.
68. James Ballingall, clerk, now or lately residing in or near Parson Street, Townhead, Glasgow.
69. James Montgomery, manufacturing chemist, now or lately residing in or near St. James Street, Hillhead, Glasgow.
70. Alexander Reid, clerk, now or lately residing in or near Annette Street, Govanhill, Glasgow.
71. John Inglis, clerk, now or lately residing in or near Cumberland Street, South Side, Glasgow.
72. James Armstrong, clerk, now or lately residing in or near Gairbraid Street, Maryhill, near Glasgow.
73. Robert Reid, commission agent, now or lately residing in or near Bothwell Street, Glasgow.
74. James Steel, foreman, now or lately residing in or near Gairbraid Street, Maryhill, near Glasgow.
75. Thomas Venables, chemical engineer, now or lately residing in or near Holborn Terrace, Kelvinside, near Glasgow.
76. James Haire, timekeeper, now or lately residing in or near Fullarton Street, Irvine.
77. Levi Barrow, vitriol pumper, now or lately residing in or near Harbour Street, Irvine.
78. Robert Pollock, foreman, now or lately residing in or near Cochrane Street, Half-way of Irvine, in the parish of Dundonald.
79. George M'Roberts, chemist, residing at the Dynamite Factory, Stevenston.
80. Thomas Sutherland, plumber, now or lately residing in or near Glebe Street, Townhead, Glasgow.
81. Charles Johnston, plumber, now or lately residing in or near Eglinton Street, Glasgow.
82. Sarah Douglas or M'Lachlan, now or lately residing at or near Alexandra Terrace, Innellan, Argyllshire.
83. Christina Colquhoun, now or lately residing at or near Alexandra Terrace aforesaid.
84. Mary Currie or Bain, wife of, and now or lately residing with, William Bain, shoemaker, in or near Ronald Street, Townhead, Glasgow.
85. Mary Blands or Low, wife of, and now or lately residing with, James Low, in or near Ronald Street, Townhead, Glasgow.
86. Robert Munro, cab driver, now or lately residing in or near Stirling Street, City, Glasgow.
87. Myles M'Cullough, aerated water manufacturer, now or lately residing in or near Garngad Road, Glasgow.
88. Michael Buchanan, labourer, now or lately residing in or near Middleton Place, Garngad Road, in or near Glasgow.
89. John Getty, labourer, now or lately residing in or near Rosemount Street, Garngad Hill, Glasgow.
90. James Gillick, labourer, son of, and now or lately residing with, Ann Campbell or Gillick, a widow, in or near Garngad Road, Glasgow.
91. George Steed, nut screwer, now or lately residing in or near Garngad Road, Glasgow.

92. Andrew Campbell, clerk, now or lately residing in or near Crossburn Street, Glasgow.
93. John Guthrie Wight, bookkeeper, now or lately residing in or near Carnarvon Street, Glasgow.
94. Donald Campbell, now or lately day constable in the St. Rollox District of the Glasgow Police.
95. William Skene, now or lately day constable in the St. Rollox District of the Glasgow Police.
96. James M'Gowan, now or lately day constable in the St. Rollox District of the Glasgow Police.
97. John Niven, now or lately day constable in the Central District of the Glasgow Police.
98. Andrew Morrison Waddell, chemist, now or lately residing in or near South Campbell Street, Paisley.
99. Donald Sutherland, now or lately superintendent of the Paisley Police.
100. Thomas Shannon, licensed badge porter, now or lately residing in or near Cherry Lane, Marybone, Liverpool.
101. George Marsh, now or lately inspector of detectives in the Liverpool City Police.
102. Samuel Wilkinson Canning, now or lately sergeant in the Royal Irish Constabulary, stationed at Liverpool.
103. Samuel Johnston, now or lately detective constable in the Liverpool City Police.
104. Robert Fitzwilliam Starkie, now or lately district inspector of the Royal Irish Constabulary at Cork.
105. William Dreghorn, supercargo, now or lately residing in or near Rathmore Terrace, Cork.
106. Francis Scannell, now or lately clerk in the Money Order Office, Post Office, Cork.
107. Christian Jacob Donkert, supercargo, now or lately residing in or near Gratton's Hill, Cork.
108. Timothy Collopy, now or lately constable in the Metropolitan Police Force, London.
109. Joseph Schonman, now or lately residing in or near Paragon Road, Mare Street, South Hackney, London.
110. John George Littlechild, now or lately inspector of police, Great Scotland Yard, London.
111. William Melville, now or lately sergeant in the Metropolitan Police, Great Scotland Yard, London.
112. Ebenezer Mears, now or lately sergeant in the City Police, Old Jewry, London.
113. Patrick Enright, now or lately constable in the Metropolitan Police, Great Scotland Yard, London.
114. Frederick Lawley, now or lately detective sergeant in the City of London Police Force.
115. Alfred Lawrence Foster, now or lately superintendent of the City of London Police.
116. George Rose, now or lately sergeant in the Metropolitan Police, Great Scotland Yard, London.
117. George Williams, now or lately chief superintendent of the Detective Department in the Liverpool Constabulary.

LIST OF WITNESSES. 23

118. William Woodfine Marks, solicitor, Liverpool.
119. William Lamie, tailor, now or lately residing in or near Exchange Court, Dublin.
120. John Muirhead Arnot, now or lately manager of the retail department of the Glasgow Apothecaries' Company, Virginia Street, Glasgow.
121. Charles Docherty, furnaceman, now or lately residing in or near Rosemount Street, Glasgow.
122. John M'Quade, shoemaker, now or lately residing in or near Rose Street, Hutchesontown, Glasgow.
123. Mary Thomson Irvine, bookfolder, now or lately residing in or near Stanhope Street, Glasgow.
124. Charles M'Guire, now or lately acting sergeant in the Royal Irish Constabulary, stationed at Glasgow.
125. John Neil, now or lately detective officer in the Central District of the Glasgow Police.
126. William Gordon, now or lately detective officer in the Central District of the Glasgow Police.
127. John M'Kay, now or lately detective officer in the Central District of the Glasgow Police.
128. George Greer, now or lately detective officer in the Central District of the Glasgow Police.
129. John Harrison, now or lately inspector in the Durham County Constabulary, stationed at Hebburn-on-Tyne.
130. John Elliott, now or lately sergeant in the Durham County Constabulary, stationed at Hebburn-on-Tyne.
131. Alexander Gordon, now or lately detective officer in the Central District of the Glasgow Police.
132. Robert Carleton, now or lately warder in the Cork Male Prison, Cork.
133. John Shaw Peake, now or lately residing in or near Rathmines Road, Dublin.
134. Edmond O'Brien Kennedy otherwise called Timothy Featherstone, now or lately a prisoner in H.M. Convict Prison at Chatham.
135. John Henry O'Connor otherwise called Henry Dalton, now or lately a prisoner in H.M. Convict Prison at Chatham.
136. Alexander M'Call, now or lately chief constable of the Glasgow Police.
137. James Brown, officer of the Town Council of Glasgow.
138. Robert Reid, traffic inspector, now or lately residing in or near Motherwell.
139. Peter Heraty, points cleaner, now or lately residing at or near Broomfield, near Govanhill, in or near Glasgow.
140. Thomas Ballantyne, pointsman, now or lately residing in or near Martyr Street, Townhead, Glasgow.
141. James Chesney, now or lately stationmaster at the Buchanan Street Station in Glasgow of the Caledonian Railway.
142. John M'Cotter, coal dealer, now or lately residing in or near Villiers Street, Glasgow.
143. William M'Elhinny, now or lately emigration agent, and residing in or near Regent Street, Liverpool.
144. Margaret M'Guinness, wife of, and now or lately residing with,

Arthur M'Guinness, labourer, in or near Cuthbert Street, Hebburn Quay, Hebburn-on-Tyne.
  145. James Campbell, now or lately chief constable of police at Hull.
  146. John Caroll, now or lately detective sergeant in the Hull Police at Hull.
  147. Robert Burton, now or lately detective sergeant in the Hull Police at Hull.
  148. James Graham, now or lately inspector of police at Hull.
  149. William Granger, now or lately detective officer in the Hull Police at Hull.
  150. George Henry Chapman, now or lately detective officer in the Hull Police at Hull.
  151. John Edge, now or lately proprietor of the Salisbury Hotel, George Street, Hull, and residing there.
  152. Susan Edge, wife of, and now or lately residing with, the said John Edge.
  153. Robert Albert Ward, now or lately an assistant in, and residing at or near, the Mission Coast Home, Saltcoats.
  154. Patrick Murphy, now or lately foundry labourer, Turner Street, Townhead, Glasgow.   Æ. J. G. MACKAY, *A.D.*

The case having been called, counsel for the prisoners intimated that they had no objections to state to the relevancy of the indictment; and upon each of the prisoners being asked, each pleaded Not Guilty.

The following Jury was then impanelled and sworn:—WILLIAM OLIPHANT MORRISON, printer, 32 Abercromby Place, Edinburgh; WILLIAM ROBERTSON SHAND, commercial traveller, 16 Manor Place, Edinburgh; JAMES SOUTTER, toy merchant, 3 Rutland Square, Edinburgh; JOHN BRAID, joiner, 13 Oxford Street, Edinburgh; ALEXANDER JERVIS, cabinetmaker, 30 Alva Place, Edinburgh; JAMES MITCHELL, grocer, 12 Gladstone Terrace, Edinburgh; WILLIAM RUTHERFORD HILSON, joiner, 5 Guthrie Street, Edinburgh; WILLIAM TOD, farmer, Starlaw, Bathgate; JOHN ANCRUM, corkcutter, 13 Young Street, Edinburgh; JAMES M'LAREN, draper, 28 Gillespie Crescent, Edinburgh; ROBERT THOMSON, tobacconist, Murray House, Argyle Crescent, Joppa; DAVID ROSS, coal merchant, Gilmerton; JAMES ROXBURGH, brick and fire-clay goods agent, 7 Southfield Place, Portobello; HUGH RODEN, millworker, 3 M'Neill Street, Viewforth; JOHN GREEN, draper, Peebles.

WILLIAM MUIRHEAD, plumber, 9 Brandfield Street, Edinburgh, was also balloted, but before the Jury was sworn, he announced in Court that he was biassed on one side, whereupon, in answer to the Lord Justice-Clerk, the counsel for the prisoners intimated that they had no objection to his being allowed to go. He was relieved accordingly, and another juryman was balloted for in his stead, and the whole Jury sworn.

The Clerk of Court then read the following special defences which had been lodged on behalf of the prisoners:—

Terence M'Dermott pleads not guilty, and further pleads that he was in the house of his father, John M'Dermott, 452 Dobbie's Loan, Glasgow, on the evening and night of the 20th January 1883.

Thomas Devany pleads not guilty, and further pleads that at or about the hour of ten o'clock on the night of the 20th day of January 1883, he was at or near the premises, No. 40 Candleriggs, Glasgow, then and now or lately occupied by David Carrick, dealer, residing there.

Peter Callaghan or Kellochan pleads not guilty, and further pleads that he was at home in his own house, No. 14 Rose Street, South Side, Glasgow, on the evening and night of 20th January 1883.

Henry M'Cann pleads not guilty of the overt acts or deeds one or more of them charged in the second, third, and fourth clauses of the indictment served upon him on the 22nd November 1883, in respect that accused was not present at the respective places where or at the time when said offences were or are said to have been committed (on 20th and 21st January 1883), but was in his own house, No. 9 Stirling Street, Glasgow, between the hours of six o'clock P.M. on said 20th January and ten o'clock A.M. on said 21st January.

James Donnelly pleads not guilty, and further pleads that he was at home in his own house, No. 38 Villiers Street, Glasgow, on the evening and night of the 20th of January 1883.

Patrick M'Cabe pleads not guilty, and further pleads that he was in his own house and shop, No. 79 Rose Street, South Side, Glasgow, on the evening and night of the 20th January 1883.

Patrick Drum pleads not guilty of the overt acts or deeds one or more of them charged in the second, third, and fourth places in an indictment served on him on 22nd November 1883, in respect that accused was not present at the respective places where or at the time when the said offences were or are said to have been committed, on 20th and 21st January 1883, but was in his own house, No. 118 Rose Street, Glasgow, between the hours of 6 P.M. on said 20th January, and 10 A.M. on said 21st January.

Denis Casey pleads not guilty, and further pleads that he was at home in his own house, No. 72 Kirk Street, Calton, Glasgow, on the evening and night of the 20th day of January 1883.

EVIDENCE FOR THE CROWN.

1. *John Montgomerie Gibson* (5). *By the* LORD ADVOCATE.—I am a gas meter inspector in Glasgow. I am in the employment of the Corporation of Glasgow, at their gasworks at Tradeston, Glasgow. These gasworks belong to the town. My ordinary duties are to keep a record of the quantity of gas made and delivered hourly, and a record of the pressure on the mains. It was my duty to go over all the holders at stated intervals. Among other works, we have four gas-holders, otherwise called gasometers. One of these is called No. 4 gasholder. It is bounded on the south by Maxwell Road, on the north by Lilybank Road, on the east by Watson & Gow's foundry, and on the west by a rope-work and Muirhouse Lane. No. 4 gasholder was detached from the rest of the works, in an enclosure by itself. Along Lilybank Road there is a seven-feet wall on the north side of that enclosure, with an entrance to the enclosure from Lilybank Road.

That entrance is usually kept shut at night. It is not locked. Any one can open it. At that entrance there is a cottage in which a man named George Harper resides, who is my neighbour and takes shift with me. Watson & Gow's works are fenced off from the enclosure by the wall of the works. There is a woodyard between the enclosure and Maxwell Road, and a paling four or five feet high which separates the enclosure from that woodyard. There is generally a quantity of wood stacked in the yard. The only thing to prevent anybody getting from the woodyard into the enclosure is the four or five feet sleeper paling. On the western boundary there is a paling four or five feet high between the rope-work and the enclosure. That paling runs along the enclosure till it meets the north boundary of Lilybank Road. The paling along the western boundary of the enclosure is somewhat lower at the end where it joins Lilybank Road than it is at the other end. The branch of the Caledonian Railway runs along the western boundary outside of Muirhouse Lane. There is only mineral traffic upon that line. The railway is about fifty feet from the paling. The west side of the enclosure is the most unprotected, there being only the paling which I have described. The governor house is inside the enclosure, on the northern boundary. The gas from No. 4 gasholder is delivered and regulated through that governor. When on duty I visit that gasholder along with the rest every hour. I was on duty at the works on Saturday 20th January this year. I went on duty at six o'clock in the evening for the night shift. I visited No. 4 gasholder at seven o'clock and took the amount of stock. I then went to the governor house and saw that all was right and lit my safety lamp. I went round the entire holder. There was nothing unusual about it. There was nothing wrong. There was no smell of gas—no more than usual. There is always more or less of a smell about a gasholder. I visited the gasholder again at eight o'clock and took stock a second time. The third time I visited it was about nine o'clock. There was nothing unusual on any of these occasions. I again visited it at ten o'clock. I did not get round it. I took the stock. The stock was 450,000 cubic feet, and the height to which the holder was raised up was 22 feet 6 inches above the level of the copestone. It rises and falls according as it is full or empty. I went to the governor house to mark my book. While I was there the explosion occurred. It was a sharp, clear, distinct explosion, and then a rattling noise, the same as if some person had flung a lot of stones on the top of the holder. There was just one sharp, clear, distinct explosion. I was standing in the governor house just at the back of the door. The explosion shook the house from the very foundations. It swayed me to and fro. I heard no sound at that time—only the explosion. After that I heard a hissing sound, the same as if missiles were flying about. It was just the same as if there were hard substances flying round about the place. I went out and saw that the holder had exploded and the holder was in flames. Q.—What do you mean by saying that the holder had exploded? A.—There had been an explosion at the holder and the flames were flying about fifty feet above the columns of the holder. The flame appeared to be mostly on the south-west side. That was the place where, on examination, I found a column cracked. I have never heard what I knew to be a gas explosion. I have heard dynamite explosions. I wrought with dynamite and exploded dynamite when I was in the employment of the Eglinton Iron Company. I was accustomed to its use. It gives a sharp, clear, and distinct sound,—just a sharp, clear, distinct explosion, and all is over. I thought at the time that this was dynamite, and I said so to myself. I took what steps I thought proper to get the gas shut off. I afterwards made an examination of the holder. I found a rent at the south-west side. It was nearest Muirhouse Lane, on the rope-work side. There was a rent, as far as I could judge, about eight feet wide, and the sheet-iron of the holder was bulged up on the side close in to the column. I could not see the rent for the sheet iron till once it was taken out and lifted. I found the base of the column cracked, and the guide rod runner broken off. I saw nothing wrong with any of the rest of the columns. There were a great many small pieces of metal all about. Matters were left in the position in which I found them till they were examined by Colonel Majendie. I think he came on the Tuesday or Wednesday following, but I am not certain which day. Nothing was altered as far as I know. Instructions were given to leave things as they were. I did not, from my examination of the column and the rent, form any opinion as to the cause, one way or the other. The only thing was, when I got No. 2 piece of the holder mentioned in the case, which was found in Caledonia Road, I formed an opinion then as to the explosion. I found it was marked in every shape and form the same as if it had been struck with dynamite. Dynamite explosion gives a pitted appearance to metal which it has burst. This piece of metal was a bit that had been blown away, and I found it had that pitted appearance. That was the only piece of metal which I observed with that pitted appearance. On the Sunday afternoon I noticed something about the paling on the west side, at Lilybank Road—the corner as you go out to the Lilybank Road. This is the side which I described as being least protected. I found three straps off the paling, one in one place and two in another place. I had seen the paling all right on the Saturday night at seven o'clock. Somebody had taken them off between seven o'clock on Saturday night and Sunday afternoon. That was not done for any purpose in connection with the gasworks. I did not see any one about the enclosure on the Saturday night. The nearest house to that holder is in Muirhouse Lane and is about fifteen or twenty yards away. The column which I found cracked, and opposite which I found the rent, was nearest to the paling there. No. 3 column would be a little nearer to the paling. That column was not opposite any road. It was the least likely place for any person to be seen about the holder, because on the other sides there were roads. At this place there were just the backs of houses. It would not be in the view of any people going along the Lilybank Road or the Maxwell Road.

Cross-examined by Mr. RHIND.—I had had the gasholders under my charge for about sixteen months at the time of the explosion. I was for seven years a gas manager, and after that I was engaged about two years at the Eglinton Ironworks, and then I came to Tradeston Gasworks. It was at the Eglinton Ironworks that I became acquainted with dynamite explosions. Dynamite was used there for taking the iron off the bottom of blast furnaces. I have had no experience from seeing its effects upon malleable iron, such as a gasholder is made of. For anything I can tell, a gas explosion may sound the same as a dynamite explosion. As near as I can guess, the exact hour at which the explosion occurred was nine minutes past ten. There was no clock in the governor house, and I had not a watch. After the explosion the police were put to watch that nothing was touched. The two places where straps were removed from the paling were about one and a half yards distant from each other. *Q.*—Did you observe whether the straps were broken, or whether they had been taken off where they were nailed? *A.*—They were wrenched off. I do not think the explosion could have caused the straps of the paling to come off. There are two horizontal straps, one at the top and one at the bottom of the paling, and then there are straps running perpendicularly up and down. It was perpendicular straps that were taken off. The breadth of each strap was about four or five inches. I did not measure them. I did not measure how wide the entire opening was. The houses at Muirhouse Lane face towards Muirhouse Lane, and their backs are towards the gasometer. I cannot say whether there are windows in the backs of these houses. The place about the gasometer is not lighted at night. There are no lights except in the Lilybank Road, with the exception of the light in the governor house. There are lights on the Maxwell Road. I cannot tell whether there are lights in the Muirhouse Lane; I never was there at night, and I did not observe whether there were any in daylight. *Q.*—Will the lights in Lilybank Road and Maxwell Road lighten up the road where the gasometer is? *A.*—They give plenty light to walk round the place and to observe. You can see quite well.

Re-examined.—The lights that have been referred to would not show a person doing anything at the foot of the column which was cracked. The slip which was made in the paling by the two straps being taken off was big enough to let an ordinary man through.

By the LORD JUSTICE-CLERK.—I was alone all this time. I was there at seven, eight, nine, and ten o'clock. I visited the gasometer at those periods. The explosion took place immediately after I left the side of the holder after counting her. The column supports the guide rods of the gasometer, and the machinery rises and falls according to the gas that goes in and out.

2. *William Key* (G). *By the* LORD ADVOCATE.—I am manager of the Corporation Gasworks, Tradeston, South Side of Glasgow. I was on duty there on Saturday 20th January this year. I left the works that night about twenty minutes past nine o'clock. I know gasometer No. 4. I had seen it in working order at a quarter past nine before I left the works. I am able to say it was in good working order, because I had passed it, and the supply to the South Side of the city was in proper order. It was part of my duty to see that the pressure on different parts of that part of the city was right. This supply is for the South Side. I found gas of the proper quality and pressure being duly delivered. If there had been anything wrong with the gasometer that would have been seen. I was away before the explosion took place. [Shown production No. 4.] About two days after the explosion, I found that on the top of the gasometer. I would

describe it as part of a brass cap having a female screw. There was nothing like that in connection with the gasometer, or with any of our works. On the top of the gasometer there were a few pieces of broken metal lying like things that had been blown there by the explosion, and that was among them.

Cross-examined by Mr. GUTHRIE.—I have been there eight years as manager. The gasometer was built prior to my going there. I never heard that there had been complaints about the smell of gas some weeks previous to the explosion. I saw Colonel Majendie. I am not aware that he states in his report that there had been an exceptionally strong smell of gas some time before. I found the brass cap No. 4 very nearly at the centre of the crown of the damaged holder. I know from my experience in connection with gasworks, extending over twenty years, that nothing of that sort had been used in erecting the gaswork. *Q.*—Have you ever erected a gaswork ? *A.*—I have designed portions of apparatus belonging to gasworks, from the retorts to the gasholders. I have carried them out personally. That was in Dumbarton. I was manager in Dumbarton for four years, and I designed all the extensions of the works there. This brass cap No. 4 is of such a construction that I know of nothing in connection with gasworks, that I could give a similar description of. I cannot say what it is. I cannot say either that the kind of screw is common enough. I think the screw is peculiar. I do not think it is a well-known form of screw. I never saw a screw of that sort before. I never heard of a screw of that kind being used.

By the LORD JUSTICE-CLERK.—It is not familiar to me.

Cross-examination continued.—I have not built any gasholder. I have superintended five or six gasworks. I have not superintended the building of any gasholder.

Re-examined.—I am quite familiar with the mechanism of gasholders and of gasworks generally. There is nothing like that screw in them.

3. *Thomas Butler* (7). *By the* LORD ADVOCATE.—I am a carter in Glasgow. I live in Muirhouse Lane, off Lilybank Road, near to the gaswork. The front of my house looks to the lane, and the back looks to the gasholder which exploded. I was at home in my house on the evening of Saturday 20th January about ten o'clock. I was sitting by the side of the fire when the explosion took place. It was just like a great burst, as I thought. I was knocked kind of stupid. The wall was blown in where I was sitting beside the fire. I saw a great light; it blew the windows in and all. The lamp, which was hanging up at the fireside, was all blown into pieces, and I saw a mass of flame all around me. I rushed out into the street. My clothes were on fire. I ran towards the top of Muirhouse Lane, where Edward Hughes, who had been in the house with me, helped me off with my coat. My two shirts, and my gallowses, and my waistcoat were burned. I was badly burned myself. I went back to the house and lifted some of my children out of bed. There were three in bed and three on the floor. The three on the floor were burned, but the three in the bed were not. One girl was burned in the hand, and her jacket was on fire, and some gentleman put it out in the lane. My wife's head and both her hands

were burned. My wife and I and my three children were taken to the Infirmary, where we were for about three weeks. Hughes was taken to the Infirmary too.

Cross-examined by Mr. BAXTER.—Before this explosion took place I had smelt an unusual smell of gas for about three weeks, or perhaps longer. The like of me, who am working about gasworks, did not think anything of it. *Q.*—Was it more than usual about a gaswork? *A.*—Yes; I had to rise two or three different times and open the door. I felt a smell in the house. *Q.*—What was it that first attracted your attention at the time of the explosion? *A.*—I did not, for the moment, think it was the gasometer. [Question repeated.] *A.*—It was the windows and dishes and all flying about the house. I saw the flash before I heard the explosion. The windows were blown in before I heard the crack. I first saw a flash just like lightning, and then the windows came tumbling in. *Q.*—Are you sure the windows were not blown out of your house? *A.*—I cannot exactly say; there was some of the glass blown in and some blown out. I ran out of the house, and into a fair mass of flame, from my own house near up to Maxwell Road. Nobody ran with me except Hughes. As near as I can guess, the wall of my house is about forty yards from the gasholder.

Re-examined.—*Q.*—Do you often smell gas thereabouts? *A.*—I did not smell it ever since the gasometer was sorted—I mean put up again. The smell was for two or three weeks before the explosion, but I have felt no smell whatever since the new one was started. I thought that the smell was coming out of a common sewer, and I made my wife put some wet cloths on the jaw-box, but they did not do any good.

By Mr. KENNEDY.—Do you remember an explosion taking place at the gasometer a good while before this? *A.*—It was not an explosion; it went on fire. That was about four years before this. I did not see what was the cause of it, but I heard it was the dropping of a light into the naphtha.

4. *Gavin Laurie* (11). *Examined.*—I am an apprentice moulder, and live with my mother, Janet Brown or Laurie, Caledonian Road, Glasgow. I remember taking a walk in Maxwell Road on Saturday, 20th January, this year, at ten minutes to ten at night. I went along Maxwell Road and down Darnley Street. The gasworks were on my right as I was going. I observed a man between Darnley Street and Lilybank Road. He was standing with his back against the paling. His back was towards the gasholder, and his face looking towards St. Andrew's Road. I saw the side of his face. It was the shuffling of his foot that attracted my attention. I passed about two or three feet from him. I looked at him. He had a slouched hat on, a black coat, and black trousers. He was about a middling-sized man. I looked back at him after I passed him. I looked back owing to the suspicious way he was standing looking at us. I did not like his way of looking, and I looked back to see what he was doing. This was on the side of Darnley Street away from the Muirhouse Lane. The back of Muirhouse Lane and the back of Darnley Street would be towards each other. It was on the side of Darnley Street near to the Maxwell Road. Being asked to look at the prisoners, and say whether he saw

any one like the man of whom he had spoken,—the witness pointed to the second in order,—Devany. The explosion happened about a quarter of an hour after I saw the man.

Cross-examined by Mr. RHIND.—By the time the explosion occurred I had reached Dr. Jeffrey's church in Caledonia Road on my way home. One Gabriel Longmuir was with me. Two ladies passed us in Maxwell Street before we saw the man, but we saw no other man. The man was not smoking. I had never seen him in my life before that I know of. *Q.*—When did you come to think that Devany was like him? *A.*—When I saw him in the Central Police Office about seven months after the explosion. I was not told by the police that that was possibly the man. I am not sure whether he is the man or not.

By the LORD JUSTICE-CLERK.—I mark with a pencil on the sketch now shown me the place where the man was standing and the place where I was.[1] It was a good light; I saw the man quite plainly. I was within two or three feet of him. He was looking at us when I saw him first. His back was to the fence, and his face was to us as we went along. It was the way he looked at us that was suspicious; I did not see what he was doing. His hands were behind his back. He was standing still. He attracted our attention so that when we got to the corner of Lilybank Road—about twenty yards off—we turned round to look at him. It was a good long while after that when I saw the man in the police office. He was by himself. I was shown one other man before I saw him.

5. *Gabriel Longmuir* (12). *By the* LORD ADVOCATE.—I am a clerk, and I reside with my father, Matthew Longmuir, bookseller, in Eglinton Street, Glasgow. I know Gavin Laurie, the last witness. He and I were taking a walk on the evening of Saturday, 20th January, about a quarter to ten at night. We came round by Maxwell Road and Darnley Street. We noticed a man standing in Darnley Street, about fifty yards from Maxwell Road. He was standing in a recess of the paling. He was standing sideways, leaning against the paling. Laurie was next to the man and had a better chance of seeing him than I had. The man was very suspicious-like. He watched us when we passed him. I saw him turn his head, looking closely at us. I passed the remark to Laurie afterwards that "that man was on for something." We looked round, and he was still there. About a quarter of an hour afterwards, when we were in Caledonia Road, we heard the explosion. So far as I know, I have not seen the man since,—I cannot be sure. I could not identify him.

By the LORD JUSTICE-CLERK.—He was about 5 feet 6 or 5 feet 7 in height, about the average size. He was dressed in a black jacket, and, I think, dark trousers and a slouched hat.

Gavin Laurie (*recalled*). *By the* LORD JUSTICE-CLERK.—Longmuir made the observation to me about the man, "I bet you that man is on for something."

6. *Robert Aitken* (13). *By the* LORD ADVOCATE.—I am a butcher's

---

[1] These places are close to the point at which the witness Montgomery found three straps off the paling.

assistant in Glasgow. On Saturday 20th January this year I was in the employment of John Donaldson, butcher, Albert Road, Pollokshields, near Glasgow. On that Saturday evening I had been a message to Eglinton Street for my master, and I was in Maxwell Road, coming home towards Pollokshields, about ten o'clock. I know the gasometer at which the explosion took place. I was in Maxwell Road, about ten yards from Muirhouse Lane, when the explosion occurred. I heard a loud noise, like the roar of a cannon, and then I saw flames. After that I saw two men running along Maxwell Street. They came from Muirhouse Lane. They passed me in Maxwell Road, running for Eglinton Street, which is the main thoroughfare up to Glasgow. This was immediately after the explosion. I observed nothing very particular about the men, except that they were running. I was standing at the palings, looking at the gasholder at the time. One of the two men was carrying a small parcel. I turned to look at the gasholder, and then I saw other two men. They were at the head of Muirhouse Lane. They ran past me towards Eglinton Street, after the other pair. I did not see where the last two came from. I formed the opinion that they were all in company, because the first two turned round to see if the other two were coming. These men were about 5 feet 2 or 5 feet 4 in height, dressed in black clothes, and had on hats and chin beards. [Being asked to look at the prisoners and say whether he thought any of these were like any of the four men, the witness pointed to No. 2 and No. 4 (Thomas Devany and Henry M'Cann).] I say that with certainty.

By the LORD JUSTICE-CLERK.—These were the first two. I know the names of the men now—*Thomas Devany and Patrick M'Cabe.*[1] I don't know who the second two were.

Examination continued.—I am perfectly certain as to the first two. I saw them the first Sunday after they were arrested, in the Central Police Station. They were shown to me there. I saw the faces of the two men quite distinctly. There was a bright light; it was moonshine.

Cross-examined by Mr. RHIND.—I had never seen either of the four men before. It was the first two men whom I saw that I identify.

[Being asked to point out which was the man whom he called Devany, the witness pointed to the second from the end, and being asked to point out the man whom he called M'Cabe, he pointed to the fourth.]

Re-examined.—Q.—You are not an acquaintance of the men, and I suppose you do not know the names yourself? *A.*—No.

Re-cross-examined.—Q.—The man you identified at the Police Office was M'Cabe? *A.*—Yes.

By the LORD JUSTICE-CLERK.—The man whom I have pointed out as M'Cabe was one of the first two, whatever his name may be.

By Mr. RHIND.—It was six or seven months after the explosion that I was asked to identify the men.

By Mr. KENNEDY.—I saw the men one by one at the Police Office. Q.—Were you told by any of the policemen there that the name of one of the men you pointed out was M'Cabe? *A.*—Yes, after they were all out. I am out of work just now. I have been so for four or five

---

[1] The witness pointed to Henry M'Cann and misnamed him Patrick M'Cabe.

weeks. I left my employment for various reasons, because I did not like him. *Q.*—Why did you not like him? *A.*—Because he was not a nice man. *Q.*—Did he like you? *A.*—I suppose he did. My last master's name was James Train, 38 Shields Road, Pollokshields. I was previously with a man named John Donaldson. I left his employment the night of the explosion. I never went back that night, and I was told not to come back on the Monday morning. I did not go back on the Saturday night because I stood to look at the gasholder. It was my duty to go back. I was dismissed by Donaldson. I was not dismissed on a charge of thieving or on a charge of making away with something about his place. He found no fault with me in that respect. I went back afterwards for my wages and got them. I read in the bills that there was a reward of £500 offered in this case. I saw the bill offering that reward a week after I gave information to the police.

7. *Mrs. Jane Stewart or M'Kersie* (14). *By the* LORD ADVOCATE.—I am the wife of a blacksmith, and live in St. Andrew's Road, Glasgow. I remember the night of Saturday 20th January last—the night the explosion took place. My daughter Jessie and I were in the Lilybank Road on our way home that night about ten o'clock, or rather two or three minutes after ten. I remember passing the end of Muirhouse Lane. We observed a man as if he was tipsy—singing and putting his hand from one side to another. I told Jessie to come to the side of the road for fear he might strike her. After he passed I looked after him, and I saw that he was walking quite straight and had stopped singing. This was on the bridge over the Caledonian mineral line—the bridge nearest St. Andrew's Road. The man was on the bridge, and then he crossed the road to the other side. When I first saw him he was coming towards us. I think this was a little over ten or about ten o'clock. The man would be about 5 feet 10 or 6 feet in height—a pretty tall man. When I looked back after him he was walking quite straight across the road. He had begun to walk straight after he passed us. At the time he passed us I thought he was the worse of drink; he looked very tipsy-like, and he was singing something about Old England. He had stopped singing when I looked back and was going like a sober man. [Being asked to look at the prisoners and to say whether she saw any one like the man, witness pointed to No. 6 (James Donnelly).] I cannot say that is the man, but it is very like him.

Cross-examined by Mr. RHIND.—Whoever the man was, I had never seen him before. I never thought any one was like him till I saw him in the police office some months afterwards. I was not quite sure about him.

Re-examined.—The man was dressed, I thought, in a dirty moleskin suit.

8. *Jessie M'Kersie* (15). *By the* LORD ADVOCATE.—I am daughter of the last witness. I was out with her in Lilybank Road on the evening of 20th January this year, shortly before the explosion. I remember passing the end of Muirhouse Lane. A man came forward. He was coming along the road tipsy, and squalling a song about Old England. After he passed, my mother and I looked round at him. We saw him

walking quite straight over in the direction of Muirhouse Lane. He was not moving his hands or staggering then; he was walking quite straight and had stopped singing. He had on dirty moleskin trousers, a dark coat, and a hookit-down cap. *Q.*—Look at the prisoners and say if you see any one like him. *A.*—Yes, Donnelly. I cannot swear to him, but I think he is like him.

Cross-examined by Mr. RHIND.—*Q.*—Did you once say that the man you saw that night had on a blue coat? *A.*—Yes, a dark coat. I went with my mother to the police office about seven months afterwards. She and I were together when I was asked if the man I was shown was like the man I saw that night.

Re-examined.—There were a number of men passed by us one by one, and we were asked to look at them, at the police office. Both my mother and I picked that man out of the lot.

By the LORD JUSTICE-CLERK.—My mother and I were together when the men were passed along. My mother recognized this man first, and I did the same.

9. *Margaret Smith* (16). *Examined.*—I reside in Eglinton Street, Glasgow. My sister Catherine and I were convoying my niece, Miss Carr, home part of the way on Saturday night, 20th January this year. We went along Lilybank Road. We parted from her at the corner of St. Andrew's Road. That is across the road from Muirhouse Lane, the opposite side of the way, but near it. After we parted with our niece we stood a little to see her on her way. This was about five minutes past ten o'clock. While we were standing watching our niece, we observed a man. He was coming from Alexandria Street into Lilybank Road. He was dressed with a long coat. That was when we were coming. *Q.*—Did you see any other man who attracted your attention that night? *A.*—When we were going we saw a man on the bridge that crosses Lilybank Road, the mineral railway bridge of the Caledonian Railway. It was just after the bell rang ten—between the ringing of the bell and us parting with our niece. The man was dressed just like a working man. He was standing with his elbows on the parapet of the bridge, looking towards Cathcart—that is, to the south. [Being asked to look at the prisoners and say if any of these was like the man, the witness pointed to No. 2 (Thomas Devany).] I think that is the man. *Q.*—Why do you point to that man? *A.*—He is just like the man I saw. So far as I know he is as like him as can be, but I cannot swear to his face, as I did not look at his face.

By the LORD JUSTICE-CLERK.—His general appearance is like that of the man. I cannot swear he is the man, but he is like him.

Cross-examined by Mr. RHIND.—I did not see the man's face. A detective came to me about three weeks or more afterwards. *Q.*—How long after that was it that you saw him in the police office? *A.*—About a month or six weeks, I think, but I may be wrong. *Q.*—A detective called upon you one day about six weeks after the explosion, and told you to look out for a man? *A.*—He asked me if I would know the man. *Q.*—Was it the detective who told you that was the man? *A.*—No, he asked me if I would know the man. He said there was a man that would pass the window. He and I waited to see the man pass. *Q.*—Then did he ask you if you thought that was the man?

A.—No, it was my sister. They never knew I had seen anything at that time, and it was my sister whom he asked to go and see the man, if this was the man that had the long coat on, and when she was looking out of the window I came into the room. I saw the man and I said, "That is not the man my sister saw; that is the man I saw on the bridge." The detective did not tell me that there was a large reward offered about this matter. I knew nothing about it.

10. *James Davidson* (18). *By* Mr. BRAND.—I am a criminal officer in the Southern District of Glasgow. I found in the yard near the gasholder eighteen pieces of iron. I labelled these. On 23d January I found about forty-six other pieces in the grounds near the gasholder. A number of them were near the shattered column. These were marked and kept in the same place till Colonel Majendie made his investigation. On 31st August I apprehended one of the prisoners— Devany- in his house, 16 Portugal Lane. I searched his house, and I found there a revolver and a box containing a number of cartridges. [Shown No. 99.] These are the revolver and the box of cartridges which I found. They were in the bottom of a chest with a number of clothes on the top of them.

By LORD CRAIGHILL.—The revolver was a five-chambered one.

11. *James M'Murray* (20). *Examined.*—I am an apprentice pattern-maker in the employment of Laidlaw & Sons. I remember on 24th February last being sent by them to the Tradeston gasometer to take certain measures. They were employed to make a new column instead of the one that had been broken. [Shown No. 5, a circular brass cap or piece of brass tube.] *Q.*—When you were there taking measures did you find that? *A.*—Yes, that is like it. I found it on the ground about three yards from the column. *Q.*—You have no doubt that is what you found? *A.*—Yes, that is like it. I gave it to Charles Simpson.

Cross-examined by Mr. RHIND.—I never saw anything like No. 5 before. Charles Simpson was with me at the time.

By the LORD JUSTICE-CLERK.—We were getting a pattern made in order to mend the broken column. This article that I found was lying on the ground about three yards from the column.

12. *Charles Simpson* (21). *By the* LORD ADVOCATE.—I am in the employment of Laidlaw & Sons. I remember being with the last witness M'Murray at the Tradeston gasometer on 24th February last. M'Murray handed me a brass cap which he had found. [Shown No. 5.] That is what he handed to me. He pointed out to me the place where he had found it. It was about three yards in a southerly direction from the column that was broken.

THE POSSIL BRIDGE EXPLOSION.

13. *Adam Barr* (25). *By the* LORD ADVOCATE.—I am a gunner in the Royal Horse Artillery. I was at home on furlough in January last visiting my friends in Springburn Road, Glasgow. On the evening

of Saturday 20th January this year, I went with my two brothers Archibald and Matthew to the house of an acquaintance named Janet Richardson, in Wigton Street. About twelve o'clock that night I left her house to return home. My brothers, Mary Kildare or Barr, wife of my brother Archibald, Janet Watson, George Richardson, and a man named George Gee, were along with me. We went from Wigton Street to the Forth and Clyde Canal bank, along which is the nearest way home to Springburn. We reached the canal bank about twelve o'clock or about five minutes past twelve at night. We walked along the canal bank in the direction of Springburn. In walking along we came to the aqueduct which carries the canal across Possil Bridge Road. When we came up there, a lady in the party saw a box lying, and said, "There is a box," and I, being nearest the canal, picked it up. The box was lying about one foot from the water, and about the centre of the arch of the bridge. The bridge has only one arch. There is a railing between the railway and the canal, and the box was standing underneath the railing. [Shown No. 6, an oval brown japanned tin ladies' bonnet-box.] That is the box, or one like it. At all events, it is the box my brother carried down to the police station. There was only one box. When I picked up the box I found there was one padlock on it, which was unlocked. I carried it two paces, and then I laid it down and opened the lid. The moon was shining. One of the party suggested there was perhaps a child in the box, and I put my hand forward to see if there was such a thing, and as I did so the thing exploded. When I first took off the lid I saw that the box was full of some white or light material. It looked like sawdust or sand. The box was filled with this stuff to about two inches from the top. When I opened the box there was no appearance whatever of smoke or fire about it. I put my hand forward very gently, thinking I might come in contact with something soft. As soon as I touched the box, the thing went off. There was rather a sort of little noise when the thing went off, like powder going off. It was a sort of fizzing noise or puff. There was a slight puff the first time, and then the thing fizzed afterwards. When it began to fizz I told my brother to run, as there would be something the matter. I myself was obliged to remain, I was so horror-struck. I had never seen anything like that in the Artillery. When I told my brother to run, my younger brother, who was behind me, was knocked over, and he said, "Oh, you have shot me." I looked round,—my heart was so overflowing with grief that I could not say anything, but I turned round and went down Wigton Street and got a policeman. The second explosion was rather a hard sound; it sounded pretty large to my ear. My left hand and wrist were injured. I cannot say what injured me; it was something which came from the box. My hands were about two feet from the box when the second explosion took place, because as soon as the thing fizzed I lifted my hand up. The lid of the box was completely blown off and separated. It had been attached to the box before. After the lid had been blown off, the stuff in the box went on burning for about a quarter of an hour. It did not at all go off like gunpowder. One of the party after that gave the box a kick and tumbled out some of the stuff. I saw it tumbled out. I went and got a policeman, and some police came and took away the box to the police office. My wounds were dressed by the police surgeon. There were no lamps on the bridge. I did not see any fuse about the box I did not m.ke any careful inspection of the ground. I did not notice any fuse. I know the smell of gunpowder very well; the smell of this stuff when it went off was not in the least like the smell of gunpowder. I know the smell of gun-cotton; we practise with it. The smell was not like the smell of gun-cotton. I do not know any smell it was like. I have never been in the way of using dynamite. Neither I nor any of the party was smoking when we came up to the box. None of us struck a light. There was no light about any of us. None of the party did anything to put light to the box.

14. *Archibald Barr* (26). *By the* LORD ADVOCATE.—I am a furnace-man, and reside in Springburn Road, Glasgow. I am a brother of the last witness. He and I and another brother, with some friends, were coming along the bank of the canal towards Springburn, after paying a visit, on the night of 20th January, between twelve and one o'clock. In going along the bank we came to the place where the canal is carried over Possil Road by a bridge of one arch. This is in the north-west part of Glasgow. As our party were proceeding along, we noticed a box. [Shown No. 6.] That is the box. It was below the hand railing of the bridge, about the middle of the arch,—near about where the keystone would be. It was just standing there. None of us did anything to it. Some remarks were passed about the box being there, and then my brother, the last witness, took it up. It fizzed up, and then when he went back it exploded. After the explosion some of us gave it a kick with the foot, and it smouldered out the same as sawdust. The first explosion blew off the lid, and it was then open. We all got rather a fright. Neither I nor any of our party was smoking, nor had we any light about us. There was nothing done to set the contents on fire. I saw no signs of fire about the box till my brother lifted it up.

15. *Joseph Anderson* (31). *By the* LORD ADVOCATE.—I was a night constable in the northern district of the Glasgow Police in January last. I recollect being on duty in Possil Road about half-past twelve on the morning of Sunday 21st January. I was about 100 yards from the bridge that carries the canal over the road. I heard an explosion. It came from the direction of that bridge. I went down towards the bridge as quickly as I could. I met Constable Frater on the way, who told me that somebody had been hurt on the bridge. I went to the bridge, and I there met the artilleryman Barr and his brothers and the rest of his party. I found six of them more or less wounded. They told me about the box. I saw the box and picked it up. [Shown No. 6.] That is the box. There was something like burnt sawdust round the sides of it when I saw it. The lid was lying a few yards from the box. I took possession of the box and lid. I made no examination of the ground to see if there was anything else lying about; I hastened away with the people who were wounded. It wa good moonlight at the time. There are no lamps near hand. I left Frater in charge of the spot. I took the box with me to the police

office. I did not collect any of the stuff that was in it or anything from the ground.

Cross-examined by Mr. RHIND.—Possil Bridge is in the extreme north part of Glasgow, and it will be about two miles from Maxwell Road on the south side,—I do not think it will be more.

16. *Thomas Frater* (32). *By the* LORD ADVOCATE.—In January last I was a night constable in the northern district of the Glasgow Police, and I am still in the service. About half-past twelve on the morning of Sunday the 21st of that month I was on duty in the Possil district. I heard an explosion,—a loud noise. It seemed to come from the Possil Bridge, from which I was about 100 yards away at the time. I moved to the spot. I met Adam Barr, the artilleryman, who was injured and bleeding, as well as other members of the party. Constable Anderson came up, and we went to the bridge together. He took away the injured people, and I remained on the spot. [Shown No. 6.] I saw that box on the bridge that night. It was taken away by Anderson. After Anderson left I went in search of my sergeant to report the matter. I returned to the bridge about half-past one the same morning. I made an examination of the ground at the centre of the bridge, where it was said the box had been. The ground was black. I found sawdust lying where I was told the box had been. The sawdust was black, looking as if it had been burning. I saw a quantity of it collected by the inspector. [Shown No. 8.] I found these things on carefully examining the ground. I would describe them as a brass tube and a brass tap. The one is a tap or cock, and the other is a piece of a tube. They had a peculiar kind of smell,—a burning kind of smell. There was nothing else peculiar except the burning smell.

17. *Donald Ferguson* (33). *By the* LORD ADVOCATE.—I am a night inspector in the northern district of the Glasgow Police, and was so in January last. I recollect the last witness coming to me on the morning of Sunday 21st January last, and informing me of the explosion on Possil Bridge. I went and examined the place. On the ground of the bridge, where it was said the thing had happened, I found a small brass cap. [Shown part of No. 8.] I saw some sawdust lying about. I collected a quantity of that stuff, and took it to the police office, and it is labelled No. 7. It had a peculiar smell—a different smell from sawdust. On searching the ground I found a cap.[1] It was lying by itself about the centre of the towing-path on the top of the bridge, among the burnt sawdust. Frater had found the tube. The cap screws on to the tube and fits it, and I found it did so at the time. The cap had the same smell as the sawdust. Frater showed me the tube as having been found at the time.

Cross-examined by Mr. RHIND.—I cannot say whether the tap was open or closed.

18. *George Murray* (34). *By the* LORD ADVOCATE.—I am a moulder.

[1] This was part of the production No. 8, being a cap which screwed on to the end of the brass tube, and it was of similar construction to the brass cap No. 4 referred to by Wm. Key as having been found by him on the top of the gasometer.

In January this year I resided in Wigton Street, Glasgow. About eleven o'clock on the night of Saturday 20th January last, I was in Garscube Road, at Dobbie's Loan. That is not very far from the bridge that carries the canal over the Possil Road; I could walk it in about two minutes and a half. I was opposite Crossburn Street. My wife went into a butcher's shop to make some purchases, and I went into a urinal. As I went in I stumbled up against two men with a box. It was a sort of brown enamelled or japanned tin box. A tall man, about six feet high, was carrying it. Both men had not hold of it. [Shown No. 6.] That is like the box. I cannot swear to it; there are so many of them alike. It was not knocked about when I saw it; it was like a new box then. The tall man had a brown topcoat on, short—not nearly to his knees. When I stumbled up against them, the tall man said, "Hoot toots, man, where are ye stammering to?" I replied, "One would think there were surely eggs in your box that you are so much afraid my stammering would do it any harm." There was a little argument with the tall man, but I could not right say what it was. I had a drop of drink in me. I cannot say whether the two men were walking quickly when I stumbled up against them. I cannot say what direction they went in,—whether they went up Dobbie's Loan or Garscube Road; I went into the urinal, and that was all I saw of them. *Q.*—Look at the prisoners and see if there are any like the men you saw. *A.*—I cannot right say, unless that one,—No. 7 [James Kelly],—he looks like the smaller man, but I cannot swear to him. I cannot say there is any one just like the tall man.

Cross-examined by Mr. RHIND.—I had never seen the men before to my knowledge.

EXPLOSION AT THE CALEDONIAN RAILWAY STATION, BUCHANAN STREET.

19. *Thomas Smith* (40). *Examined.*—I am an engine driver in the employment of the Caledonian Railway Company, and reside in Glasgow. I was in the service of the Company on the 20th and 21st of January of the present year. On the morning of Sunday the 21st, I was in charge of my engine near a shed at the Buchanan Street Station of the Caledonian Railway. I was there shortly after one o'clock in the morning, having just arrived from St. Rollox, where I had been engaged shunting. My engine was standing, when all of a sudden I heard a noise of the shed blowing up, and saw what seemed like a rocket going up at the time. The sound resembled a cannon, but was much louder, I think. The shed was one which was used for coaling or coking engines. I heard a noise of timbers breaking, and I saw bricks and pieces of wood flying about. I saw a flame when the explosion took place. I knew a man called John Francis Kearney. He was in the employment of the Caledonian Railway Company at that time. I saw him on the morning of the 21st January after the explosion. I cannot say when I saw him last.

Cross-examined by Mr. RHIND.—There was a strike amongst the Company's servants at that time.

Re-examined.—*Q.*—Was not the strike over and the case settled between the Company and the workmen on that very day—the 20th—before the explosion ? *A.*—Yes. *Q.*—The masters and the men had come to terms on Saturday ? *A.*—Yes.

20. JAMES LONG (43). *Examined.*—I am a porter in the employment of the Caledonian Railway Company at Greenock. I was at the Buchanan Street Station, Glasgow, on the night of the 20th and the morning of the 21st January this year. I was in the points box at Buchanan Street tunnel, working with a man named John Francis Kearney. I was working under him. I had never seen him before I went to work there. I went to the points box on Wednesday night the 16th and 17th of January. Kearney, I believe, was an Irishman. I went on duty on the evening of Sunday the 20th about six o'clock, and took my place in the signal box, relieving the man who had been there before me. Kearney was on duty at the box also. He had sustained some injury in the hand, and I was there to assist him. About one o'clock on the morning of the 21st an engine came up from the goods shed. It was not passed over the points. It was stopped before it came to the points. There was an explosion took place that night at an old shed belonging to the Railway Company. I saw the explosion. The shed was blown up and the fire came right across the line. The points box where I was would be about 100 yards from the shed which was blown up. The explosion caused a loud noise. It blew the lights out of the points box, and stopped the clock. It shook the box. Kearney was standing alongside me in the box at the time of the explosion. A crowd gathered at the scene immediately after the explosion occurred. *Q.*—Did Kearney signal "danger" to the engine which you said was coming in before the explosion ? [Question objected to ; objection repelled.] *A.*—Yes. The engine was a pilot engine. There was no danger at the time that I was aware of. There was no other engine moving about near the shed that night nor any train in transit. There was a goods train farther down the line. Kearney had been out of the pointsman's box shortly before eleven o'clock on the Saturday evening. He was absent about ten minutes, I should think. From that time he was in the box in my sight until the explosion took place.

Cross-examined by Mr. RHIND.—The shed which was blown up was not in use at the time ; it was an empty shed which had formerly been used as a coaling shed. At the time of the explosion there was nothing in it, so far as I am aware.

Cross-examined by Mr. KENNEDY.—I know the man who was driving the engine to which Kearney gave the signal "danger," but I don't know his name. I have seen him here to-day. The sudden explosion took me rather by surprise. It took Kearney by surprise also. He was standing with his back to the door at the time. The door was open and I was looking out. He was about to make some tea for himself, and when the explosion occurred his hat dropped into the water-can he was lifting the water out of to make his tea. I went out bare-headed from the box, and Kearney and I ran down to the pilot engine to see what was the matter. Kearney spoke to the driver of the engine, but I did not. I heard Kearney say he would go over and see what had happened, but I and the men about advised him against doing that. Kearney suggested that some of the parties who had been out on strike had caused the explosion. There was a strike of workmen connected with the railway at that time.

Re-examined.—Q.—Hadn't there been an arrangement come to between the Company and the men on that very day—the 20th ? *A.*—Yes. *Q.*—The strike was over before the explosion took place ? *A.*—Yes.

By the LORD JUSTICE-CLERK.—Kearney was the man in charge of the points box at the time of the explosion. He had come on duty along with me on the night of the 20th at six o'clock. We were both on duty at the time of the explosion.

Cross-examined by Mr. KENNEDY.—I cannot say how long Kearney was in the Company's service after the explosion occurred, as I was transferred to Greenock the following Thursday. Up to the Thursday following he was in the Company's service.

21. *John Lambie* (42). *Examined.*—I am assistant locomotive superintendent in the service of the Caledonian Railway Company, and reside in Glasgow. I know the shed in which the explosion took place on the morning of Sunday 21st January of this year. The shed was from twenty-five to thirty-one feet long and about twelve to fourteen feet broad. It had been used for coaling engines. It had an opening of about nine feet in the end looking towards the tunnel. The floor was raised about four feet from the ground with steps leading up to it. The place below the shed was open. There was a platform adjoining the end of the shed looking towards the tunnel which was level with the floor of the shed, being practically an extension of the shed. On the side of the platform, next the permanent way, there was a narrow platform adjoining the shed and raised about four feet from the ground with steps leading up to it like the rest. The floor below that platform was open. There was a door that opened from the shed on to the platform I have last mentioned. There was an engine shed between the shed in which the explosion took place and the station, and almost adjoining it end-wise. Behind the shed, and between it and the station, there is a bridge over the railway forming part of the thoroughfare, known as Dobbie's Loan Bridge. When the shed was in use there was an iron ladder put up to let the men up and down to their work at the shed. The ladder was suspended from Dobbie's Loan Bridge. That ladder was discontinued when the use of the shed was given up. The shed had been disused from November 1882. So far as the Company were concerned, the iron ladder had been removed. It was found after the explosion that the ladder had been put up again. I never ascertained by whom the ladder had been put back. It was not needed for any service of the Company. On the north side of the shed there was an opening of three and a half feet in the floor, so that any one could get in quite easily. Any one could get into the shed by way of the passenger station, or by the ladder I have mentioned, or by going along from the tunnel. The readiest access and the least observed would be by means of the ladder which we found, after the explosion, had been put up. The ladder led from the top of the wall of Dobbie's Loan Bridge. Before the shed was disused the men got to the top of the ladder by climbing over the top of the wall from Dobbie's Loan. I was roused about four o'clock on the morning of Sunday 21st

January, and went to the scene of the explosion. I found the shed levelled to the ground almost; the chief part of it was blown over towards the foundry. The shed was blown to pieces; it was in ruins. The floor was all blown away the same as the other part—quite clear of the building. From the condition of the building, and particularly of the floor, I am of opinion that the explosion had certainly occurred under the floor of the shed. *Q.*—It must have been something blowing up from below the floor to scatter the floor with the rest of the building? *A.*—That was quite evident from the appearance of it. I saw bricks and small pieces of wood scattered all round about it. There was nothing connected with the service of the Company that could have gone off and caused such an explosion. The gas which had formerly been supplied to the shed had been shut off for some time on account of the shed being disused. There was no communication with any gas-pipe in the shed. Gas could not have had anything to do with the explosion, because the place was so open. The line was cleared for traffic after the explosion, but otherwise the place was left in the same position as I saw it in on the Sunday morning, until Colonel Majendie came. I saw the box which was found in the shed. I did not find it myself, but I saw it afterwards. There were some brass padlocks on it; but that came to nothing. The distance between the shed where the explosion took place and Kearney's signal-box would be perhaps 100 yards. It would not be 200 yards, but I should say it would be over 100.

Cross-examined by Mr. RHIND.—At the time of the explosion there was nothing of any value in the shed. The shed itself was of no particular value. It was a wooden shed with a brick foundation, about three feet up. I know that the gas had been cut off from the shed, because I saw the pipe. *Q.*—Did you examine the place to see whether the gas-pipe was not standing screwed on? *A.*—I did not; but the piping had been removed. There was no possibility of the explosion having been caused by gas. I am not absolutely sure whether the ladder which I saw at Dobbie's Loan Bridge after the explosion was the disused ladder which had been there before. The ladder had been removed in the November previous to the explosion, when the shed was disused. I cannot say how long before the explosion I had been at that shed, but I must have passed it several times. I cannot mention any particular time when I observed it previous to the explosion.

Cross-examined by Mr. KENNEDY.—Kearney was on duty as a points-man in the box adjoining the shed at the time of the explosion. I have known him for eight or nine years, but I cannot exactly say how long. I have known him to be a signalman during that time. So far as I know, he was a trustworthy man; I knew nothing to the contrary. I believe he continued in the service of the Company after the explosion, but I cannot say positively. The inspector of his district, Mr. Reid, will be able to state that. I examined several of the men when I got to the ground on the Sunday morning as to what had happened. I saw Kearney, and he told me what he knew about it. *Q.*—Did he tell you in a quite open and candid manner? *A.*—Yes; he told me what had happened.

By a JUROR.—Dobbie's Loan Bridge would be about thirty or forty yards from the nearest end of the shed which was blown up.

By LORD CRAIGHILL.—I cannot say where the iron ladder which was formerly at the bridge was removed to when the shed was disused. I did not see the ladder after it was removed, but I know it was removed because I saw the place where the ladder used to be.

22. *John Boyd* (45). *Examined.*—I am superintendent of police in the Central District of Glasgow. Immediately after the explosion at the railway shed near Buchanan Street Station, I made inquiries for a man named John Francis Kearney. I found he had left his employment about the 31st March of this year. I afterwards ascertained that he had left Glasgow. I cannot say, of my own knowledge, where he has been since. I traced him to Hull, where he was in company with a man named Phelan.

Cross-examined by Mr. RHIND.—Kearney has not been back in Glasgow since that time to my knowledge.

By the LORD JUSTICE-CLERK.—He left the service of the Company, and I have never seen him since.

23. *Colonel Vivian Dering Majendie, C.B.* (48). *Examined.*—I was formerly an officer in the Royal Artillery, and am now H.M. General Inspector of Explosives. I received information of the three explosions which occurred in Glasgow on the night of Saturday 20th January, and the morning of Sunday 21st January of this year. I proceeded to Glasgow to make an investigation into the circumstances attending these explosions, with the view of endeavouring to ascertain their cause. I arrived in Glasgow on Wednesday the 24th January. I made a careful examination of the three places at which the explosions were said to have occurred—the Tradeston Gasworks, the Possil Bridge, and the Caledonian Railway shed at Buchanan Street Station. My examination of the gasometer on the first occasion took me two days, and I was there again some weeks later, when my examination occupied another day. My examination was very careful and detailed. As the result of the examination I made, I prepared a detailed report and presented it to the Home Office in the discharge of my duty. [Report produced.] In so far as that report contains the records of what I observed and saw, and the opinions I formed, it is correct. In so far as it contains information from others, I am not in a position to speak to it. In my report I give a detailed statement of the condition of things I found, and then I give certain conclusions at which I arrived. The conclusions I arrived at are contained on p. 16 of my report. (Reads) :—

" Accordingly, I conclude without any hesitation that the explosion—

" A. Was not an explosion of gas ; but

" B. Was the explosion of some powerful explosive probably of the nitro-compound class detonated in the space between the pillar and the 12th plate from the top of the outer lift, and immediately over the cup joint (probably resting upon it) and to the right of the bracket.

" There is, I think, no reason to doubt that all the observed effects could have been produced by a charge of about 5 lbs. of well-made dynamite applied as suggested, though whether the agent actually employed was dynamite, or blasting gelatine, or gun-cotton, or lignin-dynamite (imported or manufactured for the purpose), tonite or potentite, or some other variety, it is impossible to say in the absence of more precise indications than we at present possess. That it was some explosive of this class I have no doubt whatever."

The reasons which led me positively to the conclusion that the explosion was not caused by gas are contained on p. 7 of my report, and are, first of all, the fact that the explosion, however occasioned, was external to the gasholder. From my examination of the gasholder it was quite clear to me that the explosion was from without inwards, and not from within outwards. My reasons for coming to that conclusion are stated on p. 7, commencing at the paragraph marked (*a*). (Reads):—

"(*a*) The whole of the effects produced have radiated from a centre which is external to the holder. Thus we find that the pieces of bracket and the broken pieces of guide plate are all blown to the left, the pieces of the cup joint are blown downwards, the pieces of the holder itself are all blown forward in a cone of dispersion of which the apex is immediately to the right of the bucket.

"(*b*) The whole of the effects upon the side of the holder near the point of explosion have evidently been from without, as is exemplified by the blowing *in* of the plates (*see* rent at junction of three lower plates in photograph No. 6), by the violent doubling *inwards* of a portion of the 12th plate (*ibid*), and the blowing *inwards* of the remainder, by the distribution of what may be distinguished as the holder débris in a symmetrical forward cone, and by the character and direction of the holes and bulges in the holder, which have all been made from within and in no single instance from without."

I found that the fracture or breaking of the holder had been occasioned from without inwards, and that the plates near the column were blown in and pieces blown forward partially through the top of the holder and partially through the side of the holder opposite. By the "cone of dispersion" I mean the direction in which the flying fragments had gone like shot from a gun.

By the LORD JUSTICE-CLERK.—The apex of the cone was without and immediately in front of a certain cracked pillar. I then go on to say that "It admits, I consider, of no dispute that the explosive force operated from a point immediately in front of the cracked pillar close to the right of the bracket and just over the cup joint." By "the front of the pillar" I mean the side of the pillar nearest the gasholder.

Examination continued.—I then go on to say, paragraph (3), "It follows from the two preceding propositions that the explosive force was developed not within any enclosed space or chamber but in the open air." There was no enclosed space or chamber between the pillar and the body of the holder—it was not enclosed at the top or the sides, and there was no other enclosed space there where gas could have accumulated. I go on to say on p. 9, paragraph (4), that it follows that "It is certain that the explosion was not a gas explosion at all, *i.e.* was not an explosion of a mixture of gas and air," because it is impossible to produce an explosion of gas and air of this character in the open air. Gas in the condition in which it is inside a gasholder and without an admixture of air will not explode at all, but with a certain admixture of air it will explode. It was absolutely impossible that the explosion could be inside the gasometer, apart from the facts I observed. There are two reasons to my mind which are conclusive on that point. Gas will explode if duly mixed with the necessary quantity of oxygen or atmospheric air in some confined space where it would not receive either more gas or more air. If gas had been escaping out of a leak in the gasometer, it would not explode, but would burn with a flame. It would require a confined space with a certain range of proportion of gas to air which could not be attained in the open air at the particular point at which the gas is escaping. From what I have stated I am satisfied that there had been a violent explosion outside the gasometer for the reasons stated on p. 14 of my report, viz. first, that the effects were intensely local. That is a characteristic feature of dynamite explosions or explosions caused by nitro-glycerine compounds. They differ markedly in that respect from explosions caused by gas or gunpowder.

By the LORD JUSTICE-CLERK.—Dynamite, as we understand it and as it is licensed, consists of nitro-glycerine absorbed in an inert base which is in this country an infusorial earth known as Kieselguhr, exceedingly porous in character. That is what is meant by dynamite, applying the word narrowly. The only chemical constituent in ordinary dynamite is nitro-glycerine. The Kieselguhr is simply employed to render the nitro-glycerine not liquid and safe to convey.

Examination continued.—The thing that explodes in dynamite is the nitro-glycerine, the infusorial earth or Kieselguhr being merely the thing that holds the nitro-glycerine, like a sponge, so as to render it capable of being handled. *Q.*—Therefore you use the term nitro-glycerine compounds to cover cases not only of nitro-glycerine contained in infusorial earth but any other inert substances with which you may mix it? *A.*—Yes; it is merely a matter of choice which you use. It is a characteristic of the nitro-glycerine compounds that their action is exceedingly violent, but within a very limited range. I saw the evidences of that kind of injury in this case. The evidences of that which I found are stated in my report on p. 14, paragraph (1):—

"The effects produced were of a very marked and characteristic description.

"(1). *They were intensely local.*

"Thus, as I have shown, the portion of the plate of the holder exactly opposite to the point at which the explosion undoubtedly occurred was blown into small fragments, but the area of *explosive* effect as exhibited on the holder is excessively circumscribed, being limited, indeed, to the shattered upper part of one plate, and to the portion contiguous to it which has been turned back.

"Similarly, the length of cup joint affected was small, but for this portion the destruction was complete, as exhibited by the numerous small fragments into which it was blown, and which were subsequently recovered between the sides of the tank and the holder.

"Again, while the right cheek of the bracket was blown into very small pieces, the left cheek was uninjured.

"The right face of the pillar base, being that immediately opposite the explosion, was cracked, indented, and otherwise marked. The left face was uninjured, and even the paint was scarcely disturbed.

"The portion of the stone coping opposite to the point of explosion was considerably defaced, but this effect was limited to about two feet of the coping.

"The condition and position of the portions of the half-round iron stiffener, and the fracture of the lower part of the guide plate, afford further evidence of the intensely local character of the explosion, such effects being such as could hardly have been produced except by an explosive acting with detonative rapidity."

By the LORD JUSTICE-CLERK.—A cup joint is a joint where the outer lift of the gasholder descends over the inner lift, and it has water in it, so that when the lift is down it will be closed by water against the escape of any gas.

Examination continued.—It is a water seal. Then a little lower down on the same page, I refer to the evidence showing that the effects were evidently the result of an exceedingly powerful explosive, as exhibited by the great velocity with which the fragments had been projected. I found that the iron had been broken into a very large number of fragments. I found these fragments strewn about the neighbourhood of the explosion. I cannot give any idea of what the number of fragments would be, but there was a large number. The fragments had a peculiar appearance, which aided me in coming to the conclusion that it was a nitro-glycerine compound which had caused the explosion. The appearance to which I refer is pitting—the pitted appearance of the fragments of the face of the pillar, and of the stone coping. That is a characteristic of the explosion of an exceedingly energetic explosive of the nature of the nitro-glycerine compounds, and is due to the great rapidity with which the nitro-glycerine compound acts, breaking up the envelope or case in which it is contained into a number of small pieces, and projecting them with great velocity in whatever direction it may be. If the nitro-glycerine compound is contained in a tin canister and explodes, it breaks the canister into little bits like small shot, and peppers the thing which it strikes. Neither gas nor gunpowder produces that effect at all, gas still less than gunpowder. I found that some flying bits of metal had been driven into other parts of the gasometer, and were sticking there. One piece in particular, a small rivet, had been projected across the gasometer, and had struck a plate corresponding to that which must have been opposite the explosion, showing that the rivet had travelled across 160 feet with great rapidity. I found that piece of rivet inside the gasometer, showing that it must have been fired across the inside, and had stuck there. If the explosion had been a burst from within outwards, that could not have happened. I do not know that I found any other pieces of metal sticking in that way, but I found evidences of the plates having been struck, because there were bulges inside like where bits of metal had struck and fallen. The rivet of which I have spoken could not have come from any place except from the opposite side of the gasholder, and it must have been operated upon by a force from without. I have no doubt it was one of the rivets which had been on the opposite side of the gasholder where the explosion occurred. I have no doubt it was an inside rivet which had been blown out. I do not recollect observing anything outside the gasometer, on the top, as regards material falling from above upon it. From the physical appearance, and other things I have stated, I entertain no doubt whatever as to the nature of the cause of the explosion. I further say that gas in the condition in which it was in the gasholder could not have exploded.

The plan attached to my report was not drawn by me, but I believe, speaking generally, it is correct. I saw the column which was broken. The peculiar injury which it had sustained was equally characteristic of a powerful explosive of the nitro-compound class operating from the outside. The reasons I have indicated are the chief reasons which led me to that conclusion, but I might go into it in much greater detail than I have done. [Shown No. 5.] I saw that piece of brass about a month after the explosion. I do not remember if I was shown No. 4 [circular brass cap or tube] when I first saw No. 5 [circular brass cap or tube]. I did not attach any importance to it, but afterwards I came to attach importance to it from the knowledge which I subsequently acquired, namely, the discovery of some infernal machines at Liverpool. My examinations of the portions of the machinery connected with them induced me to write to the Fiscal, to get back again the little cap No. 5,[1] which I thought, and still think, bore a strong likeness to the parts of the machines or the portions of the machines which were found at Liverpool. It also bore a likeness to what I was shown as having been found at Possil Bridge No. 8. The piece of brass No. 5 looks as if it were a bruised cap of the same kind as No. 4 is a whole cap. Q.—No. 5 is just in the condition in which one part of No. 8 would have been if the Possil Bridge explosion had succeeded and knocked everything to bits? A.—Yes; it might not destroy the whole tube, and No. 5 might be a portion that was not destroyed. Q.—And would the other, No. 4 which you are now shown, look like another portion of the same thing? A.—I think so.

Besides the ordinary kind of dynamite to which I have referred, there is an illegal dynamite, which has been made in this country. I have come across it in four instances. There are very strict Acts of Parliament regarding explosives. Lignin-dynamite is an illegal substance; it is not licensed. It is never used for any commercial purpose to my knowledge, and cannot be lawfully used. It is illegal to make it or to have it in this country. Lignin-dynamite is a name which has been applied to dynamite composed mainly of nitro-glycerine absorbed, not into the infusorial earth commonly used, but into sawdust, it may be in some instances with chlorate, or it may be simply the nitro-glycerine and sawdust. Sometimes there may be a little chalk in it as well. The sawdust does not perform any other function, except acting as a sort of vehicle for the nitro-glycerine just in the same way as, in the legal dynamite, the infusorial earth acts. The first instance in which I came across lignin-dynamite was some which was contained in ten infernal machines which were seized on board the vessels "Malta" and "Batavia" at Liverpool in 1881. The machines were not seized on board the vessels, but were found in barrels professedly containing cement, after the vessels were discharged. Those machines had come from America. The next time I saw it was some material which I was told had been picked up on the Possil Bridge. I obtained it when I was in Glasgow investigating the Possil Bridge explosion, as well as the others. The stuff which I was shown on that occasion was lignin-dynamite. The third instance was in connection with the attempted explosions at the "Times" office on the 15th of March of this

[1] See the evidence of James M'Murray and of Charles Simpson, p. 35.

year, the same night as the Local Government Board Offices were blown up. The fourth occasion was in two machines which were seized at Liverpool in the spring of this year—the machines in connection with which Featherstone, Dalton, and Deasy were tried. In the instances I have mentioned the lignin-dynamite was contained in either a tin or zinc box. In two instances it was in a tin box, but the Liverpool machines were contained in a zinc box. The infernal machines which were seized at Liverpool in 1881 were not intended to be exploded by an arrangement of the description of which the brass tubes and caps Nos. 4 and 5 are portions, but were fitted with a clockwork arrangement for exploding them by means of percussion. The Liverpool infernal machines which were seized this year on the men who were tried and, I believe, convicted.—Featherstone, Dalton, and Deasy,—had two of these taps, and some parcels containing chlorate of potash and sugar and red orpiment, and also a bottle or bottles of sulphuric acid. [Shown three tubes.] These are three tubes similar to those which were found in the infernal machines at Liverpool, and I believe they are the same. In general arrangement these are precisely the same as the one which was found at Possil Bridge. If a mixture of chlorate of potash and sugar is acted upon by sulphuric acid, it produces brisk inflammation almost amounting to detonation. By inflammation I mean ignition. If red orpiment is added to it, it makes the inflammation more brisk. Realgar is another name for red orpiment. If sulphuric acid be introduced into the top of one of these tubes and the tap be turned, the sulphuric acid would flow down and would get out through the two holes in the side of the tube on to the mixture which might be contained within the brass envelope. But, in order to prevent it from going down too quickly, the tap is wrapped round with paper, and the sulphuric acid has to eat its way through the paper, and it is a mere question of adjustment of the number of folds of paper and the character of the paper, whether, in four, or five, or ten, or even forty minutes if desired, it will accomplish this and reach the chlorate of potash and sugar mixture and ignite it. Experiments have been made with things like this [holds up one of the three tubes], and it has been ascertained that according to the number of folds of paper that you interpose between the sulphuric acid and the chlorate of potash and sugar, you can delay the explosion from five to forty minutes, so that anybody who put the thing down would have time to go away. The hole at the bottom of the tube is adapted for receiving a detonator, which is merely an elongated percussion cap of unusual size, which detonates or explodes the dynamite in which the detonator may be placed. If one of these things is placed in contact with lignin-dynamite in a tin or other light metal box, and the tap turned, letting the sulphuric acid flow in against the paper and eat its way down, it will explode in from five to forty minutes as it is intended to act. I do not know of any commercial or lawful purposes for which things of that kind are made. I never saw such things in my life except in connection with infernal machines. Q.—So that if it be the case that the one you hold in your hand was found close to a box of lignin-dynamite on Possil Bridge, would you have any difficulty in drawing a conclusion as to what it was there for ?   A.—Not now, in view of what we have learned about these machines.

By the LORD JUSTICE-CLERK.—When I first saw one of these tubes I could not make out what it was. It was subsequent to seeing the tube that I learned what it was for, and it assumed importance in my mind.

Examination continued.—Q.—Supposing it to be true that Nos. 4 and 5 were found at the gasometer, would you associate them in any way with the explosion which took place there? *A.*—Yes; it appears to me that this is similar to the cap at the bottom of the one which was found at Possil Bridge, except that it is bruised and burned, showing that there has been action. Ordinary dynamite contains a much heavier charge of nitro-glycerine than lignin-dynamite can contain safely. The lignin-dynamites I have come in contact with have varied in their proportion from about 20 to about 70 per cent. of nitro-glycerine, and they do not hold the nitro-glycerine permanently; it flows out so that the lignin-dynamite is not such a material as one could properly license. Another objection is, that if it gets wet or damp it is much more likely to expel the nitro-glycerine than ordinary dynamite. As far as its chemical action is concerned, there is no difference between lignin-dynamite and ordinary dynamite. Until kieselguhr was discovered in this country it was imported from abroad in large quantities. It is not a thing of which one can get a few pounds in the market. The only place where I know it could be obtained would be from manufacturers of dynamite. It is not sold in the market as far as I know, and is not used for any other purpose but the manufacture of dynamite. If anybody wanted to manufacture dynamite for an unlawful purpose, it would be more convenient to use sawdust, as it would be more readily obtainable.

I inquired into the explosion at Possil Bridge at the same time as I inquired into the others. I handed a sample of the sawdust which was got at Possil Bridge to our chemical adviser, Dr. Dupré. The chemical proportions of the material are stated on p. 19 of my report from Dr. Dupré's report. They are stated to be—sawdust and a little charcoal, 75·4; nitro-glycerine, 19·2; moisture, 5·4 per cent. That was the composition of the sample which I handed to Dr. Dupré as having been obtained from Possil Bridge. Q.—Did you find, adhering to the brass pieces I have shown you, and which are said to have been found on Possil Bridge, charred sawdust? *A.*—I should prefer that Dr. Dupré should speak to that. [Shown No. 6.] If it were the case that that box, filled with lignin-dynamite and with such an apparatus as I have described connected with it, was found on the crown of a bridge which carried a canal over a public road, I cannot imagine any lawful purpose for which it could be there. The conclusion which I would draw from its being found there would be that it was intended to injure the bridge. It is not a thing that people would be carrying about with them for any purpose. The box No. 6 would contain about 10 to 12 lbs. of lignin-dynamite. It is very light. The lignin-dynamite which was found in the box was, explosively speaking, very poor, as it had so little nitro-glycerine in it. There was too much sawdust in it, so that it was a very poor article. Q.—Has it been found that that kind of dynamite sometimes misses fire? *A.*—Any kind of dynamite may miss fire with an imperfected detonation. A badly made dynamite would be much more ready to

ignite than that which contained a very large charge of nitro-glycerine.
Q.—Suppose that a box like No. 6, containing lignin-dynamite, had
been equipped with the kind of brass apparatus you have described,
while the detonator was conveying the fire from the chemicals into the
box, would there be a sort of puff? *A.*—Yes; the ignition of the
chlorate mixture would create a sort of fizz or puff,—a sudden
energetic ignition,—but it would be very limited in range. If it failed
to light the dynamite inside, that might account for a small fizzing
explosion; and if any part of the dynamite had caught fire, that might
contribute to the fizzing. *Q.*—Would it be quite intelligible to you as
a scientific man, that if the dynamite were of poor quality and the
connection not very perfect, some of the stuff might go off, but the
great bulk would remain as it was found? *A.*—I do not think
that any of it could go off with what I should call a detonation and
leave any behind, but I think that a portion of it might go off in the
sense of being ignited and consumed, leaving some unconsumed. It
would be burned as distinguished from detonated. There might be a
detonation within the fuse although the dynamite did not detonate or
explode. I should like to correct my answer, however, to this extent,
that I think it possible it might even happen that a portion of the
dynamite might be detonated, only not powerfully, and yet leave some
behind, if there had been sawdust without due connection with nitro-
glycerine in the middle of it.

By the LORD JUSTICE-CLERK.—I do not think sawdust would be
readily inflammable in connection with a detonator. Lignin-dynamite
and ordinary dynamite would both produce the same effects if they
contained the same charge of nitro-glycerine.

Examination continued.—If a box of the size of No. 6 had been filled
with 12 or 14 lbs. of well-made dynamite, and the dynamite had
exploded on the top of the bridge at Possil, I think the bridge would
have been very seriously injured, but I think it is possible that it
might have escaped total destruction. The bridge might have been
blown down so as to let out the whole of the water; but that, I understand, is supposing the box to contain dynamite with 75 per cent. of
nitro-glycerine. I have seen the place where the box was found. If
the canal had been let out by the destruction of the bridge, the
consequences would have been very disastrous to the houses in the
streets below. The water from the canal would have flooded the
houses, and would have created great alarm and possibly even worse
consequences. The result would have undoubtedly been to put a stop
to navigation in the canal.

I also examined the shed at the Caledonian Railway Station. I
came to the conclusion that the explosion there had been produced by
the application of a small quantity of nitro-glycerine compound. I
came to that conclusion from the appearance of the destruction which
had been wrought upon the shed, and the impossibility of accounting
for the explosion by the presence of any other substance which could
have produced the effects which I saw. From what I saw, I formed
the conclusion that the explosion must have been above the floor of the
shed. There was ample evidence, I think, on that point. The floor
was blown down instead of being blown up, and the pieces of metal
which we recovered from the planks of the floor were recovered from

the upper sides of the planks, and not the under sides. Some portions of the wood were blown into small pieces; they were lacerated. These appearances were characteristic of an explosion from dynamite, or something of the nature of dynamite. The appearances could not have been produced by an explosion of gas. The character of the effects were such that gas could not have produced them, and in the next place there was no gas in the building. The gas had been disconnected, as I understand, some time previous to the explosion. Dynamite, even if laid upon a flat surface without a jumper hole being bored or driven into it, will cause a violent explosion, rending from above downwards, and that is the common mode of using it. When people want to blast big boulder stones or tree roots, they place a little dynamite on the top, and it blows the whole thing to bits below; it does not require tamping, nor any jumper hole.

Cross-examined by Mr. RHIND.—Dynamite does not require to be confined to exercise its full explosive effects. There are other explosives having different names which act in the same way, but all belonging to the nitro-glycerine class, and also, perhaps, to the chlorate class. Where chlorate is introduced, it renders the explosive substance more sensitive and dangerous, and there have been some explosives proposed of that kind, but they have not attained any practical importance. Dynamite is very extensively used for blasting purposes. I did not say that dynamite made with infusorial earth is better in relation to its effects than lignin-dynamite, but it is better in relation to its safety. Infusorial earth is not what is known as fuller's earth. It is composed of deposits of infusoria which had been accumulated in the process of years, and the structure of which admits of their taking up three times their own weight of nitro-glycerine. I believe deposits of this infusorial earth have been discovered in Scotland. If I wished to get some of it I should go to Nobel's Explosive Company. I know of no other place where I could get it, except a manufactory of explosives in the south of England. I am not aware that it is used for any other purpose than the manufacture of dynamite. I had to examine the gasholder before I could determine in my own mind whether it was gas that had caused the explosion or not. I believe it is possible under certain conditions to produce an explosion in a gasholder, but it was not possible that the injury to this gasholder could have been caused by that. The first point I inquired into was whether it could have been the gas that produced the explosion, before I proceeded to satisfy myself what else it was likely to have been. Under very special conditions it is possible for a gasholder to explode without explosives, in the ordinary sense of the word, being used,—not when filled with gas, but when filled with a mixture of gas and air. Gas by itself will not explode. I should prefer to leave it to some other witness to say what proportion of air it would require to make gas explode, but I believe, in the case of such a gas as is supplied at Glasgow, about eight parts of air to one of gas would make an explosive mixture. I do not believe that a great escape of gas from a gasometer and the accidental application of a light outside, such as the light from the pipe of a man who was passing, would cause such an explosion; I believe it would be contrary to all experience that it could do so. The pillars which support the gasholder are hollow. *Q.*—Suppose gas had escaped into one of these pillars until it was in the proportion of one part of gas to eight parts of air, and a light had got there, would that have burst the pillar and set fire to the gasholder? *A.*—No. In the first place, I don't think the gas could accumulate in that way, because the pillar is open at the top and has ornamental open scroll-work at the back which admits the air, so that the gas would at once be diffused and go to the upper part of the pillar. But even if the pillar had become filled with the mixture and exploded, it could not possibly have produced the effects I observed at the gasholder. My attention was directed to a portion of the gasholder which was pitted. The pitted part faced the outside of the gasometer. I have had experience of gas explosions and their effects. I have made it my business to ascertain the results of gas explosions, and I have witnessed their effects in confined vessels, and have witnessed some experiments also in connection with this inquiry. *Q.*—Have you ever examined into the case of a gasholder before this one? *A.*—I have been unable to discover any instance of a gasholder explosion. The lignin-dynamite which was found at Possil Bridge was not so weak as to be totally ineffective. It contained 19 per cent. of nitro-glycerine, and, although for commercial purposes it would be an ineffective explosive, it would be still a dangerous explosive under certain circumstances. I don't think that lignin-dynamite such as was found would have destroyed Possil Bridge. The top of the arch where the dynamite was found was the strongest part of the bridge. *Q.*—And therefore the last part, I suppose, that a person desiring to destroy the bridge would put it on? *A.*—It is a more convenient part to put it, and therefore it is possible one might have recourse to that, although the least effective mode of attack. There is no difficulty in making lignin-dynamite with a proper proportion of nitro-glycerine, if you have enough nitro-glycerine. I think the explosion of the gasholder might have been caused by dynamite as weak as that which was found at Possil Bridge, if enough of it had been used; it is a question of amount. Five pounds of ordinary well-made dynamite, I believe, would have been sufficient. Of stuff such as was found at Possil Bridge, I should think it would have required probably 15 lbs., or perhaps a little more, to have produced the effect I saw. The box No. 6 would contain from 10 to 12 lbs. of the lignin-dynamite. *Q.*—So that it would require more than that box full to have caused the effect you found at the gasholder? *A.*—I don't know that it would. I think you could produce the effects I saw with 5 lbs. of ordinary dynamite, and that would represent about 20 lbs. of the lignin-dynamite which was found at Possil Bridge. But I am not prepared to say that these effects might not have been produced with a smaller quantity. To produce the effects I found at the gasholder, the explosive must have been put in a particular position, viz. between the pillar and the gasholder. I did not say that if the Possil Bridge dynamite had exploded it would have exploded altogether. I think I corrected that statement, and said it might or it might not. The probability is that if there had been a powerful detonation it would all have exploded, but I can conceive an initial detonation not so powerful as to produce an explosion of the whole—the ignition or partial detonation, and not an explosion of the whole. *Q.*—Would it be possible for the explosion to be heard 100 yards off while part of the dynamite was left unexploded? *A.*—Yes, I think so, because the detonator undoubtedly would have contributed to that noise, and the detonator contains a charge of fulminate which makes very considerable noise when it explodes. I think it certainly would be heard at that distance. When I said that lignin-dynamite was illegal, I meant that no explosive is allowed to be manufactured or imported into this country except in virtue of a licence granted by the Secretary of State, and lignin-dynamite is not one of the licensed explosives. We have never had it submitted to us, and the samples of it I have seen are not such as I should be disposed to recommend for licence. Dynamite is used largely in mining, quarrying, clearing land of boulders or roots of trees, removing obstructions from the mouths of harbours, blowing up wrecks of ships, and for many industrial purposes. I believe it is also used to clear the remnants of iron from the bottoms of blast furnaces. No person who uses dynamite makes it for himself. When I say no person, I mean that it would be illegal to do so, and we have never discovered any illegal making of it except at Birmingham in the case of Whitehead.

Re-examined.—I never knew of lignin-dynamite being used for any lawful purpose. I never knew brass tubes of the description which has been referred to used to fire a charge of dynamite for a lawful purpose.

By a JUROR.—*Q.*—How do you connect the cap found near the gasometer? *A.*—I don't know that I quite understand the question. What I said was, that I consider that this cap looked like the cap on the bottom of the instrument which was found at Possil Bridge, with this difference, that it had evidently been subjected to some violent effect—an explosion.

By the LORD JUSTICE-CLERK.—In regard to the first explosion I am of opinion that the appearances of the gasholder could only have been produced by force from without, irrespective of what the explosive agent might be, and consequently that the pieces of iron that were projected into the gasholder were marked with the characteristic marks of a nitro-glycerine or dynamite explosive, which could not have happened if the explosion had arisen from gas and not from dynamite. I am perfectly satisfied of that. The idea of a gas explosion having caused that is entirely out of the question—it is impossible. *Q.*—And if the damaged cap which was found [No. 5] is a portion of a similar instrument to that which was found at Possil Bridge [No. 8], would you have any doubt at all in your own mind that it had been used for a similar purpose? *A.*—No. I should think it unreasonable to entertain any doubt if I found it under these conditions. I cannot imagine any other purpose for which it could have been applied. There was no explosion in any large sense of the word at Possil Bridge. There was no explosion of the compound of sawdust and nitro-glycerine, but there may have been some ignition of it. There was a compound and a detonator which would be naturally used to effect the detonation of nitro-glycerine, from which I conclude that that was the object of the detonator. *Q.*—I understand you to say that lignin-dynamite is more dangerous and that the dynamite prepared with infusorial earth is a safer compound? *A.*—Yes; in regard to the power of retention of the liquid nitro-glycerine. *Q.*—So that it is a more hazardous affair and has not been used for commercial purposes of that kind? *A.*—It has never been proposed to use it for commercial purposes, and it would not be a feasible or desirable agent to apply as an absorbent. *Q.*—For the reason that it won't retain the explosive substance with sufficient security? *A.*—It won't retain any sufficient quantity to make it an explosive fit for commercial use, but it would retain a small quantity. *Q.*—Would you carry your conclusions so far as this, that the combination of nitro-glycerine with sawdust, so as to make it lignin-dynamite, indicated an unlawful purpose? *A.*—Yes, that is my conclusion; that is the conclusion I have come to. My reasons for coming to the conclusion that the railway shed was blown up by means of dynamite, were that the effects produced were of the character, and of the character only, which could have been produced by an explosive of the nitro-glycerine nature. There was the breaking of the floor in such a way that portions of the wood were completely destroyed and disintegrated. There was the driving into the floor, in one instance to the depth of one inch, of a piece of metal which must have required a very powerful force; and generally the destruction of the shed was of such a complete and thorough character that it could not have been effected in my judgment by any other explosive. We found no traces of dynamite, but, I should say, where dynamite is effectively detonated the traces of the inert base are destroyed so completely that they are not recoverable or distinguishable. *Q.*—I understand you to say that by the chemical compound you described, which is used for the purpose of exploding the lignin-dynamite, the period may be within certain limits protracted or accelerated according as the filtration of the sulphuric acid takes a longer or a shorter time? *A.*—That is so; it is a mere question of adjustment. *Q.*—And therefore it is an advantage in that respect if you wish either to protract or accelerate the explosion? *A.*—Yes, it is very useful in that way.

The Conspiracy.

24. *John Horan* (54). *Examined by the* Lord Advocate.—I am a gas-producer in Glasgow. I identify two of the prisoners at the bar, Peter Callaghan and Henry M'Cann. I met them on one or two occasions in Lennox's public-house, but I did not know the name of the shop at the time. Lennox's shop is in Bridgegate, Glasgow. I met them in this way: I was down at the bird market one Saturday evening, and I fell in with a man where there was a discussion about the famine in Ireland during the past two or three years. The man was debating and discussing the distress in Ireland, and he came forward to where I was standing and we started to speak. He spoke to me about an organization for the distress in Ireland, and I said that I had paid into different societies, at least to different people, and he said, was I in any society for myself? I said, no, but that I paid very often to anything in the cause. Then he and I went into this beer-shop and had a glass of beer, and he introduced me to Peter Callaghan. We went into a room in the shop, and they administered some words off a paper, but I could not say what they were. I could not say if it was an oath. Callaghan did not say anything to me until I went into

the wee room in the shop. He did not say to me that they had a secret society and ask me to join it. He did not say that to me at any time. I was just introduced to the wee room, and the man I have referred to, or Callaghan, I could not say which, administered the words to me. No one in the public-house spoke to me about a secret society or asked me to join it, to my knowledge at that time. There was never a secret society mentioned to me. I was asked to join a society when I told this man that I paid into different societies—at least to funds for Ireland like. He did not give the society a name to my knowledge. I did not understand it to be a secret or ribbon society. I never understood it to be anything but a friendly society or organization. I was not told when I was taken into the wee room that the members had to take an oath; the first oath I ever took was the oath I took to-day. I never took an oath in Lennox's public-house, but these words were mentioned to me or read from a paper. I don't know whether it was Callaghan or the other man who said the words. I don't know what the words were. Q.—Why were the words read off the paper? A.—I thought it was a rule they had in this society. Q.—That you should take an oath? A.—No, oath was never mentioned. I did not hold up my hand when the words were read off the paper; to-day was the first time I ever held up my hand. Q.—Have you never said that you took an oath off that paper in Lennox's public-house? A.—I never took an oath, but I told them at the County Buildings I thought it was the form of an oath. Q.—And do you think so still? A.—I don't think anything of the kind, because it never was put to me. Q.—It was the form of an oath read off a paper, only it never was put to you? A.—It was not put to me as such. Q.—But you thought it was an oath? A.—Yes. Q.—Does it come to this, that what the man read off the paper was an oath, but you did not think you took it because it was not put to you? A.—No, and I never was told it was an oath. Q.—But you thought so? A.—I thought so afterwards. Q.—What did you think at the time? A.—I thought nothing bad about it. I was led into it innocent and ignorant. I thought it was a friendly organization. Q.—What made you think afterwards it was an oath? A.—I thought it was a form to bind me to the society. But that was never mentioned to me by anybody. I think I paid Callaghan or some one, but I do not remember the name. I cannot say how long I remained a member of the society. I should say about twelve months. I would not swear to that. I never was at any meeting of the society at all.

By the LORD JUSTICE-CLERK.—It is right that you should know that if you tell the truth in this matter you cannot be prosecuted for anything that took place upon the occasions about which you are examined; but if you do not speak the truth you do it at your own peril, and you may be punished.

Examination continued.—I never was present in Lennox's public-house to my knowledge when other members of the society were there. I never met any members in Jail Square to my knowledge, with the exception of one man, Peter Callaghan. I never met Henry M'Cann in Jail Square. I have met him in Lennox's public-house. I am not aware whether the society used to meet in Jail Square. I cannot say whether they used to meet at the corner of the Green near

the Justiciary Buildings; I never was at any of their meetings. I
think I was on two occasions in Lennox's public-house when some of
those whom I knew to be members of the society were there, but they
were not there attending a meeting. I just happened to be there on
those occasions. The men who were present are the two I have
mentioned. There were others present on that occasion; it was on a
Saturday night and the house was full. I do not know whether the
men whom I knew were acquainted with the others or not. I did not
see any acquaintance between them. I was in the room with a lot of
men. There were a lot of men and women and children there, and
discussions going on. On the occasion when I was taken into the
little room in Lennox's public-house, some words were read to me off a
paper. Peter Callaghan and the man I have mentioned were present.
Q.—Do you swear that you did not take an oath on that occasion and
join what you were told was a secret society? *A.*—I never took an
oath. This is the first one I have taken in my life. I left the society
because I thought it did not answer my purposes. To be a member of
a society you should pay in so much money to keep it up, and that
does not suit a man with a wife and family. The real reason that
I left was because the clergy of the Catholic Church, to which I
belong, are against societies or any assemblage of any class of people.
They think it leads to a bad end, and are against it, and that was what
made me leave the society. *Q.*—Was it in consequence of being warned
by your priest that you left the society? *A.*—It was. While I was a
member of the society I never heard any discussion upon any subject
whatever. I never heard anything about the blowing up or destruction
of buildings or anything; nor about buying explosives. I was led into
the society innocent and ignorant, and I left it in the same condition,
and I believe the majority of the men were the same.

25. *George Hughes* (53). *Examined.*—I am a fruit merchant in Glasgow, and reside in 57 Thistle Street, Hutcheson Street. I know the
whole of the prisoners. I have known some of them upwards of two years
and some of them perhaps about six months. Some of them are dealing men, and I have been meeting with them several times. They and I
all belonged to a society. I joined the society about three months before
July 1882. The society went under the name of a ribbon society.
I was asked to join it by Peter Callaghan, one of the prisoners.
He asked me several times to join it before I agreed to do so. He
explained to me that the society would do no harm to me—that it was
like to be in friendly terms with our brethren, so that if there was
anything happened of violence betwixt the Government or anything of
that, we required to take an oath to that effect, so that we would be
loyal to our brothers—that we should take part in anything that
happened, and be loyal. *Q.*—What was said about the Government?
A.—Anything that was said about it was, that if any of our men got
into any bother or anything such as that, we were to take part in it
as well as them. I could not give the exact words that we made use
of when the Government was mentioned; these were all the words he
explained to me at that time. *Q.*—Was anything said about getting
into a "habble" with the Government? *A.*—Yes, he said that, and
we were to stand by each other if they got into a "habble" with the

Government. I did not just know what he meant by getting into a "habble." He told me the society met on the first Monday of every month in Lennox's public-house, Saltmarket. He did not mention the names of any of the members, only some of those whom I knew. There were a great many strangers whom I knew nothing about. Amongst those whom I knew were Patrick Drum and Patrick M'Cabe. Callaghan also mentioned James Kelly, Denis Casey, and Tom Devany. When I joined the society I took an oath. There was a strange man acting as chairman at that time. He had been an old pensioner, but I don't know his name. Peter Callaghan was present when the oath was administered. It was administered in Lennox's public-house, Saltmarket, on the first Monday of the month, about three months before Glasgow Fair in 1882. Of the prisoners there were present on that occasion James Kelly, Patrick Drum, Tom Devany, Henry M'Cann, Peter Callaghan, and Denis Casey. The oath was to swear by Almighty God to stand loyal to all brothers and keep all secrets, and if any of our brothers got into bother with the Government, we were to stand by and not see one "mislisted" without the other interfering. The oath was read off a paper, and I held up my hand the same as I have done to-day. I paid 2s. 6d. of entry money. A shilling of that went, I suppose, for drink in the house, and Peter Callaghan got the remainder. Peter Callaghan was called Grand Master. I continued to attend the meetings of the society from that time until about two months after Glasgow Fair. We met once in M'Ginn's public-house in Bridgegate, but I do not exactly remember the date when that was. Besides meeting in Lennox's public-house, the members of the society also met in Jail Square. We generally met on Sunday and Saturday afternoons, and whiles on evenings through the week after we quitted work. That continued throughout the autumn of 1882 and into the spring of 1883. I remember on one occasion, about the 4th or 5th of July 1882, of being in Jail Square, when Peter Callaghan, Patrick Drum, Tom Devany, and an old man, James M'Cabe, who is now dead, were there. There was also a man named John Francis Kearney, a signalman, there. I cannot say on what railway Kearney was employed, whether it was the Glasgow and South-Western or the Caledonian. He came to Peter Callaghan, and said, "There is some person wanting to see you," and he went away, and Peter Callaghan and Patrick Drum went with him. They went towards Bridgegate, and were about three-quarters of an hour away. When they came back, I made the remark, "You have been pretty long away," and they said they were seeing two fine gentlemen who had come from America. They did not tell me the names of the gentlemen. I carry on the business of selling fruit from a pony cart, and I have a stable where my pony stays. One night, when I was coming across to my own stable, Peter Callaghan touched me on the shoulder, and said, "You are the very one I am looking for." I said, "What is it?" He said, "I want an obligement of you." I said, "If I can serve you I will do it." He said, "I want you to let in two jars of vitriol; it will do you no injury." I said, "I will do that with the greatest pleasure." There was no more said then, but on the Sunday forenoon, about eleven o'clock or a little after that, we met at the entrance going into the Green at Jail Square, and Denis Casey handed Patrick Drum a bottle of vitriol, about maybe a mutchkin or a little more, and they came over to my stable. There were present on that occasion Patrick Drum, Patrick M'Cabe, Denis Casey, James Kelly, Kearney, M'Cann, Callaghan, and one of the gentlemen who came from America named Johnston. Johnston was introduced to me as one of the gentlemen who had come from America. They came into my stable, and Kearney took a white powder out of his pocket and spilled some on the floor, and then took a small bit of stick and poked it into the vitriol and touched the white powder, and the minute he did so it made a small puff, but not a great noise. That was all that happened. I was told at that time that the gentleman had come from America for the purpose of learning them how to manufacture dynamite. Q.—Do you mean for the purpose of teaching them? A.—Yes, to learn them how to make dynamite. It was the man Johnston who said that first. He was introduced to me on the 9th July, the Sunday before we went into the stable. It was Peter Callaghan who introduced him to me. Callaghan did not say anything to me about how I was to treat him; he simply said that this was Mr. Johnston from America. Q.—Did he say anything about giving him a hand? A.—He said that we would need to give him a hand. I understood him to mean that we were to help him to carry on the manufacture of this dynamite. I knew of nothing else. The dynamite was to be for blowing up buildings and such like as that; that was the expression they came out with. I heard Johnston mentioning a number of things for making dynamite. He mentioned a great number of things, but I cannot remember that. He mentioned about vitriol and glycerine, and several other articles which I cannot remember. Johnston did not mention anything about putting dynamite into a box; it was Featherstone who explained that. After Kearney put the powder on the floor of the stable, we went out and went to the Green, and Denis Casey said he knew a young man who stopped beside him, who worked in a chemical work, and he could get as much vitriol as they liked. It was agreed on then that I was to go on Wednesday before the works would stop for the Fair, with my pony and cart, to be ready at four o'clock, and this young man would go with me to the chemical work, and I was to draw one of these carboys of vitriol. I consented to do so. Kelly was to be waiting on me at four o'clock at the stable to accompany me. They gave me money, and I was to go out with this young man who was to get the vitriol. I was not told the name of the young man who was in the chemical work. I was to give him the money, and he was to get it, and I was to draw it to my stable. I was some minutes after four o'clock in getting home, and I found Kelly waiting for me. I put the pony into the stable, and went forward to a small public-house, Douglas's in Saltmarket. When I went in there the young man was sitting, and he had a good drop of drink. When we went in he said, "Are you Mr. Hughes?" I said, "Yes." He said, "Are you ready to go for that stuff?" "No," I said; "I know nothing about you," and I jumped up and went away. I don't know who the young man was. I did not bring the stuff at that time. That is all that happened on that occasion. There was no reason given at the time. I heard that the stuff was to be used for blowing up buildings. There was no money collected on Sunday the 8th July, but there was on the 16th. We met as usual on the

16th, and Patrick Drum had some money keeping, and he handed me £2, 10s., as he said he was going away to the north, where his good-son was living. He asked me to keep the money and give it to them if they required it. I took the money, and after that Peter Callaghan lifted a collection. He said there was a poor woman in great distress, as her man was lying badly. He wanted a collection. We all gave 1s. each, and Callaghan got, I should say, about 14s. or 15s. He then said it was for the use of buying stuff to manufacture dynamite, as Featherstone's funds were running out, but he expected more daily to come from America, and that we would all get back. That was the first time I had heard Featherstone named. He was introduced to me on the 16th. [Shown Timothy Featherstone.] That is the man who was introduced to me as Timothy Featherstone. Some of us objected to what the money was being lifted for when he said it was for the use of buying stuff to manufacture dynamite—that the funds were run down, but that he would soon get plenty more sent over, and that all the money would be paid back again. There was no more happened that day. We had a meeting up in the Gymnastic Hall in the evening. Kearney came to us and said to Peter Callaghan, and Patrick Drum, and Tom Devany, and me, that we had better go up to the Gymnastic Hall. We went up and had a meeting there, and Kearney was talking about what errand they came on from New York, and what a good job it was to be—that it would learn the Government a lesson that they would not do just what they thought proper—and that it would be a very good thing. *Q.*—What was to be a very good thing ? *A.*—This dynamite when it would be manufactured—that it would be very instructive. Peter Callaghan told Pat M'Cabe and me that there was no more call for us there, and we went away. Patrick Drum, Peter Callaghan, and Tom Devany stopped behind. They were three-quarters of an hour in the hall before they came to the Green. We asked what detained them, and they said they had to take an oath, but what the oath was I cannot say. The Gymnastic Hall is in Nelson Street, City, before you go up to the Central Police Office. There was none of the other men there except those I have mentioned. I have often been in Featherstone's presence. He used to come down to the Green generally on Sunday afternoon after that, and whiles through the week, and we used to walk up through the Green and stand against the paling and such places as that many a time. Featherstone was coming about the meetings off and on for I daresay about two or three months. He was there in the months of July, August, and September. It was he who explained what the dynamite was, and that by putting some into a tin box and throwing it out of the window of a carriage that wherever it was thrown it would explode and blow up anything it would go underneath—it would blow it right up. *Q.*—Did you ever hear him saying anything about the barracks. *A.*—He explained that if you were leaving a quantity of this dynamite against the wall what effect it would have—it would blow it right in, as it was so many degrees stronger than gunpowder. Featherstone has been in Lennox's public-house, but I do not remember the date. There was nothing serious talked about, such as explosives, when he was in, because there were too many in the company, and he did not mention it. It was when he was in Jail Square, or in the Gymnastic

Hall, that he spoke about that. He was in the Gymnastic Hall again in the month of August,—about the last Sunday in August,—and he gave us a fine lecture. He told us what the dynamite would do, and the strength of it, and that by placing it against the barrack walls it would blow them right up, and that it would be a fine thing that the Government might know they were not to get it all their own way, and such things as that. There was to be a collection made to pay the woman belonging to the hall, but Featherstone paid her himself, and would not allow us to pay. When Featherstone has been talking about dynamite, I have seen present Tom Devany, Peter Callaghan, and Patrick Drum. I have seen Kearney present at times also, but he is not in Glasgow just now. The £2, 10s. I had got was to keep and give them when it was required. This was on Sunday the 16th. On Monday the 17th, which was Fair Monday, James Kelly came to my house about nine o'clock in the morning and chapped at the door. My wife answered and asked him in. He came in and asked me to come out. He said, "I want to see you." I went out, and when I went I found Johnston, and Casey, and Kearney there with him. He asked me would I come down the street. I went down to the corner of the street, and Kearney asked if I had any money. I said, "No, I have not, but I can get it." I then went into the house and put some money into my pocket. We then went across the bridge and into the small public-house. I do not know the name of it. I never was in it except at that time. I gave Kearney half-a-sovereign to buy some stuff to try and make experiments. The following week Patrick Drum came home, and the next Sunday I handed up the remainder of the £2. I said, "You can do with your money as you like." Kearney came forward and said, "I had very bad success with the 10s. worth of stuff I got. It was a failure; but I hope I will have better success next time; I will pay it out of my own pocket." They all cried, "Oh no, nothing of the kind." I was not present when any experiment was made with the stuff, only what was done in the stable with the bottle of vitriol and the powder Kearney took out of his pocket. I have seen Callaghan making collections at different times, but it was not Callaghan who got the money. It was Henry M'Cann who got it. M'Cann marked down the names of those who gave it, and gave the money to Patrick Drum to keep. I did not know what was done with the money. I am telling all that I heard about the getting of the stuff. I saw the man called Johnston at different times—a great deal oftener than I have seen Featherstone. Johnston went away before Featherstone was tried. He sailed in the "Ethiopia" for New York, and I have not seen him since. I first saw Terence M'Dermott on the first Monday of June. He and M'Culloch were made members of the society on the one night. Q.—Did you see Terence M'Dermott on any of the occasions when Featherstone and Johnston were giving instructions about the stuff? A.—I saw them on different occasions on Glasgow Green when we were talking about such things, but I never saw them in any house, such as Lennox's. They were on Glasgow Green several times. I have seen Horan—the last witness—coming in on the Sunday afternoon from Maryhill different times, but not very often. I have seen him come four or five times to the Green when I was there. But there was nothing serious talked about when he was present, only they were talking about this, and Peter Callaghan told him to try and subscribe as much money as he was able among the men in Kelvin Dock and Maryhill, as it would be all needed and the money would be replaced again. Horan said he would do his best He dropped coming to the meetings about two months after Glasgow Fair. There was a meeting in Lennox's, and he was at it and gave Peter Callaghan some money, but not a great deal. I do not know what quantity he gave him. He dropped coming to the meetings altogether after that. The last time I saw him would be about two months after Glasgow Fair. Peter Callaghan told him to see if he could get a young man in Kelvin Dock who had neither wife nor family and no care, so that if any such things as any of these explosions were taking place he would not leave any trouble behind him. Horan said he could not promise that, but he would do his endeavour. I saw him after that at Glasgow Green, and he was inquiring for Peter Callaghan. He said he was going to give up such work altogether, and that the clergy were against it in Maryhill, and he was not going to turn the clergy against him for any such nonsense. I never saw him after that except once in the Jail Square, maybe about a fortnight after. I recollect a meeting in Jail Square about the end of November 1882. The men were standing partly in the Green and partly in Jail Square on the steps at the entrance going into it. Patrick Drum, M'Cann, Tom Devany, and the old man James M'Cabe, who is now dead, were standing there, and a man called Henry Monaghan came up to me in the Saltmarket, and asked if I would be so kind as to speak to Peter Callaghan and ask when he was going to hold a meeting of the Ribbon Society. I went forward and said, "Peter, when are you going to hold a meeting? Are you to hold it on Monday night, as Henry Monaghan wants to see if you are to hold a meeting to see what you are to do, or whether you are giving it up altogether?" Henry M'Cann got into a passion, and drew his hand and said, "What have you to do here?" and struck me. I cried back to him, "If I saw a policeman, you dynamite buggar, I would have you taken," and with that he flew up the Green. I came across then towards the jail, and my mouth was bleeding, and I met Constable Porter, and said, "If I had seen you a little earlier, I would have charged a man to the office," telling him what he had done. I did not say anything about dynamite, but I said M'Cann had struck me. Porter said, "Well, you are not too late yet, come away back." I said, "The passion is off me now, let him go." We were turning back when Featherstone came near, and tapping the constable by the shoulders, he said, "Never mind them, the one is as bad as the other. Come away, Mr. Hughes, you are as bad as the other." I had not noticed Featherstone before that, but we were standing, and wherever he came from, he came forward when I was going back towards the jail, and made this remark to the constable. Monaghan was in the habit of holding meetings in the society, the same as we were doing, what they called the Ribbon Society, and I suppose he wanted to have a meeting, to see if Callaghan was to drop it altogether, or whether he was to follow this dynamite business, which of the two he was going to abide by. I never heard anything more said about the dynamite than what I have told. I have told all that I heard. Only after this explosion was in the gasworks, there was one

Saturday night I was going across into the Jail Square, and Tom Devany came forward and said, "Last night"—that would be the Friday night—"I had a very narrow escape." I said, "What with?" He said, "I threw myself down on the top of the bed to have a sleep, as I was very wearied, and I heard some one speaking to my wife on the floor. I jumped up, and there I got two detectives talking to her," and he said, "If they had made any search I would have blown them into eternity." I said, "Why, it would have been very foolish; had you anything such as that dynamite in the house?" "Yes," he said, "I had, and I had a good case of revolvers." I said, "You would be a very foolish man to risk your life for anybody." He said he would have blown them into atoms. He did not show me the revolvers. The last time, to my knowledge, that I saw Featherstone was about three months after Glasgow Fair, or maybe not so much. Glasgow Fair begins on the second Monday of July. After the occasion when M'Cann struck me, there was generally a coolness between us. I suppose they suspected when they saw me talking to the constable that I had maybe told him something. I have seen M'Dermott on Glasgow Green, and in Jail Square also. I did not hear him saying anything, but just listening the same as another. I never heard Johnston saying anything about pipes in M'Dermott's house, but about two months after the Fair, one night in the middle of the week, he came down, when Patrick Drum, Devany, Peter Callaghan, and the old man, James M'Cabe, who is now dead, were there. I was standing along with them. He said, "The neighbours, where I am manufacturing this stuff, are complaining about the pipes being burnt, and we will have to look out for another place for fear the stuff is got, for fear they make complaint to the landlord, and the landlord applies to the police, and the stuff is got." Peter Callaghan, Patrick Drum, and old M'Cabe went away to carry a share of the stuff out of the place. They called it dynamite, but Johnston spoke of the stuff he was manufacturing. I don't think he mentioned the place where he was manufacturing the stuff, but they went with him towards Townhead. M'Dermott lives up that way. On the occasion when Johnston spoke about the pipes there was none of the prisoners present except Patrick Drum, Tom Devany, Peter Callaghan, James M'Cabe, and myself. The four others went away along with Johnston to carry their share of the stuff out of the place. They said that was what they were going for. They did not say where they were going to take it to. I did not know where the stuff was, but I saw them going in the direction of Townhead, where M'Dermott lived. *Q.*—Did you ever see Johnston or Featherstone reading from any paper when they were describing the way to make dynamite? *A.*—Yes. When they were in the Gymnastic Hall—we were up in it again—Featherstone took out a paper and read out to those present how many pounds they had on hand at the present time. He said they had about 37 lbs. at that time, and he told them to see and gather as much money as they could, for he expected money daily from America. There were present, when Featherstone said there was that quantity manufactured, Patrick Callaghan, Patrick M'Cabe, Patrick Drum, Tom Devany, James M'Cabe, who is now dead, and Kearney. They did not say at that time where the stuff was. I never heard any mention amongst them of dynamite after that, unless when I came on the Green, and they would be talking of what it could do, by any person going into a carriage or any machine, and taking a small box and throwing it out underneath anything, that it would blow it up instantly. That is all I ever heard them talking about. The members of the Ribbon Society had not a number, but when M'Cann was lifting money for this dynamite affair, it was by numbers it was done. He marked down every man's name when he gave a shilling—he put it down against a number. I paid into it myself 1s. or 2s., and I know the number they marked for me was 14. I have told all that I know in connection with this matter, as far as regards dynamite. I have told to the best of my recollection all the occasions when it was mentioned and what was said. I never saw the stuff itself at any time, and I never heard any description of the particular way in which it was made. I might have heard that, but I had no great interest in it, and do not remember it. I never was present when it was being made, and I never was in the place where it was being made.

Cross-examined by Mr. RHIND.—I am fifty-four or fifty-six years of age, and was born of Irish parents. I am a Roman Catholic. I cannot tell where the prisoners were born, but they go under the name of Irishmen. I have known some of them upwards of two years, and some of them upwards of six months. I have known Patrick Drum, Patrick M'Cabe, Peter Callaghan, and James Kelly longest. Kelly wrought with me at one time when I was working at my trade. I have always been very good friends with them; there was no quarrel amongst us. I am very good friends with them still; there is no animosity between us in the least. I took an oath that I would stand by my fellow-countrymen when they got into a scrape. I swore that by Almighty God. *Q.*—Have you kept that oath? *A.*—To keep that oath I thought I would not be doing right. I would think my conscience checked me. *Q.*—When did your conscience grow tender and begin to trouble you? *A.*—Maybe a couple of months or so after Glasgow Fair. I thought I was doing wrong. My conscience is not troubling me now a bit. I think I am duty bound to tell the truth. Any information that was got from me was when I was asked to tell the truth, and I told the truth at the time these men were taken. I was not to tell a lie. *Q.*—Although you wouldn't tell a lie, you quite approved of blowing up buildings with dynamite? *A.*—No, I did not do anything of the kind. I subscribed to the funds; but when I did that, I did not know what the money was for. Peter Callaghan said there was a poor man's wife in bad circumstances, and that the man was badly, and that he was lifting a collection for him, and some of us grumbled when we heard the money was for the purpose of manufacturing dynamite. After I found out that the money was for blowing up buildings they got no more subscriptions from me. I only subscribed one or two shillings, I cannot say which. At the time I went to the meetings I did not disapprove of the objects of them, because there was no word of such a thing as dynamite until Johnston and Featherstone came from New York. Up to that time the meetings were quite innocent; they were what we called meetings of the Ribbon Society. *Q.*—That is to say, that you were to assist your fellow-countrymen in distress? *A.*—You may take what meaning you like out of it; I explained what it was, and the nature of the oath. *Q.*—But your only reason for calling it a Ribbon Society is because of the nature of the oath? *A.*—That is the name that Peter Callaghan gave to me. I was only three months a member of the society before Glasgow Fair. I was at meetings where dynamite and the blowing-up of buildings with it were talked about, but not frequently—only twice. I was frequently on Glasgow Green, but only twice at meetings in the Gymnastic Hall. *Q.*—What took you to these meetings after your conscience had begun to trouble you? *A.*—Generally, when we went there, there were preachings and the like, and maybe amongst these men regularly I just went to hear what was going on. The reward of £500 had nothing to do with my conscience troubling me. I never received a farthing, and don't want anything. I never got so much as a shilling. *Q.*—Do you know Mr. Shaughnessy, who is the agent for seven of the prisoners? *A.*—I know nothing about him. I never saw him until he called on me on Thursday last. *Q.*—Did he ask you to tell him, as agent for the accused, what you were going to say to-day? *A.*—I was not prepared to answer any person then. I am bad with shortness of breath, and on the day he called I was not fit to begin. I told him to meet me this morning, and I would tell him, and he shook hands with me, and said, "All right." *Q.*—Were there plenty other people at the meetings besides the parties whom you have mentioned? *A.*—No; generally any meetings they held in the way of dynamite, they held among themselves—these men. *Q.*—Do I understand that there was no one present but the people whose names you have mentioned? *A.*—These are all that were present. I remember that they were present, because I know the men perfectly. I am sure that each of the men was present at the particular meetings I have referred to. In giving my evidence I looked at a calendar, but only for the purpose of getting the dates. *Q.*—How does looking at the calendar remind you of the dates when certain things happened? *A.*—It will remind me of the 9th of the month or the 16th of the month. Looking at the calendar enables me to give the dates more readily. [Shown calendar.] There is a cross marked opposite some of the dates. That is what I was looking for. That is Sunday 20th January, when the explosion occurred. These crosses were put there to-day. We have been looking at it, and going over it, and talking about the date on which it was. It was not I who put the crosses there. I do not know who put them there. There is no cross there, only the man had a pencil in his hand, and was looking at it. *Q.*—Did you say about Callaghan recently that you were quite willing to be hung for him? *A.*—Nothing of the kind. I deny such a charge.

Cross-examined by Mr. GUTHRIE.—I did not see the Fiscal until the prisoners were apprehended. I cannot tell the date when that was. I saw the Fiscal the day after the prisoners were apprehended. I did not keep any account of the date, and do not remember when it was. I do not remember the date because I was taking no interest in it. I did not take any interest in my meeting with the Fiscal. I did not think I was to be a witness until I was summoned, and then it is likely I was bound to tell the truth. When the Fiscal asked me questions about the matter I told him the truth. I was not going to tell a lie in the case. I knew I would be on my oath. I did not tell the police anything particular about what I have said to-day before the prisoners were apprehended. I do not remember just now what I said to them. I told them about the meetings which we had on the Green, but that was all. It was Constable Porter whom I told. I would tell him perhaps about a fortnight or three weeks before the apprehension of the prisoners. He was the constable that I was going to give M'Cann in charge to for striking me, but when the passion was off I said he might let him alone, it was not worth the bother. I spoke to Porter about this matter because he was generally the man on that beat, and was going about that place. I did not go to speak to him, he came to speak to me. He was inquiring and asking what was M'Cann's reason for striking me. Nothing very serious passed at my interview with Porter. I told him, when he wanted to know what M'Cann had struck me for, that he had given me an ill-served answer, and had called me a name, and that I called him back his name. I added that if I had seen him (Porter) I would have charged M'Cann to the office. I did not tell Porter anything about the dynamite. He asked what gentleman had come and tapped him on the shoulder and told him never to mind, and that I was as bad, and I told him that they called him Timothy Featherstone. That is all that passed before the apprehension of the prisoners. Nothing passed about £500 reward. There never was a penny offered to me, and I received nothing from anybody. I know a man named John Ward who deals in fish. I do not remember meeting him on the Sunday after the prisoners were apprehended, nor on the Monday after the apprehension. I remember having a conversation with him. He was telling me he had been taken up to Duke Street to identify the prisoners. I cannot rightly remember where this conversation took place. I think it may have taken place on the bridge or at the foot of Crown Street. I do not remember having any conversation with him in Jail Square. *Q.*—Do you remember saying to him that you had been up at the prison and had told more than you "knowed"? *A.*—No; I never said anything of the kind. *Q.*—And that £500 was not to be lifted out of the gutter, or out of the syver, any Monday morning? *A.*—Any one who told that has been telling a great falsehood. I have never mentioned money, and money has never been mentioned to me. I told Mr. Drummond, the agent for Drum, M'Cullagh, and M'Cann, anything I knew, until he commenced to "bullyrag" me. I told him on the Saturday, and I saw him before the Saturday also. I saw him again on Sunday. I had seen him on the Thursday, but I was not in the way of answering any questions to any person at that time, as I was so hoarse with cold. I told him that any questions he had to ask me I would tell him this morning, I did not care how early, but that I was not able to answer any questions at that time. The governor of the prison was present at the interview I had with Mr. Drummond. I was originally a boilermaker, but latterly I have been a fruit merchant. I became a fruit merchant when the boiler-making business became slack. I have been handling fruit for a great many years—it is upwards of thirty-five years, I believe, since I sold fruit first. I have never been in the hands of the police except once, when I was in for having a glass of drink, and I was liberated in the morning. I think I was fined 5s. for being drunk and disorderly. I had not assaulted anybody; I was only incapable of going home. *Q.*—You told me just now that you were drunk and disorderly? *A.*—I did not say disorderly, but only for taking a glass of drink. *Q.*—You said disorderly? *A.*—No; only the worse of drink. I do not remember when that was. The society never got any money from me except 5s., and I think it was quite plenty. I was in the habit of going to Lennox's when there were meetings being held there. I was never the worse of drink when I was there. *Q.*—Have you stated to any person that you never paid any money in connection with this society except for drink? *A.*—I never paid any money into the society except for drink. Generally when we broke up there was a collection made to pay for what drink had been got in. The new members when they joined had to pay 2s. 6d. of entry money, and after that I never paid anything except 6d. or so to pay for drink consumed. *Q.*—Have you not said that you did not mind of any subscriptions being paid by any person in your presence to this society? *A.*—Not to a Ribbon Society; but I have known them pay money in for getting stuff for the manufacture of dynamite. There was no money paid to a Ribbon Society. I have not a great deal of acquaintance with the witness Horan; I never saw him more than four times. On the first Monday of the month, two months after Glasgow Fair, we met in Lennox's public-house, and I saw him give Peter Callaghan some money, but what it was I cannot say. I do not remember of him giving any to M'Cann. He handed it to Peter Callaghan, but whether Callaghan gave it to M'Cann or not I cannot say. The meetings in Lennox's were held in a back room, part of the public-house. You had to go through the bar to get to the back room. There is only one large room in the place. The shopman was going out and in with drink. His name was Tommy M'Ginnes. *Q.*—He would know what was going on in the back room? *A.*—It is most likely he would. I cannot say whether there was any other shopman there. Generally there would not be much talk when the shopman was there, until he went out. He would only be in carrying drink. I think there would not be much talk when he was there, because any time I have been there I never heard any conversation concerning anything. He left the drink in the room, and kept an account, and when we were going away he was sent for and was asked what was the bill, and he said "so much," and all the members were sixpence apiece round to pay for the drink. There was generally a man at the door to let no strangers in. *Q.*—Do you say that this room was reserved from the rest of the public during these meetings? *A.*—No, not reserved; you had to pass through the bar. *Q.*—You have said a man was put there to prevent people going in? *A.*—No, the man was standing at the door in this room, and he would let no person into the room unless he belonged to the company. I cannot say whether M'Ginnes would know that. It is most likely he would. The door would be open if any person was coming in, but it would not be standing open for any time. Any person coming in would close the door after him.

Cross-examined by Mr. KENNEDY.—I am still as friendly to M'Cann as I have always been. What animosity would I have against the man? He had done me no injury. He never did me any injury except when he struck me on the Green. I have not owed him any animosity since then. When the passion was off me I forgot it, but if I had got the constable at the time, I would have given him in charge. *Q.*—And you are quite as willing to stand by him as a brother in an honest way as ever you were? *A.*—Not in any way connected with party business. *Q.*—But in an honest way? *A.*—Yes, but in no other way. I never swore in any person as a member of the society, and I hope I never will. I never got a copy of the oath I have spoken of. I never got any person to join the society in my life. There never was any word about using dynamite for public buildings until Timothy Featherstone came to Glasgow. *Q.*—When you joined the society, the objects of it were perfectly honest? *A.*—It was told to me that it was to be on friendly terms with the brothers, and that there was to be no harm, only that if any of them got into any habble or anything with the Government we were to stand by and reveal no secrets. *Q.*—And you thought there was no harm in that? *A.*—I suppose I was foolish enough at that time. *Q.*—Did you then think there was anything dangerous or dishonest in the object of the society? *A.*—Never at all; only what I have lost by paying sixpence at each meeting, which would be for drink. That was the worst thing about the society at that time. The members had to pay a sum for what drink was consumed on the premises. Generally we all met on the Green. We did not meet there every Sunday, but we met on different occasions. There were lots of other people on the Green besides us, preaching and arguing Scripture, and the like of that; but generally when we met it was not for that. I cannot say whether the Green is the usual Sunday resort for Irishmen in Glasgow. There are generally a great number of people on it belonging to other countries as well as Ireland—Scotchmen as well as Irishmen. There are plenty people all over the Green, but not in different parts of it; there are parts where there are no people. The Green is a very large place. I don't know anything about a reward having been offered in connection with this matter. I never was offered a penny, and never have received a penny. *Q.*—Do you know that any reward was in point of fact offered? *A.*—No; I don't know anything of the kind, and I want no reward. I have seen bills offering a reward. *Q.*—Did you believe the bills? *A.*—I don't know. I believe nothing of the kind, and want nothing of the kind. The bills might be true for anything I know; but I don't want anything. I never troubled myself about them. *Q.*—Have you such a lucrative business? *A.*—I make what supports me in a decent way, and generally I make what supports me in the months while the fruit lasts. I can make then what keeps me in the winter time, although I do not work any. The winter time is the slack time with us. *Q.*—Would you take £500? *A.*—No; I don't want it. *Q.*—Will you take £500? *A.*—No; I don't want it. I want to be paid the same as any other person; but I don't want any money. I never heard the oath administered except the once. Generally, when any member was being sworn, they would take him over to one side of the room. When the two men I have mentioned were made members of the society, they had to kneel down on their knees and hold up their hands, but what was said I could not say. I had to swear by Almighty God. I had to go down on my knees. The only time I heard the words of the oath was when it was administered to myself. I don't remember the whole of the words of the oath, but I have mentioned them so far as I can remember. I cannot say what assistance we were to give to a brother who might get into a habble with the Government. It might be that we would assist him with a subscription as well as anything else; I could not say. I have just repeated the words as they were repeated to me. I saw Mr. Drummond on Saturday. Q.—Did you say to him that you could not tell what the oath you had taken was? A.—I explained everything to him as I have done now. Q.—Did you say that to him? A.—I cannot explain yet what the nature of it is more than I have told you. I told him that I could not explain the nature of the oath, as I have explained to you just now. Q.—Did you tell him what you have told us to-day about the oath? A.—No, I did not; because I was not fit to tell him. I have known M'Cann for about two years back and forward by seeing him; but I never knew him to be in terms of speaking until once I became a member of that society. Q.—Do you remember on the first Sunday in March last coming up from Nelson's Monument and meeting M'Cann along with his daughter? A.—I do not. Q.—May you have met him? A.—No, I did not. I never saw him along with his daughter; but I have seen him with his son. I never saw him with his daughter-in-law. Q.—Did you, when he was passing with his daughter or daughter-in-law, shake your fist at him? A.—No, nothing of the kind. Q.—Or say, "I will do for you"? A.—No; whoever has been telling you that has been telling you a lot of nonsense. I did not shake my fist at him on the first Sunday in March at the place mentioned and say I would do for him.

Re-examined.—Constable Porter did not speak to me about Featherstone on the night after M'Cann struck me; but afterwards he asked me who the man was that had come and tapped him on the shoulder, and I told him. I said it was Timothy Featherstone, who had come from America for the occasion of manufacturing this dynamite. I told Porter that about three weeks after the night when M'Cann struck me, and I told him the same again perhaps a few days before the men were apprehended. People assemble in groups on the Green.

By the LORD JUSTICE-CLERK.—I know all the prisoners. The only ones that were attending the dynamite meetings were Patrick Drum, Tom Devany, and Peter Callaghan. The rest used to meet on the Green, but they never went into the private meetings. There was talk about dynamite in their company, but they appeared not to be sympathizing. I did not see them paying any collection, with the exception of Patrick M'Cabe. I never saw Terence M'Dermott speaking about dynamite, but I have seen him in company with the others. I have seen him giving money on two or three occasions to Henry M'Cann for the purpose of purchasing stuff to manufacture dynamite. Henry M'Cann was at the meetings in Nelson Street, but none of the rest. I generally saw James M'Culloch in amongst the rest on the Green. He was not at any of the meetings in Nelson Street. I have seen James Donnelly on the Green also, back and forward, but I never saw him in Nelson Street in the Democratic Hall. I never saw James Kelly at the meetings either. All I know about him is that he was a member of the Ribbon Society, and that he was to go with me for the stuff on the Wednesday, along with the chap, to the chemical work. I never saw Denis Casey except at the time he handed the bottle to

Patrick Drum when they took it into my stable, and he said he knew this young man, and would speak to him about getting some dynamite, and see if he could get it. The whole of them were members of the Ribbon Society.

Adjourned.

SECOND DAY.—TUESDAY, DECEMBER 18, 1883.

EVIDENCE FOR THE CROWN CONTINUED.

26. *William Porter* (55). *By the* LORD ADVOCATE.—I am a day constable in the Central District of the Glasgow Police Force. I have been there over eight years. I know all the prisoners now at the bar. Some of them I have known for about four years, and others not so long. My beat, for the last four years, has been about the foot of Saltmarket, including Jail Square and the entrance to Glasgow Green. In that way I have had a good opportunity of observing the people resorting to these localities. The prisoners generally met at the entrance to the Green off Saltmarket. I have known some of them there since I went to that beat. They generally met at a place by themselves, as you enter to the Green, on the left-hand side. I have also seen them in Jail Square. They were always in a knot, standing together. I have known Drum, M'Cabe, M'Cann, and Kelly longest. I have known Casey the next longest. It would be about the beginning of November 1882 that the prisoners began first to attract my attention. They were in the habit of meeting at the entrance to the Green, and then walking up towards the monument, and sitting on a seat there alone, and perhaps reading some letters or something of that kind. It was their general outlook for any person passing by that I thought odd. I observed they looked out for any person passing by. I sometimes took a stroll past them. They always stopped speaking when I went near them. They seemed to keep apart and avoid letting others know what they were doing. I observed those meetings very frequently from about November. There was scarcely any evening but you would see some of the prisoners there, and on Saturdays and Sundays perhaps the whole lot. They struck me as a lot by themselves, and that was what took my attention first. I know George Hughes, who is a witness in this case. I have seen him with them. He was, I may say, almost daily among them, both before and after November. I never managed to hear what they were saying. I observed occasionally among the group other two men who were new to me and new to Glasgow, so far as I knew. I observed them during the month of November. One of these men, I have since been told, is Featherstone. I began to see Featherstone with the group about the beginning of October. I found out some time afterwards the name by which the other man went; it was Johnston. They seemed to be strange men to the place. I saw Featherstone frequently with the group in Jail Square and on the Green. I saw them on one occasion reading some papers on the Green. I could not get near, but I got a field-glass, which brought

them close to me, and I saw they were reading papers. I have tried to stroll past them when Featherstone was with them. They were speaking away about something, but I could not make out what they were saying. I recollect Hughes making a complaint to me against Henry M'Cann. This was on Saturday 11th November. He said that if I had been there a few minutes sooner he would have given M'Cann in charge for striking him. I told him it would not be too late yet—could he not point him out to me?—and then the man who I was afterwards told was Featherstone came forward and said that Hughes was as much to blame as M'Cann, and to make no police case of it. Hughes said he would never mind, or something to that effect, and went away. Nothing more happened. I met Hughes one day afterwards. I was anxious to find out the strangers' names, and I asked him who it was that took him away. He said it was a man of the name of Featherstone. That was the first time I heard the name. He said something more, but I cannot say what it was—he was going on with his van at the time. Hughes goes about selling fruit in a pony cart, and he was just going away to his stables. I have seen all the prisoners more or less with the group. I missed Featherstone for a time, some time about January. He reappeared for a few days about the latter end of January or beginning of February, and then disappeared again. The meetings of the group were kept up throughout the months of January and February of this year, and afterwards, in consequence of some information which was given to me, I began to pursue inquiries with reference to these men being concerned with dynamite. I inquired first of the witness John Ward. I had seen him with the group occasionally, but not often. He seemed excited when I mentioned dynamite in connection with the group. I got no information from him. I tried other people also, and found an indisposition to speak. I met Hughes on the street about 3rd April. He said, "I believe you have been making inquiries about the dynamite explosions." I said I had. He said, "I know the parties that were engaged in it, but you are not to bring my name to the front." I told him I could not make promises of that kind—that I would do what I could, but I could not make any promises if he knew the parties. He then put me in remembrance of the row with the man M'Cann that Featherstone took away, and said, "You was a man that was engaged in it here." Q.—Were any others named at that time? A.—Yes; he named Drum, M'Cabe, and M'Cann. I got certain information from Hughes on that and on another occasion. [Shown Timothy Featherstone.] This is the man whom I knew as Featherstone. He had a beard on at that time, and whiskers.

Cross-examined by Mr. RHIND.—It was about seven o'clock on the week-day evenings when I observed the group meeting in Jail Square or Glasgow Green. On Sundays they had two meetings—one in the forenoon and one about three in the afternoon. Glasgow Green and Jail Square are favourite places for the Glasgow Irishmen meeting. Besides the group formed by the prisoners, there were sometimes hundreds of other groups. There is a very large Irish population in Glasgow. I remember when the reward was offered in connection with these explosions. I saw two bills up shortly after the time the explosions took place. The first bill offered £100 and the second offered £500. The £100 bill was up shortly after the explosions, but I cannot say how long, and the £500 offer was up some time afterwards. It was a good while before Hughes came to me.

27. *Thomas M'Ginnes* (57). *By the* LORD ADVOCATE.—I am a shopman in James Lennox's public-house, Saltmarket, Glasgow. I have been there for about four years. [Shown the prisoners.] I know some of these men by sight. I know M'Dermott, Callaghan, No. 4 (M'Cann),— I don't know his name,—Kelly, Drum, and Casey. I cannot say whether I have seen the other men or not. I have occasionally seen the men whom I have named or pointed out resorting to Lennox's public-house at different times of the day and night. I have not seen them coming and going to the public-house for more than a year, if it is a year, but I cannot be sure of the time. I took no particular notice of them at all; only serving them. I know George Hughes by sight. I have seen him there. There is any amount of people coming and going to that public-house. I am not able particularly to say on what nights these men used to come. I served at the bar and in the rooms, back and forward. There was nothing about these men that particularly attracted my attention or to make me pass any remark about them.

Cross-examined by Mr. RHIND.—I never saw these men all coming at once to the public-house. *Q.*—Were they in a room by themselves, or did they come into a room where other people were? *A.*—Sometimes. Altogether they behaved just like our other customers.

By Mr. GUTHRIE.—Besides the front shop there were two boxes and two rooms. These rooms were open to all our customers, with glass in the doors. I went in and out of these rooms occasionally with drink, serving the customers there. These rooms were open to anybody who liked to go in. So far as I saw the prisoners in coming and going to our shop, they were just like other people.

28. *John Niven* (97). *By the* LORD ADVOCATE.—I am a constable in the Glasgow Police, in the Central District. I have been there for seven years. [Shown prisoners.] I have seen some of these men before—Devany, M'Dermott, and M'Cann. I cannot name any more. The faces of the others are familiar to me. I have seen these men in the Saltmarket and Jail Square. They were together. I cannot exactly state the number of times I have seen them there. *Q.*—Did you see them frequently together? *A.*—Yes; I have seen them several times together. I have seen them together on the Green near the Justiciary Buildings. *Q.*—Did you see another man with them at any time? *A.*—I may have seen another man. There were a number of faces of men that I do not see there. [Shown Timothy Featherstone.] I cannot say whether I have ever seen that man with them. I have seen those I mentioned together.

Cross-examined by Mr. RHIND.—When I say I have seen them together, I mean the ones I named—M'Dermott, Devany, and M'Cann. I sometimes saw two together, sometimes three, and sometimes more. *Q.*—From what you say I gather that you did not see them very often, any more than you saw other Irish going about the Green and the Saltmarket? *A.*—No; because other Irish people are there daily.

Q.—Just in twos, and threes, and singly, as you saw these men? *A.*—More; because it is a sort of place for Glasgow people gathering for debating subjects. *Q.*—In short, what you say about these prisoners you can say about dozens, if not hundreds, of others? *A.*—But we understood what they were there for. We never learned what the prisoners were there for. So far as I saw, they were doing nothing different from any other Irish people.

Re-examined.—What the other people were there for was not concealed at all. They were arguing, some about religion, and others about politics, and so on.

29. *William M'Elhinny* (143). *By the* LORD ADVOCATE.—I am an emigration agent, and keep a lodging-house in Liverpool. In June 1882 I was on the landing-stage at Liverpool when the steam-tender with passengers from the screw steamer "Indiana" from Philadelphia arrived. A man, one of the passengers, came to lodge with me. He did not give me any name at the time, but afterwards he told me he was Featherstone. He stopped with me nearly a fortnight. [Shown Timothy Featherstone.] That is the man. He told me he was a reporter for a newspaper in America. Letters came to him addressed to Featherstone. He lodged with me for about a week. He went, I believe, to Cork. He told me he was going there. In November 1882 he came back to my house again, and stopped for a night or two. He did not tell me where he was going at that time, and I did not ask him. He came back again once after that, I think in the month of December. He told me at that time that he was going back to Ireland. He did not say what part of Ireland he was going to, but he said he was going by way of Holyhead. That is the passage to Kingstown for Dublin. While he was stopping with me he used to buy the papers and read them, and I saw him writing occasionally. That was all I saw.

Cross-examined by Mr. RHIND.—I saw him writing in the room in which he slept, but I was not much in it. When he came he had no luggage except a small valise. As far as I know, he had no other luggage. By the same steamer there arrived a man named Murphy. Murphy and Featherstone were very like each other in personal appearance. Murphy stayed in my house just about the same time. He told me he was going to Glasgow when he left. He had been trying to get a situation in Liverpool, and then he said he would try Glasgow for the same purpose.

Re-examined.—With regard to Featherstone's luggage, I know only about what was brought to my house, and what I saw at the landing.

By the LORD JUSTICE-CLERK.—Featherstone got about three or four letters while he was staying with me.

30. *Mrs. Jane Ronaldson or Mitchell* (62). *By the* LORD ADVOCATE.—I am the wife of William Mitchell, hotel proprietor, 11 Cowcaddens, Glasgow. I manage the hotel, which is called the "Star Hotel." I remember a man coming to lodge in our house in February last. I did not know his name at that time. I afterwards found out that it was Featherstone. [Shown Timothy Featherstone.] That is the man. He had a moustache at that time, but no beard. He lodged in my

hotel about six times to the best of my recollection. I cannot exactly tell the period over which he lodged with me. I do not keep permanent books, but simply make up the account of each customer, which is settled and done with. The six visits were during the period from the spring of 1882 until February this year. Sometimes he stayed in my hotel for a fortnight, sometimes a week, and sometimes ten days. The shortest time he was there was the last time, when he was only four days.

By the LORD JUSTICE-CLERK.—His last visit in February extended from the 10th till the 14th.

Examination continued.—He had been there previously in December. He was not there in January. He was just once there in December. I think he was there in November. He generally came once a month or thereabout. I cannot precisely say whether he was there in October. Featherstone once told me that he was engaged in the newspaper way, and I understood he was a reporter. He had no visitors whatever coming about him when he was with me. [Shown prisoners.] I think I have seen most of these men in Duke Street Prison. I am not perfectly certain whether I have seen any of them outside the prison. I thought I had seen one of them, but I cannot positively say.

Cross-examined by Mr. RHIND.—It was about the middle of December when Featherstone stayed in my hotel in that month. He was about a week in the house at that time. I think he came about the middle of December. I cannot say how long he was there in November. He generally was there a week or ten days, except the last time, when he was four days. I cannot tell what time he was there in November. He generally went out about eleven or twelve in the forenoon, and perhaps he would come in for dinner, but very seldom, and he was generally in the house before ten o'clock at night, or about that time, as far as I remember.

Re-examined.—[Shown hotel bill, No. 37.] That is one of our hotel bills against Featherstone. It begins on 10th February, and there are charges for apartments on the 11th, 12th, 13th, and 14th. He appears to have had his breakfast on the 14th, and not to have slept in the hotel that night. That account is correct.

31. *John Mitchell* (63). *By the* LORD ADVOCATE.—I am a son of William Mitchell and of the last witness. My father and mother keep the "Star Hotel" at Cowcaddens, Glasgow. We have no servant, but just work the hotel with our own family. We do not keep any permanent books, but merely make out the customers' bills, and they pay them, and the bills are not preserved. I recollect a man coming to lodge in the hotel on some occasions last year and this year. He gave no name while he was stopping with us, but I afterwards learned at Cork that it was Timothy Featherstone. [Shown Timothy Featherstone.] That is the man. I was told at Cork, after seeing him in the prison, that Featherstone was his name. I recognized him at Cork as the man who had lodged in our hotel. He lodged in the hotel at least six times last year and this year. The last occasion was in February this year, for which No. 37 is the hotel bill, signed by me. It is made out in my hand. There is nobody's name put upon it, because we did not know his name. I think it would be in May 1882 that he began

to come to the hotel, but I am not certain. Between that time and February this year, he was there about six times. He was not there in January this year. He was there about the middle of December. He stopped for over a week then, but I cannot say whether he was there in November. The longest time he ever stopped at once was over a fortnight. That was about the first of his visits. He spent his time in the hotel generally in reading and writing. He never gave me any letters to post. No communication ever came to the hotel addressed to him. Any communication he had to receive or despatch, he did it outside.

Cross-examined by Mr. RHIND.—I saw nothing peculiar about his conduct.

32. *John Bunting Guthrie* (67). *By the* LORD ADVOCATE.—I am a manufacturing chemist in Regent Park Square, and a partner of M'Geachie & M'Farlane, manufacturing chemists at Port Dundas Road, Glasgow. [Shown Timothy Featherstone.] I have seen that man before. I saw him in Cork prison. I first saw him on 9th December 1882, in the office of our firm, 82 Port Dundas Road. He called there and asked for nitric acid. He wished to know the different strengths, and what strength we could give him. He said he wanted it very strong,—the strongest made. I told him that we had it in stock from 66° to 84° Twaddle,—that is, by the hydrometer, which is one of the modes of testing these things. He asked if we could give it stronger. We said we could make it stronger, but did not keep it in stock. He did not state what strength he wanted. He did not say anything about 100°. He bought a carboy of nitric acid ready made, at from 82° to 84°, which was the strongest we had. He paid us for it, the price being £2, 15s. 6d. I have our books, with the entries applicable to that transaction. [Nos. 13 and 14.] He gave us a paper with an address on it, to tell us where to consign the carboy to. [Shown No. 41.] I understand that is it,—"D. O'Herlihy, 10 Great George Street West, Cork." That was the address he gave. I am quite certain that is the paper we got. That address was written by Featherstone in my presence, and handed by him to me. We accordingly did despatch a carboy of nitric acid by the Clyde Shipping Co.'s steamer. The entry in our sales book is under date 11th December 1882:—"D. O'Herlihy, 10 Great George Street West, Cork, 1 carboy of extra nitric acid, 148·114, £2, 15s. 6d., and 1 carboy basket, 4s. = £2, 19s. 6d." That is a correct record of the transaction. Featherstone did not tell us his name when he gave that order; he just told us where to send the carboy. He said he wanted the nitric acid for an ink manufacturer. That was all he said about it. There were 148 lbs. of nitric acid in the carboy. So far as I know, the only purpose for which such strong nitric acid is used is engraving.

Cross-examined by Mr. RHIND.—We could have supplied Featherstone with stronger acid than he bought, and we told him so. We do not sell a great deal of such acid. *Q.*—But it is of common occurrence? *A.*—Yes. I do not think nitric acid is used in the manufacture of ink. It was used at one time for making dyes. The dyes are used for making coloured inks. We asked the man whom the acid was for, and he gave the address to which we were to invoice it. That was all that was necessary. There was nothing out of the way in his not giving us his own name in addition to that of the consignees. We do not sell acids for explosives in our trade if we are aware of it. We have been asked to supply dynamite manufacturers, but we have not done so. I know what strength of acid is required to make nitro-glycerine. I have made nitro-glycerine. To make it economically, it would require nitric acid from 90° to 100°.

Re-examined.—Featherstone wanted the strongest acid he could get. There is only one dynamite work in Scotland. I do not know whether there is more than one in England. Their supplies will be in very large quantities, so that buying acid for dynamite is not a usual proceeding at all. If we had known this nitric acid was to be used for that purpose, we would not have sold it. Featherstone said nothing about making dyes. In saying that it was the practice at one time to use nitric acid for dyes, I meant that that practice had ceased, so far as I know. I had in view what are known as aniline colours. I do not know how they are made. So far as I know, there is no nitric acid bought from us for making these dyes now, nor has there been for some time. We have not been selling anything for that purpose since before December last.

By a JURYMAN.—Nitric acid at 84° will make nitro-glycerine. I have made it at that strength.

By the LORD JUSTICE-CLERK.—We sell nitric acid principally for engraving and electro-plating. These operations require strong acid,— 84° or 82°.

33. *James Ballingall* (68). *By the* LORD ADVOCATE.—I am a clerk in the employment of Messrs. M'Geachie & M'Farlane, of which firm the last witness is a partner. I was so in December last year. I remember a man coming and asking for nitric acid at our place in December last. [Shown Timothy Featherstone.] I have seen that man before, in Glasgow, Cork, and Liverpool. It was he who came asking for nitric acid in December last year. He came on 9th December. I saw him before Mr. Guthrie saw him. He asked if we made nitric acid. I said we did, and asked him what kind he wanted. He said he wanted strong stuff. These were his words. I went out and told Mr. Guthrie about it, and he came in, and a bargain was made, and a carboy was bought. I saw Featherstone writing the address to which he wanted the carboy to be sent. [Shown No. 41.] That is the paper he wrote. He wrote it in my presence, and handed it to Mr. Guthrie. The carboy was sent off by the Shipping Company's steamer.

34. *James Montgomery* (69). *By the* LORD ADVOCATE.—I am a manufacturing chemist in St. James Street, Hillhead, Glasgow, and carry on business at 18 Bishop Street, Port Dundas, Glasgow, under the firm of J. Montgomery & Co., manufacturing chemists. About the middle of February this year, a man came asking to buy something at our place. He said he wanted sulphuric acid. He spoke about nitric acid also. He wanted both acids. [Shown Timothy Featherstone.] That is the man. He said he wanted the nitric acid strong.

He spoke of acid about 90°—from 90° to 100°. We are not usually in the way of keeping or selling acid so strong as that. Q.—Do you know any commercial or chemical purpose for which acid of so high a strength is used? A.—Yes. I know it is used for making gun-cotton. It is not used for anything else that I know of. It would make nitro-glycerine. I do not know of any other purpose for which acid of so high a strength is used, except for making explosives of one kind or another. It is not used for the ordinary purposes of commerce. We said we did not keep it in stock, but we could make it for him. I think he asked what was the highest strength that we had in stock. I told him the highest strength we had was an acid about 84°. He said he would go back to Cork and consult his partner. He did not say who his partner was. He said he wanted the acid for a patent process for preserving meat. I never heard of nitric acid of 100° being used for preserving meat. I do not know what it might do to the meat. That was all that passed about the nitric acid at that time. He said he would require sulphuric acid. He said he wanted it for the same purpose—for preserving meat. He asked about the strengths of the sulphuric acid. We did not make a bargain about the sulphuric acid at that time. He asked what strength we made it at, and we told him 166° to 168°. He went away. [Shown No. 40.] We afterwards received that letter dated Cork, 17th Feb. 1883. We sent the acid as requested.

Cross-examined by Mr. RHIND.—We sent the acid to O'Herlihy & Co., Cork, on 21st February. Very strong nitric acid is used for making dyes. Q.—Acid of 100°? A.—Not usually—not so strong as that. Q.—Did you not say when examined as a witness in Liverpool, "Nitric acid of 100° is used for dyes"? A.—It may be used for dyes. I believe sulphuric acid is used for the preparation of dyes as well as nitric acid. Q.—Of similar strength to nitric acid? A.—I do not understand the meaning of similar strength. Strong sulphuric acid is not used for making aniline dyes. It is used in dyeworks, but I do not know the process. Q.—Is the acid used in dyeworks strong sulphuric acid? A.—Yes; it may be used. I saw no reason to doubt our customer's word when he said the acid was for a patent meat-preserving process. I believe acids are used for producing cold, as refrigerators.

By the LORD JUSTICE-CLERK.—The strength of nitric acid used in making aniline dyes is 90° Twaddle.

By Mr. KENNEDY.—We dilute nitric acid with water. Supposing we had it at 100° we could weaken it to any degree of weakness by just adding water. Q.—Then it would be cheaper to buy it strong? A.—No; quite the reverse. If you buy a small bottle of strong nitric acid the carriage may be less. The man who understands it can weaken it to his own mind.

Re-examined.—Q.—Would it be a better bargain to buy it of the high strength and dilute it, or of the ordinary strength and pay any difference in carriage? A.—The difference in carriage would not compensate for the strength at all.

By the LORD JUSTICE-CLERK.—The strength at which sulphuric acid is used for dyes is 166°.

By a JURYMAN.—Sulphuric acid and vitriol are the same thing. Nitric acid and vitriol are not the same.

35. *Alexander Reid* (70). *By the* LORD ADVOCATE.—I live in Glasgow, and am a clerk in the employment of J. Montgomery & Co., of which firm the last witness is a partner. I recollect a man coming asking about certain acids on 12th or 13th February last. [Shown Timothy Featherstone.] That is the man. He inquired the price and strength of sulphuric acid, and the price of nitric acid of 90°. Mr. Montgomery saw him. The man said he wanted the acid for meat-preserving. He said that he and his partners were going to take out a patent for meat-preserving. After he went away the letter No. 40 came, and the acid ordered in it was sent to Cork as directed, on the 21st February.

36. *John Inglis* (71). *By the* LORD ADVOCATE.—I am a clerk in the employment of the Clyde Shipping Company, Glasgow, and was so in December last. I have a manifest of 11th December 1882 [No. 17]. It contains an entry of one carboy of acid. That manifest is applicable to one carboy of acid shipped to D. O'Herlihy, Great George Street West, Cork. We received that carboy on the 11th and shipped it on the 13th. Looking at No. 21 [Manifest of the steamer "Ballycotton," from Glasgow to Cork on 13th December 1882], I find that on the 19th February we shipped a carboy of acid sent by A. Hope, Jun., & Co., to D. O'Herlihy, Cork. From No. 23 [Manifest of the steamer "Amsterdam," from Glasgow to Cork, 21st February 1883], I find that on 21st February one carboy of vitriol, from J. Montgomery & Co., was shipped to D. O'Herlihy, Cork. I have no business documents showing who took delivery of these at Cork. On 2d April 1883 I find from No. 24 [Manifest of steamer "Copeland," from Glasgow to Cork on 2d April 1883] of process, that two carboys of acid were despatched by A. Hope, Jun., & Co., to D. O'Herlihy by our steamers. These carboys were brought back some time afterwards by the police.

Cross-examined by Mr. RHIND.—There was no attempt at concealment with regard to the goods that were sent. Some of the carboys were consigned to us as acid, and others just as one carboy or two carboys, as the case might be, without saying what the contents were. The weight of each—carboy and all—is generally about two cwt.

By the LORD JUSTICE-CLERK.—I understand that some of the carboys contained nitric acid and some vitriol. I only know that from the documents.

37. *James Johnston* (64). *By the* LORD ADVOCATE.—I am a manufacturing chemist, and reside in Rutherglen. I am sole partner of Alexander Hope, Jun., & Co., manufacturing chemists, Coatbridge Street, Port Dundas. I recollect a man coming and buying a carboy of nitric acid from us in February last. The man was not previously known to me. He called and inquired about the price and strength of nitric acid. He did not say what strength he wanted, he just made inquiries about the different strengths. He said it was for some patent for preserving meat. [Shown Timothy Featherstone.] That is the man. I mentioned the strength we made. The man did not buy anything at the time, but on 19th February we received a letter ordering a carboy 90° strong, with a post office order for the amount. No. 38, dated 17th February 1883, is the letter we received. On the

same day we sent a carboy, for which we were paid. [Shown No. 39.] We received that on the morning of 30th March this year. The empty carboy came back. [Shown No. 32.] That was the ticket on it, bearing to be from D. O'Herlihy. In response to the letter of 29th March [No. 39], we sent two carboys on Monday 1st April, of 92° strength. These were sent back from Cork, full, by the police. The entries in our books applicable to these transactions are correct.

Cross-examined by Mr. RHIND.—The first carboy was despatched on 19th February to O'Herlihy & Co., Cork, in the ordinary way of business. There was no attempt at concealment as to its contents; in fact, it was shipped as nitric acid, which it was. I think we received the empty carboy back on the morning of 2d or 3d April. Carboys are sometimes kept a longer and sometimes a shorter time by the customer; there was nothing peculiar in this case. The empty carboy came from Cork. We have sold stronger acid than that which we sent to Ireland.

38. *James Armstrong* (72). *By the* LORD ADVOCATE.—I am clerk in the employment of Clolus & Co., glycerine manufacturers, at Ruchill Glycerine Works, Maryhill, Glasgow. I was in their employment last year. In November last year the business was carried on by Mr. Victor Clolus, a partner of the present firm, in his own name. Mr. Clolus was a wholesale dealer. I recollect in October last year a young man coming into our works at Ruchill and asking if we sold glycerine in small quantities. The exact day I am not sure of, but it was about the end of October. [Being shown the prisoners at the bar, witness identified Terence M'Dermott as the man who came on the occasion referred to.] I am quite certain of that. He asked if we sold glycerine in small quantities. I said I was not sure, but I would ask my manager and see. He said he wanted it to apply to wounds on a horse's back. He did not say what quantity he wanted. He did not give any indication about the amount. I communicated with Mr. Venables, our manager, and got permission to sell it. I sold M'Dermott 10 lbs. of glycerine on that occasion. I don't know whether that would be a good deal for a horse's back. He had nothing with him to put the glycerine in. He went away and came back with a tin can, which from its smell appeared to have been used for paraffin oil. I got the can cleaned, and put in the glycerine. I don't remember M'Dermott saying anything about filling the can up when I had weighed out the quantity. I charged him 7½d. per lb. I don't remember asking the young man whether he had ever used glycerine before. He said he had bought glycerine from the Glasgow Apothecaries' Company. That was on my asking him. If I remember right he said he had paid 10d. per lb. for it, and he said he considered it rather weak for the purpose for which he wanted it. The only purpose he had named was the horse's back. The same young man came back again about eight or ten days afterwards. He asked for the same quantity of the same thing which he had asked for formerly. I don't remember whether he said anything about his previous purchase. He said it had been all used. I again applied to Mr. Venables as to whether we should sell it. Mr. Venables seemed to have a doubt about supplying it. Ultimately it was supplied. M'Dermott was told at the same

time not to come back again. The first glycerine which was supplied was what is termed dynamite glycerine white; and the second was dynamite glycerine ordinary. On both occasions it was what we call in the trade dynamite glycerine, and has been supplied for that purpose. There are three qualities of glycerine—crude, refined, and pure. The refined is termed ordinary dynamite glycerine, and the other has the other designation which I have given. When the young man bought the glycerine he gave the name of James Bolyn, Gallowgate; the exact number I don't remember. On both occasions he took the glycerine away with him. Referring to our sale books Nos. 9 and 10 of process, I find the entries of both transactions—paid for at works by Mr. Bolyn —and the transaction is entered in the ordinary way. The first bears to have been paid on 31st October, and the second on 7th November 1882. Those entries were made afterwards. This book is entered up at the end of every month. I cannot swear that the entries I have referred to were made within a day or two, but they were made within three or four days. I don't remember anything being said on the second occasion as to the purpose for which the glycerine was wanted.

Cross-examined by Mr. RHIND.—I did not for a moment think that the glycerine was to be used for improper purposes. What is called in the trade dynamite glycerine is used, I understand, for many other purposes than the manufacture of dynamite. I had never seen the young man before, so far as I am aware. The last time I saw him was at the corner of Port Dundas Road and Water Street. I don't recollect the exact time of the year, but it was about a fortnight before he was apprehended in Glasgow.

By the LORD JUSTICE-CLERK.—When he was apprehended I was asked to go and see him in the Central Police Office. I do not remember when that was.

By Mr. RHIND.—When I saw him about a fortnight before he was apprehended I thought he was the same lad that had bought the glycerine from us. *Q.*—Are you quite sure that you are not mistaken with regard to the person of M'Dermott? *A.*—No; I am quite sure he is the young man who bought the glycerine. I don't remember how long he was in our warehouse on each of these occasions. He was more than a minute or two, because it would take at the very least a quarter of an hour or twenty minutes to fill the glycerine. In the first case he was under our observation almost the whole time he was in the place. *Q.*—You paid no more attention to him than to any other customer? *A.*—No more.

Re-examined.—*Q.*—And no less? *A.*—No less.

By the LORD JUSTICE-CLERK.—We told him not to come back because we did not sell in such small quantities as he asked for. We were not in the habit of selling them. That was the only reason.

By a JURYMAN.—The smallest quantity we ever sell ranges from 10 to 15 tons in the ordinary trade.

By Mr. RHIND.—The lad did not ask for ten lbs. of glycerine. When he brought the dish he asked it to be filled. I filled it, and it contained ten lbs. He did not ask to get the smallest quantity; he only said he wanted a small quantity.

By the LORD ADVOCATE.—When he brought his dish he asked the dish to be filled.

By a JURYMAN.—The smallness of the quantity did not excite our suspicion.

By the LORD JUSTICE-CLERK.—It was only that in our ordinary trade we did not care about selling such a small quantity.

39. *James Steel* (74). *By the* LORD ADVOCATE.—I am foreman in the employment of Messrs. Clolus & Co., Ruchill Glycerine Works, Maryhill. I was in their employment last autumn. I recollect a man coming and buying 10 lbs. of glycerine at the works. I was present on that occasion. [Shown Terence M'Dermott.] That is the chap. Mr. Armstrong served him with glycerine on the first occasion, and I washed out the dish, which had been smelling of paraffin, as near as I can recollect. This was about the beginning of November, but I cannot give the exact date. I did not keep the books or make entries in them. The same young man came back a second time. I saw him. He did not speak to me. Mr. Armstrong cried me over, and said he was going in to fill some more dynamite glycerine for this young man. Q.—Did Mr. Armstrong use that expression in the presence of the young man? *A.*—Yes; he shouted it out. Q.—That he was going to fill some more dynamite glycerine for this young man? *A.*—Yes; from the stock tank. The young man heard that said. I did not see the can filled. I kept outside with the young man in the yard. Mr. Armstrong took the can in to the stock cask and filled it. I remained outside with the young man. There is no permission for strangers inside. I did not ask the young man his name at any time. I did not hear him give his name. I did not hear any one mention his name in his presence till I was taken to the Central Police Office to identify him. Q.—Did you hear the name of James Bolyn mentioned? *A.*—Yes, on the first occasion, when the clerk asked him what he was going to do with the glycerine. He said it was to put on a horse's back. I heard him mention the name of Bolyn, but not as his own name. I think he said that the stuff was for one Bolyn, a contractor in the Gallowgate. That was all I heard. He took the stuff away with him, so that we had no occasion to send to the address.

Cross-examined by Mr. RHIND.—We have a large business, and there are a great many customers coming about the place.

40. *James Haire* (76). *By the* LORD ADVOCATE.—I am a time-keeper in the employment of the Irvine Chemical Company. [Shown the prisoners.] I recognize Terence M'Dermott. He was in the employment of the Irvine Chemical Company from 21st May 1882 to 9th October 1882. He then left the employment; and I did not see him again till 8th May 1883, when he applied for and got temporary employment, and was there till the 16th. In these works vitriol or sulphuric acid is kept in large quantities in lead cisterns. It is easily accessible to the workers.

Cross-examined by Mr. RHIND.—It is used in the course of operations at the works.

41. *Levi Barrow* (77). *By the* LORD ADVOCATE.—I am a vitriol pumper in the employment of the Irvine Chemical Company, and have been so for about two years. [Shown the prisoners.] I know Terence M'Dermott. He was in the employment of the Company

some time last year. I recollect his coming to me about the month of September last year, when I was pumping vitriol, and asking me to get him a bottle of vitriol to clean a chain. I refused it. He had a bottle with him which he wanted filled. He went back to his work, and nothing happened then. There was a large quantity of vitriol about in these works. It is produced there as a by-product. If anybody working in the place wanted to help himself to a bottle of vitriol, he would have no difficulty in doing so without observation.

Cross-examined by Mr. RHIND.—Vitriol is used for cleaning chains.

42. *Thomas Sutherland* (80). *By the* LORD ADVOCATE.—I am a plumber in Glasgow. I do repairs on pipes in the property in Dobbie's Loan of which Mr. Miller is the factor. I find that in December last year I sent a man to repair some pipes in a house, 448 Dobbie's Loan, occupied by Terence M'Dermott. *Q.*—In saying Terence M'Dermott, is that only a name to you? *A.*—I just got the order from the proprietor to go to M'Dermott's house in 448 Dobbie's Loan, where I was pretty well acquainted, and do some repair to the pipes of the jaw-box. I do not know who Terence M'Dermott is. I sent a man, Charles Johnston, to do the work. I got a note of the repairs that required to be done, and that were done. No. 118 is the note which was furnished to me at the time. Johnston brought back piping which he said had been taken out.

43. *Charles Johnston* (81). *By the* LORD ADVOCATE.—I am a plumber in Glasgow. In December last I was sent by the last witness, Sutherland, to repair some piping in M'Dermott's house in Dobbie's Loan. I do not know who M'Dermott is. I merely know that that is the name which was given to me. I examined the trap-pipe leading from the jaw-box of the house to the conductor and drain. I found it all eaten away into holes. To the best of my opinion, it had the appearance of a trap that had been used for urine. *Q.*—Would a strong acid of any kind do it? *A.*—I do not know anything about acids. The pipe was eaten away with holes, and the neighbours had been complaining. I cut it out and put in a new one. It was not a place where urine would usually be run. It had no smell of urine.

Cross-examined by Mr. RHIND.—The holes were such as you would find caused by urine. *Q.*—And seeing it, you had no other idea at the time? *A.*—No, no idea of what had done it.

44. *Mrs. Sarah Douglas or M'Lachlan* (82). *By the* LORD ADVOCATE. —I am the wife of John M'Lachlan, an engineer, at present in China. From Whitsunday 1882 to Whitsunday 1883 I occupied a house, one stair up, at 35 Ronald Street, Townhead, Glasgow, where my mother lived with me. In the second week of January this year I put up a ticket indicating that lodgings might be had in my house. On the following Monday a man came asking for lodgings. I think it was the 15th January. It was just the Monday after I put out the ticket. I put out the ticket about the 8th. The man looked at the room, being a parlour with a concealed bed, and I mentioned 7s. a week was the rent. He became my lodger. I did not ask his name that night, but next day he said his name was Moorhead, and that he was a

F

commercial traveller. *Q.*—How long did he lodge with you? *A.*—He entered into the eighth week. I recollect on the Saturday night after the first Monday he came to lodge with me, he was out till after one o'clock on Sunday morning. *Q.*—You say he came to lodge with you on the Monday, which was the 15th, and the first Saturday after that would be the 20th? *A.*—Yes. In consequence of his staying out that night so late I objected to keeping him. He had not stayed out so late before. He said that a friend had been ill, and that he had been searching for a doctor. On that Sunday about six o'clock in the evening the bell rang and somebody called for him. I cannot tell who the man was who called. From his tongue I thought him an Irishman. I recollect him bringing a man to the house the night before he left. *Q.*—Do you know who the man is? *A.*—Dalton. [Shown Henry Dalton.] That is the man whom he brought. *Q.*—You say Moorhead entered into the eighth week; the Wednesday in the eighth week would bring you to the 8th of March. *A.*—Counting it up, it brought us to the 8th of March. Moorhead said this was a friend of his that had come from Dundee. Dalton remained all night with Moorhead. Between seven and eight next morning a young man called for them—the man M'Dermott that I saw in Glasgow. [Shown Terence M'Dermott.] That is the young man. He only asked for Moorhead. Dalton was with Moorhead at the time. I took the young man into the kitchen to wait till Moorhead and Dalton got up and dressed. M'Dermott might be half an hour in the kitchen with me. I had plenty of opportunity of seeing him. Moorhead had told me a week previously that he was going away on that Thursday. He said he was going to London. I asked M'Dermott if he was going along with Moorhead to London, and he said, yes, he was. This occurrence took place on the Thursday morning, 9th March. Moorhead came out and called M'Dermott into the room. He was with them for some time. Between nine and ten o'clock Moorhead paid his bill. I cannot say whether the three men went away together. I had seen them all in the room together, and while I was in the kitchen they had breakfast, and after breakfast I heard the door open and shut and a cab driven off. When I went into the room the whole three men were off. On the night Moorhead brought Dalton to the house, Moorhead brought in a brown tin box, like a lady's bonnet-box. I cannot say whether it was a new-looking box. [Shown No. 6 and No. 20 (Tin box found near the "Times" newspaper office, London, on the occasion of the explosion there, on 15th March).] I cannot say as to the exact size of the box, but that was the kind of it.

By Mr. RHIND.—It was a very common kind of box; I have seen plenty of the same. It was the night before Moorhead left that he brought it. He did not leave it in the house. I did not see him go away, and I cannot say from eyesight whether he took it, but it went away as the rest of his luggage did. I did not see it after it came into the house. It was only one night in the house. I thought it belonged to the gentleman whom he brought with him—Dalton. Dalton and he came in together. It was Moorhead who brought the box in. *Q.*—Had Dalton luggage with him? *A.*—That was all the luggage. I did not see whether the box contained clothing or not. Moorhead went away as if to get the London train. I don't know whether

Dalton and M'Dermott went to the station, or whether they parted at the door. Dalton did not come back again.

Re-examined.—I never saw a lady's bonnet-box used for gentlemen's luggage.

By Mr. RHIND.—I had never seen M'Dermott before. I never saw him afterwards till I saw him in the Central Police Office in Glasgow. I was not told that that was likely to be the man. It was in August that I saw him in the Central Police Office.

By the LORD JUSTICE-CLERK.—I recognized him at once when I saw him again.

By a JURYMAN.—Moorhead came to my house on the 15th of January. He was out late on the evening of Saturday the 20th and the morning of Sunday the 21st. Dalton came the night before Moorhead left. I think that was Wednesday the 8th of March. Moorhead left the following morning between nine and ten.

45. *Christina Colquhoun* (83). *By* Mr. BRAND.—I am mother of the last witness. I lived with my daughter, Mrs. M'Lachlan, in Ronald Street. [Shown prisoners.] I recognize one of these men. [Points to Terence M'Dermott.] I remember him coming to see a man named Moorhead the morning Moorhead left our house. He came before breakfast-time. He did not take breakfast. He went away with Moorhead and another man. I do not know what o'clock it was; but it was after they took their breakfast.

Cross-examined by Mr. BAXTER.—I was in the kitchen with M'Dermott when he was waiting for Moorhead. M'Dermott stayed till they were ready for him, and then Moorhead called for him. I cannot say how long M'Dermott would be with Moorhead and the other man alone; but it was not very long. *Q.*—Twenty minutes? *A.*—Likely it would be that.

46. *Mary Currie or Bain* (84). *By the* LORD ADVOCATE.—I am the wife of William Bain, shoemaker, 35 Ronald Street, Townhead, Glasgow, and I live there. I know Mrs. M'Lachlan. I recollect her coming to live there at Whitsunday 1882. I remember a lodger coming to her house in the beginning of January, but the precise time I do not recollect. I saw him going out and in. I did not know his name. [Shown prisoners.] I have seen that man [pointing to Terence M'Dermott]. I have seen him in the stair of 35 Ronald Street, going up and down. I do not know whom he was going to see. It was at the time that Mrs. M'Lachlan had the lodger. I have seen M'Dermott going up and down that stair about three or four times while Mrs. M'Lachlan had the lodger.

Cross-examined by Mr. RHIND.—There were a great many other people living in that stair.

47. *Robert Munro* (86). *By the* LORD ADVOCATE.—I am a cab-driver in Glasgow. [Shown prisoners.] I have seen Terence M'Dermott and James Donnelly before. These are all I have seen. I first saw M'Dermott and Donnelly on the second Friday of the present year. They came and hired my cab from St. Vincent Street over to Portugal Lane, which is near Main Street, on the south side of the

Clyde. I drove them to the corner of Ronald Street after that. When I drove them to Portugal Lane they went into the Lane, and I waited fifteen or twenty minutes, and then they came back and entered my cab again. They had a parcel when they went into the Lane. They had nothing when they came out. A man came to the end of the lane with them and spoke to them. I could not recognize the man. [Shown Thomas Devany.] I cannot recognize him. I drove M'Dermott and Donnelly after that to the corner of Ronald Street, where they paid me off. Four or five days after that Donnelly hired me again in St. Vincent Street, and I drove him to the corner of Corn Street and Garscube Road. This would be on the Wednesday following the Friday. There was nobody with Donnelly on that occasion. He paid me off at the corner of Corn Street and Garscube Road. I was in the service of James M'Coy, a cab-owner. I cannot say whether he was known to the prisoners. [Shown Henry Dalton.] *Q.*—Did you ever see that man in Glasgow? *A.*—He resembles a man very much whom I saw speaking to James M'Coy. I am not very sure of him in that garb. I saw him in Glasgow about the same time that I drove M'Dermott and Donnelly.

Cross-examined by Mr. RHIND.—It was between nine and ten o'clock at night when I drove M'Dermott and Donnelly. My hire altogether lasted three-quarters of an hour, and twenty minutes of that time was spent waiting at Portugal Lane. I believe it was Donnelly who carried the parcel into Portugal Lane. I noticed the parcel when I was hired at St. Vincent Street. Donnelly had it then. It was a brown paper parcel about the size of the Glasgow Directory. The man whom I saw with them at Portugal Lane did not accompany them to Ronald Street. They had no parcel from Portugal Lane to Ronald Street. It was about nine o'clock in the evening when Donnelly himself hired me on the subsequent occasion. He had a parcel with him on that occasion also; it resembled the other. I never saw M'Dermott and Donnelly except on the occasions I have spoken of. I am quite sure they are the men. I identified them in Duke Street Prison about the month of September of this year. I had no difficulty with Donnelly. I had a little difficulty about M'Dermott—not much.

By the LORD JUSTICE-CLERK.—I was not quite sure about M'Dermott.

Re-examined.—I am quite sure now.

48. **Myles M'Cullough** (87). *By the* LORD ADVOCATE.—I am an aerated water manufacturer in Garngad Road, Glasgow. I have premises at No. 81 there, and carry on business under the name of Myles M'Cullough & Co. Michael Buchanan had, at one time, a small share in the business. I use weak vitriol in my business; it is a class for the purpose. I get all my vitriol from Alexander Hope, Jun., & Co., Coatbridge Street, Port Dundas. John Getty is a vanman in my service, and has been so for eighteen months. Buchanan acted as salesman during December last. There is a yard at my premises with an inside gate where there is a piece of ground common to me and certain other neighbours. It is a kind of thoroughfare—a wee bit of an inshot. It is not in my premises. I remember one evening in

October last being inside my gate when I saw a man. He was carrying a jar and was going out at the time. I did not know who the man was. I made a remark about it to Getty or some of them, and asked what that man was taking away. I thought he was perhaps taking my vitriol. I did not know whether it was vitriol or not, but it was like it. He was about where the vitriol was at the time.

Cross-examined by Mr. RHIND.—It might be a three, four, or five gallon jar that he had. It was somewhat dark at the time, in the gloaming.

Re-examined.—I do not use any strong vitriol in my business. That would not do for me. I had not given any sanction to the storing of any other body's vitriol there.

49. *Michael Buchanan* (88). *By the* LORD ADVOCATE.—I am a labourer in Garngad Road, Glasgow. I was for about eighteen months with Myles M'Cullough, aerated water manufacturer, the last witness. I know James M'Cullagh, a furnaceman, who sometimes worked in Tennant & Co.'s works while I worked there. [Shown the prisoner James M'Cullagh.] That is the man. I recollect him coming to me on one occasion, as near as I recollect, in the end of July last year. He asked me if I could get him a bottle of vitriol. I am not very certain what I said. I said I might, but I told him that I did not go for the vitriol now, so far as I remember. He did not say where he wanted me to get the bottle of vitriol. He gave me £1 to buy vitriol for him. He asked me if I would get him a bottle of vitriol. I said I was not in the habit of going for it, but I would ask the man in the yard if he would get it. The name of the man to whom I referred was John Getty. M'Cullagh said that, for fear he might not see me again before I saw Getty, he would give me the money, and he gave me 20s. to get the vitriol. He said it was the strongest vitriol he wanted. I gave the message and the money to Getty, and asked him to bring the vitriol, and he said he would. A carboy of vitriol came for James M'Cullagh. It was put in the yard outside of the work. Q.—Was it put outside Myles M'Cullough's vitriol and apart from it? A.—There was a difference between the two of some wood and sticks. It was separated from my master's vitriol. I cannot say how long it remained there, because I was in the habit of going away in the morning about eight o'clock, and I would not be back till eight or ten o'clock at night, and I did not see him for a week or a fortnight afterwards.

By the LORD JUSTICE-CLERK.—I think this was in August 1882. I made a mistake in saying July.

Examination continued.—I cannot say how long the carboy remained in the yard. I do not know who took it away. It was taken away. I got the change back from Getty in a week or a fortnight afterwards, and gave it to James M'Cullagh, with the receipt for the money. I don't recollect how much I gave him back. I cannot say in what month it was, but James M'Cullagh spoke to me on another occasion, and asked me if I would get him another bottle of vitriol. He gave me some more money, as near as I recollect 12s. 6d. I gave that money to somebody to get the vitriol for him, in the same way as before. A carboy came for James M'Cullagh, and was put down in the same place as before, I understand. I cannot say how it was taken away. I did not see it taken away. *Q.*—But you saw it there? *A.*—I cannot say I saw it, but I heard it had been put there. I never saw it again. I was asked, perhaps eight or ten days afterwards, to get a third carboy for James M'Cullagh. It was got in the same way, and brought to our place, and afterwards taken away. M'Cullagh gave me money to pay for the third carboy.

By the LORD JUSTICE-CLERK.—I heard the carboy had been taken away, but I did not see it taken away.

Examination continued.—Before any of these purchases were made, M'Cullagh asked me to get him a sample of the vitriol which Myles M'Cullough used. I have not the date of that, but it was before any of these businesses had occurred. I gave him a sample in a gill or half-mutchkin bottle. James M'Cullagh took it away, and as near as I remember, he said afterwards that it was not good enough or strong enough for him. He did not tell me what he wanted these carboys of vitriol for.

Cross-examined by Mr. ORR.—I had known M'Cullagh for some years before this. He worked for some time in the same work that I did. I knew him for four or five years. From all reports, I heard he minded his work pretty well. With regard to the first bottle of vitriol which I got for him, I did not see who took it away. The second bottle, according to the information I had, was put into the yard in the same way as the first, and I heard nothing more about it. I cannot say who went for it. I never instructed any person, only John Getty. He was the man who went for it when it came to his turn. He went for it when it answered for himself. I did not see the second bottle in the yard. I did not see either the first, or the second, or the third removed from the yard. It is not the case that I assisted to remove one of them from the yard. It is not the case that I got 2s. from a man to assist him in doing so. I never said so, and I never saw the man who took it away to my knowledge.

50. *John Getty* (89). *By the* LORD ADVOCATE.—I sometimes work as a vanman to Myles M'Cullough & Co., aerated water manufacturers. I was doing so last summer. I remember being asked by Buchanan, the last witness, to get some carboys of vitriol for a man. On the first occasion, I believe it was in the month of September last year, but I cannot tell the proper date. Buchanan asked me to get it, and gave me money to pay for it. He asked me to get strong vitriol. I sent a boy for it to Alexander Hope, Junior, & Co., and gave him the money, and told him to get a receipt for one carboy of strong vitriol. I cannot tell which boy it was, there were so many of them. I cannot tell whether it was James Gillick. A carboy of strong vitriol came for Buchanan's friend. It was in the yard, but outside the works gate. It was kept separate from Myles M'Cullough's vitriol. I put it there when the boy brought it back, and I saw it standing there. I cannot tell who took it away. I was asked on a second occasion, some five or six weeks afterwards, by Buchanan, to get another carboy for his friend. I again got money from Buchanan in the same way, and I gave it to one of the boys, and told him to order the vitriol. The second carboy was brought to Myles M'Cullough's place, and put down

at about the same place as before. *Q.*—Do you know who took that away? *A.*—I can identify one of the men, but not the other; it was in the dark that it was taken. [Shown the prisoners.] It was not one of these men. I was asked a third time to get a carboy for Buchanan's friend. That was nearly four weeks after the second, I should think.

By the LORD JUSTICE-CLERK.—The third occasion was nine or ten weeks after the first.

Examination continued.—The third was brought by one of the boys as before, and paid for with money which I got from Buchanan and gave to the boy. This carboy also was set down in the yard, and taken away. The same man took it away who took the second. He is not amongst the prisoners.

Cross-examined by Mr. ORR.—He was not a very heavy-built man. He was a kind of round-shouldered, and had a kind of light-coloured coat, with ruddy whiskers. He would be about 5 feet 6 inches or 5 feet 7 inches in height. He had stubbly red hair about his face.

51. *James Gillick* (90). *By the* LORD ADVOCATE. — I am in the employment of Myles M'Cullough. I drive a horse and van. I remember last year the witness, John Getty, asking me to get some vitriol. It was in the latter part of the year, but I do not remember the month. He gave me money to pay for it. The vitriol he told me to ask for was the strongest acid. I went to Alexander Hope, Junior, & Co., and asked for a carboy of strong vitriol. I paid for it with the money which Getty had given me, and brought it back to Myles M'Cullough's place, and saw it set down. It remained there one night. Two strange men took it away. I would not know them if I saw them. About a week or two afterwards Getty asked me to get a second carboy. *Q.*—Do you recollect how long it was after the first? *A.*— Whenever the first one was done. I got a second of the same kind from Alexander Hope & Co., and paid for it with money which Getty gave me. I brought it back in my cart and got it set down in the yard. It remained there for one night. It was lifted by one of the strange men. I think Micky Buchanan was there and helped him to lift it, but I would not swear to that. There was another boy named George Steed driving for Myles M'Cullough. [Shown the prisoners.] I have seen M'Dermott about our yard. I heard his name in connection with this case. I saw him coming about the place and coming inside Myles M'Cullough's store. He was doing nothing, just looking about him. That was before the time the carboys were got. I also saw that other man [pointing to Devany]. I saw him coming about the place in the same way as M'Dermott. He came by himself. I do not know what brought him there. It was about the time the carboys were coming. He was not there when they were lifted. *Q.*—Do you know any of the others? *A.*—That young man next M'Cullagh [pointing to Donnelly]. I saw him speaking to Michael Buchanan in Garngad Road. I have seen him going about Myles M'Cullough's place. I saw him in the outside yard. It was in the outside yard that the carboys which I was asked to bring by Getty were put. It was after the time that the carboys were coming when I saw Donnelly there.

Cross-examined by Mr. RHIND.—I think it was about a week before the carboys were brought that I saw M'Dermott. That was the only time I saw him. It was a week before I was told to go and get the first carboy. I never saw him again until to-day. *Q.*—How did you know his name to be M'Dermott? *A.*—By hearing up in the prison from one of the men who took me down to see the prisoners about two months ago. That was the first time I had seen him since I saw him before the time the carboys came.

By the LORD JUSTICE-CLERK.—It was in the prison that I heard his name.

Cross-examination continued.—The detective who took me mentioned his name. He took me to see all the men. *Q.*—And you thought you had seen M'Dermott in the yard? *A.*—Yes. These were the only two times I ever saw him in my life until to-day. I saw him in the yard about five or ten minutes; he just went in and out again. He was not speaking to anybody. *Q.*—Is it a common thing for people to go into the yard? *A.*—Yes, strange people often go in. It was just about the time the first carboy was in the yard that I saw Devany about the yard. He was doing nothing then. I did not see him speaking to any one. He stayed about five minutes.

52. *George Steed* (91). *By the* LORD ADVOCATE.—I was in the employment of Myles M'Cullough, aerated water maker, last autumn. I remember Getty giving me a message. He gave me about £1 to fetch a bottle of strong vitriol. I do not right mind the time when it was. *Q.*—How long ago? *A.*—About nine months since. *Q.*—Is it not more than a year? *A.*—Yes; it is more than a year. I got the vitriol at Hope's in Coatbridge Street, and drove it in my van to Myles M'Cullough's yard, and put it down there. Two or three days afterwards I saw the bottle lying empty. I do not know whether it was ever taken away bodily or not. *Q.*—Do you think it was emptied there? *A.*—Yes; it was emptied there, but I never saw anybody emptying it. I saw it full, and then I saw it empty. [Shown the prisoners.] I never saw any of these men coming about the place.

53. *Andrew Campbell* (92). *By the* LORD ADVOCATE.—I am a clerk in the employment of Alexander Hope, Jun., & Co. Myles M'Cullough, aerated water manufacturer, is a customer of theirs. He gets weak vitriol for the purposes of his business. I know his boys, Gillick and Steed, who come and lift vitriol for him. I recollect these boys buying carboys of other vitriol. I have our books here. No. 11 is the Outward Book of Alexander Hope, Jun., & Co. I find an entry made, date 4th September 1882:—"M. M'Cullough, V. 1." That is, one carboy of strong vitriol and three carboys of weak vitriol. The carboy of strong vitriol was ordered by the boy who came for the vitriol. He paid for the strong vitriol. The weak vitriol was paid for also at the time by the boy. There is another entry under date 21st October:—"M. M'Cullough" again—for the same, namely three weak and one strong. That was paid for, both weak and strong. Again on 6th November there are three weak and one strong. I cannot say whether the strong vitriol was used in Myles M'Cullough's business at all. I think it was; it could be used. *Q.*—But you don't know? *A.*—No. On each of the dates I have mentioned there was a

carboy of strong vitriol taken away and paid for by one of the van boys.

By a JURYMAN.—The weak vitriol is 144° and the strong is 168°.

54. *Archibald Carmichael* (61). *Examined.*—I am a sub-inspector in the detective department of police, Glasgow. Acting under instructions I made certain measurements yesterday. I visited the scene of the explosion at the gasometer, and measured the distance between the head of Muirhouse Lane at Maxwell Road and the gasometer. The distance from the corner of Maxwell Road and Muirhouse Lane to behind the gasometer is 140 yards. From the gasometer to the corner of Darnley Street and Princes Street is 180 yards. From the gasometer to Possil Bridge the distance is about 2¾ miles—about forty minutes' walk. From the railway shed where the explosion took place to the railway station platform, Buchanan Street, the distance is 300 yards; and from the same point to the signal box where Kearney was stationed the distance is 140 yards. From the shed to the bridge at Dobbie's Loan the distance is 40 yards. From the houses in Muirhouse Lane to the part of the gasometer where the explosion occurred the distance is 60 yards—that is, from Butler's house and the others. I know Terence M'Dermott's house, 452 Dobbie's Loan. To go from his house to the railway bridge near where the explosion occurred it would take three or four minutes. To go from M'Dermott's house to Possil Bridge, where the box was found, would take about ten minutes. I know Devany's house in Portugal Lane. It would take about twelve or fifteen minutes to go from his house to the gasometer. To go from his house to the railway shed, where the explosion occurred, would take about fifteen minutes, and to go to Possil Bridge about twenty-five minutes. I know the houses of Callaghan, M'Cabe, and Drum in Rose Street. To go to the gasometer from their houses would take from fifteen to eighteen minutes; to go to the railway shed twenty minutes, and to Possil Bridge thirty minutes. I know M'Cann's house in Stirling Street. To go from it to the gasometer would take twenty-five minutes, to the railway shed fifteen minutes, and to Possil Bridge about twenty-five minutes. I know Donnelly's house in Villiers Street. To go from it to the gasometer would take about forty-five minutes, to the railway shed twenty minutes, and to Possil Bridge about thirty minutes. I know Kelly's and Casey's houses in Kirk Street. To go from there to the gasometer would take about twenty-five minutes, to the railway shed twenty minutes, and to Possil Bridge about thirty minutes. I know Portugal Lane; it is on the south side of the Clyde. The main street on the south side of the Clyde is Eglinton Street. Portugal Lane is on the east side of Eglinton Street. Mains Street, Gorbals, is another principal street on the south side of the river, and is on the east side of Portugal Lane. Portugal Lane is only a short distance from Stockwell Bridge. It would take about twelve minutes to go from George Square to Portugal Lane. Ronald Street is in the Townhead district of Glasgow, or St. Rollox district, and is about ten minutes' walk from George Square. It is a short distance from the cemetery. It is a little to the south-east of the Buchanan Street Station of the Caledonian Railway Company. Corn Street is in the northern district of the city, and

within a short distance of Possil Bridge; it is off Garscube Road. Dobbie's Loan is within two or three minutes' walk of Corn Street.

Cross-examined by Mr. RHIND.—I walked the distances which I have given, and measured them in that way. In stating the time it would take to go between the various places I have mentioned, I am speaking from having walked the distance,—I walked every step in each case. M'Dermott's house consists of two small rooms and a kitchen. There was a lodger in the house when I called, a young man. I believe the house was used by others besides himself when he was living there.

Cross-examined by Mr. KENNEDY.—I superintended in some cases the arrangements by which the proposed witnesses were taken to identify the different prisoners. I recollect being present when the witness Robert Aitken, the butcher's boy, was brought to identify some of the prisoners as the men he had seen running out of Muirhouse Lane. The prisoners were brought in, and as they came in I asked their names, and they answered. The witness Aitken identified two of the men shown to him as men he thought he remembered having seen. These were Devany and M'Cabe.

55. *William Dreghorn* (105). *Examined by the* LORD ADVOCATE.—I am a supercargo in Cork in the employment of the Clyde Shipping Company. I produce the quay book No. 25 of process. It extends from January 1882 to February 1883. I find an entry in that book applicable to the steamer "Ballycotton," which left Glasgow on 13th December 1882 and arrived at Cork on the 20th. The steamer brought a carboy of acid addressed to D. O'Herlihy. Denis Deasy came and took possession of that carboy. He produced a document for it. [Shown No. 26.] That is the document which he brought.

Mr. RHIND.—I object to the evidence of this witness as to anything that was said or done by Denis Deasy. The evidence of Featherstone is the best evidence. If he is to be called and examined, I do not object; but if not, I do.

The LORD JUSTICE-CLERK.—We cannot stop the examination of this witness at the present stage. Repel the objection.

Examination continued.—When Deasy got away the carboy he signed the receipt, No. 25 of process, for it. On 22nd February the steamer "Cedar" arrived at Cork, bringing another carboy of acid from Glasgow, also addressed to O'Herlihy. The manifest, No. 22 of process, bears that the carboy was consigned from A. Hope, Jun., & Co., Glasgow. That carboy was received by Denis Deasy.

By Mr. RHIND.—*Q.*—Do you know that yourself, or only from the writing in the book before you? *A.*—I have it in my memory; I can speak from memory as to those dates. I can speak from memory as to the steamers and the dates and who the carboys were from. *Q.*—And the man who took delivery? *A.*—Yes.

Examination continued.—I have the signatures of the man.

By the LORD JUSTICE-CLERK.—One or two of the signatures were got in my presence. The signatures were got in the ordinary course of business on delivery being given.

Examination continued.—On 25th February 1883 a carboy of acid arrived at Cork by the steamer "Amsterdam" from Glasgow. I can swear that I saw Denis Deasy sign for one carboy. The carboy which came by the "Amsterdam" was consigned by J. Montgomerie & Co. to O'Herlihy, and delivery was taken by Denis Deasy. Two carboys arrived on the 5th of April by the steamer "Copeland" from Glasgow. The manifest shows that it was consigned by A. Hope, Jun., & Co. to D. O'Herlihy, Cork. These two carboys were on hand for a considerable time. I advised O'Herlihy of the arrival, but he never came to lift them. Denis Deasy never appeared to lift them either. I afterwards returned them to Glasgow. The police intervened, but I cannot swear whether it was under their directions that the carboys were sent back to Glasgow. The carboys were returned full as they had come. There were two carboys returned empty from Cork to Glasgow.

Cross-examined by Mr. RHIND.—I can swear of my own knowledge as to who took delivery of one carboy, but as regards the rest I am only speaking from what appears in the books when I say that delivery of them was taken by Deasy.

By the LORD JUSTICE-CLERK.—There were three carboys consigned altogether from Hope & Co. Of these Deasy took delivery of the first. I don't think he brought any authority with him, but so far as our books show he got delivery. There was no application made for delivery of the second two.

By the LORD ADVOCATE.—When Deasy got delivery of the carboy which arrived on 20th December, he presented the delivery order which is now shown me. He presented it to me.

By the LORD JUSTICE-CLERK.—I would have delivered the carboy to anybody who would have brought that paper.

By the LORD ADVOCATE.—The carboys which came on the 22nd and 25th of February respectively were also delivered to Deasy. On the 5th of April two carboys arrived, for which nobody came, although I advised O'Herlihy, whose name appeared as consignee, and these were sent back to Glasgow after the police intervened in the case.

56. *Christian Jacob Dankerk* (107). *Examined by the* LORD ADVOCATE. —I am a supercargo in Cork, and am employed by the Clyde Shipping Company. I was in Cork when the steamer "Ballycotton" arrived on 20th December 1882, bringing a carboy of acid consigned to D. O'Herlihy. The carboy bore to be consigned by M'Geachy and M'Farlane. That carboy was called for by a man named Denis Deasy. [Shown No. 21.] That is the manifest of the vessel proving what I have stated. [Shown No. 26.] That is the delivery order which Deasy brought and on which he got delivery. I was present when a carboy arrived by the screw steamer "Cedar" on the 20th of February. It came from Alexander Hope, Jun., & Co., and was delivered to Denis Deasy on the 24th of February. He signed the delivery order. Another carboy arrived on 23rd February, by the screw steamer "Amsterdam." Denis Deasy took delivery of that carboy also. Our outward cargo book contains entries of the return of two empty carboys on 30th March.

Cross-examined by Mr. RHIND.—I know it was Denis Deasy who took delivery of the carboys, because he signed the book. I saw him write his signature in the book in every case.

By the LORD JUSTICE-CLERK.—I know his signature.

Cross-examination by Mr. RHIND *continued.*—Q.—Do you know anything more than this, that the man came and said his name was Denis Deasy and signed his name in that book? *A.*—I know his name to be Denis Deasy. I did not know him before he came for the carboys. *Q.*—Then whether he was Denis Deasy or not you cannot say? *A.*—I could not say.

Re-examined.—*Q.*—Whether he was Denis Deasy or not, was he the man convicted in Liverpool under the name of Denis Deasy? *A.*—Yes. I gave evidence at the trial in Liverpool.

57. *Francis Scannel* (106). *Examined by the* LORD ADVOCATE.—I am a clerk in the money order office of the post office, Cork. [Shown Nos. 33, 34, and 35 of process.] These are requisitions for money orders. They were passed in to our office. One of the requisitions is "Payable at Glasgow to Alexander Hope & Co.," and signed "D. O'Herlihy, 10 Great George Street West, Cork." Another is in the same terms; and the third is "Payable to J. Montgomerie & Co.," and signed "D. O'Herlihy, 10 Great George Street West, Cork." From the stamping on these requisitions, I can say that orders for the amounts mentioned in these requisitions have been given to the person who handed them in. [Shown document forming part of No. 45.] That is a requisition for an order for £3, payable at Glasgow to J. Montgomerie & Co., signed "D. O'Herlihy, 10 Great George Street West, Cork." That requisition is in the same handwriting as the three to which I have already spoken, and is written on the same kind of slip. I cannot say whether that requisition has ever been actually presented to the post office and an order got upon it. If it had been presented, it should have had the stamp of the office and the number upon it. I would infer from the absence of these marks upon the requisition that it never has been presented.

Cross-examined by Mr. RHIND.—There was a man named O'Herlihy at No. 10 Great George Street West, Cork, but he is not there now. I cannot say whether he lived there when the requisitions I have spoken to were presented. He was tried at Liverpool and acquitted.

Re-examined.—I may have been present when the conversation between the judge and counsel upon which O'Herlihy was acquitted took place, but I don't remember.[1]

58. *Robert Fitzwilliam Starkie* (104). *Examined by the* LORD ADVOCATE.—I am a sub-inspector in the Royal Irish Constabulary, and have charge of the crime department. On the evening of the 29th March of this year I arrested a man named Timothy Featherstone. I knew him quite well. I arrested him in a house in Warren's Place, Cork, and made a charge against him. When I apprehended him I found certain documents upon him. [Shown Nos. 44 and 45.] *Q.*—

[1] After the evidence for the Crown had been concluded before the Liverpool Assizes, t the trial upon 7th, 8th, and 9th August 1883, of Timothy Featherstone, Daniel O'Herlihy, Denis Deasy, Patrick Flannigan, and Henry Dalton, the SOLICITOR-GENERAL said, "The case against O'Herlihy is on a different position from that of the four other men. The case seems to depend upon this— that O'Herlihy knew his name and address were being used by the other prisoner, Featherstone, for the purpose of procuring these materials. The letters from the chemists in Glasgow were left by the letter-carrier at his house, addressed to him."

Mr. JUSTICE STEPHEN.—I think the case against O'Herlihy very weak.

The SOLICITOR-GENERAL.—I admit that, and if your Lordship's view is that this

Did you find these documents on the person of Featherstone when you apprehended him in Cork?

[Mr. RHIND.—I object to the question. This is on the 29th of March 1883, and the documents are offered as evidence to prove a conspiracy between Featherstone and the panels, alleged to have existed during the previous year. It is proved that Featherstone was sometimes with the panels, and his name is in the list of witnesses for the Crown.

The LORD JUSTICE-CLERK.—If the evidence is to be believed, he came on purpose to communicate with the panels regarding the manufacture and use of dynamite.

Mr. RHIND.—The Crown, I submit, must first call Featherstone.

The LORD JUSTICE-CLERK.—There can be no objection to those documents being produced at the present stage. We repel the objection.]

Examination continued.—A.—I did.

[The Lord Advocate proposed to read the document No. 45 to the Jury.

Mr. RHIND.—I object to No. 45 being read. It is not the best evidence. The Crown must first call Featherstone.

Objection repelled.]

Examination continued.—[Document read.[1]] The envelope is addressed "J. Montgomery & Company, manufacturing chemists, Port Dundas, Glasgow, Scotland." [Shown No. 44—Receipt for the preparation of explosives.] *Q.*—Did you get that document upon Featherstone? *A.*—It was found on him in my presence by a constable.

[*The* LORD ADVOCATE proposed to read No. 44 to the Jury.

Mr. RHIND.—I object to this document. Everything depends on when and where it was written. It is found on the 29th of March 1883.

The LORD ADVOCATE.—Featherstone is proved to have been ordering goods, and there is found upon him written directions showing a particular mode in which these articles may be used, and that is evidence that they were intended to be used in that way.

The LORD JUSTICE-CLERK.—We repel the objection.]

The following document, on Green Paper, containing a Receipt for the Preparation of Explosives, was then read :—

No. 44. " Dissolve in bi-sulphide of carbon all the phosphorus it will dissolve, then add third of methylic alcohol usually called wood naptha,

is a case which should not be left to the jury—that it would be undesirable to leave it to the jury—my only desire is to do what is right for public justice, and if you intimate that it is a case which ought to be withdrawn, I am content that that course should be taken.

Mr. JUSTICE STEPHEN.—That is my opinion (addressing the jury). I think the case with regard to O'Herlihy is so weak that I think you ought to acquit him. If you are of the same opinion, he may be acquitted from this indictment, though there may be other things for him to answer to.

The Foreman of the Jury intimated that they acquitted O'Herlihy, whereupon the Court directed that he should leave the dock, but that he should not be discharged for the present.

[1] This was a letter bearing to be from D. O'Herlihy, dated 29th March, containing an order for four carboys of acid, with envelope addressed, and a requisition for a post office order for £3, payable to J. Montgomery & Co. [See the evidence of the previous witness, Francis Scannel.]

and one third benzine (used to clean clothes, be sure and get that kind). The more phosphorus the sooner will it act, but it will not act when raining.

"If you want instantaneous results, tie a glass test tube filled with strong sulphuric acid outside the bottle containing the other fluid, throw the two together. The moment both break, you have the result you want. Try a small quantity some place as experiment and make sure. This is the best cure for Govt. known.

"Here is the way to fix the bottles :—

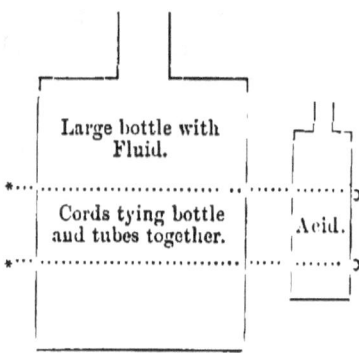

When thrown the large one breaks, so does the tube. *This is instantaneous.*"

Examination continued.—In addition to these, there were some other papers got upon Featherstone, including an hotel bill of the Star Temperance Hotel, signed by John Mitchell. [Shown No. 67.] That is a glass test tube which was found in a portmanteau in Featherstone's room. [Shown No. 36.] That is an envelope addressed to Mr. D. O'Herlihy, 10 Great George Street West, Cork, and was found on Featherstone's person. There were other articles found on Featherstone besides these, but they were not put in evidence. The test tube [No. 67] was broken at the edge, as it is now, when I got it. With the lip off in that way, it would fit quite close to the side of a bottle. That is what I understood when I saw it.

59. *Thomas Shannon* (100).—*Examined by the* LORD ADVOCATE.—I am a badge porter in Liverpool. I met the cargo boat called the "Upupa" at the Liverpool landing-stage on the 28th March of this year. A man came off the boat and engaged me. I found afterwards that his name was Denis Deasy. He asked me to carry a box from the boat to 34 Regent Street.

[Mr. RHIND.—I object to Deasy's movements as evidence against the panels. There has been no connection proved between him and the panels.

The LORD ADVOCATE.—I have proved that the carboys of acid were taken delivery of by Deasy at Cork, and it is, I submit, plain on the face of the evidence that Featherstone was taking possession of them by Deasy.

The LORD JUSTICE-CLERK.—I think this is a little delicate. You had better delay your examination on this point.
The LORD ADVOCATE.—Then call No. 101, George Marsh.]

60. *George Marsh* (101). *Examined by the* LORD ADVOCATE.—I am an Inspector of Detectives in the Liverpool City Police. On the evening of 28th March of the present year, about seven o'clock, I, in company with Detective Canning and other officers, waited the arrival at Prince's Landing-stage of the steamer "Upupa" from Cork. I saw a man named Denis Deasy coming off the vessel. I saw him speak to the last witness, Shannon, who is a porter. They went together to the fore end of the vessel, and when they came back the porter was carrying a box. They then proceeded along the landing-stage together towards Waterloo dock gate. I followed them and stopped Deasy. I asked him what he had got in the box. Deasy was afterwards searched in my presence.

[Shown Nos. 42 and 43, and asked] Did you see those documents found on Deasy's person ?

[Mr. RHIND.—I object to any evidence as to what was found upon Deasy.

The LORD JUSTICE-CLERK.—In repelling the objection we do not decide meanwhile what the effect of these articles and documents may be. We only decide that it may be proved where they were found.]

Examination continued.—*A.*—I did. *Q.*—Look at these documents [Nos. 42 and 43].

[Mr. RHIND.—This is using them as evidence.

The LORD ADVOCATE.—Then I will not pursue this matter further.]

Examination continued.—On examining Deasy a purse was found in his possession, and in the purse there was a key. I found that the key opened the box which Deasy had with him. [Shown No. 58.] That is the box which Deasy had. *Q.*—Did you find what was in the box?

[Mr. RHIND.—I object. Deasy seems never to have been in Scotland, and without some more intimate connection being proved between him and Featherstone or the panels, the evidence of articles found in his, Deasy's, possession at such a distance from the panels is, I submit, incompetent.

The LORD JUSTICE-CLERK.—There seems to us no objection to proving what was in the box, and the time and place where it was found.]

Examination continued.—*A.*—I did. There were two tin canisters in the box, very securely packed with sawdust and hay. [Shown two tin canisters, No. 59.] These are the canisters which we found in the box. [Shown No. 60.] These brass tubes were also found in the box. They had all caps screwed on the end when they were found. In the tin canisters there was a quantity of sawdust and a liquid. The canisters and their contents were handed over to Dr. Campbell Brown, a chemical gentleman in Liverpool. They were handed over to him in the condition in which they were found, and he opened one of them in my presence. There was paper wrapped round the bottom of each of the tubes forming No. 60 of process. The paper was wrapped round the end of the inner tube. There are two holes in the tube, one on each side, and there are also two slight grooves on the tube. The inner cylinder does not fit close to the outer one, and according as more or less paper was wrapped round the inner cylinder, it would oppose a greater or less thickness between the holes I have mentioned and the sides of the outer tube. The paper was tied round with a string. There were also found in the box a package of chlorate of potash and a packet of powdered sugar. I know that the packets contained these things because they were marked on the outside, and they had on them the name of a chemist in Cork. Dr. Campbell Brown was present, and saw these packets found in the box. There was also found a bottle containing a liquid. I handed that over to Dr. Campbell Brown in the condition in which I found it. *Q.*—When Deasy was asked what was in his box, what did he say?

[Objection taken by Mr. RHIND, and question not pressed.]

61. *George Williams* (117). *Examined by the* LORD ADVOCATE.—I am chief superintendent of detectives in the Liverpool police. I recollect of Denis Deasy being apprehended. I saw the box which was found with him opened. [Shown Nos. 58 and 59.] No. 58 is the deal box which was found in Deasy's possession, and No. 59 are two tin boxes which were found in the deal box. Each of the canisters was neatly rolled up with canvas, and there was a hole in the canvas corresponding to the hole in the canisters. Between the canisters there were several small parcels. One of these parcels was labelled chlorate of potash and another powdered sugar. [Shown Nos. 62 and 63.] These are the remains of the parcels of chlorate of potash and powdered sugar which Dr. Campbell Brown did not use. [Shown No. 64.] That is a small parcel of red orpiment or realgar, which was also found in the box. [Shown No. 60.] These brass tubes were also found in the box. The centre of each of these tubes was neatly wrapped round when they were found with very thin porous paper, such as newspapers are printed upon, and the paper was tied on in each of the slots, which you will notice, with very fine twine or cord like fishing-tackle twine. They were prepared for some use or another, and we experimented with them to find out what. When I say we experimented, I mean Dr. Campbell Brown and myself. There was also found in the box a bottle containing sulphuric acid or vitriol. I do not think there was anything else. [Shown No. 61.] That is the bottle of sulphuric acid which was found.

Cross-examined by Mr. RHIND.—I tried the contents of the bottle No. 61. *Q.*—And you found it to be a corrosive acid? *A.*—Yes; I applied it to chlorate of potash and powdered sugar, and ascertained its effects. I am not a chemist; but I knew it was vitriol from my general practical experience.

Re-examined.—*Q.*—Was there sawdust and some fluid in the canisters? *A.*—No, not in the canisters. The box contained the sawdust, and the canisters contained nitro-glycerine. They were full.

By Mr. RHIND.—I think I know nitro-glycerine when I see it.

62. *Robert Carleton* (132). *Examined by* Mr. MACKAY.—I am a warder in the county prison of Cork. [Shown No. 46.] I saw Featherstone write part of one of these letters—part of the one signed, " Yours, Fetherstone."

Cross-examined by Mr. RHIND.—I cannot say when I saw Featherstone writing the part of that letter. It was in the spring of this year, but I cannot recollect the exact date. I think Featherstone was about three weeks in Cork prison, but I cannot say distinctly when it was that he was there.

Re-examined.—It was shortly after he was arrested and put in prison that I saw him write the portion of the letter I have spoken to.

63. *John Shaw Peake* (133). *Examined by the* LORD ADVOCATE.—I am a professional expert in handwriting. I have been examined now for nearly twenty years in nearly every part of Ireland and in England in matters of handwriting. I am the Government expert in Ireland. They are my principal clients, and I do all their expert work of that kind in Ireland. I was examined at the Liverpool trial of Featherstone, Dalton, and Deasy, and my evidence was accepted by the Court. [Shown Nos. 41, 42, 43, 45 with its enclosures, also Nos. 33, 34, 35, 38, 39, 40.] I have had all these documents in my possession, and have studied them. *Q.*—Do you draw any conclusion as to the identity of the person who wrote them ?

[Mr. RHIND.—I object to this evidence. The witness never saw Featherstone write. The evidence of an expert who is unacquainted except *comparatione literarum* with the handwriting of the person whose writing he is called on to prove is incompetent in criminal cases.

The LORD ADVOCATE.—It was decided in the case of John Porteous, High Court, July 2, 1867, Irv. vol. v. p. 456, that the evidence of experts *comparatione literarum* was competent. I am not going to ask this witness who wrote these documents. I am going to ask him only, Do you think they are all written by the same hand ? I will prove by other evidence that some of them, at all events, were written by Featherstone, and of course the Jury will weigh the evidence and give to it such effect only as they shall think fit.

The LORD JUSTICE-CLERK.—I do not see my way to exclude this evidence as incompetent. I am not friendly to the extensive use of the evidence of experts. It may guide and assist the Jury by directing their attention in comparing the writing of the documents for themselves; but it is possible also that they may be led astray by it. They are quite at liberty to reject the evidence and form an opinion for themselves.

LORD MURE.—There is no doubt of the competency of this species of evidence. The point is not open for decision. But it is for the Jury to say what weight they will attach to it.

LORD CRAIGHILL.—I am of the same opinion. Whatever may be its weight, the evidence is quite competent. The point was settled in 1867 by the case referred to by the Lord Advocate, in which it was ruled that although this kind of evidence is open to observation, and may not be very sufficient, it is nevertheless quite competent.

Objection repelled.]

Examination continued.—A.—I formed the opinion that they were written by the same person. I desire to give some reasons which led me to come to that conclusion. I observe, however, the absence of one document here which was a very material one—indeed, the principal one—in the formation of the opinion to which I came.

G

[Shown No. 46.[1]] With No. 46 I have now the documents on which I formed my opinion.

[Mr. Rhind objected to the witness speaking to the documents forming No. 46.

Objection repelled.]

Examination continued.—Taking No. 46 as the basis of comparison, and comparing the other documents now shown to me with it, I can point out combinations of words, single words, and letters, some of them of peculiar form, which occur through the other documents, and which are identical with them. Some of these features are quite distinctive. As an instance, there are two forms of the letter X, which is regarded as a crucial letter in these matters. The writer makes use of two forms, neither of which is in general use. One of them seems to be peculiar to himself, so far as my experience goes. I can go into minute detail with regard to the handwriting in these documents if I am required to do so.

Cross-examined by Mr. RHIND.—Q.—The principal feature is the formation of the letter X, is it not? *A.*—I give that as an example. The letter X occurs in the letter in No. 46, commencing "Miss O'Connor," four times, twice in one form and twice in another. Neither of the forms is common. They are both peculiar. One of the forms occurs in the document No. 40, in the words "exclusively" and "expected," and the other form occurs in another document, No. 38. If it were not for No. 46, there is no similarity between the X's in Nos. 38 and 40. The X's in Nos. 38 and 40 are dissimilar, and it is only by taking the letter in No. 46 beginning "Miss O'Connor" that I can connect the two.

By LORD CRAIGHILL.—There is only one of the documents which have been shown to me in pencil writing. The writing in it is sufficiently distinct to be compared with the others, and I have no doubt whatever it is in the same handwriting as the other documents, apart altogether from No. 46. Comparing it with the other documents, I have no doubt it is in the same handwriting independently of No. 46, but I was given No. 46 as a specimen of the man's handwriting.

George Marsh (recalled).—*Examined by the* LORD ADVOCATE.— Q.—You have spoken to Timothy Featherstone; is there any other name by which you know him? *A.*—I forget it at the present moment. [Shown No. 116.] Q.—Do you now remember any other name by which he goes? *A.*—Edmond O'Brien Kennedy.

Cross-examined by Mr. RHIND.—Q.—Do you know anything of that except from what you see from the document No. 116? *A.*—I heard, when he was in Liverpool, that that was his name. Q.—In the court in Liverpool? *A.*—Yes; I do not know personally whether the prisoner ever went under that name.

64. *Joseph Schonman* (109). *Examined by the* LORD ADVOCATE.— I came to England recently from America. I left America on the 24th of February by the steamer "Celtic." I became acquainted on the voyage with a man who gave me the name of Johnston. I have heard lately that he went also by the name of Dalton. [Shown Henry Dalton.] That is the man who came across with me in the "Celtic," and

---

[1] See the evidence of the preceding witness, Robert Carleton, p. 96.

who went under the name of Johnston. I had conversations with him frequently. He and I landed at Liverpool at the same time. We occupied the same state-room on the voyage. He told me he was going from Liverpool to Glasgow. I told him I was going to London. He told me he would be in London shortly, and I gave him my address. He wrote it down in my presence. [Shown entry in pocketbook, No. 48 of process.] That is the entry which I saw Johnston make at the time. The entry is "J. Schonman, 20 Edward Road, South Hackney." That is the address I gave him, and which he wrote down in my presence.

Cross-examined by Mr. RHIND.—I cannot tell the exact date when Johnston wrote down that address, but I should say it would be when we were about the middle of the voyage. He wrote it while we were promenading on the vessel; it was very steady that day. I think he gave me the name of Johnston about the first morning that we saw each other. I cannot exactly say how he came to give me his name, but I suppose it was because we were travelling together. I am sure I did not mistake Dalton for Johnston. I never saw him after we landed at Liverpool until I saw him in custody.

65. *John George Littlechild* (110). *Examined by the* LORD ADVOCATE. —I am an inspector of police in Great Scotland Yard, London. On the 24th of March of this year, my attention was called to the prisoner Dalton at Charing Cross. He was joined by another man at the time. [Shown Henry Dalton.] That is the man whom I saw at Charing Cross. I watched him and his doings for a considerable time. I found out that he lived at 2 Eaton Place, Pond Place, Fulham Road, with his father and mother. His father's name was O'Connor. I found out the prisoner's real name to be John O'Connor. *Q.*—Was it John Henry? *A.*—I only knew him as John O'Connor. I made a search for documents in his father's house under authority. [Shown No. 50 of process.] *Q.*—Did you get that?

[Mr. RHIND.—I object to the contents of the pocketbook being proved. The only connection between Dalton and any of the panels which is said to have been proved, is that M'Dermott called upon Moorhead when Dalton was living at Mrs. M'Lachlan's at Ronald Street, Glasgow, and that he left with Moorhead, who said he was going to London. [See evidence of Mrs. M'Lachlan at pp. 81 and 82.] Dalton is never seen with Hughes or any of the panels, except M'Dermott. The evidence is for the purpose of blackening Dalton's character, without any connection between him and the panels being proved.

The LORD JUSTICE-CLERK.—Dalton is one of the conspirators. Repel the objection.]

Examination continued.—*A.*—I did. I found that document on his person. There are four entries in the pocketbook in pencil:—

"L. 6. 3. 83.
"G. 8. 3. 83.
"Ln. 17. 3. 83.
"M'D. 24. 3. 83."[1]

[1] These, it was contended, were intended to mean, "Liverpool, 6th March 1883; Glasgow, 8th March 1883; London, 17th March 1883; M'Dermott, 24th March 1883,"—the latter referring not to Terence M'Dermott, but to an American of that name.

All the writing which is in the notebook now was in it when I found it. [Shown No. 48.] That pocketbook was found by Constable Enright in my presence in the house at Eaton Place,—the house of O'Connor's father. All the writing which is now in that pocketbook was in it when it was found, with the exception of what may have been put on it by the officials through whose hands it has passed. [Shown No. 49 (addresses on card found on Henry Dalton : "10 George Street West," "J. F. K., 41 Stanhope Street, G.").] I have seen that card before. It was found in the pocketbook No. 48. There are some addresses written upon it. One is "J. F. K., 41 Stanhope Street, G." There is another address on the card which has apparently been rubbed out with the finger, and below it there is the entry, "10 Great George Street West." [Shown No. 51.] I have seen that pocketbook before. It was found at 2 Eaton Place, the house of O'Connor's father, by me. The name J. H. O'Connor is written in that pocketbook. I found in that notebook an entry in pencil as follows :—"That where there is a circle interfered with in its working by any body of men hostile in policy, that such centre should be in communication with the centres living nearest his district, whereby they may assist the centre whose circle is so attacked, and so assist the visiting committee in their duties, who may not be able to be at hand when needed." I found Nos. 52 and 53 in O'Connor's father's house also. [Shown No. 56.] That is a letter written from Glasgow. It was found in the same room with the other things which I have mentioned. [Shown Nos. 54 and 55.]

[Objection taken by Mr. RHIND, on the ground that the letters are dated more than ten years back.

The LORD ADVOCATE stated that he only wished to ask where these letters were found, and to prove them for the handwriting.

Evidence allowed.]

Examination continued.—[Shown Nos. 54 and 55.] I found these letters in O'Connor's father's house.

[*The* LORD JUSTICE-CLERK.—You had better not read these letters just yet.

The LORD ADVOCATE.—Very well, my lord.]

Examination continued.—[Shown No. 57, receipt signed H. Dalton.] I saw Dalton write and sign that document.

Cross-examined by Mr. RHIND.—*Q.*—Of your own knowledge, you don't know whether Dalton is John Henry O'Connor or not? *A.*—He is, according to my knowledge, and as far as my inquiries enable me to say. I never knew anything about him until I found him in London in March last. I did not know him as Dalton until I arrested him, and he gave me that name. I arrested him simply from description. I knew him, of course, some days before, but only from description. *Q.*—Then, in fact, you don't know what the name of the man was who lived at Eaton Place? *A.*—I know that the prisoner O'Connor was living there with his father and mother. *Q.*—But whether he is called Dalton, or O'Connor, or both, you cannot say? *A.*—Certainly; he gave me the name Dalton, and I knew him as that. But prior to that, I had seen him on several occasions in the neighbourhood of Eaton Place, and I then learned that his name was John O'Connor. I ascertained that from several persons who had known him from childhood. He never told me himself that his name was John O'Connor. He gave it to me as Dalton, but I knew his name in the same way as I know other people's, simply from hearing it. The house No. 2 Eaton Place is occupied, I think, by about three families, but the room that I searched was occupied by O'Connor's father, mother, and brother.

Re-examined.—I found the different documents to which I have spoken in the room which was occupied by the prisoner's father, mother, and brother, and by himself, I take it.

66. *Ebenezer Mears* (112). *Examined by* Mr. BRAND.—I am a sergeant in the City of London Police. On the evening of Thursday 15th March last I was on duty in Queen Victoria Street, City, London. About eight o'clock in the evening I heard a loud noise like a fog-signal. It came apparently from the back of the "Times" office. I at once went to Playhouse Yard to see. I saw a tin box of an oval shape, and smoke coming from it. I kicked the box, and stamped out the fire with my feet. I saw something fall out of the box,—pieces of paper and pieces of towelling. Some officers came to my assistance. I found in the inside of the box, when I examined it more closely, some sawdust. Outside and lying near the box I saw a thing like a brass tube. [Shown No. 60.] The tube which I saw was very similar to these. I took it to the station, and it afterwards went amissing in the hands of the police. I took the box to the station also. I don't think there was any damage done to the "Times" office. The windows were blackened. I gave this evidence at the trial of Featherstone and Dalton. I did not see anybody near the box when I found it.

67. *Frederick Lawley* (114). *Examined by* Mr. BRAND.—I am a detective sergeant in the City of London Police. On 15th March last I received from the last witness, Mears, a tin box in the police office. Superintendent Foster took possession of the lid of the box and a brass tube which I got from Mears, and also some of the contents of the box. I got these things back from Mr. Foster, with the exception of the brass tube. It went amissing in Mr. Foster's hands. I delivered the contents of the box to Colonel Ford at the Home Office, for examination by Colonel Majendie. I made an examination of the place where the box had exploded, and found that the surrounding railing had been blackened.

68. *Alfred Lawrence Foster* (115). *Examined by* Mr. MACKAY.—I am a superintendent of the City of London Police. I received from the last witness, Sergeant Lawley, a tin box and a brass tube, with the object of showing them to Colonel Fraser and Colonel Bowman. I unfortunately lost the brass tube. [Shown No. 60.[1]] It was a tube similar to these, except that it had not the projecting parts that these have. *Q.*—Had it a cap? *A.*—The cap, I presume, had blown off. In other respects the tube was similar to those now shown me. I had never seen such a tube before.

69. *James Campbell Brown* (50). *Examined by the* LORD ADVOCATE. —I am Professor of Chemistry, University College, Liverpool, and Doctor of Science, and I hold several public appointments as analyst. On the evening of 28th March last I was called to the detective office, Liver-

[1] See the evidence of James Campbell Brown, the next witness.

pool, and shown a wooden box containing some things which I was asked to examine. The box contained two tin cases, each of which was stitched in canvas. I opened one of the boxes at the bottom. [Shown Nos. 58 and 59.] No. 58 is the wooden box, and No. 59 are the tin boxes which were shown me. The box which I opened I found to be full of a mixture of nitro-glycerine and sawdust, and a little chalk. I ascertained the proportion of the nitro-glycerine at the bottom next day. At the bottom the proportion was 83 per cent., and at the top about 60, the average being about 75. There was not an average of 25 per cent. of sawdust, only about 23 per cent., and 2 per cent. of chalk. There would be about 21 lbs. of nitro-glycerine in the box in round numbers. There was a hole in the tin canisters, and a corresponding hole in the canvas with which they were covered. The hole in the canisters led up to a tin cylinder, $1\frac{1}{2}$ inches in diameter, and 5 inches long. The cylinder was open top and bottom. The canister was filled with sawdust and nitro-glycerine, with the exception of the tin cylinder. The stuff which was in the canister is known by the name of lignin-dynamite. It was very strong, containing 75 per cent. of nitro-glycerine on an average. It was a highly destructive article. That is a combination that is used for no commercial or lawful purpose that I know of. I found the three brass tubes, No. 60 of process, in the wooden box. I took one of them home for careful examination. I also found in the box a parcel labelled chlorate of potash, and another labelled sugar. These are Nos. 62 and 63 of process. I also found a parcel, No. 64 of process, containing a piece of realgar or red orpiment. I also found a bottle containing strong sulphuric acid. The bottle which I found is No. 61 of process. I took one of the tubes, No. 60 of process, to pieces. I found on the inner cylinder a piece of paper carefully and tightly rolled, covering the two holes. It was very tightly tied by a piece of fishing-tackle cord. The paper was a thin kind of printing paper—paper which is used by lithographers. I tried to ascertain if such an article was used for any commercial purpose. I asked a veterinary surgeon if he knew of such an article being used. It suggested itself to me to ask the veterinary surgeon, because when the man in whose possession the tubes were found was asked what it was he had, he said it was cattle spice. I was not able to find any lawful purpose for which such tubes were used. I then puzzled out for myself the purpose for which they were intended. I performed this experiment: I filled the space between the inner and outer cylinders with a mixture of chlorate of potash and sugar—the two things I had found in the little parcels in the box. I then screwed on the outer cylinder, and unscrewed the upper cap on the upper portion of the cylinder, closed the tap, filled the upper cavity with sulphuric acid from the bottle, and then replaced all the screws and taps as they were before, and placed the tube in an upright position, supported by some bricks. I then turned the tap open and retired to a safe distance to watch it. It did not act for some time, and I went cautiously back and unscrewed it again and looked to see in what condition it was. I unrolled the paper and found that the acid had only eaten half way through it. That was in about ten minutes. I then replaced the portion of the paper which had been eaten through by a fresh portion which had not been acted upon, and mounted the whole apparatus again as before, and retired for a longer period. The tube then exploded. I forget the exact time after which it exploded, but I calculated the period at which it would have exploded had the same thickness of paper been on as was on at first, and made it to be twenty-two minutes. When I say it exploded, I mean that the sulphuric acid, in coming into contact with the chlorate of potash and sugar, caused an explosion. *Q.*—Would such an explosion, supposing that apparatus had been fitted into the hole of the box containing the lignin-dynamite, have been well fitted to set off the dynamite? *A.*—It might; it would have fired it in some way. It might have been with explosive violence or it might not; I could not say that with certainty. It would depend upon the lignin-dynamite partly, and partly also upon whether it were tightly packed or not. If to the chlorate of potash and sugar there had been added some of the realgar or red orpiment which was found in the other parcel, it would have made the explosion somewhat more violent. But I believe the hole in the bottom of the canisters was intended to hold an ordinary exploder. If that hole was intended to hold an exploder or detonator, and the whole thing had been fitted into a box with lignin-dynamite, and the apparatus set in motion, the whole material in the box would have exploded with enormous violence. Such an explosion would cause great damage, and would reduce everything within a certain range to powder. I am satisfied, from finding these things in the same box, that they were all parts of one mechanism, and directed to one end. They were all equipped with the kind of things requisite for exploding them, with the exception of detonators, but I should say that a mixture of chlorate of potash and sugar alone is capable of being made into a detonator by enclosing it tightly in an enclosed space, either by ramming it very tight, or by ramming the copper cap very tight with the mixture. I made some subsequent experiments to ascertain how long an interval might elapse between the turning on of the apparatus and the exploding of it according as more or less paper was wrapped round the inner cylinder. The time depends on the number of folds of paper, and that depends on the space between the inner and outer cylinder. The maximum time would be some hours; even with the cylinders as they are, the time might be made to extend to some hours. In my experiments the time was never longer than 40 minutes, because I never put on a thicker roll of paper. [Shown No. 48.] *Q.*—Look at the leaf that is turned down; is that a receipt for an explosive, and if so, what is the explosive?

[Mr. RHIND.—I object to these entries being read.

The LORD JUSTICE-CLERK.—You may go on with your examination to the effect of informing us what the characters inscribed in the book signify.]

Examination continued.—*A.*—The entry is as follows:—
Baume N. A. S. A.
Twaddle. 150°
M. 2 Sa 1 Na ⅛ G.
F 2 Chl Pot 1 Sul ars 1 P. S.
S A = Na—cop.
N. A = S. A Ch P.
N A – specific gravity 1·52
Glass Hydrometers.
Kisselguhr = or infusorial silicous.

Baume and Twaddle are the names of hydrometers. The first line of the entry means, make a mixture, 2 of sulphuric acid and 1 of nitric acid, and ⅛th of glycerine. These are the proportions suitable for making nitro-glycerine. The next line means Fuse, 2 chlorate of potash, 1 of Sul. of arsenic, and 1 of powdered sugar. That is a mixture for filling the fuse. The three things which I found in the parcels in the box, I should say, would make a suitable mixture for filling the fuse. The next line means sulphuric acid = nitric acid and copperas. The next line means nitric acid = sulphuric acid and Chili saltpetre. The reason I come to the conclusion that that is Chili saltpetre is because there is another entry in the book explaining that. The next line means nitric acid = specific gravity 1·52, which is correct. Below the entry which I have quoted there is a note, "Glycerine is used for lubricity," and there are various other entries on other pages. Amongst others, "chlorate of potash—sulphurate of red or realgar arsenic—sugar produced, carbonate of soda." That is the red orpiment which I have stated would help the explosion, and which is mentioned in the receipt for the fuse. I also find in the book a minute description for making fulminate of silver and fulminate of mercury. These are the ingredients used for filling ordinary detonators. If that had been found in addition to the other mixture, the whole thing would have been quite complete. There is also a description for another kind of fuse in the notebook. [Shown No. 44. See page 93.] That is a receipt for an ordinary mixture for setting fire to a building. It has been frequently called Greek fire and Fenian fire. It has been called Fenian fire for the last twenty years. It is not used for any commercial or industrial purpose. It is a dangerous thing if it is thrown into any combustible—into a room. [Shown No. 67, a glass test-tube.] I have seen that test-tube before. It has contained sulphuric acid. I know that because I tested the cork. There is a rough drawing on the paper No. 44 showing a large bottle containing fluid, and a small bottle or tube tied close to it containing an acid. There is a bit out of the lip of the tube No. 67, which would enable the tube to lie closer to a bottle. If these two bottles were broken, the result would be a great blaze, sufficient to set fire to anything combustible within reach. [Shown No. 8, the brass tube and brass tap found on Possil Bridge.[1] That is a brass tube, and is practically identical with one of the tubes which was found in Deasy's box at Liverpool. If it had the upper cap it would be identical with the tubes which were found in Deasy's box. It has contained some of the mixture which has been fired. I found that it has had some of the mixture of chlorate of potash and sugar in it. I find some burnt sugar adhering round the inner sides of it. I found the same appearances in this tube that I found in the one I experimented with at Liverpool after I had used it. [Shown No. 5.[2]] I never saw that before. It seems to have been under fire. It corresponds exactly with the under-piece of one of the tubes which have been shown to me, and contains the hole through which the explosion passes. It appears

---

[1] See the evidence of Thomas Frater and Donald Ferguson, p. 38, who found these on Possil Bridge.
[2] See evidence of James M'Murray and Charles Simpson, p. 35, and of William Key, p. 29.

to have been fired. If there had been a successful explosion firing the dynamite, it would quite account for the knocked-about and burnt appearance which that cap No. 5 has. [Shown No. 4, a piece of a circular brass cap or tube.[1]] I have never seen that before. It seems to be part of the mechanism of one of these brass tubes, but I cannot very well say what part it is. Supposing it to be part of one of these brass machines, there would be use for both it and No. 5. I think No. 4 is a portion of the upper cylinder where the acid goes in.

Cross-examined by Mr. RHIND.—No. 4 is merely a piece of the brass cylinder. No. 5 exactly corresponds with a part of No. 8. I do not know anything else that it corresponds with. No. 67 is an ordinary test-tube, except that there is a piece very carefully cut away from the edge. I think there is no doubt that it has been carefully cut away. *Q.*—The drawing on No. 44 [see p. 94] represents the small bottle as not requiring to be quite close to the larger bottle? *A.*—It does not represent its projecting rim, so that if the bottle or tube was in the shape of the drawing, it would fit as close as this test-tube with the notch out. The drawing of No. 44 is merely diagramatic; it is merely a rough drawing to show how the thing has to lie. It represents the two things as some distance apart. The tube or small bottle is put into a position in the drawing which it would be impossible for it to remain in. I have heard of the mixture, a receipt for which is contained in No. 44, having been employed some twenty years ago in this country. I have never met with a case of its being used, but I have used it myself. When the liquids in the two bottles come together they make a great blaze. They would not blow up a building, but they would set it on fire. It would be of very little use in the way of blowing up a building. Taken in the connection in which they occur, it is manifest what the letters and figures in the receipt contained in No. 48 mean, and other parts of the book explain it.

By the LORD JUSTICE-CLERK.—*Q.*—All these words together could not possibly refer to anything but an explosive mixture? *A.*—No; and in other parts of the book there are explanations. I drew my conclusions after reading carefully through the whole book.

Cross-examination by Mr. RHIND *continued.*—There is no conceivable meaning I could think of applying to that entry, other than the meaning I have given. The letters and figures represent not merely nitro-glycerine, but the absorbent material is mentioned also—Kisselguhr. That, together with nitro-glycerine, is what makes dynamite. Kisselguhr is infusorial earth. I do not remember that sawdust is anywhere mentioned in the book as useable in the manufacture of dynamite, but it may be. I saw lignin-dynamite in the machines that came to Liverpool from America three years ago, and also in connection with the canisters which were found in Deasy's box. These are the only two occasions I have seen it. The lignin-dynamite which I saw three years ago was sent from America in a cask of cement. I have reason to believe it was not sent for any lawful purpose; there was clockwork provided to fire it. I do not believe a mixture of sawdust and nitro-glycerine is used anywhere for any lawful purpose. Ordinary dynamite would be quite as powerful for unlawful purposes as lignin-

[1] See evidence of James M'Murray and Charles Simpson, p. 35, and of William Key, p. 29.

dynamite if it were made up in the same quantities, but it never is. You never get a quarter of a hundredweight of dynamite in one mass.

Adjourned.

THIRD DAY.—WEDNESDAY, DECEMBER 19, 1883.

EVIDENCE FOR THE CROWN CONTINUED.

70. *August Dupré* (51). *By the* LORD ADVOCATE.—I am professor of chemistry, and Fellow of the Royal Society. I am chemical adviser to the Explosives Department of the Home Office. On 2nd April this year I received from Colonel Ford a small parcel of powdered sugar, also of chlorate of potassium, and a small parcel of a mixture of these two in about equal proportions, also a lump of the realgar or sulphate of arsenic,—red orpiment; two bottles of strong sulphuric acid; and a canister containing 28 lbs. 8 oz. of lignin-dynamite. In that sample there was 70·9 per cent. of nitro-glycerine. That was the Liverpool one. There was also a brass tap given to me by Colonel Ford next day, similar to the one produced in this case. I made an experiment with the view of testing the working of these taps. There was some paper loosely round the inner cylinder of the tap. I refastened it. I put some of the sulphuric acid out of one of the two bottles handed to me by Colonel Ford into the upper part, and put a small portion of the mixture of sugar and chlorate below. I then turned the tap, and watched it, and in 3 minutes 40 seconds after the turning of the tap, the mixture of chlorate and sugar took fire; a drop of sulphuric acid came out and set fire to the mixture. I then—because the paper had been somewhat crumpled—took a fresh piece of paper, and very carefully tied it round, and made the same experiment, and then it lasted nearly 41 minutes before it took fire. I felt no doubt in my mind that this was an apparatus for applying those compounds towards lighting something. I also became satisfied that the time interposed between the turning of the tap and letting on the acid and the explosion could be regulated within very wide limits. It would be possible, by wrapping more paper round or arranging it differently, to leave a longer time; it all depends on the number of folds and the nature of the paper. I took great pains to try to find out whether such an apparatus was used for any commercial or scientific purpose, and I could not find any. Indeed, I could find no other purpose for it than an unlawful one. On 27th January last I received from Colonel Ford a small quantity of lignin-dynamite, and later in the same day I received an oval-shaped tin bonnet-box, which also contained a small quantity of lignin-dynamite, from Colonel Majendie. On the 2nd February I got from Colonel Majendie two small brass tubes. I found that both of these had contained sulphuric acid. [Shown No. 6.] That is the box. [Shown No. 8.] These are the tubes. They are what are known as the Possil Bridge tubes. I satisfied myself that the Possil Bridge brasses had contained sulphuric acid. I did not at

the time satisfy myself whether they had contained anything else, because I had not the slightest suspicion at the time what the tap was used for. I had an opportunity, later on, of examining one of them, and I found chlorate of potassium had been in it. That was one of the two chemicals which I found in the Liverpool box also, and one of the two which I found to ignite with sulphuric acid. There is no doubt that the tap had actually been used with the very chemicals which were found in the Liverpool box. The Liverpool sample was a mixture of sawdust with nitro-glycerine, the nitro-glycerine being there in the proportion of nearly 71 per cent. of the whole. Nitro-glycerine is produced by acting on glycerine with a mixture of nitric acid and sulphuric acid, and it becomes nitric ether,—that is analogous to sweet spirit of nitre, only made with glycerine. To put it popularly, there are three things, and no more, necessary to make nitro-glycerine,—glycerine, sulphuric acid, and nitric acid. I have made an analysis of the sample of lignin-dynamite which I got from Colonel Majendie, and which is known as the Possil Bridge sample. I found it contained about 19·1 per cent. of nitro-glycerine, and the rest was sawdust and moisture. That was a much less powerful explosive than the other sample I described. Still it was an explosive nitro-compound. I have no doubt it would have gone off if it had been properly detonated. Comparing that sample with the Liverpool one, the proportions of nitro-glycerine and sawdust are just in the reverse ratio. Comparatively speaking, the Possil Bridge sample was poor as to its actual power. It would be a comparatively poor explosive as compared with the 71 per cent., but it would be a powerful explosive in itself,—a serious explosive. I had so little of the stuff given to me, that it is not easy to make a calculation from a few grains what box No. 6 would contain, but I should say it would have been between 11 and 12 lbs. of the sort of stuff I saw. Supposing 11 or 12 lbs. of that stuff had been properly detonated, it would have produced a very serious explosion. It is the quality of nitro-glycerine explosives that they are exceedingly violent locally. If you put them even upon a flat surface, that violent action is so great that even where the resistance is most, it is very strong. If you put it on a stone, it pulverizes it. If you put some of it on the top of a big boulder, it will shatter that boulder to pieces. It is a well-known way of shattering such boulders. *Q.*—Do you think that if such a quantity as that had been placed on the arch of a bridge carrying a canal, it would have endangered that bridge or canal if the explosion had been successful? *A.*—It is very difficult to say; I never saw the bridge, but I think this stuff would not have broken a strong bridge.

By the LORD JUSTICE-CLERK.—I mean, with the contents I have described.

Examination continued.—Supposing the proportions had been reversed, as in the Liverpool sample, it might have shattered a very strong arch then, and, shattering the arch, let out the water.

Cross-examined by Mr. RHIND.—I do not say that these taps could not be used for a lawful purpose; I say that I have taken great pains, but have not been able to find out any lawful purpose. Where dynamite is exploded, it is necessary that the workmen should have time to get out of the way. Such taps as these might be used for producing an explosion, but it would be a very expensive and clumsy way. No one would dream of doing it in ordinary life. In exploding by dynamite, whether for lawful or unlawful purposes, it is necessary that some time should elapse between the firing of the charge and the explosion. The whole object of these taps is to give time. This is so much more an expensive way of giving time than the ordinary way employed, that I do not think any one would for a moment attempt such a thing. The ordinary way by which the necessary time to escape is given, is by attaching to the charge a safety-fuse of varying length, which burns at the rate of a yard in three minutes. You put on half a yard, or two yards, or three yards, according to the length of time you wish to elapse. *Q.*—Then the only difference between that and the firing by means of taps seems to be that the fuse would be more likely to be seen by passers-by? *A.*—I suppose so; and a fuse must be lighted by striking something, whereas this tap is turned and there is no light. It can be turned in the dark without any notice being given. I think these tubes have been devised not by an ordinary labouring man, but by a man who very well knew what he was about. I think they might be constructed by an ordinary labouring man if he once saw a careful drawing. They are very roughly made. It is the idea that requires somebody with a head. To construct them, it would certainly require somebody having a knowledge of brassfounding. It would scarcely require a brass-founder to make them, because I suppose the various parts might be obtained in ordinary commerce. They are ordinary things; it is just the combination which is the peculiarity. *Q.*—Could no other explosive than dynamite have caused the explosion about which you were consulted? *A.*—It need not be what is generally known as dynamite, but it must be a substance of the nature of that. It might have been gun-cotton or any nitro-compound which is characterized by intense local action. Gun-cotton has an intense local action. *Q.*—Can you mention any other explosive that could have caused the effect? *A.*—No explosive that is at all in use, or that I think could be used in quantity sufficient. There are some chemical compounds which would produce it, but they would be so dangerous to handle that they could not be used practically.

By Mr. ORR.—Sulphuric acid by itself is used for a very great many purposes, commercial and scientific, and even domestic purposes, such as scouring copper. It is used in constructing galvanic batteries.

By the LORD ADVOCATE.—In any ordinary or lawful use of dynamite, the common cheap fuse is quite enough to let people get away. The action is very strong locally, but you do not require to go very far away. You can let a great many pounds of dynamite go off ten or twenty yards away. The length of this court would be quite safe, particularly if you could go round the corner, so that you would not get the direct blast. Each explosion would infer the expenditure and waste of the brass apparatus which we have called the tap. You do not require anything that would enable you to go to a distance which would take forty minutes to travel.

By the LORD JUSTICE-CLERK.—It is like laying a train after the old fashion of gunpowder, and the fuse is a more convenient way of doing it. This apparatus gives much more time, and is much more secret than the fuse, because it requires no light to be struck. The time might be extended or shortened within very considerable limits. I think no great amount of mechanical skill is required to make a tap. I think any ordinary brassfounder could easily make it after he had the instructions. These things are not artistically made; they are roughly made. Not having seen the masonry, I do not know whether the box No. 6, if exploded upon the arch of Possil Bridge, and assuming a minimum amount of strength, would have made a rent in the masonry; but it might, and probably would have blown a hole through it, even if the masonry had been several feet thick. Mixtures of chlorate of potassium and sugar are used lawfully by artillery and engineers in war, but I know of no other lawful use.

By a JURYMAN.—That mixture is used for setting fire to mines in war, and for setting off torpedoes and shells occasionally, always for the purpose of producing an explosion. I am not aware that the kind of taps we have here has ever been used lawfully. I have taken great pains to find out some use for them, because at first I was not aware what they were used for. I could find no use for them lawfully or commercially. I do not know where they are made.

Archibald Carmichael (recalled). By the LORD ADVOCATE.—I know the hall in Nelson Street, Glasgow, which goes by the name of the Democratic Hall. I have heard it also called the Gymnastic Hall. There is no other hall of that kind in that street where meetings are held. It is within a very short distance of the Cross, running from Trongate to Bell Street. I made careful inquiry in Glasgow to find out whether there was anybody of the name of James Bolyn about Gallowgate or in any other part of the town, particularly any men of that name keeping a horse or horses—a carter or contractor. I was not able to find any such person in Glasgow. I made careful inquiry, in particular, about the Gallowgate. I am quite satisfied there was no person of that name in or about the latter part of last year either keeping horses or not keeping horses in Glasgow. I have several times seen the prisoners meeting together in Jail Square. I saw all the prisoners frequently, with the exception of M'Dermott. I saw M'Dermott only upon one occasion. That was on the night I apprehended him, and he was then along with the prisoner Drum. I have seen all the prisoners other than M'Dermott meeting together frequently in Jail Square since the beginning of June of this year. I was not observing them last year at all. *Q.*—Was there anything that struck you about the manner or place in which they met? *A.*—I first saw them in the beginning of June 1883.

[Mr. RHIND.—I object to any question relating to the period subsequent to June 1883. That is, after the time libelled.

Question not pressed.]

Examination continued. — I apprehended the prisoner Terence M'Dermott. He was living with his father and mother at 452 Dobbie's Loan. His father's name, I think, is Thomas. Drum was with M'Dermott when the latter was apprehended. [Shown No. 86.] I found that envelope in M'Dermott's house. It bears the Glasgow postmark of 19th July '83, and is addressed: "Mr. John Kearney, 41

Stanhope Street," and "452 Dobbie's Lone," in pencil, on the envelope. [Shown No. 85.] That is a copy of "Penny Pictorial News" for Saturday, September 1, 1883. I found that on M'Dermott's person. It has a picture of O'Donnell, the murderer of Carey.

[Mr. RHIND.—I object to the admission of No. 85. This newspaper is found in M'Dermott's possession on 31st August when he is apprehended, and there is no evidence as to how he became possessed of it. Supposing it was purchased, it amounts to nothing.

Objection repelled.]

Cross-examined by Mr. BAXTER.—The Gallowgate is one of the most thickly populated districts in Glasgow. I did not go to any of the post offices to make inquiry whether there was any one of the name of Bolyn in the neighbourhood, but I turned up the Post Office Directory. I also saw the constables in all the eastern part of the city, and asked them if they knew any person of that name in their respective beats. I also made inquiry myself amongst contractors and others. The population of the Gallowgate is a very fluctuating one. Jail Square is a popular place for all the Irishmen in Glasgow meeting, and for others too.

By a JURYMAN.—There are many contractors and carters in the neighbourhood of the Gallowgate.

By Mr. BAXTER.—I apprehended M'Dermott on the night of 31st August.

71. *Donald Sutherland* (60). *By* Mr. MACKAY.—I am a criminal officer in the Central District of the Glasgow Police. I made a search of the prisoner M'Cann's house in Stirling Street, shortly after his arrest. [Shown Nos. 102, a small notebook; 103, a small notebook; and 104, a passbook.] These are three notebooks which I found there. The two smaller ones had several leaves torn out. I also found the pamphlet No. 101 [entituled "The Castle Government of Ireland, a Lecture by Michael Davitt"] in M'Cann's house. I searched the house of the prisoner Donnelly shortly after his arrest, in Villiers Street. I found in his house the prospectus No. 107 [subscription sheet for the paper called the "Irish Democrat"] and the two letters Nos. 108 and 109. I also found Nos. 110 [a copy of the paper called the "United Irishman" of Saturday, July 28, 1883], 111 [supplement to the "Cape Times" of Tuesday, July 31, 1883], and 112 [supplement to the paper called "The Weekly Freeman," of June 2, 1883] in Donnelly's house.

[Mr. RHIND.—I object to these newspapers being produced.

The LORD ADVOCATE.—These papers may, we submit, have a bearing on the question of design.

The LORD JUSTICE-CLERK.—We don't say that they are incompetent, but they are dated in June and July 1883; and if they are adduced as evidence of a conspiracy entered into in 1882, it seems rather remote.

The documents were accordingly withdrawn.]

Cross-examined by Mr. BAXTER.—There was just one room in Donnelly's house. His wife and child live there.

By Mr. KENNEDY.—I arrested M'Cann on the evening of the 31st August last. I cannot tell how many people live in his house, but there were a good few there when I made the apprehension. The stair is thickly populated. I found the largest of the three notebooks [No. 104] in the room where M'Cann works, in a safe, and the two smaller ones and the pamphlet I found in the kitchen. M'Cann is a shoemaker to trade.

72. *John Neil* (125). *By* Mr. BRAND.—I am a detective officer in the Central District of the Glasgow Police. On the 31st August I proceeded to Portugal Lane and apprehended the prisoner Devany. I found him in bed. In a press of the house I found a brass tube. I found a number of papers in the house. [Shown No. 97, supplement to paper called "United Ireland," dated 10th September 1881.] *Q.*— Did you find that?

[Mr. RHIND.—I object. This is found on 31st August 1883, but there is no evidence when it was got or how, whether Devany took it approvingly, or criticizingly, or how. It bears date nearly a year before the earliest date libelled, and is altogether too remote.

The LORD JUSTICE-CLERK.—It is dated before the explosions. I can see no objection to it. It can do no harm.

Objection repelled.]

Examination continued.—I found that paper. I also found Nos. 87, 89, 90, 91, 92, 93, 94, 95, 96, and 99 [see inventory of productions, p. 16] in Devany's house.

Cross-examined by Mr. RHIND.—So far as I am aware, no person lived in Devany's house except his wife and family. I only saw one child besides his wife in the house. I found the papers and the revolver in a chest in a room of his house. The chest contained clothing and a number of other articles. No. 90 [a membership card of Thomas Devany of the "Irish National Land League"] was found along with the other papers.

73. *John Elliott* (130). *By* Mr. MACKAY.—I am a sergeant in the Durham County Constabulary at Hebburn-on-Tyne. I was present when the prisoner M'Cullagh was arrested on 8th October in Hebburn-on-Tyne. I made a search in the lodgings where he resided. These lodgings were kept by Mrs. M'Guinness. [Shown No. 113.] *Q.*— Did you find that letter in his house?

[Question objected to and not pressed.]

74. *James Chesney* (141). *By* Mr. BRAND.—I am stationmaster at Buchanan Street Station of the Caledonian Railway. John Francis Kearney was signalman at the north end of the tunnel at the time the explosion took place in January last. I remember placing a man named Long beside him. I did so because Kearney came to me and told me he had fallen and hurt his hand, and was unable to pull some of the levers. I sent a man accordingly to assist in pulling the levers. I saw that Kearney's hand was injured, and that he was unable to work the levers. This was on the Wednesday before the explosion. The explosion occurred on the Saturday night or Sunday morning. Kearney did not leave the service till 31st March or 1st April. He gave no reason for leaving, and I have not seen him since.

75. *Patrick Murphy* (154). *By* Mr. MACKAY.—I live at 50 Turner

Street, Townhead, Glasgow. John Francis Kearney is a brother of my wife. He lived in Stanhope Street. I last saw him about the middle of March. His wife came to live in my house shortly after that, I think about the first week of April. She died in my house on the 10th June. Kearney did not return at the time of her funeral. I do not know where he went to. I do not know where he is.

Cross-examined by Mr. RHIND.—Kearney and I were not on very good terms for three or four years. I never was in his house in Stanhope Street. I was in his house when he lived in Murray Street, about eighteen months ago or more. From that time till he left Glasgow I was never in his house, and he was never in mine.

76. *George Henry Chapman* (150). *By* Mr. BRAND.—I am a detective officer in the Hull Police at Hull. I made inquiries with regard to a man named John Francis Kearney. He had an injury to his right hand, to the best of my knowledge. I had occasion to observe his movements in Hull. I first saw him there on Saturday, 23rd June, this year. I saw him the following day. The last time I saw him was on Monday the 25th, when he was going into his lodgings in West Street. I never saw him after that.

77. *William Lamie*[1] (119). *By the* LORD ADVOCATE.—I am a tailor in Dublin. *Q.*—Were you a member of an organization called the Fenian Brotherhood?

[Mr. RHIND.—I object to the witness being asked generally whether he is a member of this society.

The LORD JUSTICE-CLERK.—Your objection comes too early.]

Examination continued.—I was sworn a member of that organization in 1867, in Dublin, and I continued a member of it down to this year. *Q.*—You say you were sworn a member of it. Tell us the terms of the oath you took.

[Mr. RHIND.—I object. This is in 1867, seventeen years ago. It is not said where or when this society was formed, or whether the witness ever saw any of the panels present at any meetings, or that they were members of the Brotherhood, or had any connection with it.

The LORD ADVOCATE.—I do not propose to bring any of the panels directly in contact with this society. But we say in the indictment that the panels were guilty of the statutory crime and of the conspiracy libelled, in so far as, they being all members of a Ribbon Society having amongst its objects and purposes the subverting and overthrowing by force and violence the power and authority of Her Majesty in Ireland, and of compelling or constraining Her Majesty to change her measures or counsels relating to the constitution or government of Ireland, etc., did certain overt acts. The question is, what were the objects of the panels' devisings, etc., and what were the objects of the conspiracy. We say that they were to depose Her Majesty, and to levy war against her, and also to over-

---

[1] This witness was examined as an informer in the trials for the Phœnix Park murders, and at the trial of Featherstone and others at Liverpool, on 7th, 8th, and 9th August 1883. He was also a witness at the trial of Joseph Poole, his brother-in-law, who was executed on 18th December 1883, for the murder of an informer named "Kenny," eighteen months previous.

throw by force and violence her authority in Ireland. It might be pleaded that it is current history that these are the objects which are avowed by the Fenian Brotherhood and other societies in Ireland, but it would be objected that that is not sufficient in a criminal trial. And it is in order to prevent its being said that there is no proof of there existing any organization in Ireland having for its object to depose or levy war against Her Majesty, or to overthrow her authority in that part of the United Kingdom, that this evidence is adduced. I submit, therefore, that it is competent to prove that such societies exist. By this evidence the Jury may also be enabled to judge of the meaning of allusions made by the panels, such as are contained in No. 51 [excerpt from the pocketbook found in house in Chelsea, of O'Connor, Dalton's father].[1] The matter was fully considered in the trial of Featherstone and others at Liverpool. Lamie was adduced as a witness for the prosecution in that trial, and on his evidence on this point being objected to, Mr. Justice Stephen, in repelling the objection, said he would not say how far the principle would extend, but if a conspiracy existed now or recently to change the measures of the Queen by force, or seek to depose her, it would be a matter which the Jury might take into account in considering what purpose those things which were found in the prisoner's possession were intended for.

Mr. RHIND.—It is impossible from a newspaper report to say what was the evidence adduced, or what was said by the judge in that trial. What has been quoted, therefore, by the Lord Advocate is not of much authority. In that case, besides, all the persons accused were men who were traced to Ireland. The further you get from the conspiracy charged, the less competent is this evidence. Here there are no acts said to have been committed by any of the panels in Ireland.

The LORD ADVOCATE. — We say that two of the conspirators, Featherstone and Dalton, committed acts at Cork, and we charge the conspiracy as having run into all the three countries of the United Kingdom. We say that the effect of the conspiracy is to affect the constitution of measures regarding Ireland, by acting in Glasgow, and that the acts were done with special reference to Ireland. If, then, it is a matter of common notoriety that societies for the above purpose exist in Ireland, we are entitled to prove the objects of this Fenian Brotherhood, not as an entirely independent conspiracy, but as being ancillary to the conspiracy we charge, and an element which the Jury are entitled to take into consideration in judging of the question of design. We say that the evidence of this witness will explain the conduct of Featherstone and Dalton.

The LORD JUSTICE-CLERK.—My lords, there is some novelty and some difficulty in the question of evidence that has been raised. It is proposed, in order to prove the facts set forth in this indictment, to examine a witness for the purpose of showing the objects of an alleged association or combination, which is not libelled in the indictment. The charge under the indictment is twofold : first, a charge under the statute 11th and 12th of the Queen ; and secondly, a common law charge, both of these charges setting out in detail a conspiracy to alter

[1] See p. 100.

the laws of this realm, and to assail the Queen's power, evinced by certain acts of outrage and violence. The two charges substantially proceed upon the same facts. That is the conspiracy which is alleged. It is alleged also that these acts of outrage were committed by means of the exploding of dynamite, and that two persons, the one called Featherstone, and the other called Dalton, had come from Ireland for the purpose of giving instruction in the mode in which dynamite, to produce these effects, ought to be prepared and used. The prisoners are resident in Glasgow, and the facts took place in Glasgow. Now it is proposed by Her Majesty's Advocate to call a witness to show that there are some people in Ireland called Fenians, that there is a Fenian Brotherhood, and that the object of that Fenian Brotherhood is to alter the laws of the realm, and alter the laws of Ireland by the means alleged here. My lords, I must own that the admissibility of such evidence would by itself, if it were without authority, have been a matter of great doubt, so far as my mind is concerned. I should have doubted whether under this indictment, alleging a specific enough conspiracy, entered into by the men at the bar, it could be affected or in any way proved by the existence of another conspiracy in another part of the empire, in Ireland, for purposes no doubt specific enough, but which they are not alleged to have participated in as members of that other association. I think it is a matter of grave doubt, and I further think it is a matter of very little moment, because I fancy that the objects of the Fenian Brotherhood are matters of notoriety and history by this time, and that it was scarcely necessary, perhaps, to raise this question of law for the purpose of proving it. These objects have been the subject not only of public discussion, but of judicial examination and judicial verdict before this. But, on the other hand, I find that in a prosecution proceeding on the same ground as the first charge in this indictment, proceeding on the same statute, on the same clause of the statute, and against two of the alleged conspirators in this particular conspiracy, I find that the same witness was tendered, and was, after discussion, admitted by the presiding judge. I am not disposed to make any ruling inconsistent with that judgment, and therefore on the whole matter, though not without difficulty, I am of opinion that this witness's evidence cannot be excluded. As I have said already, if it were necessary for the case of the Lord Advocate here, to show that the objects of the conspiracy alleged in the indictment were the same as those of the Fenian Brotherhood, I am not at all sure that that would require to be proved by separate testimony, under the circumstances in which we are now placed. On the whole matter, I repel the objection, and I think your lordships agree.

LORD MURE.—I concur in the result your lordship has come to. If this question had been raised for the first time under this indictment, I think it would have required perhaps more deliberate consideration than we have now had time to give to it; but I think, having regard to the fact that in a trial which took place with reference to two of the persons with whom these prisoners are said to have acted in concert,—Featherstone and Dalton,—which took place at Liverpool, evidence upon this point was admitted, there is no sufficient objection stated to us to warrant us or lead us to exclude evidence of the same description in a trial under the same statute in this country. I am satisfied, on the ground your lordship has stated, that the same decision should be pronounced here.

LORD CRAIGHILL.—I have come to the same conclusion. Like your lordships, I have not reached it without difficulty, and I am not sure that, but for the authority of the decision of the learned judge who tried the case at Liverpool, I ever would have been able to reach that conclusion. At the same time, this must be said, that according to the allegation which is set forth in the indictment here, the prisoners at the bar not only conspired among themselves, and with others who are not named, but they are expressly said upon p. 4 of the indictment also to have conspired with Featherstone and Dalton; and if, therefore, there is evidence which may be adduced for the purpose of showing what were the views of either Featherstone or Dalton, for the accomplishment of that end which is said to have been the purpose to be accomplished by the prisoners at the bar in their conspiracy, it may at least be very doubtful, apart from authority, whether after all there would have been sufficient ground for admitting that evidence which the Lord Advocate proposes now to bring forward. But as I am influenced greatly by authority,—and, indeed, I may say I have reached this conclusion in respect of that authority,—it is not necessary to say what, apart from authority, would have been the judgment in which I would have been disposed to concur. I concur with your lordships in the judgment.

Objection repelled.]

Examination continued.—*Q.*—Now, tell me what were the terms of the oath you took. *A.*—" I solemnly swear to become a member of the Irish Republic, now virtually established in Ireland; never to divulge the secrets of the organization or the names of any of the members. I also solemnly swear to take up arms at a moment's notice in defence of the Irish Republic, and to obey the lawful commands of my superior officers. Should I ever divulge the secrets of the organization or the names of any of the members, I deserve death by the hands of my fellow-men. I take this oath with the true spirit of a soldier, free from any obligation whatever; so help me God." That was the oath in use to be administered to the other members of the organization. It is a numerous organization. Its membership is not limited to Ireland. There are members in England, Scotland, and America. I continued a member of the organization down to the present year. The organization was existing during last year and this year. I left Dublin for a time in 1868 and went to Liverpool. I returned to Dublin about four or five weeks afterwards. The members of the organization in Dublin generally met twice a week, unless called for a special meeting. The members present at a meeting varied, fifty, twenty, thirty, and so on. At these meetings there was drilling and the gathering of civil money. The civil money was to support the organization. There was arms money. There were two kinds of money subscribed, one called civil money and the other arms money. There were people called centres in that organization. A centre was over a circle. A circle consisted, it may be, of fifty or a hundred men. There were also sub-centres. I was a sub-centre for a few months, and a centre for a few months. There were also people called "B's" and "C's." A "B" was over a company. There might be only fifty in a company.

A "C" is over nine men. The objects of that organization were those expressed in the oath.

Cross-examined by Mr. RHIND.—I subscribed, but only when I lived in Dublin. There were drills in Cuff Lane and Peter Street. I cannot tell you all the places in which drills were held; there were different places, all in Dublin. *Q.*—You did not know whether there were drillings in any place except in Dublin. *A.*—I did not know the places, but I knew that drilling was carried on so far as I heard of. I heard it was so, but that was all. There were Fenian meetings held in Liverpool by the Irish there. I did not attend them. I heard there were such; that is all. I got arms. I ceased to be a member of the Brotherhood when I gave information. I did not get anything for giving information. I gave information because I did not like the system of murder that was going on. There was a man called James Poole executed for murder the other day in Dublin, on evidence given partly by me. That man was my brother-in-law.

DECLARATIONS OF TERENCE M'DERMOTT, THOMAS DEVANY, PETER CALLAGHAN or KELLOCHAN, HENRY M'CANN, JAMES M'CULLAGH or M'CULLOCH, JAMES DONNELLY, JAMES KELLY, PATRICK M'CABE, PATRICK DRUM, and DENIS CASEY.

DECLARATION OF TERENCE M'DERMOTT.

At Glasgow, the 4th day of September 1883 years. In presence of Walter Cook Spens, Esq., Advocate, Sheriff-Substitute of Lanarkshire.

COMPEARED a prisoner, and the charge against him having been read over and explained to him, and he having been judicially admonished and examined thereanent, Declares and says, My name is Terence M'Dermott. I am a native of Ireland, County Leitrim, twenty years of age, a hammerman, and live in 452 Dobbie's Loan, Glasgow. I am not guilty of any of the charges preferred against me, viz. of conspiring against the Queen, in contravention of the third section of the eleventh Victoria, chapter 12, or of conspiring against her at common law, or any way, nor am I guilty of the acts of malicious mischief set forth, viz. destroying a gasometer in Lilybank Road on 20th January last, or of attempting to blow up Possil Bridge on or about said date, and injuring certain people by an explosion which thereafter took place, or of blowing up a shed at the Buchanan Street Railway Station on or about said date. I remember the occurrences referred to in the petition. On the night the gasometer was blown up, I was not near it, being in my own house, which is at the other side of the town, nor had I been near that gasometer at any part of that day, nor was I near the Buchanan Street shed on that night, but I may explain that my house is about 200 yards from the shed. My house is three miles from the gasometer, and about a mile from Possil Bridge. I am not acquainted with any of the other accused, with the

exception of Drum, from whom I have bought some clothes, and M'Cann. I am not acquainted with men of the name of Featherstone or Dalton, or a man who went by the name of Moorhead, nor did I visit at a Mrs. M'Lachlan's house at 35 Ronald Street. I am not acquainted with a man of the name of George Hughes. I am not a member of the Society of Ribbonmen. I was not present at a meeting in Jail Square shortly after Glasgow Fair of 1882, at which a shilling was handed by each of those present to M'Cann. I was not acquainted with a man of the name of Kearney. I have never been in London. I did not purchase any glycerine in November last, nor on any occasion, at the Ruchhill Glycerine Works, Maryhill, nor had I ever any glycerine in my possession. It is not true, therefore, that I gave the name of James Bolan to a clerk at Maryhill when purchasing glycerine. All which I declare to be truth.
(Signed) T. M'DERMOTT.
Etc.

DECLARATION OF THOMAS DEVANY.

At Glasgow, the 4th day of September 1883 years. In presence of Walter Cook Spens, Esq., Advocate, Sheriff-Substitute of Lanarkshire.

COMPEARED a prisoner, and the charge against him having been read over and explained to him, and he having been judicially admonished and examined thereanent, Declares and says, My name is Thomas Devany. I am a native of County Derry, Ireland, forty years of age, a quay labourer, and live in Portugal Lane, South Side, Glasgow. I am not guilty of any of the charges preferred against me. I have not conspired against the Queen, either in the sense of the Act of Parliament eleven Victoria, chapter twelve, section three, or at common law, nor had I anything whatever to do with the blowing up of the gasometer in Lilybank Road, or with the explosion that happened at the Possil Bridge, or with the blowing up of the shed at the Caledonian Railway Station at Buchanan Street. I remember the night that the explosions referred to took place. I was at a Temperance Hall in Dunmore Street, in the South Side, from 6 to 9 o'clock. I came direct from there down to the Candleriggs to the Twisters' Hall, and I talked to a woman there, and did not leave till about 10 o'clock. I then went home direct and found the streets all dark, and heard that the gasometer had exploded. I am not acquainted with two men who went under the names of Featherstone and Johnston. The other accused I am not acquainted with, with the sole exception of Callaghan. I have known him about twenty years. I am not a member of a society of Ribbonmen. I am a member of no secret society whatever. I never heard Callaghan making any statement whatever about vitriol. Callaghan introduced to me no man under the name of Johnston. It is not the case that I was ever present in the Democratic Hall when Callaghan introduced a man as a Mr. Featherstone from New York. It is not the case that I, on any occasion, had in my house any dynamite or other explosive materials or anything to make any explosive material. The only thing that I had in my house, that could come near that, was cartridges, which I had with a revolver. I had them because I got an offer of them very cheap. I got them from a man who has a watchmaker's shop, about a year ago. He goes by the name of Gentleman. I remember about a year ago some detective officers searching my house after a man deserting his wife. I was in bed sleeping at the time they came in, and they wakened me. I know a man of the name of George Hughes very slightly. I have very seldom ever spoken to him. I remember that I did say to Hughes, but simply as a joke, that if the detectives had discovered the dynamite, I would have blown their brains out with a revolver. It would have been hard for them to discover what there was none to discover. I simply said it as a joke. I know M'Cann by sight, but I am not personally acquainted with him. I never upon any occasion gave M'Cann money. I had no acquaintance whatever with a man of the name of Kearney, who is stated to have been a signalman on the Caledonian Railway. I was not in the habit of going to Jail Square on Sundays, though I have occasionally gone down to hear them debating there. I would say that the Temperance Hall I spoke of is about a couple of miles from the gasometer in Lilybank Road. I was not in Garscube Road on the night of Saturday the 20th January 1883 at all. I had no tin box in my possession that night. All which I declare to be truth.—(Signed) WALTER C. SPENS. Further Declares, being shown a piece of cord with sealed label attached, docqueted and subscribed as relative hereto, Says, There are two pieces there. One is a bootlace, and the other is a rope yarn. We use such rope yarn to tie to trucks in connection with the unloading of ships. Being shown a piece of pipe with sealed label attached, docqueted and subscribed as aforesaid, Says, That is a piece of pipe which, I understood from my wife, was picked up by one of the children. Shown packet containing a white powder, docqueted and subscribed as aforesaid, Says, That packet contains chalk or whitening, which I may have used in connection with billiard-marking, or my wife may have had for the purpose of whitening the fireside. Shown book titled "Thomas Devany," docqueted and subscribed as relative hereto, Says, That book is in the handwriting of a man named James Vallery. It was in connection with a building society which has since come to an end. This I also declare to be truth.

(Signed) WALTER C. SPENS.
Etc.

DECLARATION OF PETER CALLAGHAN.

At Glasgow, the 4th day of September 1883 years. In presence of Walter Cook Spens, Esquire, Advocate, Sheriff-Substitute of Lanarkshire.

COMPEARED a prisoner, and the charge against him having been read over and explained to him, and he having been judicially admonished and examined thereanent, Declares and says, My name is Peter Callaghan. I am a native of County Armagh, Ireland, forty-seven years of age, a labourer, and live in Rose Street, South Side, Glasgow. I am not guilty of any of the charges preferred against me. I have not conspired against the Queen in the sense of the third section of the eleventh Victoria, chapter twelve, nor conspired against her at common law, or any other way, nor had I anything whatever to do with the blowing up of the gasometer in Lilybank Road, or the Caledonian Railway shed, or the explosion that took place at the Possil Bridge, on or about 20th January last. I am not a member of a society of Ribbonmen or any secret society, and never have been. I am acquainted with the eight other accused. I have not, to my knowledge, seen men who went under the names of Featherstone and Johnston. It is not the case that I ever administered any oaths, in connection with any secret society. I was never acquainted with a man named Kearney, a signalman on the Caledonian Railway. It is not the case that two Americans were introduced to me last year at all. I am acquainted with a man named George Hughes. He keeps a pony and van. It is not the case that I ever asked Hughes, on a Sunday in July or at any other time, to take a bottle of vitriol from the east end of the town to his stable. I did not make the statement to Hughes or to anybody else, that vitriol was to be used to mix up stuff to blow up buildings. I never had any conversation whatever with a man named Johnston. Shown photograph, bearing to be the photograph of Henry Dalton, and which is docqueted and subscribed as relative hereto, Says, I am not acquainted with, and never saw the man of whom that is a portrait. Shown another photograph, said to be the photograph of Featherstone; and another, which is also docqueted and subscribed as relative hereto, Says, I never to my knowledge saw the smaller of the two men in the photograph. I have seen M'Cann getting subscriptions; but the only occasion I saw him getting these was for the purpose of paying the rent for a poor woman whose husband was lying in the Infirmary. It is not the case that I was present on a Sunday, after the Fair Saturday in 1882, in Hughes' stable, or at any other time, when a small quantity of a white powder was exploded. I have been in Hughes' stable, but I never saw any vitriol or any combustible there. I did not, on the Sunday afternoon after the Glasgow Fair of 1882, ask Drum, M'Cabe, and Hughes, to go up to the hall in Nelson Street to see a man from America; and I never was in that hall when a man was making a speech about blowing up buildings. I have a wife and six children, and too much to do to support them to be meddling with such things. I cannot write. All which I declare to be truth.

(Signed) WALTER C. SPENS.
Etc.

DECLARATION OF HENRY M'CANN.

At Glasgow, the 4th day of September 1883 years. In presence of Walter Cook Spens, Esquire, Advocate, Sheriff-Substitute of Lanarkshire.

COMPEARED a prisoner, and the charge against him having been read over and explained to him, and he having been judicially admonished and examined thereanent, Declares and says, My name is

Henry M'Cann. I am a native of County Fermanagh, Ireland, fifty-seven years of age, a boot and shoe maker, and live in 9 Stirling Street, Glasgow. I am not guilty of any of the charges preferred against me. I have not conspired against the Queen, in the sense of the third section of the eleventh Victoria, chapter twelve; nor have I been guilty of any conspiracy, nor had I anything whatever to do with the blowing up of the gasometer and the Caledonian Railway shed, and the explosion which took place at Possil Bridge, on or about 20th January last. I was not treasurer of a society of Ribbonmen, nor have I been a member of any secret society in my life. I have not tasted whisky for the last three or four years; and I have not been in any public-house during all that time. The only one of the other accused that I am acquainted with is Patrick Drum, who, I think, is a dealer. It is not the case, therefore, that I ever had a meeting in a public-house when Callaghan, Drum, Devany, and James and Patrick M'Cabe were present. I have not been in any public-house in the Saltmarket for the last three or four years. I have already said that I have not been in any public-house for that time. I am not acquainted with a man of the name of Featherstone, and never saw him that I know of. Shown photograph, docqueted and subscribed as relative hereto, Says, I have never to my knowledge seen the original of the smaller of the two men shown in that photograph. I can write, but I never kept a subscription book. The only subscription I ever collected was for a poor woman whose husband was in the Infirmary. I did not know a man of the name of Kearney. I know a man named George Hughes by sight, but I have never spoken to him. It is not the case that I ever struck Hughes. He is a drunkard, and a man I would not associate with. I am not acquainted with the accused M'Dermott. It is not the case that I ever got any money from him. Being shown book, docqueted and subscribed as relative hereto, Says, That book contains entries of subscriptions of the Teetotal Society with which I am connected. I wish to add, that that book is in connection with the ladies' department. All which I declare to be truth.

(Signed) HENRY M'CANN.
Etc.

FIRST DECLARATION OF JAMES M'CULLAGH.

At Glasgow, the 8th day of October 1883 years. In presence of Walter Cook Spens, Esquire, Advocate, Sheriff-Substitute of Lanarkshire.

COMPEARED a prisoner, and the charge against him having been read over and explained to him, and he having been judicially admonished and examined thereanent, Declares and says, My name is James M'Cullagh. I am a native of County Derry, Ireland, 33 years of age, a chemical worker, and last lived at No. 16 Cuthbert Street, Hebburn-on-Tyne, a place about five miles from Newcastle. I am not guilty of any of the charges preferred against me. I have not conspired against the Queen in the sense of the Act of Parliament 11 Victoria, chapter 12, section 3, nor at common law, nor do I know anything whatever about the blowing up of the gasometer at Tradeston,

DECLARATION OF JAMES M'CULLAGH.

or of the Possil Bridge explosion, or of the blowing up of the Caledonian Railway shed. A man came to me some time before the New Year to my house. I think it was about a couple of months before the New Year. He gave me his name as "Bill" afterwards, but not on the occasion referred to. He also gave me his second name, but he spoke so quick that I did not catch it. This man asked me if I was James M'Culloch. I spell my name either M'Cullagh or M'Culloch. I told him I was, and he then asked if I worked in the chemical works. I was working at that time in Tennant's. I said I did, and he then asked if they made vitriol there. I said they did. He said he would require a small sample of vitriol if he could get it. I said I did not know whether I could get a small quantity. He then said he understood I could get it either at the works or from my namesake up the road, referring to a soda-water maker named M'Cullough in Garngad Road. I then asked him what he wanted it for. He said he would let me know by and by, after I had got the sample, if it was strong. I understood from that that he would tell me what it was for, if the vitriol was strong enough for the purpose for which he wanted it. I said I was acquainted with one of M'Cullough's men. The man to whom I referred was Michael Buchanan. After the man left, I did go to Michael Buchanan. I met Buchanan either that night or very shortly afterwards. I told Buchanan that a man had come to me wanting a sample of vitriol, and I asked if he could get it for me. He said that he did not know whether Myles (meaning his master, M'Cullough) would sell any or not, but that he (Buchanan) could get a bottle if I wanted it. I did get from Buchanan a small bottle containing vitriol that night, and this bottle I took away with me and gave to the man, who called a night or two after. He took the bottle away with him, but came back some days afterwards—I am not sure of the precise time—and said it was not strong enough. Buchanan had told me that if the sample was not strong enough, stronger he could get. I told the man this, and he then asked me to get a carboy of the strongest vitriol they had. I did go to Buchanan, and asked Buchanan to procure for me a carboy of the strongest vitriol he could get. I gave Buchanan a sovereign which the man had given me, and I got back from him, I think, about 11s. Buchanan told me that the carboy was left sitting in M'Cullough's yard. I went along with the man, and he and I emptied the vitriol into two or three jars, which were put in a sack. I carried the sack up to about the centre of the street on the left, up the Garngad Road from M'Cullough's yard. I am not sure of the name of the street. The man then told me that he had another party to help him to his destination, and he did not require me more. He told me, however, to wait at the foot of Garngad Road for him, which I did. He did appear about half an hour after this at the bridge. This was at night, but I cannot say what the hour was. I asked him what the vitriol was for, and he said it was for a new patent galvanizing battery. The man was a small man, about 5 feet 5 inches. He had no beard or whiskers, but there was about a week's growth of red stubbly hair. I would know him if I saw him again. The man came back again about a fortnight or three weeks after, I think, but I am not sure, and I got a second carboy in the same way from Buchanan, which I also helped to carry in the same way from M'Cullough's yard. The man also in the same way got one or two more carboys, but I did not help him to carry them. I explain that I am not sure whether it was the first and second carboys or the first and third carboys I helped to carry. I think 9s. 7d. was what I paid to Buchanan for each carboy. I paid Buchanan for all the carboys. The man gave me money to pay for the carboys, and I returned the change to him, except on one occasion, when I took off it a treat I gave to Buchanan. The man always treated me, but that was all I got. I got no money from him. I am acquainted with James Donnelly. He wrought in Tennant's Chemical Works along with me. I believe I have met him on occasions in Jail Square, but not when he was in company with the other prisoners. The only other of the prisoners that I have any acquaintance with, are Peter Callaghan and Patrick Drum. I do not remember speaking to either Callaghan or Drum in Jail Square, but I have seen them there. My opinion was that the man to whom I have referred was an American. I thought this from the way in which he spoke. I was slightly acquainted with John Kearney, railway signalman. The way in which I became acquainted with him was that he was pointsman near the St. Rollox Work. I cannot say where I was on the night the explosion took place, it is so long ago, and I was not taking any note of it at the time. I am neither a Ribbonman nor a Fenian, nor am I a member of any secret society. I wish to add that Donnelly has been frequently in my house. His wife comes from the same part of Ireland as I do. With regard to a letter of mine which was taken possession of at Newcastle, and which is docqueted and subscribed as relative hereto, I wish to explain with reference to the expression in that letter of "burning the things," that I came to make this reference in consequence of my wife sending a letter in which she told me she had burned everything in the house, in consequence of my being so intimate with Donnelly. I was merely writing to say that it was nonsense of her doing such a thing, as I had nothing to fear in the matter. Although that letter bears to be written by me, neither my wife nor I can write, and have to get people to write for us. That letter was written by my landlady. I can only write my name. All which I declare to be truth.

(Signed)   JAMES M'CULLOCH.
      Etc.

SECOND DECLARATION OF JAMES M'CULLAGH.

At Glasgow, the 15th day of October 1883 years. In presence of Walter Cook Spens, Esquire, Advocate, Sheriff-Substitute of Lanarkshire.

COMPEARED James M'Cullagh, presently prisoner in the prison of Glasgow, and the declaration emitted by him on 8th October 1883, which is now docqueted and subscribed as relative hereto, having been read over to him, and he having been again judicially admonished and examined, Declares, My previous declaration is all correct. I have been brought here at my own request. I wish to add that on the night the explosion of the gasometer took place, I was in Sherries'

public-house in Castle Street. I went there about a quarter past ten
P.M. I stayed there about a quarter of an hour, and then I went
straight home. I also wish to say that my reason for leaving for
England, which I did on the last Saturday of January last, was
because my wife had brought me into some debts. I never saw
Donnelly in company with the man whom I call "Bill," and I do not
know whether he was acquainted with him or not, nor had Donnelly
any conversation with me about the vitriol. I wish to add that the
persons with whom my wife contracted debt were Matthew Hall and
John M'Peak, the first a grocer, and the second a grain merchant who
keeps groceries. I wish further to add that I came to Glasgow in July
last for a week, looking for work; but Tennant's Work being closed,
I could get no work, and went back to England. I would have made
the statement which I have made about the vitriol to the police, but I
thought it would be better to wait till I was taken before the Sheriff.
All which I declare to be truth.

(Signed) JAMES M'CULLOCH.
Etc.

DECLARATION OF JAMES DONNELLY.

At Glasgow, the 4th day of September 1883 years. In presence of
Walter Cook Spens, Esquire, Advocate, Sheriff-Substitute of
Lanarkshire.

COMPEARED a prisoner, and the charge against him having been
read over and explained to him, and he having been judicially
admonished and examined thereanent, Declares and says, My name is
James Donnelly. I am a native of County Armagh, Ireland, 35 years
of age, a labourer, and live in 33 Villiers Street, Glasgow. I am not
guilty of any of the charges preferred against me. I have not conspired against the Queen in the sense of section 3 of 11 Victoria,
chapter 12; nor have I been guilty of any conspiracy whatever; and I
know nothing whatever of the blowing up of the gasometer, or
Caledonian Railway shed, or the explosion at Possil Bridge on or
about 20th January 1883. I am not acquainted with any of the other
accused. I was not acquainted with men of the names of Featherstone
and Johnston, said to have been in Glasgow in 1882. I was not
acquainted with a man of the name of Kearney. Shown piece of
paper, on one side the words "Your old comrade, John," and on the
other side with writing, docqueted and subscribed as relative hereto,
Says, I don't know anything about that piece of paper. It does not
belong to me. On the night of Saturday, 20th January last, I went
home at five o'clock at night; and as I had to go out early next morning to work in Tennant's Chemical Works, I did not go out all that
night. My wife was in the house with me that night, but there was
no other person. It is my ordinary habit since I came to the town to
go down to the Jail Square on Sunday afternoons, and occasionally on
Saturday afternoons. All which I declare to be truth.

(Signed) JAMES DONNELLY.
Etc.

Declaration of James Kelly.

At Glasgow, the 4th day of September 1883 years. In presence of Walter Cook Spens, Esquire, Advocate, Sheriff-Substitute of Lanarkshire.

COMPEARED a prisoner, and the charge against him having been read over and explained to him, and he having been judicially admonished and examined thereanent, Declares and says, My name is James Kelly. I am a native of County Sligo, Ireland, 50 years of age, a hammerman, and reside in 72 Kirk Street, Calton, Glasgow. I am not guilty of any of the charges preferred against me. I have not conspired against the Queen in the sense of the third section of 11 Victoria, chapter 12; nor have I been guilty of any conspiracy whatever, and I know nothing whatever of the blowing-up of the gasometer, or of the Caledonian Railway shed, or of the explosion at Possil Bridge on 20th January last. I know all the other eight accused to speak to. I see them in Jail Square when I am taking a walk on Sundays. I am not a member of a society of Ribbonmen or of any secret society. I was not acquainted with men named Featherstone and Johnston, but I remember a man named Hughes told me that men of those names were in Glasgow. I never came across Featherstone on any occasion. It is not the case that upon a Sunday in July 1882 I came to the Jail Square and handed a bottle of vitriol to Patrick Drum. It is not the case that Callaghan, in my hearing, said, "I have a bottle of vitriol here, and I'm going to see how it works." I remember Hughes saying in the Police Office on Sunday last that either Casey or I gave a bottle of vitriol to Drum, but I know nothing about it. I was not in Hughes' stable when some white powder was exploded. I know nothing whatever about that. I cannot write. All which I declare to be truth.

(Signed)   WALTER C. SPENS.
                                         Etc.

Declaration of James Kelly.

At Glasgow, the 19th day of September 1883 years. In presence of Walter Cook Spens, Esquire, Advocate, Sheriff-Substitute of Lanarkshire.

COMPEARED James Kelly, presently prisoner in the prison of Glasgow, and the declaration emitted by him on the 4th curt., and which is docqueted and subscribed as relative hereto, having been read over to him, Declares, That declaration is quite correct. I have been brought before the Sheriff at my own request, because I wish to add something to that declaration. When I was brought before Captain M'Call on Saturday the 1st of September, he told me there was no charge against me, and that there would be nothing against me if I became a witness against the men who were taken. I told him I could not be a witness against them, as I knew nothing against them. I was let home on the Saturday, but was told to come back on Sunday at ten o'clock; and when I came back I was detained. George Hughes was sitting in Captain M'Call's room, and he said to me before Mr. Boyd, I think, that it was a bad job, and that he and I knew nothing about it. I said, No, we did not. Hughes then said, "Do you mind coming down to the foot of the Saltmarket to Douglas' public-house on Fair Wednesday (I think he said Fair Wednesday) with a bottle of vitriol?" I said, No, I did not. "Oh yes," Hughes said; "you were down and gave a bottle of vitriol to Pat Drum." I said, No, I didn't, and he then said, "Either you or Casey did it." All this was said before the Captain of Police. It was after this that the Captain of Police, whom I supposed to be Mr. Boyd, said he would require to send me up to Captain M'Call. I was taken up to Captain M'Call, and then Captain M'Call said to me that there was no charge against me, but that if I would not become a witness he would need to make a charge of conspiracy against me along with the others. I said, Very well, I could not help it. I should have made this statement in the first declaration, and it was because I had not done this I wanted to be brought before the Sheriff again. All which I declare to be truth.

(Signed) WALTER C. SPENS.
Etc.

DECLARATION OF PATRICK M'CABE.

At Glasgow, the 4th day of September 1883 years. In presence of Walter Cook Spens, Esquire, Advocate, Sheriff-Substitute of Lanarkshire.

COMPEARED a prisoner, and the charge against him having been read over and explained to him, and he having been judicially admonished and examined thereanent, Declares and says, My name is Patrick M'Cabe. I am a native of County Monaghan, Ireland, 50 years of age, a general dealer, and live in 79 Rose Street, Glasgow. I am not guilty of any of the charges preferred against me. I have not conspired against the Queen in the sense of the third section of the 11 Victoria, chapter twelve, nor have I been guilty of any conspiracy against the law of the land, nor had I anything to do with the blowing up of the gasometer and the Caledonian Railway shed, and the explosion which took place at Possil Bridge on or about 20th January last. I am not a member of any society of Ribbonmen, or of any secret society. I have no acquaintance whatever with the other accused. I never was present at any meetings which were held in Lennox's public-house in Saltmarket. I never saw men who went under the names of Featherstone and Johnston, and who were said to come from America. I was not acquainted with a man named Kearney. I know a man named George Hughes by sight, who is a fruiterer, and has a pony and cart. I know Callaghan by sight. I never heard Callaghan, on a Sunday in July 1882, or at any other time, asking Hughes to take a bottle of vitriol to his (Hughes') stable, nor did I hear Callaghan make any statement about vitriol being used to mix up stuff to blow up buildings. Shown photograph, which is docqueted and subscribed as relative hereto, Says, I never saw the original of the smaller of the two men shown in that photograph. All which I declare to be truth.

(Signed) PATRICK M'CABE.
Etc.

Declaration of Patrick Drum.

At Glasgow, the 4th day of September 1883 years. In presence of Walter Cook Spens, Esquire, Advocate, Sheriff-Substitute of Lanarkshire.

COMPEARED a prisoner, and the charge against him having been read over and explained to him, and he having been judicially admonished and examined thereanent, Declares and says, My name is Patrick Drum. I am a native of County Meath, Ireland, 64 years of age, a hawker, and reside in 118 Rose Street, Glasgow. I am not guilty of any of the charges preferred against me. I have not conspired against the Queen in the sense of the third section of eleven Victoria, chapter twelve, nor have I been guilty of any conspiracy, and I had nothing whatever to do with the blowing up of the gasometer, or the Caledonian Railway shed, or the explosion at Possil Bridge, on or about 20th January last. I am acquainted with the accused, Callaghan. I remember once being with Callaghan in a public-house in Saltmarket. I think it is about twelve months ago. Not that I am aware of have I ever seen men who went under the name of Featherstone and Johnston. It is not the case that I was ever present when an American addressed me and others about blowing up public buildings. I am acquainted with Patrick M'Cabe. I cannot write. All which I declare to be truth.

(Signed)   WALTER C. SPENS.
Etc.

Declaration of Denis Casey.

At Glasgow, the 4th day of September 1883 years. In presence of Walter Cook Spens, Esquire, Advocate, Sheriff-Substitute of Lanarkshire.

COMPEARED a prisoner, and the charge against him having been read over and explained to him, and he having been judicially admonished and examined thereanent, Declares and says, My name is Denis Casey. I am a native of County Armagh, Ireland, 39 years of age, a scavenger, and reside in 72 Kirk Street, Calton, Glasgow. I am not guilty of any of the charges preferred against me. I have not conspired against the Queen in the sense of section 3 of 11 Victoria, chapter 12, nor have I been guilty of any conspiracy whatever, and I know nothing whatever about the blowing up of the gasometer, or of the Caledonian Railway shed, or of the explosion at Possil Bridge on or about 20th January last. I am acquainted with James Kelly, and with Patrick Drum and Patrick M'Cabe. The other accused I do not know. I am not acquainted with men who went under the names of Featherstone, Johnston, or Kearney. I know a man of the name of George Hughes by sight. It is not the case that I had a bottle of vitriol in my possession on a Sunday in July 1882. I could not, therefore, hand such a thing to Patrick Drum. I never knew where

Hughes' stable was, and never was in it. I cannot write. All which I declare to be truth.

(Signed) WALTER C. SPENS.
Etc.

The LORD ADVOCATE.—That is the case for the Crown.

EVIDENCE FOR THE DEFENCE.

EVIDENCE FOR TERENCE M'DERMOTT.

1. *John Hesson.* *By* Mr. BAXTER.—I am a labourer. I work in Maryhill Gasworks. I was not working at the Tradeston Gasworks at the time the explosion occurred last January. I was living at 385 Eglinton Street at that time. My house was about a quarter of a mile, I suppose, from the gasholder that exploded. I remember the night of the explosion. I was sitting at my own fireside; I heard a noise. I went out. I saw tank No. 4 blazing. I knew its number. I had done work upon that tank before the explosion in July and August last year. I had charge of the painting of it. There were some little escapes about the tank at that time, at the top, about the rivet heads. That was towards the Muirhouse Lane side. I did not know what column it was principally at. There was nothing done with those escapes; they were not thought so wrong. The escape of gas at that time was not very much. There was one at the back side where there was a good deal. I was not in the neighbourhood of the tank immediately before the explosion occurred. I was about five months away from the tank at the time the explosion occurred. There was no one with me except my wife and children when the explosion occurred. I made no remark to her.

Cross-examined by the LORD ADVOCATE.—I did not think anything of these escapes.

2. *Andrew Logan.* *By* Mr. BAXTER.—I am a master cartwright and joiner at 269 Eglinton Street, Glasgow. I remember the night of the explosion of the Tradeston gasometer, last January. At the time it occurred I was just stepping on to the bridge to cross into Eglinton Street, about two minutes' walk from the gasometer. Shortly before that I had been in the house of Thomas Butler, carter, Muirhouse Lane. When I was there I smelt a fearful smell of gas. I went into Butler's house about twenty minutes before ten. Butler and his wife were not in, and I stopped for a wee while till they came in. There was a very heavy smell—a nuisance of a smell. When I came out of the house I still felt the smell of the gas strong till I went to the bridge, about a minute and a half before the explosion. I did not see any persons running out of their houses after the explosion. I did not see any persons running in my neighbourhood. I did not know George Hughes, a fruit dealer.

Cross-examined by the LORD ADVOCATE.—There was generally a very bad smell of gas about that tank for two or three years back. I have frequently gone about it. Q.—You do not like to live near a gas tank? A.—There was a fearful bad smell; there must have been a tremendous escape about that gaswork, or it could not have had the smell it had. For years past it was much the same. The railway is only about seventy yards from it, and sparks from the engines fly on to the top of the tank.

3. *James Campbell.* By Mr. BAXTER.—I am a provision curer, and live at 55 Muirhouse Lane. I remember the explosion at the Tradeston gasometer on 20th January last. For some time before that I had observed a strong smell of gas. It caused me annoyance in my house. The smell was increasing before the explosion; the leakage was getting worse. When the explosion occurred I was in St. Andrew's Road, a short distance from Muirhouse Lane, on my way home. I know Butler, a carter, who lives in Muirhouse Lane. I was not in his house shortly after the explosion, but I was at his house. I observed the windows of the house. They were blown out, either out or in; they were smashed out at any rate. I cannot just say distinctly that they were blown outside, but they were smashed out of their place and a wreck. I saw fragments of the windows lying outside of the house and some inside too. I saw Butler and Edward Hughes running from the house, and Butler's vest was on fire. I know Edward Hughes. I did not see any other person running in my neighbourhood, but there were several constables and strangers about the place at the time.

4. *Mary M'Dermott.* By Mr. BAXTER.—I am a sister of the accused Terence M'Dermott. I remember the night in January last when the explosion occurred at the Tradeston gasometer. I do not remember the day of the month, but I remember it was on a Saturday night. I heard nothing of the explosion till the Sabbath day. On the Saturday my brother was in our house, 452 Dobbie's Loan. He was complaining of not being very well, and was expecting his brother in from Coatbridge, so he did not leave the house. In the afternoon I went out some messages, leaving him in the house, but I did not delay very long. I cannot say for certain what was the longest time I was out, but I am quite sure I was not half an hour out at any time. When I went out I left my brother there, and he was there when I came back. I cannot tell what time all this was, but it was in the afternoon. My brother never went out to my knowledge till he went to bed at night, except once to the back court, and his brother Patrick was along with him. I cannot exactly tell at what time he went to bed; it was not very late and it was not very early, but I passed no remark upon the time he went to bed. It was at his usual time so far as I recollect. It was at the back of eleven. Q.—After eleven? A.—Yes. I never went out after nine o'clock. Q.—Was your brother there during the whole of that time till he went to bed? A.—Except once when he went to the back court, and he was not out longer than seven or eight minutes, and his brother Patrick was with him. He went out in his shirt sleeves. In addition to Terence, his brother Patrick, Patrick's wife, my father and mother, and I were in the house that night.

Cross-examined by the LORD ADVOCATE.—Q.—You told us you paid no particular attention at the time to this explosion? *A.*—I did not say that; Terence and Patrick and I went to the back room window to see what was the cause of the noise, and we saw nothing. Terence said it might perhaps be the boiler of the work that my father wrought in that had exploded, and Patrick said no, perhaps it might be the boiler of a train. These were all the remarks we passed. *Q.*—How do you happen to remember so particularly what Terence was doing that Saturday? *A.*—Simply because he was complaining of not being very well. *Q.*—How does that enable you to remember that Saturday so particularly? *A.*—The noise after that; I can remember it quite well. *Q.*—Had he been in the house more days than that one Saturday or not? *A.*—I did not need to pass remarks on what Saturday he was in the house. He was in the house many a Saturday this year. *Q.*—Is he generally in on the Saturdays? *A.*—Yes, for he would be working about the house. He was a dutiful boy to his father and mother, and did not go out very much. He was many a Saturday in the house. *Q.*—Was he more in than out, or more out than in? *A.*—I never marked it down with pen and paper. *Q.*—And you did not mark this Saturday down more than any other? *A.*—I did remark when the question was put the length of me about the noise. *Q.*—Can you tell us how long before the noise it was that he was out seven or eight minutes? *A.*—It would be between nine and ten o'clock.

By Mr. BAXTER.—*Q.*—Was it the fact of the explosion that impressed that particular Saturday upon your mind? *A.*—Yes, because when I heard the noise I went to the window. *Q.*—Was there a good deal of talk afterwards about the explosion that had taken place? *A.*—Well, I was not out to hear the talk. My brother Terence has always been a good worker, and he brought his wages home with him regularly.

5. *Elizabeth Corbett or M'Dermott.* *By* MR. M'LENNAN.—I am the wife of Patrick M'Dermott, Coatbridge. My husband is a brother of the accused, Terence M'Dermott. Terence lives with his father at 452 Dobbie's Loan, Glasgow. I remember one Saturday night in January last going with my husband to Terence M'Dermott's father's house. *Q.*—Did anything happen that night to fix it in your memory? *A.*—Yes, I heard an explosion while I was there. It was between seven and eight o'clock when we got to Dobbie's Loan. We found in the house, when we went there, my good-father and good-mother, Terence, and his sister, the last witness. Terence was out once that night after we went there. *Q.*—At what time was that? *A.*—It was late. My husband was with him. They were out between eight and ten minutes. They went to the back court. They did not go out to the street. This was after the explosion. Terence had not his coat on when he went out,—he was in his shirt sleeves. My husband and I stayed there that night, and did not go home.

By the LORD JUSTICE-CLERK.—I cannot say where the report was which I heard.

Examination continued.—I remember the whole of us looking out at the window when the explosion took place, and speculating as to the cause of it. I thought it was a boiler that had burst. I afterwards

I

heard outside about explosions that had taken place. I am sure that Terence was in all that night except during the ten minutes after the explosion.

Cross-examined by the LORD ADVOCATE.—The explosion took place between ten and eleven o'clock. Terence had not been to bed before the explosion. He went to bed with my husband, going on to twelve o'clock, a while after the explosion. When he went to the window to look out he had been sitting with the rest of us in his clothes.

Re-examined.—I did not hear more than one explosion that night. I cannot say what time it was, except that it was about ten o'clock.

6. *Patrick M'Dermott.* *By* Mr. M'LENNAN.—I am a miner, and reside at 40 Back Row, Rosehall, Coatbridge. I am brother of the accused, Terence M'Dermott. I remember the night of the explosion in January last. It was a Saturday night. I left my home about five o'clock that evening, and went to my father's house in Dobbie's Loan along with my wife, the last witness. We arrived there about twenty minutes past seven. I found my father, who was lying badly, my mother, my sister, and Terence in the house. We stayed there all the evening, and slept there that night. Terence was never out that night after we arrived, so far as I remember, except once when he and I went to the back court before we retired to go to bed. He went down in his shirt sleeves. I remember hearing an explosion that night. To the best of my opinion, that would be about ten o'clock. We all looked out at the window and had some conversation as to what was the occasion of it. I slept with Terence that night. We went to bed between eleven and twelve o'clock. I heard just the one explosion. Terence remained in bed with me all night.

Cross-examined by the LORD ADVOCATE.—I cannot say whether Terence and I both went to bed at the one time or not, but it was within a little of each other. So far as I remember, the explosion took place about ten. Terence had not been in bed before the explosion at all. He was sitting talking like the rest of us.

EVIDENCE FOR PETER CALLAGHAN.

7. *Ann Callaghan.* *By* Mr. BAXTER.—I live with my father, Peter Callaghan, at 14 Rose Street, South Side, Glasgow. I remember the night when the gasometer at the South Side exploded last January. I was on the street at the time. My father had sent me for a paraffin lamp that was being repaired at the oil-shop. He had sent me from the house. He had been in his house from the time he came home from his work, about half-past three or four o'clock, until half-past ten, when he went out for a paper. *Q.*—Was he in the house up to the time he sent you out for the lamp? *A.*—Yes. When I went out for the lamp the explosion occurred; the gas had gone out lower down. I met my sister Mary Callaghan when I was out. I was out about ten minutes altogether. When I came back to the house my father was still there. He had had a newspaper before I went out. My father is a quay labourer. He has been in regular employment. There are six of us in the family. My sister Mary is a weaver, and I

am a servant with my aunt. After I came back from getting the lamp, my father went out for another newspaper. That was about a quarter before eleven o'clock. He was out just about five minutes. He had just to go to the close-mouth for the paper. It was the "Universe" that he went for. After that he was not out of the house any more that night. We all went to bed at the same time. My mother is alive. She was in the house that night too.

8. *Peter Callaghan. By* Mr. BAXTER.—I live with my father and mother at 14 Rose Street, South Side, Glasgow. I remember the night last January when the gasometer in Tradeston was blown up. My father was in the house that afternoon. I came in about six o'clock, and remained in the house until my mother sent me down to the oil-shop for sticks to kindle the fire on Sunday morning. I don't remember whether that was before or after the explosion occurred. I did not hear the noise of the explosion. I was about five minutes out of the house on that message. I saw my father in the oil-shop getting a paper, and I stood at the window till he came out, and after he came out, I went in and got my message, and he was in the house when I went up. He had been down before me. He went out for the newspaper. I went straight back to the house. I was in the house all night after that. My father was there all night too.

9. *Mary Callaghan. By* Mr. BAXTER.—I reside with my father at 14 Rose Street, South Side, Glasgow. I remember the night when the explosion took place at the gasometer at Tradeston last January. I was in Cansh's. It took me about ten minutes to walk home. I heard the noise, and saw the gas going out. I met my sister Ann shortly after that. She was out for messages. I had left the house at half-past six that night. My father was sitting reading when I left. I went back to the house at about twenty minutes to eleven. I went back with Ann. I found my father there. I was not out again that night. My father did not go out again that night that I remember. When I returned to the house, he was reading the paper. Our house is not supplied with gas; we use paraffin lamps.

EVIDENCE FOR JAMES DONNELLY.

10. *Patrick M'Kenna. By* Mr. M'LENNAN.—I am a labourer, and reside at 33 Villiers Street, Glasgow. I know the accused Donnelly. He lived in the same stair with me in 33 Villiers Street. I remember well the night of the explosion of the Tradeston gasometer. There was a good deal of speaking about it at the time. I came home at five o'clock to my own house. My sister, who is married to Donnelly, came in at half-past six with Donnelly's boots. She asked me to heel them. I am not a regular shoemaker, but I do a little work in that way. I did heel Donnelly's boots that night. I commenced to them about seven o'clock, and was done about half-past ten. When I did the boots, I asked Mrs. Donnelly if he was needing the boots that night. She said he did not need them, for he was in the house, and was not going out. The boots remained in my house till Sunday

morning, when Mrs. Donnelly took them away. Donnelly is a labourer. He has one child, about a year old. His wife is about twenty-eight or twenty-nine.

Cross-examined by the LORD ADVOCATE.—I did not see Donnelly that night. I do not know where he was.

EVIDENCE FOR PATRICK M'CABE.

11. *Mary M'Cabe. By* Mr. BAXTER.—I am a daughter of Patrick M'Cabe, one of the accused. My father is a general dealer at 73 Rose Street, South Side, Glasgow. There are six in our family. I assist my father in the shop. I remember the night of the explosion in January last. I did not hear it. I was busy in the shop that day, the same as any other Saturday. It is our busy day, and we do not shut till eleven o'clock. I was in the shop that night. I would be there about nine o'clock, when the shop opened in the morning, and stayed there till it closed at night,—the whole time. My father was in the shop the whole day; he never leaves on the Saturday at all. He was there along with me during the whole time. After the shop was closed, I went out for messages. I left my father in the house. Our house was at that time connected with the shop. I left my father there about eleven o'clock, after the shop was closed. I cannot just say when I came back, but I came back shortly after fetching my messages. I would be in before half-past eleven any way. I remember the gas going out. My father was in the shop at the time that occurred. He sent my little sister for candles to light the shop. This was the only occasion on which the gas has ever gone out except from frost in the winter time. I cannot say what put the gas wrong at that time. I saw Mrs. Freeman that night in the shop with her little boy. She was there, I think, about five minutes from ten. The gas was blinking when she came in. I do not remember whether it went out while she was in the shop. After I came back from doing my messages, my father was still in the house. He stayed there till he went to bed. He never goes out after he shuts the shop any night. We all went off to bed at the same time. I am seventeen years of age. I am the eldest child, and the youngest is two years old. None of the other children assist in the shop. None of them are able to do anything for themselves except Patrick, who is working. My mother is alive, and sometimes assists in the shop.

12. *Catherine M'Cabe. By* Mr. BAXTER.—I live with my father at 73 Rose Street, Glasgow. I remember one night last January when the gas went out in our shop. I was sent out for candles by my father. He had been working in the shop that day. I brought the candles back. My father did not leave the shop after that. He had been in the shop working that evening before he sent me out. Q.— During the whole time? A.—During the time the gas was going out. Q.—But was he in the shop the whole evening? A.—Yes; he did not go out after the shop was shut.

13. *Elizabeth Gardner or Freeman. By* Mr. BAXTER.—I live at 11

Sandyfauld Street, South Side, Glasgow. I remember one night last January the gas going out in our street. I afterwards knew that to be the night when the gasometer was blown up. There was a great deal of talk about it. I know the accused, Patrick M'Cabe. I was in his shop that night just at the time the gas went out. His daughter Mary was at the door. She seemed to me as if she was going a message. M'Cabe was in the shop. I was in the shop just a few minutes. He gave me his answer, he had not got what I wanted to purchase. I know the M'Cabe family. I always found M'Cabe himself most attentive to his business and his family. I never called there any night but he was there. My son James was with me on the night of which I have been speaking.

14. *James Freeman. By* Mr. BAXTER.—I know Mr. M'Cabe's shop in the South Side of Glasgow. I remember being there with my mother one night last January when an explosion occurred. Some of the gas went out and some was blinking. M'Cabe was in the shop when we went to it. I know him well by sight.

EVIDENCE FOR DENIS CASEY.

15. *Rose Ann Casey. By* Mr. M'LELLAN.—I am a daughter of the accused Denis Casey, and live at 72 Kirk Street, Glasgow. There are six of us in the family, of whom I am the eldest. My mother is alive. I remember an explosion taking place in the South Side of the city in January this year. I did not hear about it till the Monday morning. On the Saturday my father came home between half-past three and four o'clock. He had some drink in him, and he fell asleep on a chair at the window with his drawers on. He had taken off his working trousers and coat. He did not go out again that day. He fell asleep with his arm on the window and slept all afternoon. He was not out on the Sunday because he had no clothes to go out with; he had nothing but his working clothes.

EVIDENCE FOR HENRY M'CANN.

16. *John M'Cann. Examined by* Mr. KENNEDY.—I am a son of the prisoner Henry M'Cann. I am an iron moulder to trade. I am married, and my wife is here to-day. At the time of the explosion at the Tradeston gasometer I was living about a quarter of a mile from my father's house in Stirling Street. I remember reading about the explosion on the Monday after it occurred. I work at the Etna Foundry in Lilybank Road, and I could see the gasometer from the back yard of the foundry. The foundry is not so far out the road as the gasometer. I remember going up to my father's house on the evening of the Saturday that the explosion occurred along with my wife. We went about seven o'clock. I went to get my boots soled and heeled; my father is a shoemaker. I took my boots with me on my feet; I had no other pair. I found my father in when I went to the house. My sister Catherine, Robert Barclay's wife, was there also,—she came in shortly after I went. I took off my boots and gave them to my father, and he

commenced working at them, and after he was done I put them on and went away. I was in the house the whole time. It was going on to the "chap" of eleven o'clock when I went away. The only time my father left the room was when he came into the kitchen to take his supper. I was in the kitchen when my father was working at my boots. He went back again to the room to work after he had got his supper. I remember remarking to my father that it was time we were off—going home—that it was about eleven o'clock, and when I came down-stairs with my wife the whisky shops were shut. My sister Mrs. Barclay had left the house before that—about nine o'clock, as far as I remember.

Cross-examined by the LORD ADVOCATE.—I recollect the Saturday on which I went to my father's particularly, because my mother was very ill at the time. I was first asked to recall the events of that particular evening in the County Buildings last Friday. Till then I had not returned to the subject or thought of it. I do not recollect the events of any other Saturday since 20th January with the same precision.

Re-examined.—I never went to my father's house any other Saturday night last winter to get my boots soled and heeled.

17. *Mrs. Maggie Hurst or M'Cann. Examined by* Mr. KENNEDY.—I am the wife of John M'Cann, the last witness. I remember the explosion of the Tradeston gasometer in January last; it was on a Saturday. I remember, on that Saturday night, going along with my husband to his father's house, about seven o'clock in the evening, to get his boots soled and heeled. It was the boots he had on his feet he wanted repaired. We found Mr. M'Cann in when we got to the house. He was just done with his day's work, and said he was tired enough to begin to my husband's boots, but he would do it. My husband and I waited till his father finished the boots, and then my husband put on the boots, and we went away. It was close on eleven o'clock when we left. When we left, old Mr. M'Cann was still in the house. I was never up with my husband at his father's on any other Saturday when he was getting his boots soled and heeled.

Cross-examined by the LORD ADVOCATE.—I remember that this was on Saturday 20th January last, because my husband never before got a pair of boots soled and heeled by his father. I recollect it was on the 20th January that event occurred, by hearing read out of the papers, on the Monday night following, what had occurred,—about the explosion. *Q.*—But what makes you recollect it was on that Saturday more than any other that you made this visit to your husband's father's? *A.*—Just through the boots soling and heeling; that is all.

18. *Mrs. Catherine M'Cann or Barclay. Examined by* Mr. KENNEDY. —I am a daughter of the prisoner Henry M'Cann, and wife of Robert Barclay. I lived, in January last, in the same stair as my father, but in a different house, and I do so still. I live up one stair, and my father lived three stairs up. I went up to see my father very often. I remember the Saturday when the Tradeston gasometer exploded. I heard of the explosion shortly after it happened; my father read it out of the paper on the Monday following. I went up to my father's

house on the Saturday evening about seven o'clock. I found my brother and his wife there. My father was a kind of late stopping with his work that night, and he had to commence again to my brother John's boots. It would be about nine o'clock, I think, when I left. My brother and his wife remained in the house after I left, and my father was still working at the boots. My mother was ill at the time. My father has been in regular employment. He has been working lately to one Ferguson, I think, whose shop is near St. Enoch's Square. He took his work away and did it at home. My father is a member of St. Alphonso's Chapel, Great Hamilton Street, of which Rev. Michael M'Ginn is the clergyman. I sometimes went to the church with him. I think the occasion I have mentioned is the only one when my father ever soled and heeled a pair of boots for my brother.

Cross-examined by the LORD ADVOCATE.—*Q.*—Was it much spoken of at the time, or was it merely a small event? *A.*—It was only a small event; it was not regarded as of importance at the time. I do not know when my father began to the boots; I was busy in the house, and did not pay much attention. My father was working when I went in. My father was very tired, and said he would rather go to bed than start to the boots. He was working at them for about two hours. I cannot say whether he was nearly done at nine o'clock or not; I left him working at them when I went away. Sometimes my father went out for a walk after dinner on Sundays, and sometimes he took a sleep, and then went out, perhaps, about the tea-hour. Sometimes he went to the Green on the Sunday afternoons. He very seldom went out on the afternoon of Saturday. I remember that the occasion when my father was working at my brother's boots was on the 20th January, because my child was badly at the time with chincough, and I had to bring her to the doctor that evening. That is the only way that I mind about the day. I have not it written down anywhere. *Q.*—How does your child having the chincough fix the date as being that on which the explosion occurred? *A.*—Because I remember my father reading the paper on the Monday night following. *Q.*—But how do you associate the two things? *A.*—My mother was badly at the time, and that brings it to my memory, because I had to do everything in the house for her. *Q.*—But how does that connect it with the explosion? *A.*—That is the only way I remember about it.

By the LORD JUSTICE-CLERK.—I do not remember anything that happened on any other Saturday in January, or on any Saturday in the month following. I cannot tell anything my father did on any of the Saturdays in either January or February. It was about three months after that before my child was better of the chincough. I do not remember anything that occurred on the second Saturday after the one I have spoken to.

19. *Rev. Michael M'Ginn. Examined by* Mr. KENNEDY.—I am a Roman Catholic clergyman at St. Alphonso's Chapel, Great Hamilton Street, Glasgow. I have been incumbent of that chapel for eight or nine years. Great Hamilton Street, where my chapel is situated, is quite convenient to Glasgow Green. There is just a row of houses between the street and the Green. Glasgow Green is, I believe, a great resort of Irishmen; indeed, of people of all sorts. It

is a resort of working men in general, as far as I know. The Jail Square is quite near the Green. I pass it frequently, and I always see it crowded—especially on Sundays. I have known the prisoner, Henry M'Cann, as one of my congregation pretty well for the last two years. He has belonged to the congregation, so far as I know, for some six or seven years; but during the last two years he has taken a much more active part in the affairs of the congregation, and has been connected with the Total Abstinence Society in the parish. The Total Abstinence Society is one to which men come and take the pledge on the Monday evenings. We have a hall where they assemble during the week; and they have weekly meetings on the Mondays, for the purpose of giving an account of the income during the week, and also for the purpose of admitting new members. The hall is at 146 London Street, on the top flat. That is also in very close proximity to Glasgow Green, and quite near the chapel. The society is in connection with my congregation. There are no female members in the society. It is for men only. I can pledge women as well as men, but we have not them in the same regulated form as we have the men. The women do not meet at the hall I have mentioned; they meet in a large room attached to the school in Greendyke Street. Henry M'Cann had to do with the women's society in this way, that he was sent down from the men's society very often to take a note of the names of the women who wished to take the pledge on the Monday evenings,—enter their names in a book, and give each one a medal. When the women took the pledge and got the medal, they had to pay a subscription of 6d. That was the amount of the subscription of members; but occasionally less than that was given. I have visited M'Cann in his own house. His house was clean and comfortable for a man in his position. He seemed to be in pretty regular employment. From my knowledge of him, as one of my congregation, and from my intercourse with him, I formed the opinion that he was a decent man for his position in life—sober and industrious. So far as I saw, the man had a kindly disposition. I think he was a regular attender at church. The hours of service at St. Alphonso's Chapel on Sundays are eight, half-past nine, and eleven in the morning, and seven o'clock in the evening. The weekly meeting of the Men's Total Abstinence Society was held on Mondays at nine o'clock in the evening. I nearly always attended these meetings, unless I was away on vacation or the like. I frequently saw M'Cann there during the spring and summer of 1882, and since that time. What I have said as to his regular attendance at church applies to the last two years.

Evidence for Patrick Drum.

20. *Mrs. Isabella Drum or O'Brien*. Examined by Mr. GUTHRIE.—I am a daughter of Patrick Drum. My husband is a French polisher, and we live at 118 Rose Street. I remember the explosion at the gasworks in January of this year. I was living, at that time, at 118 Rose Street, along with my father. I lived there from the time of my marriage until the 1st of June last. I remember that night

quite well, because the gas went out when my husband was reading the paper to my father. My father can neither read nor write. When the gas went out, my father sent me to the woman next door to tell her the gas had gone out. This would be about ten or half-past ten o'clock at night. He asked me to see if the gas had gone out next door. The house I went to was Mrs. Stewart's. Mrs. Stewart is here to-day. When I was rapping at the door, Mrs. Stewart came out and told me that her gas was out also. I roared into my father that Mrs. Stewart's gas was out also, and he told me to go down to the baker's, as he was in the habit of putting lighted coals on the pipes in the close. I went down and found there were no lighted coals on the pipes. I then went back to my father again, and he sent me for a candle. The lights in the street were out, and I told my father that when I came in. He went to bed that night about half-past eleven. My mother is alive, but she is in feeble health, and my father has been in bad health for four or five years. He went to bed before I went. No one went out of the house that night. I lay in the room, and I was next the door, but I did not hear any one going out. If any one had gone out, I would have heard him quite well. My father has been in bad health for some time. He has been bad with his heart and with his breath, and he had a sore leg at one time. His leg swelled, and he had to go to the Infirmary and get bandages for that. He was very often confined in the house. About a week or a fortnight before the explosion took place, he was confined to the house with illness, but he had recovered and was out on the day the explosion took place. He is a dealer in clothes. He buys old clothes and sells them to people to make them up. He has followed that business regularly since I remember, when he was in health. I have often had to go with him, on account of his feeble state of health, to carry some clothes for him, as he was not fit to manage them. I have seen him sitting down on stairheads from weakness. My father went to chapel regularly every Sunday when he was in health. He went to ten o'clock mass. He never went out in the evenings in winter; but in summer he would go out for a little walk, and then come straight home again.

21. *Henry O'Brien. Examined by* Mr. LYELL.—I am a French polisher and the husband of the last witness. I was married on the 16th of February 1881, and lived with the prisoner Drum in family until June last. I remember the evening of the explosion at the gasometer. I was reading the paper to Mr. Drum at the time. I was sitting next the fire in the kitchen reading the paper, and suddenly the gas went out. We were quite alarmed, and Mr. Drum went behind the door to see what was wrong with the meter; and afterwards he told Bella, my wife, to go down for a candle. She went for the candle, and when she returned she said the gases in the street were out. I remember quite distinctly that Mr. Drum was there all that time. I went to bed that night about an hour afterwards. I think this took place between ten and eleven o'clock. Mr. Drum has been in bad health for three years to my knowledge. He had a very sore leg at one time, and attended the Royal Infirmary to get bandages, and they cured the leg. It was better for a good while. After that he was bad with his chest and heart, and Dr. Rankine

attended him. In the winter time he never went out at all unless any person left a note for him to call at the house in connection with business. He was a hawker, and bought old clothes.

22. *Mrs. Cecilia M'Intyre or Stewart.* *Examined by* Mr. GUTHRIE.—I am the wife of Thomas Stewart, lithographic printer, Glasgow, and live at 118 Rose Street, next door to Patrick Drum. I remember the night when the explosion took place at the gasometer. The gas went out, and immediately after a knock came to the door. I went to the door and found it was Mrs. O'Brien, the wife of the last witness. I had a conversation with her. After that I heard her father, Patrick Drum, telling her to go down-stairs and see if the baker had been putting anything on the pipe at the close. The light in the stair went out that night also. I was not out on the street, and cannot say if the lights were out there. Mr. Drum lived beside me for about three and a half years. I considered him a very quiet, respectable man, and a decent neighbour. I used to hear the door of his house locked between half-past nine and ten o'clock every night.

23. *Francis Canning.* *Examined by* Mr. LYELL.—I am a wholesale clothes dealer in Saltmarket, Glasgow, and formerly I had a place in Steel Street also. I do a very extensive business, the largest of the kind in Glasgow. I know the prisoner Drum. I have known him about twelve years. He is a hawker, and used to come and sell clothes to me. He would come to my place of business sometimes three and four times in a week. He had considerable dealings with me. He always bore a very good character, and was respected by all who knew him. I remember about twelve months ago his legs and feet were swelled, and I have noticed that he has been failing for a while back. He complained several times of having difficulty in coming up my stair.

24. *Dr. John Francis Sutherland.* *Examined by* Mr. LYELL.—I am prison surgeon, Glasgow. I have had occasion to attend the prisoner Drum since his apprehension. He was placed on the sick list some time about the middle of November. The day after his admission to the prison he was very weak, and he was allowed to take less exercise; he was allowed to walk in the inner instead of the larger ring. In November he was seriously ill with bronchitis and weakness of the heart. The weak action of his heart I believe to be due, in a man of his time of life, to fatty degeneration. I should say his illness was chronic, with acute periods. I had considerable difficulty in getting him to understand my questions. I thought he was a man of low intelligence. The affection of his heart would cause his legs to swell.

GENERAL EVIDENCE IN DEFENCE.

25. *James Cogans.* *Examined by* Mr. M'LENNAN.—I reside in Muirhouse Lane, South Side, Glasgow. Muirhouse Lane is just opposite the gasometer where the explosion took place in January last, and runs between Maxwell Road and Lilybank Road. My house is the

farthest up the lane in the direction of Maxwell Road. Between my house and the corner of Maxwell Road there is a space of about sixty yards with no houses on it. There is a yard in that space, which is railed off from the road by a fence some feet in height. I have a piggery at the back of my house, and at the time when the explosion took place I had about fifty pigs. I have a good right to remember the explosion; I hope I will never hear the like again. On the night of the explosion I was working at the end of my house, outside the piggery, and close to the fence between the end of my house and the corner of Maxwell Road. There was only the paling between me and Muirhouse Lane. I was working there in and out most of the night. I began before it got dark, and I was working on at the time of the explosion. It was a beautiful, clear moonlight night, and, in addition to that, the place was illuminated by Dixon's blazes. I could see all around me quite well. It would be at the outside from seventy to eighty yards from where I was to where the tank blew out and burst. I could see the column where the explosion took place quite well. There was a small paling at the back of my house, and between it and the gaswork ground, and I had a wee garden just at the back of the house. That was the only obstruction there was between me and the gasometer. I could see over the paling as plain as I could see in the middle of the street. When I was working at the place I have mentioned on the night of the explosion, I did not see any one at or near the gasometer. I did not see anybody near it or running away from it shortly before the explosion took place. I was so near Muirhouse Lane that I could see everybody who went from Muirhouse Lane to Maxwell Road. There is a barricade across the lane, and only just entry for persons to walk by, and that barricade is just outside the paling where I was working. *Q.*—And you have a gate there into the lane? *A.*—I have a gate into the back side. I was in my yard at the time the explosion took place. The first men I saw that evening running out of Muirhouse Lane in the direction of Maxwell Road were Thomas Butler and Edward Hughes. Their clothes were on fire, and I cried to Butler to wait until I would put them out, but he ran away like a man mad, back into his own house after having come out. He cried out, "My weans are all burnt." The next man I saw passing was a man named Fearns, who lived beside me, and a man named Stoddart. They came running into the lane for their lives. They ran to their own houses, which were inside of mine. Fearns' windows were smashed. In about ten minutes after the explosion there were hundreds of people there. I did not see any strange men running out of Muirhouse Lane into Maxwell Road that night about the time the explosion took place, or at all, and there was only about three feet wide opposite me where they could pass out of the lane. *Q.*—Was it possible that two men could have run out of Muirhouse Lane into Maxwell Road about that time without you seeing them? *A.*—They could not.

26. *Patrick M'Kenna. Examined by* Mr. KENNEDY.—I am a holeborer at Dubs' in the High Street, Glasgow. I have lived in Glasgow for some years. I have known the prisoner Henry M'Cann for a considerable time. I have visited him at his house. I attend St.

Alphonso's Chapel, and I have seen him there. I have frequently seen him during the last two years on Glasgow Green on Sunday. Sunday is a great day for people on the Green. I never heard about M'Cann holding religious disputations. Q.—Or being present at religious disputations on the Green? A.—No. Q.—Have you been with the prisoner listening to debates between Mr. Harry Alford Long and some Catholics? A.—Yes. I know George Hughes, one of the witnesses in this case, by eyesight, but not otherwise. I did not see him here yesterday nor the day before. I never saw him on the Green along with the prisoner M'Cann and others. I have seen him on the Green on Sundays. I remember one Sunday night in March last being down at the Green, and coming along near Nelson's Monument with Henry M'Cann. There was no woman along with M'Cann. There was no one along with him but myself. I remember of a man coming up and speaking to M'Cann. He said he would do for him. M'Cann and I were coming along, and the man shook his fist at M'Cann, and said he would do for him. Q.—He said, "I will do for you"? A.—Yes. It was at M'Cann the man shook his fist. M'Cann asked me did I hear what the man said, and he laughed. The man passed on. [Shown George Hughes.] That is the man who passed us on that occasion, and shook his fist at M'Cann.

Cross-examined by the LORD ADVOCATE.—I did not think much about what took place at the time. There was no one else present.

Examined by Mr. BAXTER.—I know a man John Ward, a fish dealer, by sight. I never saw him on the Green with Hughes.

27. *John Ward.* *Examined by* Mr. BAXTER.—I am a fish dealer in Govan Street, Glasgow. I know a man named George Hughes. Q.—Do you remember that man making a strange statement to you on the Green not very long ago? A.—It was not to me he made it altogether. [Shown George Hughes.] That is the man to whom I refer. I remember meeting him on the Green after the accused had been apprehended. There were four or five of us standing together on the Jail Square, at the foot of Saltmarket, when Hughes came down the street, and a man stopped him and asked if he had been up in the office. He said he had, and the man asked him what they had taken him up for. He said he was going to lie in under no man's dirt, and went there to tell what he knowed—£500 was not to be lifted every Monday morning in the syver. Q.—Did he say anything more than that he would tell what he knowed? A.—He said he would tell what he knowed and what he did not know. These were the words he used; and he walked away then.

Cross-examined by the LORD ADVOCATE.—Q.—Why did you not put in the second set of words when you were asked the question first? A.—I forgot it. Q.—What brought it to your memory again? A.—When I was asked. Q.—Were these second words ever used? A.—Yes, they were. One of those who was present when Hughes said what I have stated was a young man M'Kenna,—the last witness. Unless he was deaf he could not help hearing what Hughes said. Hughes spoke so that you could hear him half roads across the square. The four or five who were there could all hear. I don't know their names; I cannot tell their names. *Q.*—Were you talking to four or five men whom you did not know? *A.*—Yes, I was; and I am talking to hundreds I don't know unless by eyesight. One of the men I was speaking to was Pat Byrnes. He heard what Hughes said. He is a dealing man. Another man who was present was named Skillan. These are the only ones whose names I know. The others heard what Hughes said also. I am not a friend of the prisoners. I often met them in Jail Square, and I sometimes went about with them. I was not a friend of Kearney, but I remember seeing him once. I don't remember ever seeing him with the prisoners. I never met the prisoners in M'Ginn's public-house in Bridgegate, but I have gone in along with one or two of them into it. I never saw Kearney along with the prisoner M'Cann, to my knowledge. *Q.*—Did you ever subscribe in M'Ginn's public-house to a fund which the prisoners were raising, called the Defence Fund? *A.*—Not to my knowledge. I have subscribed twenty or thirty different times to charitable purposes in the Jail Square and in the street. I have heard a Defence Fund mentioned on behalf of the prisoners which George Hughes himself subscribed to. That fund was raised about a fortnight or ten days after the prisoners were apprehended. *Q.*—Then George Hughes did not want them to be convicted? *A.*—I cannot tell you. *Q.*—Did you not at any time before the explosions subscribe to a fund the prisoners were raising, called the Defence Fund? *A.*—Not to my knowledge. *Q.*—May you have done it without knowledge? *A.*—I may; but not to my knowledge.

Re-examined.—I have never subscribed to the fund to defend the prisoners; but it was allowed to be a fund to defend them that Hughes subscribed to. At the request of Mr. Shaughnessy, who acts for the prisoners, I made an attempt to find the addresses of the men who were speaking to me when Hughes came up in Jail Square. I found out that Byrnes' address was 12 Crown Street, but I could not get Skillan's address.

Mr. RHIND.—This closes the evidence for the defence.

THE LORD ADVOCATE'S ADDRESS.

THE LORD ADVOCATE.—May it please your Lordships.— Gentlemen of the Jury, you have now heard, and I am sure you have given very careful and patient attention to the voluminous evidence which has been laid before you in this very important case—a case of very great importance, both to the public and to the unfortunate prisoners who are placed at the bar; and it is my duty at this stage to state the grounds on which I shall ask at your hands a verdict of guilty against the prisoners upon the evidence which has been led. Before proceeding, however, to examine the evidence, it is right that I should shortly explain to you the nature of the charges, so that you may the more readily follow the application of the evidence to those charges. If you will have the kindness to take the indictment, you will find that there are two charges or groups of charges contained in it. There is first what we call a statutory charge under the Act of 1848, entitled "An Act for the Better Security of the Crown and Government of the United Kingdom;" and then there is a common law charge, as to which I shall say a few words afterwards; but perhaps you will kindly follow on the first page of the indictment, while I read the clause under which the statutory charge is preferred, and I shall then explain it to you in a very few words. The third section of the Act provides [reads]. Now that is the section of the statute under which this charge is preferred, and I do not think I need enter into any detailed criticism of its terms. It is enough to say that the part of it with which you are more immediately concerned is the part nearest to the foot of the first page (see page 2), and that the general effect of the statute is to make criminal the compassing, imagining, devising, or inventing things which shall compel Her Majesty or Parliament to change their counsels, and shall give—what is important and what you will keep in view—evidence of that intention by overt acts. That, I think, is shortly the sum and substance of this statutory provision. Now, gentlemen, the importance of keeping that in view is this, that in general it is not in law a crime merely to entertain particular intentions. Generally speaking, if these intentions do not result in some sort of act, it is not a crime merely to entertain them; but in this section of the Act of 1848 there is a peculiarity, inasmuch as the intention is made the substance of the crime, provided that intention is manifested by certain specified kinds of overt acts, such as by uttering or declaring by publishing any printing or writing or by open and advised speaking—that means, speaking that is not merely rash or hasty speaking—or by any other overt act or deed. So that the two things required in order to entitle you to find that this statutory crime has been committed are, in the first place, that you should be satisfied that intentions of the particular class imputed to these prisoners were entertained by them; and secondly, that they should have manifested these intentions by some overt acts. An overt act, as you know, simply means an open act, and lest there should be any doubt as to what the meaning of an overt or open act is, you have illustrations given of the kind of overt or open acts by which the intention may be manifested, those that are given, being by printing or writing or by open or advised speaking or any other act, meaning of course any other overt act. So you see it is not necessary in order to the statutory crime being committed, that a blow shall have been struck or a force have been placed in the field, or any act of violence in the ordinary sense committed. It is enough—of course, I am stating the law subject to direction from the bench—but, subject to that direction, I state to you that upon a just construction of this statute, it is enough if a person is proved by some open manifestation to have cherished the particular class of intention which the statute describes, and I only say further upon that point, that if you shall come to be satisfied that there was a conspiracy amongst the prisoners at the bar, or any two or more of them, to carry out by the use of explosives the kind of criminal intention imputed in the statute, that is, either to compel Her Majesty or the Houses of Parliament to change their counsels with respect to Ireland, then such a conspiracy or compassing would have been an overt act within the meaning of this statute, even although there had been nothing done in the way of using the explosives at all. That is an important point, and therefore I should ask your Lordships' attention to a decision by the highest tribunal in the land, I mean the House of Lords, in which upon an appeal from Ireland a ruling was given to the effect which I have just explained. Your Lordships will find the case I refer to, being the case of "Mulcahy against the Queen" [June 29 and 30, and July 3 and 10, 1868], in L. R. III., Eng. and Ir. App. p. 306. There were various points decided in that case, but the one with which we are here concerned was the rejection of a construction of the statute on which it had been contended that something in the nature of violence—an act other than the mere making of a conspiracy and agreement—was requisite in order to constitute the statutory offence. The decision was given in that case in the sense I have explained, it being laid down,—

LORD MURE.—Where is this?

LORD ADVOCATE.—At page 306 of the L. R. vol. III., Eng. and Ir. App. It was laid down that while conspiracy cannot exist without the consent of two or more persons, their agreement is an "act in advancement of the intention which each of them has conceived in his mind." So that is a decision by the House of Lords, that an agreement of the nature which we have here charged is an overt act within the sense and meaning of the statute, in advancement, and is evidence of the intention which is here imputed. Now I mention that for the purpose of showing what we mean when we allege in what is called the minor proposition of the indictment—when we set out the things which we undertake to prove were done by the prisoners at the bar, we say that this was a crime in so far as all and each or one or more of you, being members of a secret society having for or amongst its objects the subverting of authority and constraining a change of the counsel and will of Parliament, and acting in concert with certain other persons, did prepare certain explosives, and so on. That is an allegation of purpose and intention. Then there is a further allegation on page 4 at the middle of the page (see page 4), practically an allegation of the criminal intention which is of the essence of the statutory offence. Then the way in which the overt acts are alleged you will find to be that they "did express, utter, or declare by the following overt acts or deeds or one or more of them," the first of which is a conspiracy "for and concerning the secret purchasing or procuring of chemical or other materials to be used in the preparation or manufacture of dynamite, lignin-dynamite, or other explosive substance or substances, and the secret preparation or manufacture of dynamite, lignin-dynamite, or other explosive substance or substances, and for or concerning the clandestine laying or placing and exploding by you or one or more of you, or by your agents and abettors to the prosecutor unknown, of the said dynamite, lignin-dynamite, or other explosive substance or substances at or near public buildings, or buildings used for the service of the public or other buildings or works in or near Glasgow, with the wicked and felonious intent and design of destroying or seriously injuring the said buildings or works, and of destroying the lives, persons, and property of the lieges, and with the further wicked and felonious intent and design by means of such explosions and the terror and alarm to be thereby created in the mind of Her said Majesty to change her measures or counsels, or to intimidate or overawe both Houses, or either House of Parliament." [See page 5.]

LORD JUSTICE-CLERK.—Do you mean it would have been sufficient without overt acts if they had agreed to use these things?

LORD ADVOCATE.—Yes, that is my point; I am going to explain to the Jury that if no explosive had ever been applied to any building, if they are satisfied upon the evidence that a conspiracy to this effect, as alleged, existed, that is an overt act manifesting intention within the meaning of the section.

LORD JUSTICE-CLERK.—Refer me to the part of the indictment where this is charged.

LORD ADVOCATE.—Your lordship will find that allegation of intention at large in pages 2 and 3, and you will find in the middle of page 4, that, using the statutory words, we say that the prisoners, who are all named, "did all and each or one or more of you" do certain things. Now your lordship will find that the first overt act we allege is simply conspiring, and that was not objected to as irrelevant.

LORD JUSTICE-CLERK.—"Wickedly and feloniously meeting and conspiring together." [See top of page 5.]

LORD ADVOCATE.—Yes, to the effect set out. The allegation of that conspiracy ends in the middle of page 5 [see page 5], and we simply charge the conspiracy as an overt act which is evidence of the criminal intention. Then the second overt act which we charge is the blowing up of the gasometer; the third is the attempt to blow up the Possil Bridge; and the fourth is the blowing up of the railway shed. Now, I pray you, gentlemen, to keep that in view, because you will see that in some aspects of the case it is of great importance. We allege, in short, that criminal intention was manifested by four acts—first, by entering into a conspiracy, which would have been enough, even if nothing had followed upon it; second, by blowing up the gasometer; third, by trying to blow up Possil Bridge; and fourth, by blowing up the railway shed. But what I wish you clearly to comprehend is that these last three overt acts were simply evidence of the intention in the same way as the first overt act, and accordingly, although I do not for one moment say it is unimportant—on the contrary, I say it is very important—that you should arrive at a conclusion on the question whether the prisoners had or had not to do with the actual blowing up—because if they had, that would be the clearest evidence of such conspiracy and intention—even if you should think that the evidence is insufficient as regards all or any of these explosions, to connect all or any of the prisoners with them, there would still remain sufficient ground for a finding of guilty under this statute, if you should come to be of opinion that the prisoners, or any two or more of them, had conspired to the effect which we allege.

LORD JUSTICE-CLERK.—It is a conspiracy to levy war.

LORD ADVOCATE.—Very much that, and it was held by the Lord Chief Justice Coleridge.

LORD JUSTICE-CLERK.—But how do you put it?

LORD ADVOCATE.—We do not use that particular expression, but it is substantially that. I put it thus, that if there is a conspiracy to put fear and terror, either upon Her Majesty, or the Houses of Parliament, or upon those whom Parliament represents, so as to compel those persons and bodies, that together constitute the legislature of this kingdom, to alter their counsels with respect to Ireland, then that is an overt act, and that is the act that we allege.

LORD JUSTICE-CLERK.—But that is not quite the phraseology of the Act, for it is either to deprive or depose Her Gracious Majesty, etc., or levy war against Her Majesty, Her heirs or successors, within any part of the United Kingdom, in order by force to compel them to change their measures; and therefore a levying of war, as I understand, but of course it must be constructive.

LORD ADVOCATE.—As your lordship well knows, it was a question raised repeatedly whether levying war required that armed force should be put in the field, and the contention that it did was overruled.

LORD JUSTICE-CLERK.—Levying war is just subverting the laws by force.

LORD ADVOCATE.—It is simply subverting, as your lordship says, the laws by force instead of by legitimate means,—by reasoning, argument, persuasion,—appeals to the mind and conscience of the Queen and Parliament, and those who make Parliament—the people of this country. It is seeking to put fear and force upon them to get the laws altered in that way instead of in the other. Now that is the substance, turned into popular language, of the conspiracy which we allege; and while I shall maintain to you upon the evidence, that it is sufficiently proved that at all events some if not all of these prisoners were concerned in carrying out the conspiracy by blowing up the buildings, or some of them, I pray you to note, that even if you should think that there was no proof with respect to any of the explosions, if you should be of opinion that the conspiracy is proved, then that is enough. That, then, is the effect of the statutory charge. But in the law of Scotland it has generally been found—better, perhaps, than south of the Tweed—that there is enough of native vigour to meet any dangerous public crime or offence without the help of statute, and, accordingly, there is a common law charge here, which you will find set out in the middle of page 2 [see page 3], that, "albeit by the laws of this, and of every other well-governed realm, the wickedly and feloniously conspiring to effect an alteration of the laws and constitution of the realm by force and violence is a crime." Now, although I do not think you will have any difficulty in understanding the nature of the statutory charge, after the explanations I have given you, I feel sure you will encounter no technical difficulty upon the charge I have now read. It is couched in the plainest and most popular language, and what we allege in it is the same thing as we have alleged under the other and statutory charge. We allege conspiracy almost in the same words as before, to procure an alteration of the laws, particularly with respect to Ireland, by putting force or constraint upon the Queen or upon Parliament; and then that that conspiracy was carried out by the blowing up of the buildings. But there again I may say to you—again subject to the direction you will receive from the bench—that if you should be satisfied on the common law charge, as on the statutory charge, that there was that conspiracy, even although you should think that it is not proved that the prisoners were concerned in carrying it out by the actual use of explosives, it would still be your duty to find a verdict under that charge. Now I do not know that there is any other point that I need dwell upon, in explanation of the indictment.

LORD JUSTICE-CLERK.—If the conspiracy and object and purport of it are proved, that is a sufficiently overt act to satisfy the statute.

LORD ADVOCATE.—Yes; and I say in like manner, it is a conspiracy enough to satisfy the common law charge.

LORD JUSTICE-CLERK.—Because it is an illegal conspiracy.

LORD ADVOCATE.—Yes; such a conspiracy as is here alleged. But while I say there might be a question under the statute, as to whether an overt act did not mean something like putting force in the field, no such point could have been raised under the common law charge.

LORD JUSTICE-CLERK.—Whatever the ultimate act upon it was, it was a crime in itself. It was an illegal compact, and constituted a crime, although it never went any farther.

LORD ADVOCATE.—That is so, and as your Lordships are well

aware, the point was settled in Scotland in the case of James Cumming and others, High Court, Nov. 7, 1848, J. Shaw, p. 17. I think, therefore, gentlemen, I need not say anything more about the indictment, and I now proceed to examine the evidence which has been adduced before you. I may say at the outset, that I am sensible you must have felt that the evidence in the case is somewhat detailed, and perhaps, sitting as you did and hearing it coming out from one witness after another, a little difficult at first sight to follow. But I hope that, now that you have listened to the whole of it, with such aid as it will be in my power to give, you will have little difficulty in applying it to the facts of the case. You must be well aware that a conspiracy, of which it is the essence that it is secret, occult, and hidden, is not easily proved by direct evidence. It is very seldom that the Crown or those charged with the duty of laying before a Jury a case of this kind are able to adduce direct evidence of the conspiracy. We have, however, some such evidence here. But even although there were no direct evidence of the conspiracy, it would be for you to judge, whether on the whole facts that you have had laid before you, the reasonable and fair inference is not that a conspiracy to the effect alleged was actually entered into. And the more, I might almost say, that the evidence is minute and detailed, the more that it comes from different quarters and from different persons, the more almost one might say that it is circumstantial, it grows stronger, because you then must be satisfied that it is not merely a statement of some person or persons who might be mistaken or might not be speaking the truth, and conviction is carried to the mind as the inevitable result of many and various proved facts.—Before I proceed to examine the more material parts of the evidence, I think there is one part of it as to which I may say a very few words and then pass it by altogether, as a matter which does not admit of controversy—I mean the facts relating to the three explosions which occurred on the night of the 20th and morning of the 21st of January. Now what you have heard proved to have occurred on that night and morning was of a very significant kind. On the same night and morning, within three or four hours—within an interval not exceeding, I think, three hours—three explosions occurred, two of them very violent, and another less so only because it was a failure. Well, to what were these explosions due? To what physical agency were they attributable? I think you can have very little doubt that they were all due to substantially the same cause— to what we may popularly call dynamite—to some compound of the nitro-glycerine class. It has been suggested that the gasometer was not blown up by dynamite or other nitro-glycerine compound. That I contest. Gentlemen, I think it would be almost trifling to go into that matter after the evidence you have heard. You heard Colonel Majendie and others explain the nature of the resulting injuries. There was a great rent in the outside of the gasometer close to the column. That column itself was cracked. Large numbers of fragments of iron, individually small, had been sent flying about, and what is quite conclusive upon this matter is that these fragments were shot from without the gasometer inwards and broken up into small bits. If the gas had been ignited and burst inside the gasometer it would have shattered it outwards, and would not have broken it into such small pieces. But, you will recollect, you saw some of the fragments which were exhibited, and you heard Colonel Majendie describe how inside the gasometer, opposite where the rent in the column was, he had found a nut actually shot into and sticking in the metal on the opposite side. I need not say what degree of force it must have required to detach a nut,—which no doubt was an inside nut where the rent occurred,—what degree of force it must have been which, striking an outside plate and rending the plate, would detach the nut from the bolt and send it over as if it had been shot out of a gun or cannon, so that it would stick into the metal on the other side. There were other instances of the same kind, but that was the most distinct. Then you saw some of the bits of iron, and you observed how they were pitted in a way which indicated that some very violent explosive had been applied to them. That, Colonel Majendie explained, was the distinctive appearance due to the bursting of a nitro-glycerine compound, and the breaking up of the tin or zinc box in which it had been contained into such minute fragments that they are really like pellets fired out of a gun, and acted with such force as to indent the iron. You had a number of other indications—the column cracked outwards, the notion being that the dynamite was placed between the column and the gasometer—making it clear it was not an explosion of gas. But then, you will recollect also that Colonel Majendie said this,—and he has not been contradicted on either of these points,—that it is a known physical fact that coal gas in the condition in which it was in that gasometer will not explode at all. The kind of gas which was there burns. When we turn on our gas it does not explode—it burns, and so it would have burned if a rent had been made and it had come out into the air, and a light had been applied, just as it did when the dynamite had broken it, because after the explosion there was a great blaze. There was not another explosion or succession of explosions. The first explosion did not exhaust the gas, and there was a burning until the gas was burned out. Now it is quite true, as Colonel Majendie explained, that under certain conditions and with certain proportions of air and gas you may have an explosion. Of that we have known instances. But these conditions could not exist inside the gasometer, he said, nor could they exist outside the gasometer, because the moment the gas got out at any kind of rent it would spread in the air—there would be such a large volume of atmospheric air outside, that it would reduce the gas below that particular proportion which makes it explosive. Accordingly the kind of place in which gas explodes is where it gets into a confined space, where it so happens that the gas and air are mingled in particular proportions. But except in that condition it won't explode, and therefore it was physically impossible in this case that it should explode. It was suggested by my friends on the other side that perhaps the gas might have gathered in the pillar. But Colonel Majendie answered that conclusively. He said the pillar was open at the top; and I do not see how it was to get into the pillar. But then if it did, it would have got out, so that that theory must be altogether abandoned. You, no doubt, will bear in mind there were two brass articles found, viz. a brass cap on the top of the gasometer, and a brass tube near the foot of the shattered column, which, although not thought important at the time, were afterwards identified as being practically the same as those which were used for the Possil Bridge attempted explosion and inside the infernal machines found at Liverpool; so that, on the whole, I leave that point without further observation than that I think you will have no difficulty in arriving at the conclusion that dynamite was the cause of the gasometer explosion. Well, gentlemen, this explosion happened about a quarter past ten o'clock, and very singularly, on the same night about twelve o'clock, when Adam Barr, the artilleryman, and his friends were going home, they found a box on Possil Bridge. That box you have seen, and I do not ask you to look at it again. It is an ordinary tin bonnet-box. He proceeded to open it. It was, of course, darkish, but there was a certain amount of moonlight, and after he had been looking at it a little, a slight explosion occurred, after what he described as a fizzing; then a second explosion took place, the box was turned over on its side, and its contents smouldered away. The explanation of all that is now perfectly plain. We know from analysis that what was in that box was lignin-dynamite, that is to say, a kind of dynamite not lawful in this country—because all explosives need to be licensed in this country—not useful for any commercial purpose; but easily made because the ingredients of it are easily got. Ordinary dynamite requires as the inert base an infusorial earth commonly called kieselguhr, but it is not sold in the market, and is only imported in quantity by the two great firms which make the dynamite lawfully used in this country. But that was the stuff. It was a poor dynamite, because it appears only to have had 20 or 25 per cent. of nitro-glycerine, and 75 per cent. of sawdust. But dynamite it was. Probably the poorness of the composition arose from the want of complete knowledge, on the part of those who compounded it, or from their having run out of materials; but as to that, it is not necessary that we should inquire. Well, at the time, Barr did not notice anything further about the box and its contents, but a constable going past later took up the very strange apparatus which you have seen, and have now become familiar with, and which I hold in my hand [No. 8, a brass tube]. That, we now understand from the explanations given to us, is an apparatus not used for any other purpose, except for exploding infernal machines. There is no man whom we have been able to find, and there is no man whom the prisoners have been able to find, we are entitled to assume, who can say that a thing of that sort is used for any lawful purpose. The men of skill who have been examined tell us that it had been used— that there had been sulphuric acid in one part, and chlorate of potash and sugar in another. Now we know from what was found in Liverpool, that these are the things of which a mixture is made, for lighting explosive dynamite for illegal purposes. You combine together the chlorate of potash and sugar, you tie round the inner part with paper thicker or thinner, with more or fewer folds, according as you wish it to act slowly or quickly, and then you put sulphuric acid into the tap, open the tap and go away. You see that that apparatus can be plunged into the dynamite—no light needed—nobody sees how you do it—all in the dark. You have simply to turn the tap and let the acid eat through the paper, and an explosion will take place, in time, according as you make the paper thicker or thinner. I think we have the explanation of what happened to Adam Barr in this, that the fizzing he first heard was probably the acid getting in amongst the chlorate of potash and sugar—that was probably the first little explosion— and then when it got to the detonator, which is put into the end of the apparatus, that probably was the second explosion. But whether there was a detonator, or whether it was a certain amount of dynamite which exploded, is not material, because, most providentially, the great body of the dynamite did not explode. But I think you can have no doubt that that was simply—to use popular language—an infernal machine laid down upon the middle of that bridge, and in the middle of the night. Now I ask you, gentlemen, for what purpose but one could it have been left in that place? It is inconceivable that it was for a lawful or innocent purpose—none has been suggested. For what purpose but one could any human being be in possession of such mechanism? There has no lawful purpose been suggested. If you come to the conclusion that it was left there for the purpose of destroying or damaging that bridge, then I think you will be of opinion, that whoever left it there was about the most wicked of mankind. Whether they precisely knew the quality of the dynamite, or whether they thought it would succeed in breaking the bridge, and flooding a populous part of the great city of Glasgow with the water of the canal, is a matter we need not inquire into. But whether they were right or wrong in supposing that the intended explosion would bring about such disastrous results is not material. It has been proved to you that, poor as the dynamite was, if it had gone off, it would have done great damage. You see its power from the explosion at the gasometer. I therefore say there is absolute evidence that in all the three explosions of that night, there was ingenuity of the most wicked kind brought to bear, for the injury of property, and possibly of life. Then what about the third explosion? That took place about an hour or three-quarters of an hour later still. About a quarter past one the shed at the Caledonian Railway Station was blown up; and there again, it has been proved by Colonel Majendie, and there has been no attempt made to contradict it, that the shed was clearly destroyed by dynamite, or other nitro-glycerine compound, and nothing else. The notion of gas is excluded; there was no gas there. The shed had been disused, and there was no gas there. But gas would not have done it. The floor was blown down, and the other parts of the building were blown up, and the judgment of Colonel Majendie is that it must have been a nitro-glycerine compound; because he found bits of metal, which he thinks were parts of the tin case which had contained the dynamite, driven into the wood, in some cases, to the depth of an inch. I think you will have little difficulty in concluding that that explosion, like the others, was due to dynamite, and of course to dynamite maliciously used. It is, then, a very singular thing, that in three places in one night, and within two hours, these things should have happened; and you will have very little difficulty in drawing the conclusion, as reasonable men, that it was the same organization who did these three things. Such things do not happen by way of coincidence. They have not happened before, and they have not happened since, and I hope they won't happen again. But when you find three such things occurring in one city in one night, I think you can have no hesitation in reaching the conclusion that in pursuance of some conspiracy—I am not saying at this moment who it was—some man or men did these things for the purpose of injuring property, and either injuring life, or producing alarm in that great city. I pass from these matters as not susceptible of controversy. There is another matter to which I ought to refer in passing—some questions Mr. Rhind put, but which I hope he did not mean to adhere to,— and that is the suggestion that the blowing up of the Caledonian shed might possibly have been due to the strike. Now, I am sure, you would not believe,—and none of us will believe,—in the absence of evidence, that a body of railway servants, even if they had a dispute with their masters, would have done any such thing. We are not accustomed to that in Scotland, and I do not think you would readily accept such a suggestion. But it happens that the strike was over on the Saturday, hours and hours before the explosion occurred. So, that being the sole suggestion with regard to the shed, it may be dismissed from your minds, as I daresay you will also dismiss from your minds the idea that the gasometer was blown up by gas. We start, therefore, with this, as I submit, a proved and incontrovertible fact—that there was some agency at work in Glasgow that night, and that it must have been an agency not dealing with the property of one person, but dealing with the property of more, and bent upon causing alarm, if not destroying life, in the city, for purposes which I think we shall afterwards see clearly enough. Of course, what I have said down to this time does not in the least bring any of the prisoners into contact with this evidence. I have merely proved that three dynamite explosions happened that night; but I am sure the mere fact of these things occurring would not in your minds lead, without reasonable evidence, to your connecting the prisoners, or any one of them, with those occurrences. No mere general feeling that somebody must be punished would influence your minds without sufficient evidence, and I would not ask you to arrive at any such conclusion. But, gentlemen, if we can prove that side by side with these explosions there was a conspiracy in Glasgow— that the members of that conspiracy had been purchasing and obtaining explosives, for the purpose of destroying buildings, with the view of striking terror and alarm, and causing the Queen and Parliament to change their counsels, in terms of the indictment— then, I think, the connection between the two simultaneously occurring things would be easily established. And now I propose to ask your attention to the evidence by which, I submit to you, is established against all the prisoners—although against some more and some less, yet against all of them sufficiently—the fact that they were members of an organization or conspiracy having the objects which are set out in this indictment. Now the first evidence upon that matter that has to be considered is the testimony of Hughes. Of course, gentlemen, if you believe Hughes, the conspiracy is proved. You will no doubt be asked to disregard his evidence; and I do not for a moment say that Hughes, without corroboration, would be sufficient to establish so grave a charge. But I do submit this to you, that Hughes' evidence is not to be rejected without cause shown. Still less is Hughes' evidence to be rejected, if you shall think that it fits in and agrees with the other evidence in the case, converging from many quarters, and upon which no adverse comment can be made. I hope to be able to show to you that Hughes' evidence is amply corroborated—that there is corroboration of many and various kinds—and, indeed, that you might almost have enough to prove conspiracy without his evidence at all. It will be said, no doubt, that Hughes is an informer, and that he broke away from those with whom he was in association; and this is perfectly true, and has no doubt to be kept in view by you in considering his evidence. But what you will have to make up your minds upon is this, whether, after you have seen him and heard him, that is sufficient cause for rejecting his evidence, if it is otherwise corroborated. No doubt, breaking away from an organization renders a person liable to observation; but I venture to say, gentlemen, that if the organization is of a criminal and illegal character, it is surely not wrong to break away from it; and if he came to think that he had had long enough to do with this conspiracy, and that it was getting into close quarters with violence and crime of a kind that he did not approve, and from which he shrank, I do not think you would blame him for parting from it, or for telling the truth in regard to it, in the interests of public justice. There is a great difference between informers according to the extent to which they have entered into crime, and I am perfectly content to leave it to your judgment, whether the extent to which Hughes had gone into this conspiracy was such as to make you disbelieve him when he says that he left it, and is now telling in the interests of public justice what had been going on within its circle. I now ask your attention, that you may have consecutively in your minds the story that Hughes tells; and I may say, gentlemen, that I propose to follow the order, first, of asking you to bear in mind the evidence of Hughes, and of the others bearing upon the conspiracy generally, without at this moment seeking to put together the evidence bearing upon each particular charge preferred. I propose to do that later, because it would not be wonderful, with ten prisoners in the indictment, if you had a little difficulty in applying the evidence to each. But I intend later to give you such aid as I can upon that point. In the meantime, I ask you to attend generally to the evidence we have of such a conspiracy as we have set out. Now you will recollect what Hughes' evidence amounts to. He says that about the first Monday of March, I think, he was sworn in a member of a secret society called a Ribbon Society. He was sworn in at the request of the prisoner Callaghan. Now this society had a meeting in Lennox's public-house, at which Devany, M'Cann, Drum, Kelly, and Casey were present. Then he gave the oath as far as he could recollect. It was read off a paper, and one point of it was that the members of this society were to stand together, if they got into any "habble" with the Government. Well, one does not see how people could get into a "habble" with the Government, or need to stand by each other in such a "habble," if there was not something illegal in the things that they contemplated doing. That seems to me—if you believe Hughes—almost to import a mark of some kind of illegality in this organization or society, although his evidence upon it is rather vague. He says not much happened for some time; but in order of dates, I think the next event I should ask you to recollect is, that Terence M'Dermott and James M'Cullagh were sworn in members of the society on the first Monday of June. Terence M'Dermott was not apparently a member down to that time, but he was sworn in on the first

Monday of June, and so was James M'Cullagh. Hughes says that down to about the beginning of July he heard nothing about dynamite, or about anything criminal in connection with this society. But at the time which he mentioned, the Tuesday or Wednesday before Glasgow Fair, when Devany, M'Cann, Callaghan, Drum, and Kearney, the signalman, were along with him in Jail Square, Kearney took away Callaghan and Drum aside with him. He said, "Some person wants to see you," and these two went away. That is what Hughes says, that Kearney took Callaghan and Drum away with him; and in about three-quarters of an hour Callaghan and Drum returned, and said they had met two fine gentlemen from America. Now, I am not to pause at this time for corroboration of that, but I daresay it is in your memory, that this is about the time Featherstone and the man named Johnston are proved by independent evidence to have come to this country, and to have appeared on the scene. That is the statement of Hughes, and apparently he did not know very much more about what happened at that time. The two fine gentlemen turned out to be Featherstone and Johnston. Then a few days after that, Callaghan (who seems to have taken rather an active part in this matter, as I shall show, all through,—he was always present at the swearing in, and invited people to join in the society—he invited Horan), according to Hughes, about the 6th or 7th of July, asked Hughes if he would allow a few jars of vitriol to be placed in his stable in Market Street, saying it would do him no harm. It is an important circumstance, that this request should have been made within a few days after the two fine gentlemen from America appeared on the scene. Hughes seems to have known at that time nothing about dynamite or its component parts, and he agreed to store the vitriol, as he was asked. The next thing that happened was a few days after, when—Hughes being with Callaghan, Devany, Drum, M'Cabe, Kelly, Casey, and Kearney—Callaghan, who again seemed to take the leading part, introduced Johnston to the group, as a gentleman from America, who had come over for the purpose of doing what Hughes in the box described as "larning" them to make dynamite, which you will of course understand to mean, teaching them to make dynamite. Johnston's object was disclosed then—he was introduced as one of two gentlemen who had come to teach the making of dynamite; and it was explained then that the object of the dynamite was to destroy buildings. That is Hughes' story. They then went to Hughes' stable in Market Street, where there was to be an experiment made, and Hughes described the way in which some white powder was put down, and one of them had a bottle of vitriol, and a stick was dipped into the vitriol and put on the powder, and it exploded. Casey, Drum, and Kearney were in the stable on that occasion. It was a small experiment which was made. According to the statement of Hughes, Johnston said, at that time, that they should endeavour to get some young men who had no ties or connection, and who, if caught, would have no dependants, actually to do the thing. I ask your attention to that, because you may have some conclusion to draw upon that subject, in regard to the evidence which has been led, as to some of the older men being at home on the night of the explosion: but it was quite evident that the notion of these people was, that while the older heads should plan and find the money, they should get as the actual operators some young men who had no dependants, and, if they were caught, there would be no great harm done. That at least is Hughes' story. Now there is another circumstance very significant and important in this matter, that Callaghan, within a very few days, asked Hughes, with his cart and pony, to get vitriol on the Wednesday following; and Hughes agreed to go, but seems afterwards to have repented. I think he said he went and found a young man who was to accompany him rather tipsy, and he did not like the business and went away home. That was on the 12th of July. Hughes says he went with Kelly to M'Dougall's public-house in Saltmarket, and there they found the young man rather the worse of drink, and Hughes went away home. But passing from this, gentlemen, and still continuing Hughes' narrative, no doubt you will keep in view, in considering his credibility, that afterwards we have other evidence that these men did begin to get vitriol—evidence as to which there is no doubt whatever. The next circumstance spoken to by Hughes was that about the 17th of July, Kelly came to Hughes' house and asked him to come out and speak, and when he did so he found outside Johnston, Kearney, and Casey. They asked him if he had any money, which Kelly said they wanted to buy stuff. Hughes says he had been entrusted with £2, 10s. by Drum, and apparently they were wanting some of it. I think he said he gave them half a sovereign, and that they then went away. Then, gentlemen, the next thing that Hughes says is, that on Sunday about the 23rd July, being in Jail Square with Callaghan, Devany, Drum, M'Cabe, M'Cann, Kelly, and Donnelly, Kearney, who had been a very active man, and who has disappeared, as you have heard, came there with Featherstone. The other man who had been on the scene on the previous Sunday was Johnston. Featherstone went on and explained the use of dynamite, according to Hughes, and said that it would give the Government a lesson. You see the importance of all references to the Government, and I pause upon this, to call attention to it as a fact that shows the design of dynamite being used—not malice to private persons, but to frighten the Government and give them a lesson. We have ample and independent evidence that Featherstone did come from America about that time. The nature of the contents of his pockets you have seen already, and I do not think I need to call

your attention to that again. That is Hughes' testimony. Of course
you see I am putting this before you, mainly for the purpose of
afterwards asking you to consider how far Hughes is corroborated.
On the afternoon of the same day, a certain number of them were
invited to go to what we call the Democratic Hall, but which
Hughes called the Gymnastic Hall, and which appears to go sometimes by one name and sometimes by the other. Hughes mentions
that Kearney, Callaghan, and Devany, went to the hall, and, thereafter, Featherstone delivered a lecture upon the use of dynamite.
They had plenty of dynamite prescriptions with them. Hughes
also says, that after a time he and M'Cabe were told that they
were no longer wanted. I think you must have seen traces
throughout that there were different degrees of confidence in this
conspiracy, and that they do not seem to have been quite sure
about Hughes. There appears to have been things they did not
wish him to hear. He was not invited to see Johnston the first
day, and M'Cabe and he, on this occasion, were no longer wanted,
and Drum, Callaghan, and Devany remained behind three-quarters
of an hour with Featherstone, in that hall; and he, Hughes,
afterwards learned that they had taken an oath. That brings us
down to about the 23rd July, according to the dates, as near as
I can gather. And then on the 30th, Hughes says, that being with
Callaghan, Devany, Drum, M'Cabe, Kelly, Casey, Donnelly, and
others in Jail Square, Callaghan made a collection of money. He
said it was for some poor woman, but Hughes afterwards found
that the money was to buy materials for making dynamite. He
said apparently that money would be coming from America. There
were £2 gathered on that occasion. We do not find, as far as I
can recollect, much in the month of August. Probably you will
think this important when I come to trace Featherstone's movements; but, according to Hughes, on the first Monday of September
there was a meeting in Lennox's public-house, where Callaghan,
Devany, Drum, M'Cann, and others, were present, and on that
occasion Johnston attended, and the man Horan was also present.
M'Cann on that occasion made a collection. The witness
Hughes says that Horan about that time—the Sunday after the
17th—told him he was going to leave the society, because his
priest had told him it was wrong to be in this society, and he had
better leave. Now, that is just what Horan himself told us did
happen, and there you find a plain corroboration of Hughes' statement. Towards the end of September, Hughes says that Callaghan,
Devany, Drum, and Hughes himself being in Jail Square, Johnston
came and said complaints were being made about the pipes in the
house where the stuff was being manufactured, and that it must
be removed; and most of the party went away in the direction of
Townhead. Now, the suggestion we make upon that is, that they
went to Terence M'Dermott's house in Dobbie's Loan, where we
have proof that in the end of September there had been com-

plaints about the pipes, although that is suggested to have been due to another cause. But it is not immaterial on the question of Hughes' credibility. About the end of October there appears to have been a quarrel between Hughes and M'Cann, and on that occasion M'Cann struck Hughes.

LORD JUSTICE-CLERK.—What was the date of that?

LORD ADVOCATE.—About the 11th of November,—Porter gives the time exactly,—and here we again run up against outside and independent corroboration. Now, what happened on that occasion is rather important. There was this quarrel, and Hughes went away. He seems to have been offended at this blow, and he got into conversation with Constable Porter. He said to the constable, "If you had been here a little ago, I would have given M'Cann into custody." Porter said, "It is not too late yet." Hughes replied, "The passion is off me now." At that time the party came strolling up.

LORD JUSTICE-CLERK.—What was the quarrel about? I never clearly understood that.

LORD ADVOCATE.—It is not very clear, but M'Cann admits that the quarrel did take place. I rather gather it was something about calling a meeting. Hughes asked him when he was to call a meeting, and apparently, whether M'Cann had felt offended at anybody interfering or not, it resulted in a slap in the face. But here, as to the main facts there is no doubt, because I think M'Cann admits this quarrel himself; at all events, Porter tells what happened; and here we meet with direct corroboration of Hughes; because Hughes says that while he and Porter were talking the others came up, and Featherstone spoke to Porter and said, "Never mind, the one is as bad as the other." So there you have got an outside person coming into contact with this transaction, and seeing Featherstone among them. Now, it would seem as if from that time onwards Hughes did not associate so much with them, but he certainly did go with them sometimes, and he says that he frequently saw the parties now at the bar meeting in Jail Square. It is only right here, before passing from Hughes, that I should recall to your recollection the answer which he gave in response to a question by his lordship in the chair, who asked him the names of those who were present at the dynamite meetings. I think he then spoke of Drum, Devany, and Callaghan, as having attended the dynamite meetings, and of having seen M'Dermott give money for the stuff, and about Kelly going to the chemical works for the stuff. Now, you will judge of that answer, gentlemen, but I submit to you that the meaning of that, taken along with the rest of his evidence, was plainly this: he was there speaking of the specific dynamite meetings and not about the general meetings—about the lecture in the Democratic Hall, and the meeting in the stable, and otherwise. He cannot have meant to say, that at all those numerous meetings in Jail Square and the Green, nobody but those three were present.

LORD JUSTICE-CLERK.—No, he says the reverse immediately afterwards. I understood that it indicated a greater amount of confidence in the limited number, than in the whole.

LORD ADVOCATE.—That is precisely so, and that there was an inner circle, if I may say so, within this larger group. Now, gentlemen, that is Hughes' story, and it is for you to judge whether it is all an invention. I submit to you it is not, but on the contrary, that it is corroborated in almost every essential particular, except one, which you will have very little difficulty in inferring from the other evidence,—the actual communings between the conspirators, which, of course, nobody was let in to hear; and I shall ask your attention shortly to the corroboration of Hughes upon these points. Now, gentlemen, there is one thing perfectly certain—that is, that all those men were in the way of meeting at the places where Hughes says they met. They sometimes met in Lennox's public-house, and they much more often met in the Jail Square and the Green. Of course, I do not say that that carries us very far, but it is something to begin with; it is not all an invention. The meetings of these men are proved by very ample independent evidence. You have the constable Porter, whose beat includes Jail Square and the foot of Saltmarket, and he says that he observed these ten men and Hughes with some others, associated in a way that attracted his attention from about, I think, he said the month of November 1882. Now, will you kindly recollect, in the question whether you are to believe Hughes or not, the sort of description that Porter gave of the meetings of those men. My learned friends, quite properly doing their duty for the prisoners, asked the question, "Are not there plenty of people who go to Lennox's, and who meet in Jail Square and on the Green?" No doubt there are, but then Porter told you that the group now at the bar, with Hughes, and Kearney, and Featherstone, and others, when they appeared kept apart from the rest. People break up into groups on the Green, but this group was in the way of keeping by themselves, avoiding observation, and above all, apparently not letting anybody hear what they said. The very fact of this group thus exciting the attention of Porter is not insignificant in that matter; and Porter evidently suspected them, because he strolled slowly past, as a policeman would do, with his ears open, and tried to pick up what they were saying, but they stopped speaking. He describes the way in which they sometimes withdrew away to a distance, and so great were his suspicions, before he ever heard of Hughes, that he took a field-glass to look at them, to see what they were doing, as they were too shy when he got near them, and he saw them reading letters and papers. Now, that, gentlemen, is evidence, which I think you can have no difficulty in believing, of the fact that the men were assembling for some purpose—what it was you will judge—in the numbers and at the times and in the modes of which Hughes speaks. So far, therefore, Hughes is corroborated. Of course, what I have stated thus far would not be a reason for your inferring without other evidence that they were plotting dynamite outrages. But still, it is a step. Another witness who speaks to the assembling of these men, is Constable Niven, who corroborates Porter as to the association of three of the prisoners. He speaks of seeing M'Dermott, Devany, M'Cann, and perhaps Kelly. I think that was what he said in his evidence, and you will judge whether he tried to stretch the point at all, when he mentioned three, and perhaps four. The fact that these men went to Lennox's public-house is also proved; it is proved that all the accused, except Casey, were frequently in that public-house down to about November 1882. You heard M'Ginnes, the man who serves in the public-house, and he proved that he has seen Callaghan, M'Dermott, M'Cann, Kelly, Drum, and Casey, and also Hughes, on Saturday nights in the public-house; but he does not identify Devany, M'Cabe, Donnelly, or M'Cullagh, as having been in the party. There again, it is not an invention on the part of Hughes that the prisoners frequented that public-house. But it is suggested that although they went there, they had no opportunity of doing the things they are said to have done. Now, I would ask your attention to what Hughes said they did there. He does not say they plotted dynamite there. The question was put to him, and he says, "No; it was too public a place;" but they sometimes retired into an inner room and swore in members. He himself was sworn in there, and so was M'Dermott and some others. Well, M'Ginnes, without any disposition to interfere and hurt his customers or say anything against them, says they came and went like others. But there was one part of his evidence, where he said they sometimes went into an apartment with others, and sometimes they went into a room by themselves. Now, that is all that Hughes says. He does not say that every time they met there there was something illegal done. There were four rooms in Lennox's public-house with glass doors, besides the public front door, and according as the house was thronged or otherwise, or as they wanted to swear in a new member or not, they would go into the private room, or simply mix with the general customers in the parlour. So that there again you have further corroboration of what Hughes says. The next point I should bring under your notice is the evidence of Horan, and I daresay you must have been a good deal struck with it. Horan tells you he was invited, I think by Callaghan, who seems to have invited most of the people to join the society which met in that public-house. You will judge whether he was telling all he knew. I submit to you he was not. He at once began to speak about its being a friendly society, and that being all he understood. I asked him, "Did you take an oath?" No, he did not. But then it turned out in the end that that was a question of words, because it appears that something was "mentioned off a paper" which he afterwards found out to be an oath; and the way in which he felt himself justified in saying he did not take an oath, was that his mind was not running along with this being an oath at the time. That is rather a question of fencing with words, and I think you will have little doubt, that on Horan's evidence, it is proved that there was put to him and administered to him something in the nature of an oath, regarding the society in that very public-house. There again you find corroboration of Hughes. Horan was most unwilling to speak, and tried all he could to avoid speaking, but he could not help admitting that, as Hughes said, he had been sworn in in that place, for that is what Horan's evidence comes to, discounting the particular language he used when he did not want to be committed to the oath. Hughes does not say that Horan was very deep in these things, and Horan himself says he was seldom there, and that his priest, when he came to know he was a member of a secret society, gave him good advice, to the effect that these societies were apt to lead to a bad end, and advised him to get out, and so he got out. But there again you have an important piece of corroboration—most unwilling corroboration—of Hughes, as to the fact that a secret society met in Lennox's public-house, which Callaghan asked him to join, and on entering which he swore an oath. At this point, I think I may take up as still further corroborating Hughes, and also as coming from important independent sources, the evidence of the arrival and doings of Featherstone in Glasgow, because that not only corroborates Hughes, but really establishes apart from him, I submit, the whole of this conspiracy. You have it proved by the witness M'Elhinny, that Featherstone landed at Liverpool in the month of June 1882, and we have very distinct evidence, from two most respectable witnesses, Mrs. Mitchell and her son John, who keep the Star Hotel, Cowcaddens, Glasgow, that on six occasions, between an early period in 1882—they seem to think it was rather before July, I think one of them said about May—between the spring of 1882 and the 14th February 1883, Featherstone lodged in their house; in particular, he lodged on the last occasion for four days, from the 10th to the 14th February, when he paid the hotel bill, which was found in his purse when he was apprehended. The other times Mrs. Mitchell was not quite sure about; but it was at intervals between the month of June and the month of December. Now, what was Featherstone doing in Glasgow? That is important. He did not tell his name to the Mitchells, but he said that he was connected with the American Press,—that he was a reporter for the American Press,—and apparently, as far as she saw, his time was chiefly employed in reading newspapers and writing. But he seems to have been careful to post his own letters, for he never asked anybody to do that, and he did not get any letters addressed to him there; so that, although he had been six times living in this very respectable hotel, he took care that the people in the hotel neither knew his name, nor what he was about. But, gentlemen, we know what he was about. We know that he was mingling with those men. Hughes says he was teaching them to use dynamite, and we know, from sources altogether independent of Hughes, that he was buying the materials for making it. Hence it becomes important, I think, that at this stage I should bring under your notice the witnesses who establish Featherstone's doings during the time he was in Glasgow.

LORD JUSTICE-CLERK.—It would be convenient if you can follow the order of time, as to what he did in Glasgow.

LORD ADVOCATE.—I shall endeavour to do so as nearly as I can. I need not say more about the evidence of the Mitchells; but we find that while Featherstone was in Glasgow, he bought acids appropriate for making dynamite—you will see afterwards whether they were for that purpose—he bought the kinds of acids requisite for making dynamite. His first purchase was upon the 9th of December 1882, from the firm of M'Geachie & M'Farlane. That is proved by the witness John Bunting Guthrie, who is a partner of that firm, and Ballingall, his clerk. Now I would ask your attention to what passed on the occasion of this purchase. On the 9th of December he asked for nitric acid, and he was very particular, as he always was, about its strength. He asked what strength they had, and they told him that they had it at 66 to 84 Twaddle, which is a well-known hydrometer for measuring specific gravity. That was not strong enough; he wanted something stronger, but he had to be content with what he could get, and he bought a carboy containing 148 lbs. of nitric acid, the strongest they could give him. It was from 82° to 84°. These purchases are proved by entries in the books, as well as by the witnesses, and he gave what you will probably consider important in other aspects of this case—he wrote, in the presence of these gentlemen, that address. [Showing No. 41.] He gave the address, D. O'Herlihy, 10 Great George Street (West), Cork. Now I am going to submit to you, that for the purposes of this nitric acid, D. O'Herlihy is just Featherstone. There is a D. O'Herlihy, and to this first firm Featherstone said that the nitric acid was wanted for ink manufacture. It is only right to say that O'Herlihy does apparently carry on ink-making in a small way.

LORD JUSTICE-CLERK.—If he is an ink manufacturer, how does that appear in the evidence?

LORD ADVOCATE.—It does not appear in the evidence here.

LORD JUSTICE-CLERK.—I did see something about it among the documents.

L

LORD ADVOCATE.—It may be in the address, but it is the case that he is an ink manufacturer, I believe, in a small way. Although he was given notice of as a witness for the defence, he has not been examined. There is evidence that he left the address 10 Great George Street (West), Cork. But, gentlemen, you will no doubt recollect, that the partners of the firm of M'Geachie & Macfarlane, when they were asked, was such strong acid used for making ink, said, no. Then it was suggested, it might be for making coloured ink. Thereupon I asked the question, had it been at one time used for making aniline dyes, and the answer was, "At one time, but not now." Accordingly, you are left in this position, that, as far as the evidence goes, it negatives the idea that this strong kind of acid which Featherstone bought was suitable for ink-making at all. But I do not think you will find that very important, when you keep all the evidence in view. The next purchase was from Montgomery, when a different account was given of what the acid was wanted for. It is proved by Mr. James Montgomery, of Montgomery & Co., and by his clerk, Reid, that Featherstone came about the 12th or 13th February 1883, and proposed to buy nitric and also sulphuric acid. I pray you to note that. He wants to buy from these people two of the components of nitro-glycerine. Formerly he had bought one. He had once bought sulphuric acid and nitric acid, and he spoke of having a partner, and communicating with him about the acid. He was asked, as you will recollect, what he wanted to do with it, and I think he said, at this time, it was for a patent for preserving meat. Well, he went away, having made this call on the 12th or 13th February, to consult his partner, and he wrote from Cork—at least the letter received by Montgomery & Co., I think you will see, is in Featherstone's hand. [Reads No. 40.] It is dated Cork, 17th February 1883, and in it he says, "Gentlemen, upon the report of my partner, who was recently in Scotland, and who called upon you, I am inclined to try your acid, and will thank you to send me one carboy, graded 160 T. I enclose 16s. 4d.—12s. 6d. for the acid, and 4s. for the bottle. I have deducted five per cent., which I understand you allow for all cash orders. If this works as well as expected, I shall deal exclusively with you." I ask your attention to that, because he wrote at the same time to the next firm, that he would deal exclusively with them. I put it to you whether this letter, which I now show you, is in the same hand. That letter is signed D. O'Herlihy, and I ask you to consider whether that is not Featherstone. It is important to notice also, that when he was asking for that acid, he asked it 90° and 100° strength. No human being says that that is suitable for preserving meat, and nobody says that O'Herlihy had anything to do with preserving meat.

LORD JUSTICE-CLERK.—What was the date of that transaction?

LORD ADVOCATE.—His first visit was on 12th and 13th February, and his letter from Cork was dated the 17th.
LORD JUSTICE-CLERK.—That is, after this explosion.
LORD ADVOCATE.—Yes.
LORD JUSTICE-CLERK.—That shows what he was trafficking in.
LORD ADVOCATE.—It does, and the suggestion I make is, that the stuff which he got in answer was what was made into dynamite in Cork, and came back in the infernal machines, which were brought by Deasy. It was too late to be used for the explosions of the 20th and 21st January. Then, he attempts to make the third purchase from another firm, viz., Messrs. A. Hope, Jun., & Co. It is proved by Mr. James Johnstone, the sole partner of that firm, and by William Johnstone, his clerk, that Featherstone came in February 1883, wanting to buy nitric acid; and he asked it strong there also, and got it. I should say he purchased from Montgomery, and he got it at this other place also. And here he told the same story, about wanting it for a patent for preserving meat. On the same day that he wrote that letter from Cork—the letter which I suggest to you is his; and which is signed D. O'Herlihy—he wrote this letter, which is No. 38 of process, to A. Hope, Jun., & Co., and which is almost in identical terms with the other, which you have before you. [See pages 77 and 97.] He says there, as he did in the other, "The spring season is nigh at hand, and if successful in our operations, we will be good customers." Now, I put it to you whether that is not just Featherstone again. These, gentlemen, are the three purchases by Featherstone, and I would now ask your attention to what became of these things which were thus bought. It is proved that they were sent to Cork. That was proved by the Shipping Company's people, and it was proved by the witnesses we examined from Cork, that the three carboys were delivered to and signed for by Deasy at Cork. That was proved by the shipping documents, and I think you saw the receipts which were signed for them, and I need not trouble you by showing you them again. Well, the last consignment that was made to him was stopped by the police, because the thing was found out. To make my narrative complete, I should have told you that on the 29th of March he wrote to Alexander Hope, Jun., & Co. for another consignment of sulphuric acid. He says, that having used their last consignment and having been satisfied with it, he was now to give them a further order, and he wants other two carboys. These carboys were sent, and they were the carboys that were stopped by the police and sent back full. Now, that letter is signed D. O'Herlihy also, and it is proper at this stage that I should show you another letter which seems to have been the draft of this one, of the same date, and which was actually found in the pocket of Featherstone, and signed D. O'Herlihy, like the other. He had, apparently, been getting ready, because we find within it a requisition for a money order. The requisitions for the money orders were proved by

the post office clerk, from Cork, without saying who gave them in. There are three requisitions for money orders, all signed by D. O'Herlihy, and they were all to be for carboys sent, and I put it to you whether these are not all sent by the same man who wrote the order which has been already spoken of. Then, last of all, this [showing No. 45] was found in Featherstone's pocket, being again a requisition to pay Montgomery. [See page 93, footnote.] But you find no stamps upon it, and the inference I am disposed to draw from that is that Featherstone was apprehended when he was on his way to the post office with this letter and order, signed by O'Herlihy, in his own pocket, showing that he was receiving letters addressed to O'Herlihy. There is an envelope which was found in his pocket. [Showing No. 36. See page 94.] Now, gentlemen, in that state of the evidence, I think you can have no difficulty—there are other documents which we proved by one of the witnesses, which you can see if you desire it—on the question of handwriting. But I do not wish to delay you upon that, because there are so many details to be pieced together that I do not desire to detain you more than is necessary on that point. What happened next was that a man named Denis Deasy appeared on the quay at Liverpool with a box which contained two infernal machines. The police had fortunately information, and they were on the quay, and this gentleman was met.

LORD JUSTICE-CLERK.—What was the date of that?

LORD ADVOCATE.—I think it was about the 15th of March, but I will inquire as to that, and give your lordship the exact date. It was thereabout, and he had what I think you will agree with me was a most wicked sort of luggage: there were two tin canisters containing very strong dynamite; the proportion of nitro-glycerine in the sawdust was about 75 per cent., being a most strong and dangerous compound. There were also in the box these three things [showing No. 60], with packets of chemicals appropriate for firing the dynamite. There was a bottle of sulphuric acid, a parcel containing chlorate of potash, a parcel containing powdered sugar, and a parcel containing realgar or red orpiment; the one last mentioned, as the chemists have told you, if mixed with chlorate of potash and pounded sugar, making the explosion more violent; so that this box had two machines with everything necessary for firing them. Now, who was this man Deasy? you will naturally ask, at this stage. I submit he was simply an agent of Featherstone. There were two letters found upon him, which were put to the witnesses, and which, I shall now ask you to conclude, established that agency. He had a letter of introduction to a person called Pat Flanagan. The letters to which I refer are marked Nos. 42 and 43 of process [see pages 95 and 97], and are signed, "Yours, etc., Edmond." Now, I put it to you whether there can be the smallest doubt that these are in Featherstone's hand. There is no doubt as to why he signed "Edmond," because that is his real name. His real name was not Featherstone, as has already been proved to you, but Edmond O'Brien Kennedy; and so, although he thought it necessary to assume a false name in dealing with the honest public, in the letter of introduction which he gave to his agent with his two infernal machines, he signed with his own first name, Edmond. Now, it is by pursuing that course of reasoning that I think you will have very little doubt that the stuff that was sent from Glasgow came back among the sawdust as part of the nitro-glycerine, and that Featherstone was connected with all these things. But, gentlemen, if there was any doubt as to Featherstone's real character—and this is very important on the question of the object or design of this conspiracy —there was a green paper which has been referred to—No. 44 [see page 93]; I suppose the colour was symbolical—which contained a receipt for making Fenian fire, and a picture of how you were to tie the two bottles together, if you wanted to produce an instantaneous effect. I do not know that I need read it again. It is only fair that I should say that this is not in Featherstone's hand, but it was in his pocket, which comes to the same thing. It bears to be a copy of a cure "for Govt.," but whether it was for the gout or the Government does not much matter.

LORD JUSTICE-CLERK.—It did not much signify, because it was not intended as an honest receipt for the gout.

LORD ADVOCATE.—Certainly it was a recipe for a most mischievous, I was going to say, explosive, but that would be hardly correct, because it is proved that this is not for exploding, but for setting fire to a place. When you fling the two bottles down, a blaze is set up. Now that, I think you will agree with me, is a most unfortunate kind of companion for the prisoners to be associating with. We know now enough of Featherstone, who is getting his deserts in Chatham Prison; but that is the kind of man who made these visits to Glasgow, between the beginning of June last year and the 14th February this year, and who, by many witnesses— not by Hughes alone, but by other witnesses—was seen associating with these men on the Jail Square and in the Green, and who, Hughes says, lectured to them in the Democratic Hall. When, therefore, Hughes tells you that Featherstone came to teach the making of explosives, can you doubt it? The man was all round with receipts for explosives, and he was buying materials for them in Glasgow. Therefore, I submit to you, there is most ample corroboration of Hughes upon this point. But, whether there is corroboration of Hughes or not, supposing he was out of the case altogether, we have had proof beyond doubt, that a man of the character of Featherstone, carrying on what Featherstone was doing, and laden with the kind of things that we find him with, and sending over his agent, Deasy, with these machines to Liverpool, was certainly a very bad associate for these men to be with; and you could even from that evidence—if you are satisfied it is true and sufficient—draw the inference that he was with these men for the purpose alleged by Hughes. Now that is Featherstone, and I do not know that I need say any more about him. I think, perhaps, at this stage, it would most contribute to clearness to take up the case of Dalton, as another instructor in those malicious arts. There seems to be some little doubt whether Johnston and Dalton were the same. I would rather say they were not, but you will judge. Hughes says Johnston went away shortly to America; and, although it does appear from a passenger who came home in the American steamer with Dalton that he sometimes called himself Johnston, I do not think he was the same Johnston, I do not ask you to take it that Dalton and Johnston are the same, because I do not think that would be sustained by the evidence; but still, Dalton does play an important part in these transactions, and the evidence about him is very material, as showing the real character and the doings of some of the prisoners, and, particularly, of Terence M'Dermott, regarding whom you will have observed that, down to the point I am now coming to, there has been less evidence than about most of the rest. But you will hear enough about his part in these transactions before we have done. The evidence about Dalton proves that he came across in the steamer "Celtic." That is proved by the witness Schonman, who knew him as Johnston, and who saw him write. Schonman deponed that he was going to London, and that Dalton said he was going to Glasgow.

LORD JUSTICE-CLERK.—They agreed to meet in London.

LORD ADVOCATE.—Yes; and the address was given in Dalton's hand; but, gentlemen, what is not unimportant in regard to Dalton is the card that he had, to which I would ask your special attention. There is his pocketbook, containing the address of Schonman, written by the man himself. Now, he had also a card in his pocket when he was apprehended. [No. 49. See page 100.] It has an important bearing on this case, and its importance you will see when I show it to you. Upon that card he had three addresses written. One of the names in the middle of the address is rubbed out with the finger, but that is no matter, because we have got the address itself, and it is 10 Great George Street (West). Now that was O'Herlihy's address, to which Featherstone got his nitric acid and sulphuric acid sent; so that this man Dalton has what I might venture to call Featherstone's address. But he has another address, which is not unimportant in this case, and it is this: "J. F. K., 41 Stanhope Street, G." Now, we know who this is: that is, J. F. Kearney, an associate of these men, who was a pointsman on the Caledonian Railway, and who has disappeared. This is a very singular circumstance; most important, as showing the association of Dalton, not only with Featherstone, but with Kearney, who was a leading man in this dynamite manufacture. The other thing that this man, whose name is Dalton, had, was an entry of three pages which are important, and of which I may say something immediately. We know from witnesses of undoubted credit that Dalton came to Glasgow; and here it becomes necessary that I should bring under your notice evidence of which, perhaps, you may not have quite understood the importance at the time it was led. We brought evidence to prove that a man Moorhead, whom we believe to be another of these people, arrived in Glasgow, and took lodgings with Mrs. M'Lachlan. Mrs. M'Lachlan told you that she put out her ticket on the first Monday of January, and she got as a lodger Moorhead, on the Monday after,—that would be the 15th,—and from that time she said that Moorhead lodged with her till, I think, the Thursday eight weeks after.

LORD JUSTICE-CLERK.—Who was Moorhead?

LORD ADVOCATE.—Another like Featherstone and Dalton, but he has disappeared. But I am going to bring Dalton and Featherstone into his company. We believe he was an American Irishman. Moorhead lived with Mrs. M'Lachlan for these eight weeks. We do not know precisely what he was doing, but we know he was associating with the prisoners to a certain extent, because, you may recollect that on the night before he left, which would be the 8th of March, Mrs. M'Lachlan says that he brought home a friend with him, who, he said, was a friend from Dundee, and whom she identified as Dalton. They had with them a very singular piece of luggage, a lady's new bonnet-box, like the one found at Possil Bridge. This, of course, was later than the time of the explosions in Glasgow. The box was more like the one found at the "Times" office. It was, however, a lady's bonnet-box, which is a favourite article of use with the dynamite school. Well, having appeared with this luggage, I would ask your attention to what happened next morning. Next morning, before Dalton and Moorhead had risen, M'Dermott, the first prisoner, called for them, and that it was M'Dermott is left beyond doubt, because Mrs. M'Lachlan said that he had to wait in the kitchen with her about half an hour, until Moorhead and Dalton were up; so that she had the most ample opportunity of identifying him. But his identification does not stand upon Mrs. M'Lachlan's evidence alone, because she had living with her her mother, Christina Colquhoun, and I think she also identified Terence M'Dermott without any difficulty. But, gentlemen, his identification does not stop there, because we have Miss Mary Bain, who lived in the same landing, and she had seen Terence M'Dermott, not on that occasion only, but on other occasions, coming up that stair, so that Terence M'Dermott was a visitor in that stair. Who he was calling for you may conclude. We are not able to prove for whom he called on the other occasions, but he was met repeatedly by Mary Bain in that stair; and we know that on the morning of the Thursday I have mentioned, he called for Moorhead and Dalton there. Well, then, what did they do? The two men, Moorhead and Dalton, got up and breakfasted, Terence probably having had his breakfast before, and Moorhead asked for his bill and paid it, and Mrs. M'Lachlan did not watch them more. She asked where he was going, and Moorhead said he was going to London. She asked Terence M'Dermott was he going, and he said he was going to London too. Now, gentlemen, that is identified as the 9th of March, and something took place seven days after, as you may recollect, but whether that was connected with these men, we do not need to inquire. There were two explosions in London on the 16th,—the explosions at the "Times" office and at the Local Government offices. That, however, is hardly here, and I do not therefore pursue it: but they went away that day. Now it is very singular that in Dalton's notes we find corroboration of things that you would hardly have expected to get there, showing the accuracy of Mrs. M'Lachlan. We find in his notebook this entry, L. 6/3/83. That is evidently Liverpool, 6th March 1883. Then we find G. 8/3/83, which we suggest is Glasgow, 8th March 1883, the very day Moorhead brought him in. He brought him on the 8th and kept him until the morning of the 9th, and then we find another entry, Ln. 17/3/83. That we read as London, 17th March 1883. Whether he went to London at once on leaving Mrs. M'Lachlan is not material. There is a letter produced, from which it would appear as if he had been in Glasgow on the 13th, but that is not material. So that I have now shown to you by evidence beyond doubt, that Dalton, whom I have connected with Featherstone, who had Featherstone's Cork address and Kearney's Glasgow address in his pocket, was an associate of M'Dermott and of Moorhead, who has disappeared. I must ask your pardon, gentlemen, for going into these details; but their importance I am sure you will appreciate. You here have Dalton brought into connection with at least three members of this conspiracy, Featherstone, Kearney, and M'Dermott. These three he is in contact with, and M'Dermott went away with him and Moorhead. Well then, gentlemen, upon this matter of Dalton, I do not know that I need go into any further evidence. There is a letter, No. 43 [see p. 95], which we had some question about, but if your Lordships think there is the least doubt about its admissibility, I won't read it.

LORD JUSTICE-CLERK.—You had better not.

LORD ADVOCATE.—I will not read any letter about which any doubt exists. As to the handwriting of Dalton there is no doubt, because there is a receipt for what was found in his pocket, and you have his own pocketbooks. Dalton, again, like Featherstone, had in his pocketbook two things, which I submit to you are of importance in this case. He had receipts in these pocketbooks for making very dangerous explosives, and in particular he had a receipt for making nitro-glycerine and dynamite. Like Featherstone, he had receipts upon him, so that there is very little doubt what he came from America for. But there is another thing which he had, which may not be without its importance, as showing the design and object of these persons, and that is an entry which you understand now after Lamie's evidence. "That where there is a circle interfered with in its working, by any body of men hostile in policy, that each centre should be in communication with the centres living nearest his district, whereby they may assist the centre whose circle is so attacked, and so assist the visiting committee in their duties, who may not be able to be at hand when needed." We now know that that is Fenian language. A circle is an area of the Fenian organization, and a centre is the chief of the circle; so you here get Dalton, and through him the other conspirators brought into contact, perhaps not very directly, but quite sufficiently, with the Fenian organization, and you have them by other documents, brought into contact with a number of Land League papers, which were found upon some of them. Now, gentlemen, I think I need not delay you by saying more about Dalton; but I venture to submit that both of the persons whom we charge in the indictment as having been members of this conspiracy are proved to have been people of a very dangerous kind, and who had plainly come to this country for no good end, but for the purpose of instructing in the use of dynamite persons in this country. Before passing from Dalton, there is only one other point I should refer to, and that is the evidence of Monro, the cab-driver. He on a particular evening drove first to the place where Devany lived, and a box or parcel was taken in there, by Donnelly and another, and they then drove up to the street in which M'Dermott lived. It is quite true that we did not absolutely prove they met this man, or that they were seen, but you have as an incident that at all events Donnelly, certainly and possibly one of the others, was driven between these places. That, however, does not come to much. Donnelly and M'Dermott are the two who were driven, and I ask you to conclude what they were driven between those places for.

A JUROR.—There is no doubt that they were driven; I have their names. The doubt is about Dalton.

LORD ADVOCATE.—The doubt is about Dalton.

Adjourned.

FOURTH DAY.—THURSDAY, DECEMBER 20, 1883.

THE LORD ADVOCATE.— May it please your Lordships: Gentlemen of the Jury; I shall now resume the narrative of the facts proved in this case. I was last night, when our proceedings were brought to a close, about to bring under your notice some very important evidence, regarding the purchases by M'Dermott and M'Cullagh, of materials suitable for making dynamite, and the bearing of that will be at once obvious to your minds. The evidence of it is perfectly clear. You will recollect that James Armstrong and James Steel proved that M'Dermott came to the premises of Clolus & Co., manufacturing chemists, at Ruchill Glycerine Works, on 30th October 1882, and again on 6th November of the same year, and that on each occasion he bought 10 lbs. of glycerine. It appeared that it was not in the ordinary course of business for that firm to sell such small quantities of glycerine, and they seem to have made some demur to doing so,—in answer to one of yourselves, it was brought out that from 10 to 15 tons was the quantity they were in the way of selling, and the proposal to purchase a small quantity was not a kind of thing they were accustomed to. But, at all events, on each of these two occasions, there can be no question that M'Dermott did go and ask for glycerine. On the first occasion he was served with a kind the name of which I don't think was given, but, on the second occasion, what he got was called "dynamite glycerine," not by him, but by the person who served him; that being the trade name of the particular kind of glycerine, of which there are three qualities sold by that firm. Now, it is very important in this connection that you should keep in view precisely what M'Dermott said on the occasion of these purchases, as bearing on the question whether the purchases of that glycerine were for some necessary or lawful purpose, or whether they were for some illegal purpose. He first seems to have gone and asked in general terms whether he could have a small quantity of glycerine,—apparently small, with reference to the kind of business which these gentlemen carry on,—and after some demur they agreed to give him it. They asked, in the first place, what he wanted it for, and he said he wanted it for a horse's back. The question then was about the name, and it does not quite clearly appear whether the name given was his own name, or whether it was the name of the person for whose horse he said he wanted the glycerine. I rather think it was the latter, and as that would be probably the more favourable for M'Dermott, I am quite willing to put it to you, on the footing that that was what he said. Taking it that he did not give the name as his own, but as the name of the owner of the horses, he said it was for John Bolan, contractor in the Gallowgate. That was what passed on the first occasion. About a week after—because you will see it is just a week between the 30th of October and the 6th of November —M'Dermott came back again, and said that the glycerine he had got was done. Now, supposing, gentlemen, that the glycerine had been wanted for lubricating a horse's back, or any sore of that kind, you would hardly expect him to use 10 lbs. in a week. But that is not worth commenting on here, because it is perfectly evident that this was altogether a falsehood. He got on that occasion a second quantity of 10 lbs., and was told not to come back again. From what was said by the witnesses, they did not like this selling to an unknown person in small quantities, and he was told not to return. In regard to the quantity, you have the evidence, and no doubt recollect it, that when he was asked whether he had anything to put the glycerine in, he said, no, and then he went away and came back with a can, which smelt of paraffin oil, and the witness Steel cleaned it out, the glycerine was put in; and you may recollect that when it was being filled up, he did not ask for a particular weight, but said, " You had better fill the can." So that what he wanted was just the fill of that very considerable vessel, which it was proved contained 10 lbs., and substantially the same thing happened upon the second occasion as upon the first. Now, gentlemen, if it had been true that this was for a man named James Bolan, a contractor in the Gallowgate, M'Dermott would have been able to prove it, or at least to give the information necessary for enabling this man Bolan to be produced. But what is said by M'Dermott in his declaration? He denies that he made these purchases at all, and he denies that he ever gave any such name as Bolan, so that I think it would be almost needless for us, representing the Crown, to pursue that matter further. But, lest there should be any doubt about it, and in order to get at the truth, we caused most careful investigation to be made, whether there was such a person as James Bolan in the Gallowgate, or anywhere else, and you heard the constable who made the investigation in the Gallowgate and Glasgow generally, say that he was unable to find any such person. So that what you have is this, two purchases of large quantities of glycerine—10 lbs. purchased on the 30th of October, and other 10 lbs. on the 6th of November, on each occasion dynamite glycerine—the kind of glycerine known as dynamite glycerine —under a false name, and with a false representation as to what it was wanted for. And I think you will be satisfied that that is a very serious circumstance, not only against M'Dermott, but against all those with whom it has been proved he has been associated in this business. If you recollect the evidence of the chemist, you will see that one of these bonnet-boxes, which seemed to be used by these people, contained somewhere about 10 or 12 lbs. of stuff altogether, and if you take vitriol and sulphuric acid and sawdust, you will see what a very large quantity, first of nitro-glycerine and then of dynamite, 20 lbs. of dynamite glycerine would make. That is a very serious circumstance against M'Dermott and his associates. But then, gentlemen, that is not the only constituent of nitro-glycerine which M'Dermott was trying to get, because it is proved to you that even at an earlier time, when he was a workman in the Irvine Chemical Works, where he served from 21st

May to 9th October, he asked Levi Barrow, the vitriol pumper, to give him a bottle of vitriol or sulphuric acid. Barrow said he would not, and M'Dermott did not push the matter. But Barrow told you there was plenty vitriol lying open there, and it was quite possible for M'Dermott to help himself to vitriol, if he wanted it. I think at that time M'Dermott said it was to clean a chain, but you will judge of that. I don't want you to say, or to assume, that he took the vitriol. What is important, is that he wanted to get vitriol. In a question of design and purpose, it is enough that he wanted to get vitriol, which is one of the constituents of nitro-glycerine. You will, no doubt, have observed the dates which I have just given you. The date when he attempted to get that vitriol was, according to Barrow, in the month of September 1882, and we find him buying glycerine in the end of October and beginning of November. That was all after the American gentlemen, as they are called, were in association with the group of prisoners, instructing them in making nitro-glycerine, and you will judge whether the fair inference is not that M'Dermott was one of those who were commissioned to endeavour to get the constituents of nitro-glycerine, in pursuance of a common plan agreed on amongst the prisoners. There are some other pieces of evidence which do not go very far,—they are not quite clearly proved,—but it is right you should keep them in view, and draw your own conclusions from them. Hughes told us that on one occasion, when they were in Jail Square, Johnston, I think, came and said the people in the house where the stuff was being made were complaining of the pipes being corroded by acid. Well, it was proved to you by the witness Thomas Sutherland, and also by Charles Johnston, that in the month of December 1882, after all that stuff had been bought, the pipes in M'Dermott's house— the pipes from the jaw-box—were seriously corroded and eaten through. It is only right to say that it did not occur to Johnston at that time, knowing nothing of what may have been going on in M'Dermott's house, to associate that with any felonious or particular cause. He said it might be due to the acid in urine, but, at the same time, in answer to a question put, he stated that that was not a likely place—that these pipes were not likely pipes for urine to pass through in such a house. It was the pipes from the sink or jaw-box that were corroded with acid. But you will judge, when that fact is taken along with what was spoken to by Hughes, as to the whole party turning and going away in the Townhead direction, where M'Dermott lived, each to take his share of stuff, whether we do not get there an account of the reason for that corroded condition of the pipes which was found in M'Dermott's house. I put that before you, and you will give such weight to it as you think fit.

LORD JUSTICE-CLERK.—Where was M'Dermott's house?

THE LORD ADVOCATE.—No. 452 Dobbie's Loan, up at Townhead,

and that was the direction in which, according to Hughes, the party went to take away the stuff. Well, then, gentlemen, I referred to some other matters yesterday in connection with Dalton, with whom M'Dermott was brought into association, and you no doubt recollect that very important occasion, on the morning of Thursday 9th March, when M'Dermott called for Moorhead and Dalton, and when it was said they were going to London together. You will also bear in mind that another of the witnesses, Mary Bain, who lived in the stair, said that she had repeatedly seen M'Dermott there while Moorhead was there. Now, in his declaration, M'Dermott denies he was ever in Ronald Street, although he is identified by three witnesses as being there on the morning of 9th March, and by one witness, Mary Bain, as calling on other repeated occasions, while Moorhead was living there. So that I think you will be satisfied that a very grave and direct case is made against M'Dermott. And if you are satisfied that he was an associate of the others, then all that is made against him is also made against the others, his associates, in pursuing the common purpose. But there is another of the prisoners against whom there is serious evidence of buying explosive compounds; I refer to M'Cullagh. The evidence against M'Cullagh of these purchases is very important, because, you will observe—indeed, you will have observed already—that these purchases were made in a most circuitous and underhand way, evidently for the purpose of escaping observation, and with the view of preventing the real buyer of the stuff from being found out. The history of that is this: you have heard that there was a soda or aerated water maker, who goes by the name of Myles M'Cullough, I think, at Garngad Road. Myles M'Cullough had in his employment, at that time, a workman named Michael Buchanan, and he also appears to have had several boys, who drove the vans in the course of his business, I suppose for bringing in materials for making the waters, and no doubt for delivering the waters about town. It is proved that M'Cullagh, the prisoner, went to Buchanan, the servant of Myles M'Cullough, and asked him if he would get a jar of vitriol for him. Further, it is proved that vitriol is used for making aerated waters. That, however, is weak vitriol, gentlemen. But it was not weak vitriol that the prisoner M'Cullagh wanted, it was strong vitriol, and he gave £1 to Buchanan to get this strong stuff, and then Buchanan gave the £1 to John Getty—it passed through various hands. John Getty was one of the principal vanmen; but John Getty did not go himself, but on the first two occasions of purchase, gave the money which he had got from Buchanan to a boy Gillon,—a little boy who drove the van,—and the boy Gillon, when he was going for vitriol for his master, Myles M'Cullough, bought a jar of vitriol for the prisoner M'Cullagh, and paid for it with the prisoner M'Cullagh's money, bringing back the change he got to Getty, who gave the change to the prisoner M'Cullagh.

That happened twice, on the dates I will give you immediately. The same thing happened a third time, and on this occasion, when Buchanan was requested by the prisoner M'Cullagh to get the vitriol, he, as before, asked Getty the vanman, and Getty transferred the duty to another of the van boys—on this occasion a boy George Steel. So that you have here three purchases of three several jars of strong sulphuric acid by M'Cullagh, the prisoner, bought in this circuitous and underhand way, put down in Myles M'Cullough's yard, and lifted as I shall immediately explain. If this vitriol was wanted for an honest purpose, why did not M'Cullagh go and buy it himself? Why did he get it passed through a number of hands, and make it appear as if it was being bought by an aerated water manufacturer who had a lawful use for it? You will have little difficulty in arriving at a conclusion on this matter; it was simply to hide its purpose. If he wanted it for an honest purpose, he should have gone and bought it himself. Now, gentlemen, I will give you the dates on which these purchases were made. The first was made on 4th September 1882; the second was made on 21st October 1882; and the third was made on 6th November 1882. These were the three dates, which are proved from the books of the people from whom the vitriol was bought,—Alexander Hope, Junior, & Company. And it is not immaterial to notice that Alexander Hope, Junior, & Company was one of the three firms from which Featherstone was in the way of buying vitriol; Featherstone was in the way of making purchases at the same time, and he got vitriol consigned to Cork to him just about this time. Now, gentlemen, I have given you those dates as having a very important bearing upon the whole case in more ways than one. It will be in your recollection that it was in the month of September that M'Dermott was trying to get vitriol in the other works, and perhaps if he had got the vitriol there it would not have been necessary to buy this, but it is, at all events, to be noted that attempts were being made by one of the persons whom we charge as conspirators to get vitriol in other works. I pointed out to you a few minutes ago that the latter of these dates, the 6th of November, was the very day on which Terence M'Dermott bought his second 10 lbs. of glycerine. That is a striking fact in the case. So that you have by two of these conspirators on the same day a large purchase of two of the essential constituents of nitro-glycerine. Now, when you come to questions of common purpose and common acting, when you find identity of dates of that kind, you will have little difficulty in seeing the great importance of that identity. I do not know that I need delay you longer upon that matter, except to call attention to what M'Cullagh himself says in his declaration about these purchases, because if a satisfactory account had been given by him of them, although they look strange, and although the coincidence is unfortunate, and although the occult

and circuitous way in which he tried to hide that he was the real
buyer would create suspicion against him, these adverse impressions
might be removed. And if he had an opportunity of explaining,
and if he had shown, which he alone could do, that it was wanted
for some lawful purpose, and if his statement had been verified, he
would have had the benefit of that. But he was asked about it
in his declaration, and I shall read to you what he said about it,
because it is very important. He said: "A man came to me
some time before the New Year to my house" [reads from
M'Cullagh's declaration from the top of page 12 down to " I
got no money from him." See top of page 121]. Now, there is a
strange mixture of truth, and what you will probably be of opinion
is not truth, there. He admits the purchase, and, for anything
I care in this case, it may have been for a man called Bill; it may
have been for Featherstone or one of the others,—that is precisely
my case. But that account cannot be true, because it is not
credible that a man would come up on the street to another, and,
merely saying, "I am Bill," ask him to get him carboys of vitriol,
supplying the money for the purchase, and rewarding him afterwards by giving him a drink,—it is not credible that there would
be three or four consignments of vitriol got by a man named Bill
in that way; and where this man came from or went to is not
explained. That is just the kind of story you are acquainted
with in ordinary thefts,—where the thief says, "I got it from a
man on the street whom I never saw before and have never seen
since." That will not delude anybody, and I think, when you find
the attempts at concealment made by M'Cullagh in buying the
vitriol, which he admits was wanted to be of the strongest, and when
you find these purchases going on at the time when glycerine was
also being got, you will have no difficulty in reaching the conclusion
that these purchases, which M'Cullagh admits were made, were
truly for the felonious and illegal use of making nitro-glycerine.
There is another point, namely, that the jars were left in the
outside of Myles M'Cullough's yard, and you no doubt will
keep in view also that it is proved that Donnelly, M'Dermott,
and Devany were seen about the gate of that yard about
this time. They were not seen inside apparently, and no wonder,
because the vitriol was left sitting in the outer yard. Very
probably they were the men who filled it into the jars and
took it away in the sack. At all events, it is very singular that
while we find one of the prisoners, M'Cullagh, buying vitriol in
this circuitous way, two or three others are found hovering outside
at that very time. I submit, then, that these purchases, like the
purchases of glycerine by M'Dermott, shed a very important and
very dark light upon this part of the case. I think that concludes
the evidence I have to bring under your notice regarding the
actual purchases by the accused. Now, gentlemen, I wish to pass
to another part of the case, intending shortly to make some

observations of a general character upon what I have already said, and also upon the part of the case to which I am now coming. I shall submit to you that the evidence to which I have already referred amply and sufficiently proves that there was a conspiracy, to which each of the prisoners was a party along with Featherstone and Dalton, for the purpose of making explosives and using them for destroying buildings. What the ulterior object of that was I shall immediately inquire. But while we charge the conspiracy itself as an overt act within the meaning of the statute, and while we also charge the conspiracy itself as a common law crime, it is to be kept in view that we separately charge that these men had to do with the actual explosions proved to you, and therefore, before proceeding to ask your attention to a few observations on the question of the design of this conspiracy, I shall conclude the examination of the evidence, bearing upon what we say are overt acts, by which it was carried out. The first of these was the explosion of the Tradeston gasometer, and I do not repeat what I have already said to you on that point, as to what that explosion was due to, because I left the evidence with you last night, as conclusively establishing that it was due to dynamite, or some other nitro-glycerine compound. Hence it becomes very important to determine, if we can, whether the prisoners, or any one of them, were seen at the time, or about the time, at the place, or about the place, where that explosion occurred. Now, you have had evidence on that point, gentlemen, and you have had it proved to you, on testimony of which you will judge, that not fewer than three of the accused were close to the site of that Tradeston explosion. You have it proved that Devany was there, that M'Cann was there, and that Donnelly, to say the least, was not far away. And I shall first ask your attention to the evidence bearing upon the prisoner Devany, because his presence at the place is most clearly and most unequivocally proved. You may recollect the evidence given early in the case by the boy Gavin Lawrie, a smart boy of fifteen, who is an apprentice designer. What he says is that he was taking a walk with a companion named Gabriel Longmuir, also about fifteen or sixteen years of age, along Darnley Street, which is close to Lilybank Road, when they were struck by the appearance of a man who was leaning with his back against a paling. Now, Lawrie says, when they passed this man, who had on a dark hat with a flat rim, and who was about the middle size, there was something they thought suspicious about his appearance —something they did not like. He was looking apparently in an inquiring way at them—very probably to see whether they were looking at him. But, at all events, there that man was, with his back against the paling near the gasometer, at the place you have already heard described, and the description of which I need not repeat. So much was it the case that the aspect of this man struck the boys, that they looked back, and when they had got a little past the man, the second of the two boys, Gabriel Longmuir, made the remark, "That man is on for something." Now, that was a very striking remark made contemporaneously, because there is no kind of evidence so reliable as that which proves the effect produced on the mind of a person at the time the thing to which he speaks took place, and before he knew it was to turn out important, or that there would be any inquiry about it. And you know very well how, without being able to say why, we feel that there is something suspicious or strange about a person; we know such impressions are produced upon the human mind; and on these two intelligent boys there was an impression made by that man, that there was something strange about him, and that he was "on for something." Who was the man? On that point Lawrie is quite distinct. He passed the man within a couple of feet, and he says Devany is the man. Longmuir, who was farther away, is not so distinct. In fact, I do not think I can put it to you that Longmuir identified Devany at all. He said he might be like the man, but he cannot be said to have identified the man. But Lawrie identified the man quite distinctly, and he said of Devany, "That is the man." I should have said that what Lawrie and Longmuir saw was very shortly before the explosion, about ten minutes or so. They were very little past the place when the explosion occurred, and the suggestion I make is that Devany was waiting for the explosion. Probably the box had been laid, and the tap turned, and the sulphuric acid was eating its way through the paper at the very time he was waiting with his back to the paling,—waiting until it would explode. At all events, that is the suggestion I make, because the explosion occurred within ten minutes or a quarter of an hour afterwards. The evidence, however, does not stop there, because you have the butcher's assistant, Robert Aitken, who says that he had come down Eglinton Street, that he was going along that very place, and that he saw immediately after the explosion two men running out of Muirhouse Lane. Now, you may recollect that Muirhouse Lane is close to the gasometer; it is the place where poor Butler lived, whose house was shattered and who was burned with his family by the explosion. Well, two men, immediately after the explosion, were seen by Aitken running out of Muirhouse Lane in the direction of Eglinton Street, which is, as no doubt you know, the main thoroughfare south of the Clyde at that part of Glasgow. In short, two men were making away through the main thoroughfare up to the town. Most people after an explosion would wait to see all about it. A crowd gathered in ten minutes, but these particular men were in a hurry to get away. They were not anxious to wait to see about the explosion. They thought the sooner they could get into Eglinton Street and be off the better. Well, who were these two men? On that Aitken is quite distinct. He says Devany was one, and M'Cann another. I don't think he was quite so distinct as to M'Cann, but as to Devany he is perfectly positive that he is one of the two men, and he also says that the other was M'Cann.

LORD MURE.—M'Cann or M'Cabe.

THE LORD ADVOCATE.—He pointed to M'Cann and called him M'Cabe. Well, gentlemen, in that connection I would ask you to keep in view this, that according to the same witness, Aitken, there were other two men—another pair of men running up immediately after the two whom he identified, and the first two men turned round and looked towards the second two to see if they were coming. There were thus more associates than the two men there that night, for there can be little doubt that the impression produced on Aitken, if you accept his evidence, was well-founded, viz. that these four men were substantially in company—that is, the first two wanted to see if the second two were coming; and the second two, like the first two, were making off and not stopping to see, like most people, what this explosion was. Now, that, I think, is very important evidence as far as it goes, and it makes, you will observe, very clear the testimony of the second distinct witness to the identity of Devany. Of course, the boy Lawrie knew nothing about Aitken nor Aitken about Lawrie, and Lawrie says, "I saw Devany leaning with his back against the paling;" and Aitken says, "I saw him run away out at Muirhouse Lane immediately after the explosion along with M'Cann." But, gentlemen, we bring another of the prisoners into that locality on that night. You may remember Mrs. M'Kersie and her daughter Jane. On that evening they were going along Lilybank Road, which is close to the gasholder, and they met a man who appeared to be the worse of drink. He looked as if he was staggering, and he was singing songs. They seem to have been prompted by curiosity to look round, and when they did so after he was past, they saw him walking quite straight, and he had stopped his singing. They say that man was Donnelly. They both identified him as Donnelly; at all events, Mrs. M'Kersie did, and the daughter says he is very like him. What I suggest here, is that Donnelly was, like Devany and M'Cann, waiting about until the explosion occurred. And seeing two people, he did not wish to look as if he was suspiciously loitering, therefore he appears to have assumed a staggering gait, and to have commenced singing, as he stopped both when the ladies were past. But, at all events, they identify Donnelly as being there. Now, the identification of Devany does not stop with the two witnesses to whose evidence I have recalled your recollection, because Margaret Smith, you may remember—an old lady—says that she and her sister, Mrs. Kerr, were convoying a niece home along by the railway bridge, on the side of Muirhouse Lane, about ten o'clock that night, their niece being a young lady, and when they had parted with her, they stood looking after her, to see that she got on all right, I suppose. Miss Smith says, when they were so doing, they saw a man leaning on the railway bridge, at the side of Muirhouse Lane, and she says that man was Devany. So that you have three very distinct witnesses to the fact that Devany was loitering about in close proximity to that gasometer before the explosion, and that he ran away after it. There was an attempt made in cross-examination to throw some doubt upon Aitken and Margaret Smith. I don't think my learned friends attempted to say a word against Lawrie or Longmuir; but Mr. Rhind subjected Aitken to a cross-examination, to show that he had been dismissed. Aitken said candidly that he had been dismissed from his service. He said, "I did stay too long out that night; I did not go home on the night of the explosion to Pollokshields to my master, and on the Monday I got my wages and went away." But does that lead you to doubt the evidence of Aitken? As to this lady, Margaret Smith, one of my learned friends put a question. He suggested, "Was he not pointed out to you?" Well, it turned out that Devany was not pointed out to her at all, but that, when one of the police authorities was in the house, talking to her sister, Mrs. Kerr, and not being aware that Margaret Smith knew anything about this affair, she, looking out of the window, pointed to a man going along the street, and said, "There's the man we saw on the bridge;" and that was Devany. Now, I say that was a cross-examination which very much strengthened the evidence for the Crown, as, indeed, a good many of the questions put in cross-examination in the course of this case did. I therefore leave the question in your hands, whether it is not satisfactorily established that Devany certainly,—Devany by three witnesses,—M'Cann by one, and Donnelly by one, were at or about the site of that explosion on that night, loitering to begin with, and running away in the end. Now, if you have at all taken the view which I submitted to you, upon the prior evidence, that these men were all conspiring together for the purpose of blowing up buildings, I think you will have little difficulty in drawing a conclusion as to what the result on the whole evidence as to these three should be. And, gentlemen, I must tell you—and here I ask a direction from the Bench in point of law—what is the effect of one or more of the conspirators doing an act of the kind, which they had in common conspired to execute, upon the rest? I think it right to say at this stage, that I am not in a position to ask you to hold that upon the evidence any of the other prisoners at the bar were at or about the places where any of the three explosions occurred. I think the three I have named are all who were brought to the site of the gasometer. In regard to the Possil Bridge, —I may just recall your recollection to the evidence, although I cannot say it is sufficient,—you had the evidence of the man named George Murray, who told us he was in a particular street near to Possil Bridge, when two men passed him, carrying a tin box, just like a tin bonnet-box, and probably the box which was set down on Possil Bridge. He had a drop of drink; he seems to have lurched up against the men, and the men appeared to be very sensitive about being stumbled against, and George Murray said, "You have surely got eggs in your box, when you are so afraid." Probably they had got something much more dangerous than eggs. Of these two men, one, he thinks, was Kelly, but I cannot say that he stated it with such a degree of assurance, or even professed to state it with such a degree of assurance, as to make it right I should ask you to hold that Kelly is proved to have been at that spot; and therefore the result, as regards Possil Bridge, is that we have not been able to connect any of the prisoners, directly, with setting down that box. And I say the same with respect to the explosion at the Caledonian shed; we have not been able to bring any of the prisoners to the spot there, at or about the time when the explosion occurred. But we do bring very near to that spot at that very time, one of the men who seems to have been deepest in this conspiracy, and who, unfortunately, has escaped, I mean Kearney, the signalman. You will recollect that he is the man who appears to have been the first to bring the two American gentlemen into contact with the group on the Green, and he was in nearly every stage in the inner circle of this conspiracy. You will also remember that he is one of the men, whose addresses were found upon the card which Dalton had in his pocket,—"J. F. K., 21 Stanhope Street, G.," which was Dalton's sign for Glasgow. On coming from America, or, at all events, before he was found, Dalton had the address of this man Kearney, just as he had the address of what we know to have been Featherstone in Cork, nominally D. O'Herlihy, Great George Street (West). Now Kearney was in the signal-box that very night. Long, who was with him most of the time, remembers that Kearney was not out of the signal-box for a considerable period, but we had it proved that there may be almost an indefinite delay in an explosion, by wrapping more or less paper round the tap, so that there is nothing in the time that Kearney was in the signal-box to make it impossible, although it might make it improbable, that when he was out for seven or eight minutes he had set down the box. I cannot say that the evidence is such that I can ask you to believe that he did it; but that is not important, as Kearney is not here. You have also to keep in view that the site of this explosion is near Terence M'Dermott's house,—a few minutes' walk from it,—and apparently there had been a ladder put over the bridge at Dobbie's Loan very shortly before the explosion. It is proved that the shed had been disused for some time,—it was not in use at the time,—but when it was in use the quickest mode of getting to it, and the one apparently commonly used by the workers, was by the iron ladder which was hung over the bridge at

Dobbie's Loan. Well, that shed having been disused, the ladder was taken away, and it had been away for a considerable time, but on the morning after the explosion it was found to be there again. None of the officials of the railway know by whom it was replaced, and I think it is a fair inference or surmise—although I cannot ask you to take it as proved—that Kearney and some of his confederates may have put the ladder over the bridge, come down by it, and placed the dynamite in the shed. But I do not ask you to come to any definite conclusion upon that point. I say nothing more about Possil Bridge or the Railway shed, but taking it that I have proved that either Devany, or Devany along with Donnelly and M'Cann, were three of the four men who were seen running away after the explosion at the gasometer, what is the effect in law of that upon the rest? I submit to you, as a proposition true equally in law and in common sense, that if you shall come to be of opinion, upon the rest of the evidence, that these men, the three, or any one of them, who were seen at the gasometer, were confederates along with the other prisoners at the bar,—that they were acting together for a common purpose, and that that purpose was the purpose set out in the indictment, the manufacture and use of explosives against buildings,—then in point of law each one of the conspirators was responsible, legally and morally responsible, for the act of any one of them done in pursuance of that common purpose. So that it would by no means follow, gentlemen, that because only Devany, either with or without Donnelly and M'Cann, was seen and identified as being at the site of the explosion of the gasometer, they alone were responsible. I say, on the contrary, subject to direction from the Bench, that if you are satisfied there was an agreement or conspiracy amongst these men in pursuance of a common purpose, the common purpose being to make and use explosives against buildings, and if you find that any one of the men did use explosives against buildings in pursuance of that common purpose, in law that is the act of them all. Therefore, in coming to consider the evidence, you will see that it is not so material whether you can or cannot trace them all to the spot or not, if you find one of them there, and you are satisfied that he was there in pursuance of a common purpose. I shall now pass from that part of the case, and in concluding the observations I have to make to you, I shall now very shortly sum up the results of the evidence as far as I have examined it.

THE LORD JUSTICE-CLERK.—Are you not going to make any observation upon the cabman's evidence?

THE LORD ADVOCATE.—I beg your lordship's pardon.

THE LORD JUSTICE-CLERK.—I would like to know whether my impression upon it is the same as yours.

THE LORD ADVOCATE.—I shall state my impression of it.

The Lord Justice-Clerk.—It is hardly important enough to delay you.

The Lord Advocate.—The result of that part of the evidence, I think, is this: it is proved that upon a particular occasion, if I recollect right, the second Friday of January, M'Dermott and Donnelly hired a cabman named Munro in St. Vincent Street, and having hired him they drove down to Portugal Lane,—to the end of Portugal Lane,—being a place on the south side of the town. Now, it is in Portugal Lane that Devany lives. They had a small parcel with them,—not very large,—about the size of a Glasgow Directory wrapped in paper. They went into the Lane, and the cabman cannot say where they went to. I suggest that they went to Devany's house. They remained about twenty minutes, and a man returned with them who cannot be identified. Where did they go? To Ronald Street at the other end of the town. Now, who were there at that time? That was the time Moorhead, who has disappeared, was lodging with Mrs. M'Lachlan. No, I am wrong there; I think Moorhead went there on the 15th of January, and the occasion when this cab was driven there would be probably rather sooner. But, at all events, they went to Ronald Street, where almost immediately afterwards Moorhead appeared. What they did in Ronald Street is not proved, but it is a somewhat singular fact that you find M'Dermott and Donnelly, two of the most active conspirators, driving about in a cab that night, in the neighbourhood of Devany's residence, and in a place where we afterwards find Moorhead, the associate of Dalton and M'Dermott.

The Lord Justice-Clerk.—How do you associate Moorhead with these facts?

The Lord Advocate.—In this way: I shall shortly repeat it again. It is proved, gentlemen, that on the 15th of January, as nearly as Mrs. M'Lachlan can recollect, Moorhead came to lodge with her. He stayed till the Thursday eight weeks,—the last full day he was there was the 8th March. On the evening of 8th March, Moorhead came in along with Dalton, the two bringing a bonnet-box.

The Lord Justice-Clerk.—I am quite aware of the facts as to the 8th of March, but in regard to the previous facts, can you bring him into contact with them?

The Lord Advocate.—I cannot bring him into contact except in this way, that on the evening of the 8th of March and the morning of the 9th I bring him into contact with Dalton and M'Dermott. But then, gentlemen, you will see that is a good deal; it is by no means little if you bear in mind what Dalton's own pocketbook proves. He has marked " G., 3/ 8/ 83." That means 8th March 1883, and " G." stands for Glasgow ; " L.," Liverpool ; " Ln.," London ; and so you find there is no doubt that he was in Glasgow at that time. It is a remarkable corroboration of the accuracy of Mrs. M'Lachlan that we find in Dalton's diary an entry of that kind. You will believe that he was coming and going on what was an illegal errand. And there is another occasion on which Munro, the cabman, was hired by Donnelly. He is quite distinct in regard to Donnelly hiring him twice. Now, I think you will be of opinion that Donnelly is not in a grade of life or a man to be driving about in cabs at his own charges, unless he was on some errand for which other people were finding the money. There is just one other point about the cabman. He thinks, although he is not very sure, that he saw Devany talking to M'Coy, his master. But that does not come to much. Munro is in the service of a Mr. M'Coy, and he thinks he saw Devany talking to M'Coy. I think that is all that is proved by Munro'; at least there is nothing more that dwells in my mind on the subject. So that the case, so far as we have examined it, comes to this on the evidence—that you have it proved that in the beginning of March Hughes was sworn in to the secret society. In the beginning of June M'Dermott was sworn into the same society with M'Cullagh. We have not very clear evidence as to the objects of that secret society except this, that according to Hughes the import and effect of the oath were that the members were to stand by each other if they got into any habble with the Government; so that it is quite evident that the society contemplated that it might find itself in conflict with the powers that be. We do not find that for a considerable time there was any mention of the use of dynamite, or, so far as we can see, of any other illegal purpose, but on the occasion I have mentioned to you, in the month of July, in Jail Square, the two fine gentlemen from America were brought upon the field, and from that time Featherstone, and sometimes Johnstone, were in constant, or very nearly constant, association with the prisoners. We find lectures delivered by Featherstone upon the use of dynamite, and the way to make it, and its effect in blowing up buildings. We find him saying at one of these lectures, it would teach the Government a lesson, and show them they were not to have everything their own way. Now, that rather reflects back some light upon what the meaning of getting into a habble with the Government was. Then, we have it next proved, that a small bottle of vitriol and a white powder were brought into Hughes' stable, and an experiment made. Hughes was asked by Kelly to store some jars, and he was asked also by Kelly to go and drive some jars of acid. Then we have all the purchases by Featherstone, and the transmission of the materials purchased to Cork, and their coming back, as I submit to you, in infernal machines. Side by side with the purchases by Featherstone, we have the purchases by M'Dermott and M'Cullagh. Side by side with these, we have all the various other circumstances that I have referred to, and, last of all, we have the explosions occurring on the 20th of January, shortly after the materials might well have been made into nitroglycerine, and used for that felonious purpose. Now, I am not going to repeat what I am afraid I have already gone into in almost too great detail, as to the evidence upon this point, but I may say that this is one of those cases where the closest attention requires to be paid to the whole evidence. Where you are dealing with a secret conspiracy, it is seldom you get such direct testimony as we have from Hughes in this case. You are, gentlemen, put to build up a case upon minute facts, all leading with perfect certainty to one conclusion, and only one. If you shall be satisfied upon the evidence thus far, that there was a conspiracy to which all these men were more or less parties, the next point is, what was the object of that conspiracy? We charge that the object of the conspiracy was the one set out in the indictment—substantially by force and violence, by producing terror and alarm, to cause the Queen and Parliament to change their courses in regard to Ireland. That is putting it shortly. Now, gentlemen, if that was not the object, what was the object?—I mean if that was not the design of this conspiracy, what was its design? There has been no other design suggested, unless it was the strike in connection with the Caledonian Railway; and that suggestion will be at once dismissed, for reasons which I have already stated, as not having the slightest shade of probability. But you will notice, gentlemen, what is the history of the more active agency in this conspiracy. The more active part of it is done by people coming from America—American Irishmen. It cannot be supposed they knew there was going to be a strike among the Caledonian Railway servants, and, besides, the strike was over before the explosion took place. But it was not the Caledonian Railway shed only; the gasometer was assailed, and no human being has suggested any reason for destroying it. Personal malice is out of the question. The shed was owned by the Caledonian Railway Company, which is another way of saying by thousands of shareholders scattered throughout the country, and there is nothing to lead any one to suppose that the shed was blown up in malice to the Caledonian Railway Company, or the shareholders of it. But then it happens that other explosions took place. The gaswork is owned by the Corporation of Glasgow, and there has been no suggestion that anybody had malice against the Corporation of Glasgow. Then the third explosion was on the bridge of the Canal; and nobody has suggested that there was any malice against the people who own the Canal. But each and all of those explosions were exceedingly well adapted to strike terror into the general population of Glasgow. If the Canal explosion had succeeded, we cannot tell what damage might have been done to life and property, because it would have let out the water in the Canal in a very crowded part of the city. It is almost a wonder that the damage by the gasometer explosion was so little ; it was, however, considerable to poor Butler and some others, who were there. Now, when you find three explosions occurring in the same night, assailing the property of different people, and no other suggestion is made, you will probably not hesitate to conclude that ours is the only reasonable suggestion, viz. that there was a conspiracy having for its object the intimidation of the Government. And, of course, there is no more effective way of intimidating a Government than by intimidating the people who elect the House of Commons. Whether the scheme of intimidating the people, and through the people the Government, was likely to succeed or not, is a very different question, and this is not the proper time or the proper place in which to discuss it. We may have our opinions in regard to it, but the question you have to consider now and here is whether there is any other explanation that can be given of the action of the conspirators ; and if you believe the evidence, you have direct testimony that what I have stated was their object. Along with that, you will no doubt keep in view what was found in Dalton's pocket,—I mean the paper about the Fenian organization, and about circles and centres. But I won't detain you longer on this point. If you come to the conclusion that these men, or any two or more of them, were parties to a conspiracy for the use of explosives against public buildings, as sensible men of the world there is no conclusion but one which you can draw from that —that the design of the conspiracy and its object was to use these explosives for the end set out in the indictment. At this point I would conclude, but for the fact that there are ten prisoners before you, whom I have hitherto rather taken *en masse*, dealing with them as a group of conspirators; and it might aid your deliberations if I said a few words for the purpose of individualizing and bringing together very shortly, although perhaps at the risk of repetition, the points that tell against each of them. It will be your duty, taking every care, and doing every justice to the different prisoners, to have present to your minds in a compendious form the considerations which bear against each ; and I am afraid, as I have hitherto been dealing with them rather as a group, that you may possibly have lost sight of the points that bear against each individually. I propose, therefore, now to bring together the points which tell against each. I will first take the case against Terence M'Dermott. Now, gentlemen, Terence M'Dermott was sworn a member of the secret society in the beginning of June 1882. He is proved by Niven, the constable, to have been an associate of Devany and M'Cann and others in Jail Square, just at the time when this conspiracy was being hatched. You will recollect that he was chiefly at Irvine down to October, and, although he might be in Glasgow on Saturday afternoons and Sundays, his regular residence was not in Glasgow, but in Irvine ; at least I assume in his favour. You find that M'Ginnes proves that M'Dermott was seen with M'Cullagh and M'Cann, with Drum, Casey and Hughes, in Lennox's public-house, just as Hughes says. So that there can be no doubt that M'Dermott was an associate of the prisoners, and that he was sworn a member of this secret society. The next point, which it will be necessary that you should keep in view, is his attempt in the month of September to get sulphuric acid from Levi Barrow, the vitriol pumper; and next after that is the purchases of glycerine from Clolus & Co., under a false name, in the end of October and on 6th November 1882, the latter date being the same as one of the purchases of vitriol by M'Cullagh. You will no doubt keep in view that in his declaration he denies the purchases altogether. He denies that he gave the name of James Bolan, and denies the transaction altogether. The next point which I put before you in the evidence, although, perhaps, it is not so clearly brought home, is that which relates to the injury to the pipes in his house, which we suggest was due to acid. We have not been able to bring that so sharply home as we would have liked, but you will judge of its effect. You have M'Dermott next driving about in a cab visiting Portugal Lane and Ronald Street. Then you have his visit to Moorhead and Dalton, and his going away with them on the morning of Thursday, 8th March, as he said himself, to London. I think that is all I need say about him, because I have gone into the details before. I have only to repeat, that in his declaration he denies altogether the purchases of glycerine, and he denies that he visited at Ronald Street, although that is proved by the testimony of three separate and distinct witnesses. I now come to the case of Devany, who stands second in the indictment. Devany was a member of the secret society before Hughes joined, and was present when Hughes was sworn in. Devany was also a regular associate of the others at Lennox's public-house and at Jail Square, and in particular, he was at the meeting on the 4th or 5th of July, when Kearney mentioned that the two gentlemen from America were there, and when M'Cullagh and Drum went away along with Kearney and saw these two gentlemen. Then he was one of those who were present at the lectures given by Featherstone in the Democratic or Gymnastic Hall about the end of August, these lectures being about the manufacture of explosives and their use against buildings for the purpose of teaching the Government a lesson, or showing the Government they were not to have everything their own way. The next point we have against Devany is this,—Devany lived in Portugal Lane, and we suggest that he was visited by Donnelly and M'Dermott, although that is not directly proved. But what is perhaps the most fatal circumstance, and absolutely conclusive, if you believe it, upon the whole of the rest of the case against Devany, is that by no fewer than three witnesses he is identified as having been at the place of the gasometer explosion. You have Lawrie quite distinct; Longmuir says he was like him, leaning suspiciously against the paling, and Longmuir remarking, "That man is on for something." Aitken identified him, and Margaret Smith also. And I pray you to recollect what I said before, —that he was loitering before the explosion, and running away immediately afterwards. Most people stay — innocent people stay—to see what has happened, and its cause. He went away. That, I think, is the main part of the evidence against Devany. But, gentlemen, there is another circumstance against him, and I do not know that it has been clearly brought before you yet. It may be in your recollection,—and it is very important on the question of the credibility of Hughes,—that Hughes said that on one occasion Devany had told him that when he had lain down on the top of his bed to take a sleep, two detectives came in, and he was very much afraid they would find the dynamite,—meaning, of course, the dynamite he had in his house,—but if they had found the dynamite he would have blown out their brains with a revolver which he had in the house. In his declaration he admits that he made such a statement, but he says it was a joke. Well, gentlemen, it was a very singular joke; and there is one real fact about it, that when he was apprehended and his house was searched, a revolver and a case of some thirty-five cartridges were found in it. So that it is true he had a revolver, and what a working man like him would be doing with a revolver for any lawful purpose one does not see. But taking his own statement, it shows that dynamite was in his mind, if it was not in his house. And why he should say it was a joke—a good or a bad joke—to speak of blowing out the brains of the constables if they found dynamite in his house, if there was no dynamite there, it is not easy to see. Hughes says that one Saturday night after the explosion he was going across Jail Square, and Devany came up to him and said, "Last night I had a very narrow escape. I had laid myself down on the top of the bed after I came home to have a sleep, when I heard some one speaking to my wife at the door. I looked up and heard some one. If they had attempted to take me I would have blown them to eternity; I would have blown them to atoms." From this statement, it does not appear that he mentioned dynamite, but Devany admits it more fully in his declaration than Hughes puts it in his evidence. Here is what Devany says in his declaration: "I remember that I did say to Hughes, but merely as a joke, that if the detectives had discovered the dynamite I would have blown their brains out with a revolver. It would be hard for them to discover what there was none to discover. I simply said it as a joke." Now, I ask you to consider whether it is conceivable that he would have made a joke about a thing if it was not in his mind. I say that is, almost under Devany's own hand, evidence that he had dynamite stored in his house, with a pistol intended to assail anybody who came to take the dynamite. I don't think I need go into any of the other evidence relating to Devany. You will remember a number of papers of various kinds were found in his house, besides a revolver and 'cartridges. I come next to Peter Callaghan. The points bearing against him are the following: It would appear that Callaghan had taken an active part in getting members for the society, because it may be within your recollection that he had for some time been pressing Hughes to join the society, and it was very much upon his entreaties that Hughes did join. Callaghan was present on the occasion when Hughes was sworn in. He was also present at the meeting in Jail Square, on the 4th of July, when the two Americans arrived. Then he was present at the experiment in Hughes' stable on the Sunday after the 4th of July, with the bottle of vitriol and white powder. He was also present when Featherstone lectured in the Democratic or Gymnastic Hall. He was present when Kelly said he had made an unsuccessful experiment, for which he got 10s. out of the £2, 10s., which Hughes was keeping to purchase materials, and Kelly said, "I will pay that myself." Callaghan was present when Kelly made that statement. Constable Porter speaks quite distinctly to the general association of Callaghan with the others in Jail Square. M'Ginnes identifies him as a frequenter of Lennox's public-house, and Horan, the only other man—that unwilling witness—who was a member of this society who is not in the dock, says Callaghan was present when he was sworn in a member. I think these are the main points against Callaghan. There is one point more bearing upon Devany, which I should have asked your attention to; Devany gave in a special defence,—what we call an *alibi*,—alleging that he was somewhere else at the time of the Tradeston explosion. No attempt was made to prove an *alibi*, and you will draw your own conclusion from that. Notice was given telling where he was. No attempt was made to prove it. The next prisoner I come to is Henry M'Cann. Now, he is one of those identified by Aitken. And Horan says he was present when he went to the public-house,—Lennox's,—and was sworn in. Then M'Cann is also proved to have been present at the meeting when the oath was administered to Hughes. He was also at the experiment in Hughes' stable on the Sunday, when the vitriol and white powder were tried, and he appears to have been one of the men who took the most active part in collecting money. It is suggested that the money was collected for a poor woman—for a charitable purpose. It is for you to judge whether that was made out, or whether he was not a sort of collector or treasurer, for, amongst other things, getting money to purchase the stuff, as they called it. Then he was the man with whom Hughes had the quarrel, which rather separated Hughes from the rest, and Porter identifies M'Cann as constantly associating with the others at Jail Square. And you may recollect that the accident of the quarrel quite distinctly brings,—by the independent evidence of Porter—independent of Hughes,—brings Featherstone into direct contact with M'Cann and the others, because when Hughes, being rather affronted by the blow, went away and met Porter, and said, "If you had been here a little time ago, I would have given M'Cann into custody," the group came up, and Featherstone accosted Porter, and said, "The one was as bad as the other; never mind." So that you have M'Cann, not only directly associating with the rest of the group, but with Featherstone. Then he is also identified by Constable Niven, as associating with the others, not only in Jail Square, but other places. These are the main points in the case, as against M'Cann. In his declaration he denies collecting money. There were collecting-books found in his house, but the suggestion with regard to them is that they were for charitable purposes. I think the Catholic clergyman proved that M'Cann collected for a Total Abstinence Society, but I don't think the books were shown to him, or identified with that collection. But we had it from others that he was collecting money. The next prisoner to whom I shall refer is James M'Cullagh; and his case you will find attended with very little difficulty, because it was M'Cullagh who bought the sulphuric acid, through his namesake,—three carboys,—at the time M'Dermott was buying glycerine. Then there is evidence that he was associated with the rest; and you have his declaration, in which he admits the purchase of the vitriol, but says it was for the man Bill, of whom he can tell nothing. These are the main points in his case. Then you have Donnelly. That he was a member of the secret society is proved. Porter speaks to the general association of the accused, including Donnelly; and he was one of those—and this is very important—who were seen close to Myles M'Cullough's premises, about the time when the jars of vitriol were lifted. Not only so, but Donnelly is one of the men who drove in Munro's cab along with M'Dermott; and, what is perhaps most important of all, Donnelly is one of the men identified as having been at the site of the explosion on the evening of the 20th of January. Now, I do not go through the more general evidence.

THE LORD JUSTICE-CLERK.—By whom was Donnelly identified that night?

THE LORD ADVOCATE.—By a Mrs. M'Kersie and her daughter. Mrs. M'Kersie and her daughter were going along together, and met a man who seemed to be staggering and who was singing. They looked over their shoulders, and he was walking quite sober and had stopped singing. They identified him as Donnelly, the mother distinctly; the daughter says he is like him. Of course the other was the third identification of Devany. Well, Donnelly, you see, gentlemen, is brought into very close contact with many of the most important circumstances in this history. The next prisoner to whom I come is Kelly. He was present on the first Monday of March, when Hughes was sworn in; he was present on the Sunday when the experiment was tried in Hughes' stable; he was present when Johnston gave instructions in the use of dynamite, which was about the 12th of July. Hughes gave him, at his request, 10s. to buy stuff to make an experiment, and, according to Hughes, Kelly afterwards came back and said the experiment had been unsuccessful, and that he was to pay the money himself. Then Porter identifies Kelly as associating with the others. M'Ginnes speaks of Kelly frequently meeting with them in the public-house. The next prisoner is Patrick M'Cabe. He was present when Hughes was sworn in. He was present when the bottle of vitriol was brought, and the experiment made. He was present when Featherstone gave his lecture in the Democratic Hall, and Porter identifies him as one of the parties who frequented Jail Square. I think that is all that bears upon his case. Then Patrick Drum was present when Hughes was sworn in on the first Monday of March. He was present when the bottle of vitriol was brought and the experiment made. He was present when Johnston explained the use of dynamite in Jail Square. Then Hughes says that about the 16th of July, he received £2, 10s. from Drum to keep, and that was the money out of which he gave 10s. to Kelly, to make an experiment which Kelly said proved unsuccessful. Further, Drum was also present in the Democratic Hall, when Featherstone gave the lecture upon dynamite, and he is identified by Porter as one of the party who frequented Jail Square. The last of the accused is Casey. He also is said to have been present when Hughes was sworn in. He was present at the meetings in Jail Square, when the bottles of vitriol were brought and the experiments made in the stable. Then he made arrangements for Hughes going to get vitriol. Hughes was, according to his statement, asked if he would drive some vitriol, and he agreed to do so. He was told it would do them no harm, and he met a young man in the public-house to which he was assigned, rather the worse of drink, and he apparently repented and did not drive the vitriol. Then Porter identifies Casey as one of those who was in the way of frequenting Jail Square; and M'Ginnes identifies him as being frequently in the public-house, along with Callaghan, M'Cann, Drum, and Kelly. I think these are the particulars bearing upon the individual prisoners; I mean apart from the general evidence which I have already appealed to as being proof of conspiracy generally. There is only one point I think I have omitted, and that is the attempted *alibi* of M'Cann. He is one of those who is said to have been seen near the gasometer. Now, you will recollect, his is by no means a satisfactory *alibi*. In the first place, as you know from your experience on juries, an *alibi*, particularly when attempted to be proved by friends, requires to be very closely examined; and in this case the statement by John M'Cann and Maggie M'Cann is that on that particular occasion John's boots were brought to his father Henry

M'Cann, the prisoner, for the purpose of being mended; and Mrs. Barclay, a daughter of Henry M'Cann, says that he was still mending away at the boots at nine o'clock when she left. The others stayed later, and say he went on mending the boots all night. Now, gentlemen, of course you must keep in view these are all members of M'Cann the prisoner's family, and one point to be kept in view is that, not only must you be satisfied with the integrity of the evidence, but you must be satisfied that the witnesses are not applying evidence of what truly occurred on some day to the date in question. That is one thing that always requires close watching.

THE LORD JUSTICE-CLERK.—How does the *alibi* bear upon this case?

THE LORD ADVOCATE.—Only because we have a witness who says that M'Cann was at the gasometer explosion. I am not examining any *alibi* except those of the men who were at the explosion. Devany made no attempt to prove his *alibi*. I put no questions to the witnesses who spoke to the *alibi* of men whom we do not bring to the spot. There was no need that I should; I only examined those applicable to the men who were said to have been on the spot. You will judge of the value of that attempt to prove an *alibi*, and give every fair consideration to it, I am sure. The only other man who was brought to the spot was Donnelly. Now, the *alibi* attempted to be proved on the part of Donnelly is not really an *alibi* at all. It comes to this,— that Donnelly's wife brought a pair of boots to Patrick M'Kenna to be mended that night,—it is a singular coincidence that the ground of recollection of the prisoners' witnesses is that boots were brought to be mended, in the only two important defences of *alibi* in this case,—and it is said she wanted the boots that night, and that he said she could not get them. But then, gentlemen, you must know that Patrick M'Kenna never saw Donnelly that night. It is not proved that Donnelly had only one pair of boots, and he might quite well have been near the gasometer at the time of the explosion, although a pair of his boots were sent to be mended that night. I therefore submit that there is an entire failure to prove this *alibi*. Now, I shall point out the result of the evidence bearing on the cases of the individual prisoners. You will observe that Callaghan, Devany, and Drum are perhaps most distinctly proved to have been active members of the society.

A JUROR.—Is there a receipt signed by Drum for the £2, 10s.?

THE LORD ADVOCATE.—No. There is evidence of this,—it is for you to judge of it,—that all the prisoners were members of this secret society, and that they were all frequent associates, and associates when these matters were being talked over. The evidence of frequenting the society and taking an active part in it seems strongest against Callaghan, Devany, and Drum. The strongest evidence of collecting money is against M'Cann. Then, gentlemen, on the very important matter of purchases, the strongest evidence is against M'Dermott and M'Cullagh. It is only right to say that, as regards Kelly, M'Cabe, and Casey, the evidence on some of these important points is slight. The evidence, I think, as regards Kelly, M'Cabe, and Casey, points more to constant association and conference with the others, than to actual participation in the explosions. The evidence of specific acts is not so strong against these men as against the others; but there is ample proof that they were members of the society, and constant associates when those discussions about dynamite were going on. But no doubt you will consider it right in applying the evidence to each personally, to see the particular things which he did, as well as to have regard to the fact that he was a member of the society. Then, in regard to the most vital point, that of actual presence at the site of the explosion, it is strongest against Devany. I submit as to Devany, it is clear. There is evidence, which you will judge, against Donnelly and M'Cann, but it is slight. I leave you to judge of that. I say against Devany it is clear. I think I have now gone over the main points in this very detailed case. I offer you an apology for detaining you so long, but you must have observed that the evidence is exceedingly voluminous, and it was only by bringing together, in the way I have endeavoured to do, the various points of that evidence, that you could well hope to carry in your minds all that was proved before you, and to apply it to the charges against the prisoners at the bar. The very number of the prisoners makes your duty, as it makes the task of every one concerned in the case, difficult; but I submit that, as the result of the whole of this inquiry, we have established what is quite enough, either under the statute or the common law charge, against all the prisoners. It will be quite enough if you are satisfied that they were parties to a conspiracy of the character charged in the indictment, even although there were no evidence to bring any of them into actual contact with the explosions. But I say that we do bring some of them into contact with the actual explosions; and I say, lastly, on this point, that if you shall be satisfied as to the conspiracy—that they were all conspiring to this common end, and that one or more of them carried out that conspiracy by blowing up the gasometer, they are all in law, as in morals, responsible for the act. So that, probably, in the result,—although that might seem to be an important distinction—you may not consider it so very vital after all. Now, I am very sure that it is needless for me, in concluding, to say anything by way of caution or warning in regard to the manner in which you ought to deal with it, as I am confident you will deal with it rightly. I have to submit that there is no reasonable doubt; but should there be a doubt in your minds in regard to these prisoners, or any of them, you will carefully weigh the evidence before making up your minds upon it. You are the judges of the evidence, and if you shall come to the conclusion that there is reasonable or serious doubt in the case of any of the prisoners, you will give them the benefit of that doubt. But if, on the other hand, you are satisfied that these men, or any two or more of them, were associates in a wicked and dangerous conspiracy of the character and seeking to attain the objects set out in the indictment, you will not shrink from performing the duty of finding a verdict in accordance with the conclusion at which you have arrived.

MR. RHIND'S ADDRESS.

Mr. RHIND, Advocate, then addressed the jury for the prisoners M'Dermott, Devany, Callaghan, Donnelly, Kelly, M'Cabe, and Casey. He said—

Gentlemen of the Jury,—I have never before addressed a jury with more anxiety than that with which I now address you. The crime charged is so grave; the number of the accused is so large; the punishment which will follow upon a conviction will necessarily be so severe. The Lord Advocate in his address to you has adverted again and again to the atrocity of the offence of which he asks you to find these prisoners guilty. Gentlemen, it is no part of my duty, it would be inconsistent with that fairness and moderation which I trust you will find in all I have to say to you, to dispute one word of what his Lordship has said to you in that respect. But I think you will agree with me in this, that the graver the crime that is charged, the graver the result which must follow on conviction, the more it becomes a jury to pause, the more you will be inclined to hesitate, before, on evidence which is not satisfactory to the minds of every one of you, you will find a verdict which will consign these men to a dreadful doom. The case which the prosecutor has laid before you, and on which he asks you to convict the prisoners, is indeed a strange one. He does not suggest that they were guilty, if guilty they were, of the crime charged against them from any personal motive, from lust of gain, or any of the more ignoble impulses that animate human nature. If they were guilty at all, he does not question, he admits, that it was not from any motive of that kind, but because of the affection, misguided, if you will, they bear to the fair Irish land they love so well. I am satisfied that you will come to the consideration of such a case prepared to scrutinise severely the evidence brought in support of it, thinking perhaps that if these prisoners have been led into evil, and near the verge of guilt, they are yet not unworthy of sympathy; that even if, foolishly and ignorantly, they listened for a little while to the suggestion of crime, there were yet in their natures some elements of the hero.

Gentlemen, in the city of Glasgow there is a vast population of natives of Ireland, Roman Catholics and poor labouring men, who feel deeply, as I suppose every Irishman does, for what, in their expressive language, they call "the distress" of Ireland. It is nothing peculiar to the prisoners, if you should think it established against them, that they should meet together on Glasgow Green or in Jail Square on Saturday afternoons, or on Sundays, to talk over Ireland's wrongs. Hundreds and thousands of Irishmen did and do the same. Nor was it unnatural that when they talked of Ireland they should not like to do so in a policeman's hearing; not because they meant evil, but because long years of injustice and oppression have taught these poor Irish people that the very name of Ireland sounds like high treason in British ears. Recent legislation has tried to remove, but has not yet removed that feeling. And so, when you find groups of Irishmen whispering about Irish distress, it by no means follows that they are met to do anything more than talk of Ireland's wrongs, or of legitimate means for the restoration of happiness to their native land. An example of that is to be found in the card taken possession of in the house of one of the prisoners, who is a member of the Irish National Land League. The card narrates the objects of the League. I had occasion to read it to you in the course of the trial; and I put it to you, is there a word, is there a syllable in it suggestive of disloyalty, or with which any right-minded Scotchmen or Englishmen would not sympathise? Why, the Irish National Land League has not for a single one of its objects anything beyond what recent legislation of the British Parliament has tried to effect. That, gentlemen, is the sort of Irish society you have in Glasgow—poor, honest hard-working men, believing greatly in their country's wrongs.

Gentlemen, in May 1882 there visited Glasgow from America, bribed, one cannot help suspecting, with American gold, a villain of the deepest dye—one Timothy Featherstone. No one can have any sympathy for that man; and it is well for the country, and for all, that, at Liverpool in the month of August last, he and three others received as the punishment of their crime a doom which to my mind is worse than the scaffold—penal servitude for life. These three others were Dalton, Flannigan, and Deasy. Previous to that, on 11th June 1883, there had been a trial in London, the result of which was the conviction for the same offence of four prisoners, Gallacher, Whitehead, Wilson, and Curtis; and they too were sentenced to penal servitude for life. One cannot help feeling that perhaps the Crown, in these circumstances, having got those eight men, the instigators and principal actors in the dynamite outrages, confined to gaol for the remainder of their lives, might, whatever their convictions regarding the guilt of the prisoners now at the bar, have done well to let them alone. Surely sufficient punishment to satisfy the demands of justice has already been awarded: surely sufficient warning to satisfy the demands of public safety has already been given. Look at the prisoners at the bar. Look at the rags they wear. Men of no understanding, of no education, half of them unable to read or to sign their own names; if to any extent they were guilty of crime, is it not certain that they were mere tools, mere dupes in the hands of villains who tried to seduce them into wrong, dupes led astray by ignorance and what to them seemed patriotism, tools paid by no hire? But, gentlemen, the case is here, and you must try it; and if you will listen to me for the necessary space, I will show you that there is absolutely nothing against these men, nothing but the purest conjecture, mere possibilities throughout; no evidence upon which a court of law would find established an ordinary debt, far less convict of a serious crime.

Gentlemen, the learned Lord Advocate has said a great many things to you which, as you will doubtless have anticipated, it is no part of my case to dispute. It is no part of my case to dispute that the three explosions which occurred in Glasgow on the 20th of January last were produced by dynamite, and were caused by ill-disposed persons for illegal purposes. For a time, during the leading of the evidence, it rather appeared that the explosion at the Buchanan Street Station railway shed was the result of the strike among the company's men; but, having regard to the coincidence of the other two explosions, undoubtedly unconnected with railway matters, it may fairly be assumed that the origin of the whole three explosions was the same; and, indeed, I think you will perceive that it does not particularly signify to the case before you whether it was or was not. And so you may lay out of view that part of the Lord Advocate's address. But I do dispute thoroughly the position taken up by the Lord Advocate, when he suggested to you that, because of these explosions, suspicion must attach to the prisoners. At that time Featherstone and Dalton and Deasy and Flannigan were at large; and so were the four prisoners who in June were convicted in London; indeed, one of them, Gallagher, actually had a brother resident in Glasgow, and so is proved not to be unconnected with that city. And what is more probable than that Featherstone—proved to be in Glasgow a few days before the explosions, proved to be there shortly after the explosions—was also there on the 20th of January when they occurred? There were plenty of people, independent of the prisoners, by whom the explosions might have been caused, and so far as regards the mere fact of the explosions having taken place, there is nothing whatever in that to connect the prisoners with them. It is said that the prisoners, or some of them, were connected with a secret society. Well, societies for the relief of the distress of Ireland are not peculiar to the prisoners at the bar. I have no doubt there is hardly an Irishman in Glasgow—an Irish Roman Catholic, of course, I mean—who is not a member of some such society; and, for my part, I see nothing wrong in Irishmen being members of a society, secret or otherwise, whose object is either to alleviate Irish distress or to obtain, by legitimate means, redress for the wrongs of the Irish people. There are in Glasgow hundreds of societies like that to which the prisoners belonged, and the mere fact of their belonging to such a society is no more evidence of their being connected with the explosions than it would be in the case of any of the innumerable other Irishmen in Glasgow who were and are members of similar societies. Let the prisoners at the bar be ever so guilty, the mere fact of their being members of a society is no evidence of their guilt.

Gentlemen, the general evidence brought against the prisoners is of two kinds: the evidence of Hughes the informer; and the independent evidence relied on by the prosecution. In dealing with the case I prefer to reverse the course pursued by the Lord Advocate, and to ask your consideration first to the evidence as it stands without that of Hughes; for I am persuaded that if I satisfy you that without Hughes' evidence you would never dream of convicting the prisoners, then the addition of Hughes' evidence will not make any difference in the result at which you may arrive. There is first of all the evidence of the constable William Porter. Porter says that he knows all of the prisoners, that he saw them meet on Glasgow Green and in Jail Square, where they whispered together, and sometimes read letters to each other. Than the last I can conceive of no more harmless operation, or one less suggestive of evil, especially seeing that half, or more than half, of the prisoners are unable to read. And the letters can hardly be said to have come from Featherstone, for Featherstone was on the spot, and did not require to write. Featherstone was there and a man called Johnston. I think the learned Lord Advocate went rather far in suggesting that Johnston was Dalton; for if that were so, why was Dalton not exhibited for identification, as Featherstone had been, to Porter and Hughes and the rest? As for Dalton, how could the prisoners be conspirators with him? He was never in Glasgow till March 1883, long after the explosions, long after the last purchase of dynamite materials had been made by Featherstone. Porter says he was suspicious of the prisoners. Gentlemen, a policeman's suspicions do not go for much. And that is really all Porter's evidence, excepting that two men whom he believes to have been Featherstone and Johnston were occasionally to be seen in the group; and this, gentlemen, is the uncorroborated evidence of a single witness, on a point on which above all others witnesses are liable to be mistaken, namely, a question of identity. But along with Porter's statement, and completing the Crown evidence on this part of the case, must be taken the evidence of M'Ginnes and Niven, the former of whom had seen certain of the prisoners in Lennox's public-house in the Saltmarket, where he was the assistant; the prisoners conducting themselves, as he told you, just as other customers; while Niven, a constable, spoke to seeing the prisoners, or some of them, together on Glasgow Green, but not oftener than, or conducting themselves differently from, other Irish people. All that simply comes to this, that these men are Irishmen, one in country, one in religion, one in friendship, and that they met and talked together, and occasionally went into a public-house together. If they had wanted to plot dynamite explosions, the last place they would have gone to would have been a public room in a spirit shop, or among the crowds assembled in Jail Square or on Glasgow Green. What Featherstone and Johnston may have said to them does not appear, but I do not suppose they said more to any one of the prisoners than they did to hundreds of other Irishmen in Glasgow; and you will not assume that any evil suggestions they may have made were more effectual with the prisoners than with the numerous other Irish whom, doubtless, they endeavoured to prompt to crime. It is said that certain of the prisoners were present at the explosions. Suppose, gentlemen, that that were so, would that be any evidence against these prisoners? Would it not rather be evidence in their favour? Professor Dupré told you that the ingenuity of the arrangement by which the dynamite was exploded consisted in this, that it was of such a nature as not to produce an explosion for a considerable time—even forty minutes, or more if thought necessary—after it was put in action, so as to enable the operators to escape, not only beyond risk from the explosion (a very short time would suffice for that), but beyond the risk of suspicion from being found in its vicinity. You may depend upon it that the men who hung that machine between the pillar and the gasometer, the men who blew up the railway shed, and the men who placed the tin box on Possil Bridge, would go away as soon as they had laid their apparatus in position, and would be as far as possible from the scenes of the explosions before they occurred—not idly and needlessly loitering near, imperilling their own safety without the possibility of furthering in the least their evil purposes. But laying that aside, is there any reliable evidence—even if it mattered—to show that a single one of the prisoners was near any of the explosions at the time when it occurred? M'Dermott is not said to have been there, nor Callaghan, nor M'Cann, nor M'Cullagh, nor Kelly, nor Drum, nor Casey. That is seven out of the ten accused. But it is said that the witness Gavin Lawrie, a boy of fifteen, had, a quarter of an hour before the explosion took place at the gasometer, seen a man —a man who in his opinion, and possibly also in that of his friend Longmuir, was somewhat suspicious-looking — standing with his back against a paling in the neighbourhood of the gas-work, and that that man was the prisoner Devany. It is further said that Lawrie's evidence (for you will remember that Longmuir, though he saw as much of the matter as Lawrie, could not identify any of the prisoners) is supported by that of the witnesses Robert Aitken and Margaret Smith. Aitken—that is the lad, a butcher's assistant, who stood in the witness box with his hands in his pockets, and gave his evidence with a cool flippancy that suggested but little respect for the oath he had taken—Aitken said, that on the explosion occurring he saw first two, and immediately afterwards other two, men running out of Muirhouse Lane towards Eglinton Street—that is, running away from the explosion; and that the first pair of men were Devany and M'Cann. How little reliance can be placed on his testimony is seen from the fact, spoken to by Inspector Carmichael, that in the Glasgow police office he identified, not M'Cann, but M'Cabe as one of the two men. The Lord Advocate has put it to you, that the fact of the men running away showed a consciousness of guilt. Gentlemen, I do not think so. On hearing such an explosion, it is true that some men, like the witness Aitken, would out of curiosity go to the scene of it. But I think that as many men, probably more, would be influenced in quite the reverse way, and, hearing and seeing one out of several gasholders explode, would run away, fearing that the flame might be communicated to the others and cause their explosion also. There is nothing suggestive of guilty knowledge in this. Then as to the witness Margaret Smith, her pretended identification of the man she saw coming out on the Lilybank road as being something like the prisoner Devany is almost ludicrous in its weakness,—she admitted that she had never seen the man's face. A momentary sight of a man's person on a dark January night—his face never seen at all—is that evidence, I will not say reliable evidence, but any evidence at all against the person supposed to be identified? Now, gentlemen, there you have the entire evidence of identification, in the instance where the Lord Advocate told you it was strongest—in the case of the prisoner Devany—and I put it to you, is it evidence upon which you can safely or satisfactorily proceed? None of the persons ever saw Devany in their lives before. None of them ever saw him again till six or seven months after, when they were shown him in the Glasgow police office, and their suspicions and imaginations had, however honest they might be, unconsciously been stimulated by the £500 reward offered by Government. As to the supposed identification of Donnelly at the gaswork, and Kelly in connection with the explosion at Possil Bridge, all that I have already said applies to it much more strongly; for the Lord Advocate concedes that it is weak indeed when compared with the alleged identification of Devany; and, besides, the man fancied by the witness Murray to be like Kelly, or not unlike Kelly—I forget which expression he used—was not seen at the Possil Bridge; all that is said regarding him is that he was doing what for aught I know fifty other men may have been doing in Glasgow that night—carrying a japanned tin bonnet box. It is not said that any of the prisoners were at the scene of the railway shed explosion. But it is said that Kearney was there. Why, where else could he have been? He was at his signal box, engaged in his ordinary duties of signalman, and the only suggestion made against him by the Crown, as showing that he was the author of the railway shed explosion (gentlemen, even if he was, that would not implicate any of the prisoners), was that he gave some signal or other which the man, who was in the signal box along with him, did not see the necessity of, but which, had Kearney himself been here, he doubtless could have explained. Gentlemen, I think I have established to your satisfaction that there is no evidence on which you can rely to show that any one of the prisoners was present at the scene of the explosions, and that, even if any of them were present, that would be no indication of guilt.

Now, gentlemen, apart from the testimony of the informer Hughes, and from the declarations of the prisoners, I think there is only one other line of evidence which is suggested by the Crown as proving guilt; and that is the alleged purchases of materials capable of being used in the preparation of dynamite, and one or two incidental matters said to bear on the alleged possession by certain of the prisoners of explosive substances. And here let me point out to you, that much of the evidence regarding nitro-glycerine and its component parts which has been led before you has really no bearing on the points at issue. Featherstone—so the Crown has proved with great elaboration—made frequent purchases of nitric acid, and it was pointed out to you, as of value and significance in the case, that he always took care to get it of a strength not ordinarily required for innocent purposes. Well, the purchases of nitric acid by Featherstone were made on three occasions—on 11th December 1882, from M'Geachie & M'Farlane; on 19th February 1883, from Alexander Hope, Jun., & Co.; and on 21st February 1883, from J. Montgomery & Co. The first of these purchases was sent to Ireland, and never came back; the second and third of them were not made till long after the explosions in question here. Obviously none of the quantities of acid so purchased could have been used in the manufacture of the dynamite found at Possil Bridge, or exploded at the Tradeston gasworks or the Buchanan Street railway shed. These purchases may have a bearing on the guiltiness of Featherstone of the crime the punishment of which he is now suffering. They have, and can have, nothing at all to do with the guilt or innocence of the prisoners at the bar. But it is said that certain of the accused —to wit, M'Dermott and M'Cullagh—purchased, the one of them glycerine and the other sulphuric acid,—circumstances which, even if incriminating them, of course cannot affect any of the other prisoners. Looking at these matters in their true light, they do not incriminate even M'Dermott and M'Cullagh. Remember that, apart from the evidence of Hughes, neither of them knew that glycerine and sulphuric acid, or glycerine and nitric acid, combined would make nitro-glycerine. I make bold to say, gentlemen, that prior to the revelations which were made in the English dynamite cases, not many, if any, of you did. I know that, previous to that, I certainly was not aware how nitro-glycerine was made ; and glycerine seemed to me a perfectly harmless substance, while sulphuric and nitric acids were dangerous only because they were burning and corrosive agents—materials useful for many purposes ; possibly hurtful to persons carelessly employing them ; but certainly not explosives. Well, it is said that M'Dermott, while in the employment of a chemical manufacturing company, asked a fellow-workman to fill him a small phial with sulphuric acid. Granted that he did so, is that any evidence of guilt ? He said it was to clean a chain. Sulphuric acid is used for cleaning chains. If M'Dermott had been conscious of a guilty purpose he could, without asking for it, have taken as much acid as he pleased. The fact that he openly asked for it, in place of taking it secretly, seems to me to be conclusive that he at least had no intention or knowledge that it was to be put to an improper use. As regards the purchases of glycerine by M'Dermott, the facts are these. He purchased about 31st October and 7th November 1882 two quantities of glycerine of 10 lbs. each—the price being 6s. 3d. The purchases were made from the witness Armstrong, at the works of Clolus & Co. at Maryhill near Glasgow ; and we were told by Armstrong that M'Dermott, who apparently wanted the smallest supply of glycerine which Clolus & Co. would sell, represented that he wanted the glycerine to apply to wounds on a horse's back, and that he had been sent to get it by a contractor in the Gallowgate called Bolan. The Lord Advocate says these representations were not true, and that the fact that he made, when buying the glycerine, statements which were not true, shows guilty knowledge on his part. Gentlemen, it is not proved that M'Dermott's statements were untrue. It is not said that glycerine is not a suitable substance for healing wounds on a horse's back ; and although the police cannot now trace Bolan as an inhabitant of the Gallowgate of Glasgow, it does not follow that there was not such a person there in October or November 1882 ; and suppose there were no such person there, it does not follow that M'Dermott, himself innocent, was not imposed on by a person representing himself to be Bolan, a contractor in the Gallowgate. But even if M'Dermott intentionally made false statements to Armstrong, that would not prove his guilt. Remember what Armstrong told you— that he made difficulties about selling the glycerine to M'Dermott ; not because any suspicion of an improper purpose entered his mind ; but because Clolus & Co. being wholesale dealers, it was out of their way to sell so small a quantity. Suppose that M'Dermott did give an imaginary account of the purpose for which he wanted the glycerine, that would not show that he knew it was to be applied to an illegal purpose ; it would simply show that, being anxious to get the glycerine (possibly he was Featherstone's unsuspecting dupe), and finding that Clolus & Co. were making difficulties about selling it, he made use of the first fiction that occurred to him for the purpose of inducing them to sell. What I have said as to M'Dermott's purchases of glycerine of course more than answers the argument put forward against the prisoner M'Cullagh in regard to his purchases of sulphuric acid ; for in his case it is not suggested that he made any false representation, as it is said that M'Dermott did. But I need do no more than advert to that in passing; for my friend Mr. Orr, who represents M'Cullagh, will doubtless address you more fully on the matter. Supposing that Featherstone did all that the Crown attributed to him, there is nothing in the world to show that M'Dermott or M'Cullagh (assuming—what is not proved—that the glycerine and vitriol bought by them were in fact intended for the manufacture of dynamite) were anything worse than his innocent dupes. And all this evidence about the purchases of glycerine and vitriol, gentlemen, you will keep in view, even if it were evidence against the two prisoners who made the purchases,—I have submitted to you it is not,—can be no evidence against the eight prisoners who had no concern with them. I will have occasion to deal more fully with that when I come to address you on the individual cases of the respective prisoners whose interests are entrusted to my care. The witness Munro, a cab-driver, spoke to having on two occasions in January 1883 driven the prisoners M'Dermott and Devany in his cab to Portugal Lane. Surely, gentlemen, there is nothing in that. If the parcel they were carrying—a small parcel the size of an octavo volume—contained dynamite, there was no hurry with it, no necessity for conveying it in a cab. All this evidence simply comes to this, that on two occasions the men conveyed a small brown paper parcel, contents unknown, from one part of Glasgow to another. Then it is said that on the morning of 8th March 1883, M'Dermott called for a man, called Moorhead, who had since the previous 15th of January been lodging with the witness Mrs. M'Lachlan, at No. 35 Ronald Street, and that Moorhead was acquainted with Dalton, who was subsequently sentenced to penal servitude for life. There might have been some significance in that if it had been shown that M'Dermott was acquainted with Dalton's misdeeds. But it was not shown that Moorhead was aware of them, far less that M'Dermott did, who never saw Dalton save on this solitary, and, for aught that appears, chance occasion.

Gentlemen, that is the whole of the independent evidence which it is said bears against the prisoners, or some of them, excepting that which the learned Lord Advocate sought to extract from their declarations. He said—I will deal with that more fully afterwards—that certain of the prisoners in their declarations make statements which are not true. Gentlemen, I often think that too much is made by public prosecutors of falsehoods in the judicial declarations of prisoners. So much depends on a man's temperament, on the circumstances under which he is called on to make a statement before a magistrate which he knows may be used against him, but which a somewhat extraordinary law does not allow him to use in his own favour. And in the present case, what were the circumstances under which these men—being accused of dynamite outrages—were called on to emit their declarations? The declarations were made in September and October 1883, the earliest of them being dated 4th September. In the year 1882, when the purchases of glycerine and vitriol were made by M'Dermott and M'Cullagh, no one but men of skill knew that these two substances combined would make a dangerous explosive. But then there came the dynamitard's trial in London in June 1883, and the trial on 7th August of Featherstone, Dalton, Deasy, and Flannigan. The revelations which these trials (they were reported at length in every newspaper in the country) made to us all will yet be fresh in your recollection. Then for the first time the dangerous capabilities of glycerine and sulphuric acid would be revealed to such of the prisoners at the bar as had to do with them. They were accused of being dynamitards; it was blazoned throughout the land that a dynamitard's doom was penal servitude for life; they had, the Crown say (though I wholly dispute that they have proved it), been to some extent associated with Featherstone—what wonder, gentlemen, that they, ignorant and uneducated men as they are, were afraid to confess that they had bought glycerine or sulphuric acid—were afraid to confess (if they did know him) that they had associated with the convict Featherstone? Gentlemen, that does not show their guilt; it only shows that their moral courage was not of an order which is rarely bestowed on men of their class.

Gentlemen of the Jury, that is, apart from the evidence of Hughes, all the evidence—every syllable of it so far as it has any bearing on the case—upon which you are asked to find these men guilty of the serious charge made against them. I put it to you,—I ask even that one amongst you who may be least favourably disposed to the prisoners,—is there, as against the majority of the prisoners at the bar, one tittle of evidence at all? is there as against any of them evidence which establishes guilt? No, gentlemen, there is not.

And if, without the evidence of Hughes, your verdict must be one of acquittal, will his testimony change your view of the case? It is the evidence of a solitary witness—one man swearing against ten—it is the evidence of that most detestable of all characters, an informer; it is the evidence of a man who, I will show and prove to you, is a perjured liar and villain. Gentlemen, an extraordinary law—I venture to think a most unjust law—prevents prisoners at the bar of a criminal court giving evidence in their own behalf. In civil trials, whether the interests at stake be a few pence or thousands of pounds, the law allows the parties to be examined as witnesses; but where men's lives or liberties are concerned it will not allow the testimony of the prisoners; it shuts the mouths of those witnesses who necessarily know most of the case. Gentlemen, there are ten of the prisoners as against Hughes alone. Reverse the case. Suppose Hughes were in the dock on a charge of perjury; and these ten men were in the witness-box against him, could you refuse to convict him? How unreasonable then would it be, on Hughes' testimony, to find the prisoners guilty! Why did Hughes become an informer? He said his conscience pricked him—he said that when the policeman asked him he could not tell a lie. A lie!—why, he never told a greater lie than when he swore that; for the constable Porter told you that it was not he who went to Hughes, but Hughes who came to him—Hughes who volunteered his tale—a tale he never told, until when gentlemen? Until the Government reward of £500 made his conscience prick him. Hughes, forsooth, says he will not take that reward. Why, if he is an honest man, should he not? That is simply a specimen of the wretched hypocrisy that characterized his evidence throughout. Hughes told you that when he joined the secret society he took an oath; that he swore by Almighty God that he would stand loyal to all brethren. Gentlemen, on his own confession he broke that oath; on his own confession he stood in that witness-box a perjured scoundrel—false to the friends he betrayed—false to the God whose name he blasphemed. It is not on evidence such as his that you will consign these prisoners to a terrible fate.

Gentlemen, I do not think the Crown have treated you fairly, I do not think they have treated the prisoners fairly, in not putting into the witness-box the two men with whom the prisoners are alleged to have conspired—I mean Featherstone and Dalton. Their names are in the list of the Crown witnesses. They were here in Edinburgh; nay, they were actually exhibited in Court to several of the witnesses. Why were they not examined for the prosecution? It was no part of my duty, it would have been going out of my province, to have made them my witnesses, both because it is the prosecution, not the defence, that is bound to establish its case, and because it cannot be expected of the prisoners that they should call to give testimony on their behalf two men who are undergoing a sentence of penal servitude for life; and who might obtain commutation of their sentence if they got the Home Secretary to believe that through them a fresh set of conspirators had been convicted and punished. It was for the Crown to have called these men. If the case for the Crown were well founded, who are the two men outside of the dock who know most about it? Why, Featherstone and Dalton. Gentlemen, the Crown, if its case were true, has not called its best witnesses. No prosecution can succeed that, having it in its power to do so, declines to produce those witnesses who are necessarily best acquainted with the facts. The Lord Advocate told you he could not call them because their evidence would be tainted evidence. Is that a reason which you will take off the hands of the prosecution? Does the Crown refrain from leading evidence because it may be observed against it that it is tainted? You all know what Queen's evidence is. That is not only tainted evidence, but bribed evidence, and yet the Crown constantly and proverbially makes use of it. Tainted evidence, gentlemen, where you have the Crown making use of Hughes, perjured by his own confession, and whose last witness was the informer Lamie, who came here with his hands red with the blood of his sister's husband—the man Poole, who was executed in Dublin on Wednesday! Gentlemen, I am entitled to assume,—you are entitled to assume, that the Crown did not call Featherstone and Dalton simply because they knew their evidence would not support the case for the prosecution.

[Mr. Rhind then proceeded to deal in detail with the case against each of the individual prisoners whom he represented; and he concluded as follows:—]

Gentlemen, I have now done. I think I have shown you that, without the testimony of Hughes there is not one iota of evidence to establish guilt against any of the prisoners. I think I have shown you that to condemn ten men on evidence which, apart from that of Hughes, is plainly insufficient, would be monstrous; and I am sure that there is no man who has listened to this case that would, on Hughes' testimony, convict of the meanest or most trivial crime. But suppose Hughes were, I do not say a satisfactory, but even a witness whose word could at all be relied on, would that enable the Crown to prevail? Certainly not. For what, after all, would the case for the prosecution amount to? No man is a criminal simply for a thought he has in his mind. He may dream over the possibility of a crime; but many a man does that, and before action repents. Even if Hughes' evidence is true, he does not pretend to connect the prisoners with the explosions. For aught that he says to the contrary, these poor and ignorant men, animated by an insane delusion as to how they could serve their country best, were at worst only playing with fire; they never got the length of agreeing upon any criminal act; they never stepped beyond the line that separates folly from crime. Gentlemen, a great and heavy responsibility rests upon you. I know you will discharge it well. I beseech you not to suppose that because these crimes happened—that because they might have caused great destruction of life—that therefore the law demands a victim. The law demands no victim; it demands justice. In making up your minds, you will not leave out of view —a jury cannot leave out of view—the frightful doom to which a verdict of guilty would consign the prisoners; the terrible misery and destitution which it would inflict on the helpless women and children that are dependent on them. You will bring to bear on the case not only all the intelligence of your minds, but the warm and tender hearts that God has implanted in your bosoms. Gentlemen, I leave the case of the prisoners with confidence in your hands. I know you will return no verdict that does not satisfy alike the severest judgment, and the tenderest conscience, among you.

ADDRESS BY N. J. D. KENNEDY, ADVOCATE.

Gentlemen of the Jury,—I am counsel for Henry M'Cann alone, and solicit your indulgent attention while I state the grounds on which he bases his defence. That the evidence presses with very unequal weight on the different prisoners is admitted. That it has failed to bring any guilt home to him I trust to convince you by the plain and brief review of it which I will endeavour to present. But when Mr. Rhind, a veteran of the Courts, confesses himself weighed down by a sense of his responsibility, you will forgive my expressing the anxiety I feel in rising to address you after him, in reply to a case prepared with all the resources of the State, and presented with all the unrivalled power of the first law-officer of the Crown. Were the issue to be decided by skill or by sympathy, this poor man, unaided, unable to secure experienced advocacy, might well despair. I can no more presume to cope with the Lord Advocate than the prisoner can resist the armed forces of the Government, nor can my weak words oppose with effect the interests and prejudices excited by the nature of the charge. Against the danger of confounding the accused with the accusation, against the subtle influence of public prejudgment, against the secret snare of the informer there is for him no hope, no confidence, no security except in your humane and impartial discrimination.

Let us see what the Crown has undertaken to prove, and how it ought to be proved. The prisoner is charged under the statute with having levied war in order to compel some change of measures, and to have evinced his treason by conspiring to use explosives or by other overt acts; or alternatively at common law with having conspired to alter by force the constitution of the realm. It is singular that neither in the indictment, nor throughout the proof, nor in the address of the Lord Advocate, can we find any suggestion as to what the change or alteration to be effected was, or in what direction, whether of liberty or coercion. If there was a conspiracy, there must have been agreement as to what was to be conspired for. Are men zealous for an unknown object? Do men rush into serious crimes to promote they cannot say what? If you are left in ignorance of the end, how can you judge whether acts proved to have been done were means towards it or not? There was no such omission when the Chartists were tried, and not convicted. Their object was the establishment of the Charter.

Similarly, when the Fenians were tried and justly condemned, their object was known and set forth,—the erection of a republic on the ruins of the Union and the throne. But no such purpose has been so much as hinted at here.

As to the first charge, proof of the overt act is not proof of guilt. Unless the levying of war for the specific purpose is established, this charge is as harmless as sawdust without nitro-glycerine. If any prisoner belonged to a secret society, or took unlawful oaths, there are many biting statutes under which the Lord Advocate may prosecute, and no acquittal on this indictment will bar any such prosecution. But these offences will not prove the specific treason here libelled. The charge of conspiracy, always a favourite with prosecutors, also requires cautious handling. The general rule of criminal justice is clear. Each man bears his own burden and answers only for his' own acts. But when several persons conspire,—that is, when they deliberately agree to execute and take steps to execute any unlawful design, when, though there may be different parts assigned to the partners, there is yet a unity of resolved action in furthering the common, understood, criminal end,—then by a technical fiction, the acts of each conspirator done for such end may be imputed to and proved against all or any of his accomplices. But reticence or suspicion are not conspiracy. To be a confidant is not to be an accomplice. Who can insure himself against receiving dangerous secrets? No man can be safely condemned as a conspirator unless he is clearly shown to have given complete assent, intelligent approval, and actual assistance to the criminal design. These remarks apply equally to the general charge of conspiracy, and the special charge of conspiracy constituting the first overt act. It is apparently on the first overt act that the prosecutor relies for a verdict. Therefore the issue between him and this accused stands thus: Did M'Cann conspire to levy war or to effect a forcible alteration of the Constitution? Suspicion will never do. Suspicion and proof are as different as darkness and light; the one is a doubt of eventual innocence, the other a certainty of present, personal guilt.

The proofs on which the Crown case against M'Cann rests are mainly three—(1) that he was a member of a society formed and existing to execute the criminal designs libelled; (2) that he has been sufficiently identified as having been seen near the gasometer a few minutes after its explosion; and (3) that he was observed in the company of Featherstone, whose secret designs, we now know, were wicked in the extreme. I intend to test each of them, so as to satisfy your minds that what might have been sufficient has not been proved, while what has been proved is insufficient to support the weight of the verdict which the Crown demands.

Permit me, however, by way of preface, to inquire how stand the moral probabilities—for or against the accused? What is his position? his character? his means of intimidating the estates of the realm? Is he a fanatic, impelled to vengeance by any personal wrong? Is he one of those clever, shifty, subtle adventurers who prey on their Irish countrymen by pretending to carry on a piratical warfare against the English Government? No; he is a decent, dull, ordinary man, who thirty years ago made Glasgow his home, who has by steady work at his trade of shoemaking maintained himself in a creditable way and brought up respectably a large family, who are now awaiting with the deepest anxiety the issue of this trial. He has been not merely an industrious, but a religious man, whose religion bore fruit in the practical benevolence of parochial duties. You have heard how leading a part he took in the affairs and societies of the church, and how his clergyman and neighbours were impressed by his honesty and excellent principles. His heart was good, but his brains were poor enough. Indeed his activity was religious, and not political; for no scrap of paper has been produced, no word of his repeated by any witness, to show the political sentiments he entertained. What could have induced such a man to aspire to the perilous eminence of a conspirator? What could have so perverted his natural sense of right as to link him to a conspiracy of such special wickedness? Where and what was the motive? The Crown has suggested none. This man, therefore, is not the stuff of which conspirators are made. So far everything is in his favour.

Let me next examine if the prosecutor makes any stronger case on the real or material evidence. It will not have escaped you how the very points on which the Crown relies to convict the other prisoners utterly fail as against M'Cann, how of all the marks which are said to indicate guilt, because inseparably associated with guilt, and which are alleged to be found in them, not one can be discovered against *him* after a most diligent inquiry. Did *he* ever propose to buy dynamite? or any constituent or accessory of its use? Did *he* ever attempt to procure any? Did *he* ever have any in his possession or under his roof? Did *he* ever flee from justice? No; he sat at his ordinary labour until he was arrested without warning, perhaps without reason. The police instantly had his person searched, and his house ransacked; and the most skilful and keen-scented detectives have been hunting ever since in every possible quarter for the faintest trace of suspicious material. With what result? Not a single article capable of becoming evidence of guilt, not a weapon, not an acid, not a bit of brass, not a chemical conundrum, not a grain of powdered sugar, not an entry in the diary of any passenger, not a letter from anybody to anybody found anywhere, not even a *Penny Pictorial News*, such as is triumphantly exhibited in the case of another of the accused, can be produced against him. Strange, if he is guilty, that the circumstantial signs of guilt, which you were led to expect, which cannot inform or lie for reward, should be so conspicuous by their absence; but perfectly natural on the supposition that guilt is absent! Therefore thus far both moral and material proofs range themselves on the side of the accused.

But it is said that a secret society had been instituted to prepare and use dynamite in levying war or effecting some forcible change in the Constitution, of which M'Cann was a member. The evidence on this point requires rigorous scrutiny. No doubt the prisoner did belong to a club which generally met in M'Ginnes' public-house. But what is the proof that the criminal designs and acts libelled were ever entertained or attempted by *that* society? The prosecutor has called only two witnesses. Horan does not help him. Of the informer Hughes he is rather ashamed. Now we know the usual marks of a criminal conspiracy against the State; the evidence of Lamie about the Fenian organization supplies an excellent example. Its nature is to be dark and secret. It chooses remote or concealed places for its midnight meetings. There are watchwords, passwords, disguises. Its members are long known, tried, and tested before they are trusted. They are selected for audacity and resource. They avoid recognising each other in public. Their objects are clear and definite. Their oath expresses these objects, and specifies the penalty of slackness or treachery—generally death. Then turn to the contrast which all we know of the taproom society presents. Of whom is it composed? Of men, merely acquainted, introduced in the most casual public way, without any inquiry. Hughes is tapped on the shoulder while walking about the Green,—" Come in and join us." He joins them, and that is all. It matters little that Hughes calls this club " a secret ribbon society." There is no treason in a name, nor in a ribbon, though we are not even told the colour of it—red, green, or orange? Probably it was not blue! And where was the secrecy?—where even privacy? Secrecy of a conspiracy on the stage! secrecy of the most public room, opening by a glass door, of a public-house into or out of which men, women, and children were continually passing! Secrecy of the most patent squares in Glasgow at the hours when policemen, Orangemen, and promiscuous pleasure-seekers most congregated there! If this is secrecy, then what is publicity? Was this society anything but what Horan says it was?—an association, partly for pleasure, partly to help the distressed in Ireland, this help apparently taking the shape of periodic drinking to their health.

But " the oath—the oath." Was any taken? The two witnesses do not agree. The mere taking an oath, however, proves nothing. Then what was the oath? For its terms we are asked to rely on the single memory of the unprincipled Hughes, who confesses that he only heard them on the single occasion, now nearly two years ago, when he says he was sworn in. What alteration of the laws did it propose? what change was to be compelled? what penalty did it impose? what criminal purpose did it indicate? Leave out the words " with Government," which may be a gloss slipped into the text by Hughes, and not a phrase remains from which sophistry itself can extract a conjecture of suspicion. Accept his version, and what does it imply beyond such assistance as humanity may honestly give to distress? Is it to be assumed against the accused that "assistance" can only mean "assistance by dynamite"? Even the ready Hughes fears to go so far. He admits that he did not understand this oath as binding him to any conspiracy or anything worse than to subscribe for the defence of their countrymen when prosecuted by Government. Is it criminal to aid in securing a fair trial? Is it criminal in M'Cann to have understood the oath in the same sense as Hughes? But "the oath binds to secrecy." What if it does! Are Good Templars, Orange Lodges, Friendly Societies treasonable, because they have their secrets and mysteries. If any of the Jury are Freemasons, I ask them to recollect the penalty their oath annexes to breach of secrecy, and its words of obligation to aid all brethren,—words infinitely more capable than any Hughes has stated of being wrested, as the Inquisition did actually wrest them, to mean revolutionary designs against Church or State. Such secrecy, such obligations, such vanity may be in foolish taste, but no more infer conspiracy than the toy cannon of a river excursion steamer are proof that she is a pirate. Therefore what this oath contains and what it omits are so far from importing the common purpose charged that they point to a different object, which has not been brought into the most distant relation to any of the overt acts in the indictment. Nor is there any attempt to prove that this society was connected or affiliated with any other organization whatever. And even from the dangerous lips of the informer we gain another proof that its aims were not what the Crown rightly thinks it vital to show they must have been. In March 1882 this society was in full vigour. But Hughes concedes that until the end of June, when the American emissary arrived, no person had even thought of dynamite, far less designed to use it, or employed unlawful means for any object whatever. That I submit is conclusive.

It is next asked, "Why and for what did M'Cann collect subscriptions?" It is for the Crown to prove a guilty reason. *Prima facie* subscription is rather charitable than criminal. Assume that he did receive a few half-crowns of entry-money with occasional sixpences from nine or ten persons in the course of several months. Were these the funds by which the journeys, experiments, and luxuries of Featherstone, Dalton, Moorhead, and the rest fell to be maintained? Were these few halfpence the military chest for the war against the most strong and wealthy of Governments? That is not likely. It is not proved that a single farthing collected by M'Cann was expended for any criminal purpose. Even according to Hughes, these monies purchased nothing more harmful than drink to the poor. Nor would they go very far. Perhaps some of the drinkers may have indulged in hotheaded talk over their liquor at their meetings. But Hughes admits that there was not a whisper of dynamite. This club, therefore, was no conspiracy and M'Cann no conspirator.

I grant that Moorhead and Featherstone, prior to January 1883, organized a gang to blow up public works by dynamite, and by that means effected or attempted the three explosions round which this case centres. Of these facts I think there is independent proof. But you observe that with the agents and operations of that gang the prisoners are connected only by the evidence of the informer. Let me examine how far that evidence directly affects M'Cann, reserving till a later stage the credibility of that witness. If he speaks truly, three of the prisoners belonged to that confederacy, which is perfectly distinct from the convivial club to which M'Cann resorted. Its members were few. They met seldom and secretly. They bound themselves by a special oath. They procured, prepared, and employed explosives. But then M'Cann was none of them. M'Cann attended none of their meetings. If on the 4th of July Featherstone talked gunpowder politics, M'Cann was not there. If Featherstone lectured on dynamite in the Gymnastic Hall, if again he stated that there was 37 lb. of it somewhere in stock, if he did on a third occasion say that Governments might take a lesson (what Governments, what lesson, or from what the lesson, we are not informed), although mere listening were sufficient to make every hearer guilty of conspiracy, it matters nothing to M'Cann, for he was not named as even a hearer. If there was a meeting to consult about removing "the stuff" for fear of the tell-tale corrosion of M'Dermott's sink, what did M'Cann know of it? what had he to do with it? Absolutely nothing, though judged by the evidence of one who is rather an enemy than a witness. If £2, 10s. was raised for their criminal object, who collected it? Not M'Cann. The strange story that it was obtained from the Gymnastic Hall audience under pretence of charity to an old woman, and in the same breath announced to the same persons as intended to buy dynamite, may be true or false, but M'Cann was neither auditor nor subscriber. Who was the treasurer of this special fund? Hughes himself, at least *vice* Drum. Then consider this. Why was dynamite never alluded to in M'Cann's hearing? Why was no purchase, no collection, no unequivocal act of conspiracy ever done in his presence? Perfectly natural, perfectly consistent with the view which I have presented of the other evidence, but not easily reconciled with the theory of M'Cann's guilty participation in the conspiracy.

Gentlemen, I now pass from the period antecedent to the explosions to examine the alleged proof that M'Cann took part in their perpetration. That he had any hand in the two later explosions is not suggested. But it is urged that the boy Aitken recognises M'Cann as one of four men who passed him in a street near the Tradeston gasometer shortly after it was blown up. I concede that if thoroughly reliable his evidence would go further to condemn the prisoner than all the Crown's guesses, testimonies, and productions put together.

No doubt he identifies him now. But there is no more difficult subject, no more copious source of errors than identification, as jurors and jurists have had too good reason to feel. What better illustration than the incident of yesterday! The Lord Advocate, indeed all of us, in broad daylight, after having seen each of them several times, confounded together Featherstone and Dalton. On such a point three witnesses would be none too many. But let us agree to accept as sufficient one cautious witness, who has had the means and motive for distinct observation, who can recollect by specific marks or special grounds, and is unopposed and corroborated by circumstances. But do you think the ex-butcher-boy comes up to weight? Remember his cool impudent demeanour, as he lounged against the box with both hands in his pockets. Did his history inspire you with any stronger confidence? For several weeks he has been out of work. He can get no employment except to give evidence. His last masters dismissed him for reasons which he preferred to keep to himself. But his former employers also dispensed suddenly with his services. This time he favours us with the reason, or the fiction, that he had not returned to his work at midnight of this Saturday of the explosions. With such antecedents it is quite natural that he should wish to pose as a witness of importance. A reward of £500, as Hughes sagely remarked to Ward, can't be picked every day out of the gutter. Aitken does not profess Hughes' more than stoic indifference to lucre. Why should he not have his knife twice as deep into the case and the prize of the case, as any one else? Accordingly, where other witnesses can only see two men, he sees four, and points to M'Cann, whom no other person saw, as one of them.

But, were he ever so cautious and accurate, what were his means of observation or recollection? The man he had never seen before. He was not close to him. There was nothing to attract his attention or fix the identity in his mind. There was no peculiarity in dress, walk, or action, far less any mark in feature or limb. He just took a careless glance by the dim light of the moon struggling to glimmer through Glasgow smoke. Could the difficulties in the way of forming a sound judgment have been greater, or what he calls his judgment more worthless? We may gather as much from his own evidence; for he has at one time pointed out another man. He admits that, in August at the police office, he was shown the prisoners one by one for the purpose of identification, and did identify two of them. He is certain that these two were named Devany and M'Cabe, and that the second was named M'Cabe, to whom you may notice M'Cann bears some resemblance in age, type of face, and general appearance. Then comes Inspector

Carmichael, who took charge of the arrangements for identification, who was then present, and knew each prisoner thoroughly by name and person. He states distinctly that the two men whom Aitken then pointed out and heard named were Devany and M'Cabe. M'Cann he could not identify at all. Now reverse the position. Suppose that Aitken had then indicated M'Cann, but had in Court pointed out M'Cabe as the second of the men he saw, would M'Cann be touched by that evidence? Then is the actual case any stronger, because the lapse of time since that eventful night is greater? Either then or now Aitken's recognition is at fault.

But the case does not rest even there. The explosion occurred about ten, the scene of it being fifty minutes' walk from the prisoner's house. We have the direct testimony of three witnesses how, on that evening from seven till shortly after eleven o'clock, M'Cann was quietly seated with his family round him by his own fireside, mending his son's boots for the Sunday. No doubt cavils at this proof have not been spared. "Singular coincidence," says the Lord Advocate, "that one other of the accused on the same night also got a boot repaired." Were this a pure abstract reflection on the doctrine of chances, I should not think it worth while to differ. Perhaps a little research might have discovered several thousand "singular coincidences" of Glasgow workmen getting their shoes mended on a Saturday night. But the remark insinuates that this evidence is false. That suggestion is entirely gratuitous. It is hardly plausible, for two accused having a common defence, had they resolved to resort to falsehood, would scarcely have fixed on the same fiction, when so many others lay ready to their hands. It is next said that the witnesses are the prisoner's own family. Why, whom else would you naturally expect to speak to what occurred in his own house? But we may learn from the records of criminal trials that a false *alibi* is prepared in a different way. The scene of it is usually laid in some public place, the effect of it turns on some minute difference of clocks, the witnesses who support it are persons who are or profess to be strangers to the accused. Finally it is urged that there was nothing to fix that Saturday evening in the minds of these witnesses. Was the unique series of explosions nothing? By what else do the Crown witnesses refer their evidence to that Saturday? But the prisoner's son, daughter, and daughter-in-law are enabled to speak to this particular evening not only by the explosions, but by their concurrence with this single mending of the son's boots by the father, and with the illness of his wife and grandchild. Then is it not absurd to maintain that Aitken cannot be mistaken?—a rash boy, who had neither reason nor opportunity to observe nor anything to impress what he observed on his memory, who has certainly pointed out two different persons at different times with equal confidence, and whose evidence is directly contradicted by three separate testimonies.

That disposes of the only direct proof offered of the prisoner's presence at any explosion. I may remind you how the Lord Advocate's argument, at another part of his address, revolved in a vicious circle. "What proves the prisoner's design to levy war? That he exploded the gasometer;" then subsequently, "What proves that he exploded the gasometer? His design to levy war." Such fallacies, like captured guns, are readily turned against their former masters. I don't seek to return fallacy for fallacy. But this argument is legitimate. If Aitken's shaky recollection does not overcome the proof of M'Cann's absence from the place of the explosions, that absence makes against the view that M'Cann was a conspirator. On the other hand, the independent considerations already submitted, which go to negative his complicity in the conspiracy charged, thereby prove that he could not have aided in the execution of designs which he did not share, and throw into the scale another heavy weight against the reliability of Aitken. So far, then, the proof directed against this prisoner has failed to reach the mark. Perhaps you may agree with the Lord Advocate that without Hughes he has proved the existence of a conspiracy. He did not allege, nor can it be maintained, that without Hughes he has proved that M'Cann was a conspirator. Even with Hughes' evidence I have shown that he was not in the dynamite ring. But great stress is laid on Hughes' testimony as to association between the accused, and the presence of M'Cann at some experiment in his stable, of which we know very little except that it did not relate to dynamite, for dynamite was not so much as talked of until the following Sunday when M'Cann was not present. I propose to impeach his whole testimony on grounds already anticipated by the prosecutor.

That the statements of informers, a species thought to have become extinct in Scotland, ought not to be received except with the most cautious reserve, is admitted. If you honour me with your attention through an examination of this informer's credibility, I hope to show that the safer and more rational course is to reject altogether whatever stands on his sole credit. When and why is a witness worthy of belief? If you are convinced that a given witness has a sufficient sense of moral obligation, that he feels and respects the solemnity of an oath, that he is incapable of deceiving and unlikely to have been deceived, if his deposition has been consistent and confirmed from other quarters, then you may without danger adopt his testimony and believe on your oath what he has stated on his, as if your own ears had heard and your own eyes had seen. But weigh Hughes in what fair balance you please, he is found wanting. His situation in the cause exposes him to deserved suspicion. He lies open to the strongest temptations to speak falsely, interest, passion, self-preservation. Can you be sure that he has successfully resisted them? What interest had M'Cann to conspire, compared with Hughes' motives to inform?

What is his character? Need we go further for an answer than to his own evidence? His own acts declare it. Will he regard an oath? One oath he took and has not the smallest scruple to violate. Will he hesitate to endanger an innocent man? If his evidence is false, there is an end of him; if it is true, then he has proved himself capable and willing to commit atrocious crimes by infernal engines which would destroy property and sacrifice the lives of innocent women and children, whom even the stern laws of savage war would spare. But the Lord Advocate condescended to make a half-hearted apology, which Hughes' own lips effectually confute. "Hughes never went any great length, but repented, especially when sent to fetch the carboy of vitriol." No doubt he went for the carboy and returned without it. But why? Because his conscience pricked him? Nothing of the kind; but because on arriving at the rendezvous he found his confederate tipsy, and was too wary to peril his neck or risk his plot on the discretion of a drunken boy. Then what length did he go in this conspiracy? How deep may *he* involve himself and yet be excusable? If he, who was a part of every important meeting of the circle, who aided at experiments, who planned the purchase of explosives, and knew the amount of them in stock, who kept the dynamite purse,—if he, who did all these things, was rather sinned against than sinning, with what reason can the prosecutor ask a conviction against M'Cann, who did none of them? Repentance! Did he profess that he ever felt it? Indeed no profession would have much availed him. He readily closed with Featherstone's first proposals, and did his best to carry them out. Not until months after the explosions, not until the disclosures following on Featherstone's arrest had become public, not until fear of consequences and hope of reward pointed out the way of impunity, profit, and infamy, did he turn informer. Repentance! Did he, while giving his testimony, express by word, gesture, or demeanour, any contrition, shame, or regret for the parts he had played? Did he not callously detail the origin and progress of these crimes with all the glib fluency of a quack puffing counterfeit wares?

So much for the witness. Let me next consider the matter of his evidence. Here we all feel seriously crippled. Where every test together would be none too much, we have been deprived of the proper means to apply any. We cannot try it by comparison with other testimony, for the Crown has walked by the famous rule of an Irish Attorney-General,—" Never call two informers to the same plot, or their stories will clash." We cannot meet it by direct counter-evidence, for we were denied all knowledge, left in the dark without even the twinkle of a conjecture, of what Hughes was to say. In any country but Scotland, we should have seen his sworn deposition months before trial. But our law presumes that every accused, having fifteen days' notice of the names of the witnesses against him, can discover what evidence each is prepared to give. And no honest or truthful witness ever refuses to speak. But Hughes refused,—a case the law never contemplated. He would tell nothing "until Monday morning," the hour at which he would likely be put into the box, when it would be too late to make any investigation, too late to avail the accused, even if it were made, for the trial once begun, no addition to the prisoners' list of witnesses could be allowed. What cause was there for this anxious concealment, this dread of any inquiry, this resolve to spring his fictions on the defence like a sudden mine? He had reasons better than his pretext of short breath, but not so producible. If his breath had been as short as his conscience, the Crown might have been soon and sadly bereaved of this the precious jewel of its proof.

Nor can we expect many variations in the premeditated story of a clever and unscrupulous man. But in such a case any contradiction is material. One detected falsehood destroys the whole. A few such I ask you to note. While he declares with absolute confidence that he was present on several occasions when various persons were sworn in, he admits in cross-examination that he never heard the words of the oath, which he so glibly repeats, except when he alleges that it was administered to himself. Again he represents himself as having rather drawn back when the project of using dynamite to destroy public works began to be mooted. That was in response to the soft suasive suggestion of his examiner. But he also tells us that this took place early in July. Now it is just then that his activity begins, that he takes lessons in the theory and procures materials for the practice of the dynamite war, in which he continues for months afterwards a zealous combatant. Another point deserves your notice. He affirms that his connection with the club which met in M'Ginnes' public-house lasted only three months. Now we know when the connection began, for he was sworn into it early in March. We know also that he was an active member of the dynamite circle until at least the November following. Observe further that the three months calculated from March expire several weeks before Featherstone's arrival, and so before the first suggestion of any conspiracy. Therefore either Hughes is caught in a flagrant and deliberate contradiction, which ruins his credit, or his connection with this club ceased when he became a conspirator, because it neither existed for nor served any such criminal purposes,—which confirms the view of it already submitted. I close the list of his variations, which might perhaps be extended by reminding you that he has made two distinct contrary statements as to whether he mentioned dynamite to the policeman Porter. When examined in chief, he said "Yes;" when cross-examined by Mr. Guthrie, he as stoutly said "No." By these points do you not find traces distinct, if slight, of direct falsehood on the face of this evidence?

Least of all can this corrupt witness be trusted when implicating

Henry M'Cann, for against him he has a personal grudge to satisfy. He admits that M'Cann struck him a violent blow on the occasion in November when Featherstone with difficulty dissuaded him from giving M'Cann in charge. That is true. But, when we inquire what provocation Hughes gave him, comes in the fiction. Here Mr. Hughes' plausible inventiveness rather failed him. Some unnamed third person had asked Hughes when a meeting was to be held. That he says was the reason of the blow. We cannot trust Hughes' words, but the conduct of the parties, the act done, the whole scene, show the absurdity of his explanation. That M'Cann should wantonly assault his sworn confederate is not likely. That he should strike a brutal, almost murderous stroke against his superior officer, a trusted member of the executive, the vice-treasurer of the military chest, because some other man chose to ask an ordinary question about the common cause, is most improbable. That either of two accomplices in a desperate plot, linked by mutual oaths and common hazard, hating the Government and all its agents, should call the police into a dispute with the other, is almost incredible. But that of two acquaintances with no such secret ties or restraining fears one should strike the other in sudden quarrel, and that the person struck should shout for a constable, is natural enough. This incident, therefore, tends to prove either that Hughes was not a conspirator, in which case his evidence is a fabrication, or that M'Cann was not his accomplice, perhaps the more probable alternative.

That blow was remembered and resented. Indeed, resentment made Hughes forget for a moment his habitual caution. You recollect how on a Sunday night in March last, while meditating the treacherous stroke which he so soon afterwards delivered, he met M'Cann with Mackenna, and hissed in M'Cann's ear, " I'll do for you yet." Of course Hughes denies both the meeting and the menace. Why did he utter his denial with such vehemence, with changed colour, with the air of one who had expected the question? Mackenna heard the words distinctly. To both men it seemed at the time an idle threat. That tells in favour of the accused. Had Hughes held a secret which would endanger M'Cann's neck, after such a warning he would have made all haste to abscond. But he remained, for he did not foresee how that threat could be fulfilled, and his liberty waver with the breath of the informer's mouth. Nothing in Hughes' evidence is more remarkable than his singular anxiety to conceal his enmity, because he anticipates its effect, and the skill with which he moderates his direct testimony against his enemy. An ordinary informer, more revengeful than reflecting, would have set M'Cann in the front of the conspiracy. But Mr. Hughes is too prudent to overreach himself, and lose the refined luxury of perverting justice to serve his private ends. He does not waste fiction needlessly. He restrains himself to what he calculates will be just sufficient to secure a conviction. Perhaps he has left some elements out of his calculation. Why should *he* hesitate to revenge the injury done him, when some convenient stretching of the truth will do it, who did not hesitate, without any such excuse, to plot against property and life? From conscience he knows that no man can be safer. From detection he hopes to assure himself by speaking in the dark where no one can contradict, and refusing to reveal his evidence until too late to subject it to scrutiny. Should his revenge succeed, Hughes, like another informer of the purest water, may throw the chief responsibility on other shoulders, —" Don't blame me, but those who believed me."

From one point of view I may appear to do Thomas Hughes some wrong. If you take him at his own valuation, never did so upright a witness lift his hand to take the oath of justice. He is not as other witnesses are. Neither hope nor fear can move him. To gain as well as to vengeance he is insensible. He has nothing to desire, to dread, or to regret, for, whether conspiring or betraying, he has done no wrong. The Government, which a cobbler nearly subverted, this hawker has saved. Yet he is so humble that he rejects all recompense; to have done right suffices him. Wealth he despises. He saw the bills offering £500 for information before he informed, but did not quite believe them. That reward he would never accept, however honestly earned. To him, who makes a precarious living by trucking gooseberries through the Saltmarket, who sorely grudged the monthly sixpence of drink-money, £500 is mere vanity and vexation of spirit. Though M'Cann insulted and struck him, this good man never felt one movement of ill-will. "He loved him still the same." He chose to turn the other cheek and bide his time. Truth is on his lips, charity in his heart, duty before his eyes. We seem, when least looking, to have found the ideal for whom philosophers have searched and sighed, about whom poets have delighted to dream, of whom I fear that judges have doubted and theologians have despaired—the just man made perfect! How melancholy to discover that our refined gold is mere common dross! But it is well for the interests of justice that this man has protested too much, and has overacted the part he set himself to play. Once or twice he dropped his mask and enabled us to spy his true features before he could recover it, as when he subscribed for the defence of these prisoners, and up to the moment when his name appeared in the Crown's list of witnesses, persisted in the consummate hypocrisy of offering them aid and sympathy.

It is maintained, however, that if unworthy of belief, he is set up by corroboration. No doubt he has sometimes trespassed into truth. No doubt some things which he states are confirmed. Glasgow Green and Jail Square, M'Ginnes' public-house, are real places, Featherstone and Johnston are real persons. But no false witnesses, from Titus Oates downward, ever were so foolish as to build falsehood on falsehood. They know that it is not the lie direct and entire, but the circumstantial lie that is half a truth, which is difficult to detect. They speak truth where truth equally serves their purpose, or where to speak falsely would be dangerous. Hughes' own graphic words to Ward sum up their method,—" I told the Fiscal all I knew, and all I didn't know." So swindlers pay down honest cash for trifles, in hope to get credit for large orders. But corroboration, to have any effect, must bear directly on the personal guilt of the individual accused. Now, whatever may be the case with some of the other prisoners, not a solitary circumstance, not a single witness corroborates Hughes as against M'Cann.

In saying this, I do not leave out of view the evidence of the two constables, Niven and Porter. Niven, whose beat includes Jail Square, is the more exact. Porter is the more zealous, but a zealous policeman makes a bad witness. They saw the prisoners on the Green and in the Square. But how often? Several times in as many months. But when? In the year before the explosions happened. Niven only observed groups of two or three, and never saw M'Cann along with Featherstone. Porter thinks he saw the prisoners all together, and once noticed some of them reading letters. And he "suspected them." Why? of what? how much? He could not say,—perhaps "in virtue of his office." At all events he took no step. That leads me to think that he looks at August through the spectacles of January, and reflects back into a presentiment the wisdom only gained after the Liverpool trial. If presentiments are evidence, we shall next have ghosts as witnesses! Now, gentlemen, had Featherstone never existed, the accused, like the other Irish, would in the ordinary routine of his life have met his friends in the Square, disputed on the Green, and adjourned their discussions to their favourite public-house. And what does casual meeting with Featherstone matter? You are not likely to be misled by the fallacy which the Lord Advocate's argument, by tracing Featherstone's plans and movements before dealing with the individual accused, was distinctly calculated to suggest. You will not suppose that, because after two prolonged trials, aided by a troop of detectives, a legion of witnesses, and all the resources of science, we now know Featherstone's designs, therefore we can fairly impute to M'Cann any such knowledge when they met in Glasgow streets. Remember that Featherstone introduced himself as a reporter, the character which gives right of access and interview, and opens the doors of palace and hovel; as from America, which was a sure passport to every Irish heart. Then observe this contrast, that with Dalton and Moorhead, the latter the immediate director of the explosions, who kept themselves more secret, who assumed no such ostensible mission, M'Cann is not brought into the slightest connection. Not a visit, not a cab-hire, not a distant glimpse of them, not even a suggestion that he ever heard the names of them.

As this intercourse is made a corner-stone of M'Cann's condemnation, permit me by one example to test its practical value, and illustrate the extreme danger of founding on such a crumbling basis any inference of guilt. Featherstone, as we know, while brewing his plot, stayed at Mitchell's Star Hotel. Suppose that on the first fine Sunday after his arrival, he had said to John Mitchell, as respectable and loyal a citizen as any in Glasgow, "I'm a stranger here, and should like to visit some of the sights. I have come to report on the condition of the lower classes in the city, specially the Irish. Will you take me round where I can meet them?" Assume that Mitchell had been so rash as to walk with that arch-conspirator through Jail Square, crossing the beat of the vigilant Niven. Assume further, that they had wickedly proceeded to mingle in the crowd on the Green, and come within range of the lynx-eyed Porter with his deadly telescope. Suppose also that Mitchell, unconscious how he might be accused of playing an important part in a secret and tremendous State conspiracy, had committed the damning indiscretion of consenting to take a friendly glass at the same table with the truthful Hughes in that very public haunt of horrible treason, M'Ginnes' tap-room. Then I ask you to say, reviewing this boasted proof, whether the "reliable" evidence would not stand as strong and sufficient against John Mitchell as it now stands against Henry M'Cann? Would not the accusing voice of the Lord Advocate press as powerfully for a conviction? Would not John Mitchell run as serious danger of being entangled in this cunning network of appearances? Pardon me! I understate my case. Against Mitchell the argument would be stronger, for with Mitchell Featherstone lived for weeks, among his papers was found Mitchell's address, Mitchell had no occasion to take him to the Green or Jail Square on Sundays and Mondays, while the prisoner and Featherstone only met in public places casually and unfrequently, while the prisoner's active chapel duties, voluntarily undertaken and religiously fulfilled, involved his traversing these places on those days, and explain his presence, if explanation were required. I say the most innocent man in Glasgow, Liverpool, London, or any part of the globe Featherstone ever visited, might be placed in equal peril by argument similar to this makeshift guesswork, which the Crown miscalls proof. Apply to it a second test—the test of logic. Just analyze its elements. Because Featherstone and M'Cann were once or twice seen together in the street, therefore Featherstone may possibly have confided to him his specific criminal designs, therefore he did. Because he did. M'Cann may possibly have approved of them, therefore he did. Because M'Cann approved, he may possibly have agreed to put heart and hand to carry them out. Therefore he did agree; therefore he did abet, or at least some other persons did under Featherstone or Moorhead's direction, therefore he ought to be convicted. If you think such premises lead by plain demonstrative steps to that conclusion, then by all means convict.

I have now, at a length for which I entreat your forgiveness, traversed the case against the prisoner. I have submitted the grounds on which the direct evidence, at the only two points where it touches him, cannot be safely credited, because self-contradictory, contradicted by opposing testimony, and, so far as coming from an informer, leavened with falsehood, and prompted by revenge. Indirect evidence there is none, for his association was not the criminal confederacy libelled, while to the small, secret gang, by whom these crimes were organized and executed, he did not belong. Therefore, with their thoughts, words, acts, or letters he is not concerned. Material evidence against him, such as is pressed so strongly against other prisoners, there is none, and this defect speaks powerfully for his defence. Moral evidence against him there is none, while his position, his industry, the want of any motive for committing these strange, atrocious acts, and his tried character, require, to overcome them, proof of unusual directness and strength. Can it be said that you have here a body of evidence, clear, complete, such as leaves no doubt, and compels unhesitating conviction?

But when was the Lord Advocate without a resource in any extremity or poverty of proof? At one time I thought he intended to seek the means of supplying the defects of his case in the production No. 104. I watched with some little anxiety what use he might make of that church passbook found on M'Cann's table. If he could not decipher conspiracy in words, he had shown his power of twisting it out of letters. I turned its leaves to see if the prisoner had used P. S., N. B., or L. S. D., or like abbreviations. What could N. B. denote but "Nitric Bombs"? What Irishman could write P. S. except as the symbol for "Potash and Sulphuric Acid"? What could be clearer on the face of it than L. S. D.?—who runs may read—"Lignine sent by Dalton"? But no such letters occurred. This book was too clear. It contained only names, addresses, and contributions of the Women's Society of St. Alphonsus. That was the frank and truthful account of it given to the Crown by M'Cann on his examination. In case of any attempt being made to contradict him, I had some of the subscribers here to prove it.

But such argument was too unreasonable, and too easily answered. His lordship had a more strategic shift in reserve. He revived a dangerous doctrine from its long repose with other rusty engines of the old statecraft of more arbitrary times. "A conspiracy is secret, occult, hidden, proof is difficult to obtain, therefore do not expect or require it," else the Crown may lose a verdict. Gentlemen, conspiracy may be secret,—most crimes are. It may be difficult to prove, as it ought to be, especially against one who was not a conspirator. But if this canon is to rule, if you trust to appearances, magnify suspicions, and believe without a reason, if this single excuse of "occultness" is to suffice, if the utterance of the magic phrase "secrecy" is to charm all doubts into silence, then it will never be difficult to convict. Reason may fail, evidence may fall short, but bad precedents for dispensing with both in such accusations can always be found. I am confident you will not let this trial add to the roll of them, already too long. What doctrine can be more perilous to innocent men, or more deadly to the spirit of justice, which wills the safety of the accused not less than the safety of the State? No surer signs have registered the advance of our civilization than the increasing reluctance of juries to declare guilt except on direct proof of actual personal participation, their growing mistrust of suspect or infamous witnesses, and their deepening conviction that in large-hearted justice consist true safety and true strength. Therefore I appeal from this miserable figment of "secrecy" to maxims of esteemed authority, golden rules of jurisprudence, that redeem the errors into which law has too often stumbled, that half compensate for the dangers to which the infirmity of human judgment exposes the wisest tribunals, and have saved from death, or servitude scarcely less terrible, many a victim of malice, suspicion, or mistake. "Construe in favour of the accused whatever is equivocal." "Presume everything for him until proof displaces the presumption." "Convict no man except on proof absolutely incompatible with any conclusion but guilt, for it is better that ninety-nine guilty men should escape, than one innocent man be condemned." These maxims, which prosecutors are so liable to forget, it is the special honour and excellence of a jury to remember and apply. Then, where the crime is constructive, and the circumstances mysterious or conjectural, may I not fairly solicit and anticipate a verdict of acquittal?

Gentlemen, my duty, however imperfectly discharged, is almost ended. The most serious part of your duty will soon begin. The responsibility of an advocate is not small. But infinitely greater is the responsibility of those to whose final judgment the law entrusts the fate of the accused. And the gravity of the charge, the aspect of the times, the effect of the verdict, all combine to invest your functions with unwonted importance. For this trial is not acted in a corner. In our own country, in every part of their native land, and throughout the greater allied countries on the other side of the sea, each step of it is followed with intense interest. Each line of the evidence will be scanned by jealous eyes. Each grain of it will be sifted by the scrutiny of acute, often hostile judgments. Every word of your verdict will be tried in the fiercest fire of criticism, kindled by contending interests and passions. For there are some so blinded by patriotism that they despair of justice to an Irishman from a British tribunal, and seek for something which may justify that unhappy despair. Others, who live, move, and profit by trading on prejudice, and embittering national feuds, would rejoice to have the most slender handle for alleging that any one of the prisoners had been dealt with rather as an alien than a fellow-citizen. They see clearly how the least appearance of inequality, how the slightest sign of straining a point to convict, how the mere suspicion that any of these men had been involved in the crime of others without specific personal proof, would become a lever to move at their will the now quiescent mass of their countrymen. Not the triumph of fifty elections, not the terror of all the conspiracies ever planned, would so well serve their sinister purposes of separation. Defeat on a fair field of battle, however decisive, a nation may forgive, and extend to the victor the hand of cordial alliance. Subjection by a foreign power, however severe, a nation may forget, and both races, ruling and subject, may soon coalesce into one equal, strong, united, and imperial commonwealth—Yorktown and Waterloo, Norman and Saxon, are now no more than names in history. But by an instinctive law which does honour to our nature, the injustice which is swift to convict, while usurping the place and power of justice, is not so forgotten or forgiven. Its fruits are the study of revenge and the hate almost immortal, which reproduce themselves in agitation, disorder, and crime. Need I remind you how the verdicts of 1794, just, perhaps, yet unjustly obtained in this Court against "the friends of liberty," still stir the deepest currents of our own political being? Need I remind you how more than arbitrary rule, more than military oppression, convictions of conspiracy and other state-made crimes against humble men, on strained and tainted evidence, twice roused the people of both nations to overturn the throne, and consummate a revolution? And in what age or country can you find examples of this law so frequent, so instructive, so reproachful, as in distracted Ireland during that reign of terror which followed the desperate rising of '98? Did not the erring zeal of jurymen, alarmed into forgetfulness of impartial reason by their fears for the safety of the Government, yield a fatal belief to the loose surmise of detectives and the perjury of informers swearing lives away for revenge or reward? Have not impartial annalists condemned as judicial murders many of the iniquitous convictions of these dishonoured days? Did not these strike so deep into the soil of the national life,—did they not so burn into the breast of the Irish people, that neither community of interest, which often yokes discordant forces to work together towards mutual good, nor the power of time, which is wont to alleviate such evils as beset our ill-judged efforts to civilize, nor our equity of rule, which razed the monuments of ancient wrong, and made straight executive ways so long made crooked, nor even our recent generosity, which outran justice, in haste to bring atonement for the lamented past with security for a brighter future, have as yet prevailed to close this wide and grievous wound or pluck from the memory of Ireland those rooted sorrows?

These considerations I lay before your judgment, not to suggest that you should "shrink from the duty of determining according to the evidence," but that, availing yourselves of the errors not less than of the wisdom of our ancestors, you may approach that duty in the true spirit of justice, perform it with careful discrimination, and render the safe, humane, and healing verdict which your hearts will never regret, and after-times never reverse.

MR. ORR'S ADDRESS.

May it please your Lordship,—Gentlemen of the Jury, it is now my duty to address you on behalf of James M'Culloch, who stands fifth in this indictment; and when I consider the admirable patience with which you have followed the evidence and the speeches in this protracted trial, I do not need to bespeak a fair and calm consideration for the case which I have now to plead. I do not need to remind you, that for this young man the issues of this trial are of the supremest importance; for into your hands has been committed the disposal of his fate, and upon your judgment at this crisis depends, not what is to befall him during the next few months, or even the next few years, but whether his whole future life is to be one worth living at all, or whether, almost at its threshold, it is to be covered with indelible disgrace. In the light of that solemn consideration let me entreat you to dismiss from your minds every other thought, and, in the spirit of free and impartial justice, to give every weight to the considerations which I may be able to urge on the prisoner's behalf.

Let me say at the outset, that into the voluminous mass of evidence that has been led in this case I do not consider it my duty to enter at any length. I shall confine myself to one or two points in the evidence which in my judgment alone affect the prisoner M'Culloch. With what my learned friends Mr. Rhind and Mr. Kennedy have said on the general aspects of the case, I heartily concur. They have presented the case as regards their clients, first as it stood apart altogether from the evidence of Hughes, and then as it was affected by his evidence. Let me reverse the order, and consider first how Hughes' evidence affects M'Culloch, and then how the case stands apart from that, and I think I shall be able to arrive at the same result, that of innocence in his case, as my friends arrived at in the others.

As to the informer Hughes and his character, I do not intend to speak. He is an abandoned man, and a traitor to his friends; and the evidence of such a man you will receive, in so important a matter, with the utmost caution and reserve. But let me take the case presented against me by the Crown, let me suppose that Hughes is speaking the truth: what is the result? About the 1st of March 1882 Hughes joined what he calls a Ribbon Society in Glasgow, and he states that M'Culloch was sworn in a member of this Society on the 1st of June. Now, even according to Hughes, the society was at the first of a perfectly innocent character. My learned friends who have spoken before me have illustrated this to you already. Let me take a very simple test. You heard Lawrie, the Dublin informer, repeat the oath and describe the methods and operations of the Fenian Brotherhood. By that oath they swore to take up arms, and in pursuance of it they met for drill, they carried arms, they had centres and sub-centres, A's and B's, superior officers and inferior officers,—in short, they went about their organization as if they meant business, and really intended to do what they could to overthrow the Government. Contrast that with the conduct of the members of this society which Hughes and M'Culloch belonged to in Glasgow. The most deadly thing about it that Hughes could mention was that he had to pay 6d. now and again for drink. They met occasionally in a public-house, nothing serious was said, and in point of fact, you have this—that until Featherstone appeared on the scene on the 16th of July, nothing whatever had been done, no business of any kind transacted other than what could be called perfectly innocent. But even with this harmless society what was M'Culloch's connection? Hughes did not speak to M'Culloch's being present at more than one meeting. He joined on the 1st of June, and Hughes never saw him at a single meeting subsequent to that date. He never saw him give any subscription or collection. I take it, therefore, that M'Culloch's connection with this society was of the most vague and shadowy character. Even M'Ginnes the publican, who pointed out several of the other prisoners as men who frequented his house, did not know him, and had never heard his name. Let us take it that Hughes was speaking the truth, that from the 16th of July, when Featherstone appeared on the scene, matters did assume a much more serious complexion,—from the first to the last of the meetings to which he spoke M'Culloch was not present at one of them. I shall mention in detail what these meetings were. There was the meeting on the Green on the 4th or 5th of July, when we first hear of the "two fine gentlemen who had come from America." M'Culloch was not there. There was the meeting in Hughes' stable on Sunday the 9th July, when Johnstone was introduced and experiments were made with the powder by Kearney. M'Culloch was not present then. There was the meeting on 16th July, when a collection was taken up for dynamite purposes, and when Featherstone first appears on the scene. On the same evening there was a meeting in the Gymnastic Hall, when Featherstone expounded the uses of dynamite for "learning the Government a lesson." At neither of these was M'Culloch present.

The LORD JUSTICE-CLERK.—Do you say, Mr. Orr, that M'Culloch was not present on the 16th of July?

Mr. ORR.—No, my lord, he was not present on that day. Then there were subsequent meetings at which they discussed the quantity of dynamite they had made, and spoke of having to remove their operations to a different place, owing to the neighbours complaining of injury to the pipes. At not one of these meetings is it suggested that M'Culloch was present. In short, from the first day of which Hughes speaks of the dynamite meetings being held down to the last, we never hear the name of M'Culloch mentioned as being at any one of them. Now I ask you, as reasonable men, is it conceivable that he could have been so deeply involved as the Crown have suggested, when we find that for the space of three or four months he does not appear even at a single meeting? Had he been deeply involved—had he been involved at all—had he been a member of the dynamite league, or even aware of such a conspiracy, would he have been absent from all these meetings extending over so long a period of time? The inference plainly is that he was not a member of the dynamite league at all, and that he knew nothing of the existence of such a conspiracy as is here alleged. Now mark the result, it is most important as throwing light upon M'Culloch's subsequent conduct. The result is this, that even according to the story of Hughes—who was glib enough in the box, and anxious to gather as many of the prisoners as he could into his net—this man is not a member of this alleged conspiracy, he is not a conspirator with Featherstone, Dalton, and others, as he is charged with being in this indictment.

Now, gentlemen, I come to the second part of the case against M'Culloch. But you will keep in mind that we start with this, that he is not a member of any dynamite league, and is in entire ignorance of the existence of any conspiracy for blowing up buildings or the like. Now, what does he do? Here let me call your attention to a matter in which M'Culloch stands in marked contrast to all the other prisoners. Alone of the ten prisoners, he gives you in his declaration a frank and candid explanation of his connection with this whole matter: nay, he admits more—and he is the only man at the bar who is in that position—than the Crown have been able to prove against him. That is a remarkable fact, and one that tells strongly in his favour. For consider the position a prisoner is in when he makes a declaration. He is in a most trying position. A guilty man will most probably conceal what he knows; but the instinct of an innocent man is to make a full and complete explanation of all he knows, and especially if on the face of matters he appears to be compromised by some foolish or thoughtless conduct, he will hasten to make a clean breast of everything in order that false impressions may be at once removed. That is exactly what M'Culloch did. He does not deny knowing anything about the other prisoners. He frankly admits being acquainted with some of them, who were fellow-countrymen and worked in the same place as himself. He admits getting a sample bottle of vitriol from Michael Buchanan. Then he goes on to say that on three subsequent occasions he procured a carboy of vitriol from Buchanan in the same way. So far he is corroborated by Buchanan. But he goes further. The carboys were placed in the outside yard. None of the Crown witnesses can tell us how or when they were removed. But M'Culloch—going beyond what has been proved—explained quite frankly that on two or three occasions he helped the man " Bill " to remove the vitriol from the yard, and to carry it up the street, where he was told he was not further needed. But he tells us more. He tells us that the man who asked him to get the vitriol was named " Bill," and was a small man, about 5 feet 5 inches, with no beard or whiskers, but about a week's growth of red stubbly hair on his face. The learned Lord Advocate put it that this was one of those fabricated stories with which we are familiar in criminal cases, of a man appearing on the scene whom the prisoner had never seen before nor since, and of whom he knew nothing. Now that explanation might be all very well but for this curious and important fact, that M'Culloch's description of " Bill " is exactly corroborated by Getty the vanman. You will find the witnesses who speak to M'Culloch's case on page 25 of the indictment. They are Nos. 88, 89, and 90. Getty happened to see the third carboy removed, and although he was paying no particular attention at the time, he describes one of the men who took it away as a man about 5 ft. 6 in., with red stubbly hair on his face. That description precisely corresponds; and this fact alone goes very far to set up the prisoner's declaration as an honest and truthful story. But that is not all. Michael Buchanan was an unwilling witness, but Gillick, one of the boys who brought the stuff in the van, believes (though he does not swear to it) that he saw Buchanan himself assisting a strange man to remove one of the carboys from the yard. Now M'Culloch says he himself helped Bill to remove two of the carboys,—he is not sure whether the first and second, or the second and third; but whichever way it was, it exactly fits in with Gillick's evidence that on one of the occasions Buchanan was the man who gave the assistance. I have called your attention, gentlemen, to the open and candid nature of M'Culloch's statement as being in marked contrast to those of the other prisoners. Let me now ask you to observe a second point, in which he stands in equally marked contrast to the others,—I mean his frank and honest conduct. The Lord Advocate made it a point against Featherstone and M'Dermott that when they went to purchase nitric acid, sulphuric acid or glycerine, as the case might be, they acted in a disguised and dishonest manner. Featherstone went to people who knew nothing about him, he assigned a false reason for the use of the acids, and gave a false name and address. M'Dermott did the same. Contrast all that with M'Culloch's conduct. Had he been in the secrets of the conspirators, and wanting sulphuric acid to further the purposes of this conspiracy, he would probably have done the same thing. He would have gone now to one place, now to another; he would have given a false name and stated a false purpose. Instead of that, when he is asked to get the stuff, he goes down the street to his friend Michael Buchanan, whom he has known for years. He went in the most open, even careless manner, and the carboys were put into the yard, which is a thoroughfare, where everybody could see it. He says the man gave him a treat on each occasion for his trouble. Precisely so. M'Culloch was a simple, ignorant, foolish man, probably too fond of a dram, and very likely not indisposed to do a thing of this sort for the sake of a dram. It was a thoughtless and foolish act for himself, but at the time he did not think of the consequences,—only of the reward. It simply comes to this, that he says, "Well, I don't mind obliging you; I'll go down the street to my friend Buchanan and get the stuff for you." The open, careless, thoughtless way in which he went about it is entirely inconsistent with the theory of guilt, but is perfectly consistent with the idea that he did it as an outsider, as an innocent man, knowing nothing about the purpose for which it was to be used. Further, it has not been proved in any way that this man "Bill" was connected with this or any conspiracy, and this is a fatal link awanting in the case of the Crown. But assume that "Bill" was— as I think not improbable—one of Featherstone's emissaries or agents, note how he addresses M'Culloch. "This man," he says, "asked me if I was James M'Culloch. I told him I was; and he asked me if I worked in the Chemical Works. I was working at that time in Tennant's. I said I did, and he asked me if they made vitriol there. I said they did. He said he would require a small sample of vitriol, if he could get it. I said I did not know whether I could get a small quantity. He then said that he understood I could get it either at the works, or from my namesake up the road, referring to a soda-water maker named M'Culloch, in Garngad Road." He addresses him as a stranger to whom he has been sent, and I think I can see how M'Culloch comes to be connected with this matter at all. Kearney, Donnelly, and some of the others knew him, as he himself admits—knew the kind of work in which he was employed—knew of his acquaintance with Michael Buchanan; and thinking he would be a useful tool in procuring what they wanted, they sent "Bill" to him for the purpose. But when he gets the stuff, and helps to carry it up the road, as he explains, there his connection with the matter ends. That is his own account, and certainly the whole of what I may call the real evidence of the case is consistent with that explanation. When he was arrested long afterwards near Newcastle, where he was working at the time, absolutely nothing was found on his person or in his house, either in Newcastle or Glasgow, where his wife was still living,—no trace of material to connect him with this conspiracy in any shape or form, not even one of those innocent newspapers which were found on some of the other prisoners. They found not the slightest vestige of evidence to connect him with Land League, Secret Society, or anything of the kind. In short, he appears once, and once only, in connection with this matter from beginning to end, and that is when a man goes to him and asks him to purchase for him some sulphuric acid. When he has done that he disappears from the scene, and neither before that date nor after it is there any evidence at all that he was connected with this conspiracy. Again I ask you, as reasonable men, whether it is conceivable that he could have been so deeply involved as the Crown allege,—for that is the case against me, that he is one of those deepest in this conspiracy, —when you find that from first to last of it he has absolutely no connection with the matter, except that one circumstance which I have stated and explained. As my learned friends have already done, I ask you to disbelieve the evidence of Hughes; but I say that whether you believe him or not, on the worst possible case that can be made against me, M'Culloch was not connected with this conspiracy at all. As to his possible connection with the actual explosions, I am not going to trouble you with any remarks, because the Crown have not suggested that he was seen at or near the scenes of any of them, or had anything to do with them.

On the case which I have thus presented on behalf of M'Culloch, I am content to appeal to you, as I do with confidence, on the ground of bare justice, and ask you to find that of the charge of being a conspirator with Featherstone, Dalton, and others, he has not been proved to be guilty. Had M'Culloch been a Scotchman—a countryman of your own—I am convinced you would have dealt out to him the most impartial justice; but the fact that he is an Irishman, and that the excesses with which he is charged are connected with that unhappy and distracted land, will, I feel, make you doubly anxious—if that be possible—to see that he suffers no injustice at your hands.

But then, gentlemen, if there be any foundation at all for the view which I have submitted, I think I can go further, and fairly claim your sympathies on the prisoner's behalf. For the view that you will then take of his case will be this,—that this young man, honest, hard-working, respectable, as he appears to be—a young Irishman living in a Scotch town, and thrown much of necessity into the society of his fellow-countrymen—has been, unwittingly on his part, entrapped by some of the evil spirits among them into the furtherance of their dark designs. For that unconscious and innocent assistance—if assistance it was—he has surely paid dearly enough already, when he has been dragged to the bar of this Court. But you will agree that for such a man, innocent in heart and mind, yet compromised by some foolish or thoughtless action, no position can be so painful, none so fitted to call forth your sympathy and commiseration; and you will hasten, as your countrymen in these days are hastening to render what they deem tardy justice to Ireland,—so you will hasten to release an unfortunate fellow-creature from the distressing position to which he has been reduced by the cruel circumstances of his lot.

MR. GUTHRIE'S ADDRESS.

Mr. GUTHRIE then addressed the Jury on behalf of the prisoner Drum, as follows :—Gentlemen of the Jury, the importance of this case has not been exaggerated by my learned friends—its importance for the prisoners at the bar, its importance for the country. But it will not be necessary for me to detain you long, because, as you can well understand, the general considerations which have been already put before you apply equally to the whole of the prisoners at the bar. There are, however, some special matters referring to Patrick Drum's case which must be brought distinctly before you. I need scarcely say that each case must be considered by itself. And what I now ask you to do is to throw aside every prejudice or presumption which may have arisen in your minds from Patrick Drum's association in this indictment with the other prisoners, and to consider the charge against him as if he and he alone sat at that bar. He has been associated with the other prisoners by the Crown in the alleged commission of certain offences. I hope to show you that no such association in point of fact existed. What then, in popular language, are the charges against Patrick Drum? They are two in number—first, that he entered into a conspiracy with others to do certain criminal acts; and second, that he not only conspired and agreed that these things should be done, but that he actually did them, either by himself or by others who were employed by him. As to the second charge, I do not think it is suggested by the Crown that he did any of these things by himself; that suggestion would be too wild in this particular case. Looking to the man himself as you see him at the bar—a man between sixty and seventy, a man of feeble health, infirm in his limbs—it is out of the question to suggest that he himself personally could be concerned in any such undertakings. You have it also distinctly proved, not only by his family, but by neighbours, that he was in his own house on the night of the 20th and the morning of the 21st January. If so, if personal intervention must be put aside, was there any evidence that the acts in question, acts which could only be referred to in tones of the sternest reprobation, were authorized by the prisoner Drum? Was there any reason why he should be held responsible for them? Gentlemen of the Jury, those accustomed to conduct criminal proceedings of this kind can generally have a good idea of the kind of evidence which they will have to meet. But in this case, I am bound to say, we have been all at fault. We came here expecting to see the convicts Featherstone and Dalton in the witness-box, the chief witnesses for the Crown, and we had prepared ourselves to meet them. That was manifestly the intention of the Crown when this indictment was framed. It will not do for the Crown to say that they were brought for identification; they were brought to speak for the Crown, and were put into the list of witnesses for that purpose. The Crown found that they would not speak for them. Why not? These men knew that they had a chance of getting a remission of their sentence were they to favour the Crown. Does that not show that Featherstone and Dalton were utterly unable to connect the prisoner with the crimes charged against him? It comes to this, either that Featherstone and Dalton are acting in a manner entirely opposed to all the motives by which men are generally actuated, that they are men in whose breasts the love of freedom is extinguished, or that the prisoners at the bar are innocent. This is a most startling and unusual feature in the case, and one which seems to me sufficient for its decision. Gentlemen, we have not seen these witnesses in the box, as we fully expected to do. But we have had a mass of other evidence, much of it very interesting from a scientific point of view, although exceedingly remote from the questions at issue. The Lord Advocate put it that there were three kinds of evidence of immense importance in a case of this kind. The first was evidence of any of the prisoners having collected money for the purpose of procuring dynamite; the second was evidence of the purchase by any of them of the materials for making dynamite; and the third was evidence of their presence at any of the explosions. I accept the Lord Advocate's classification, and I ask you to notice what followed in the Lord Advocate's address. He started by including Drum among the active members of the society. He proceeded, as I have already stated, to define the different ways in which the members' activity manifested itself, but he failed to include Drum under any of the heads which he held to imply active participation in the conspiracy. On what then is the Crown's case as to Drum to be supported? It is not to be supported by evidence that Drum, an Irishman in a strange city, was in the habit of associating with his fellow-countrymen in public squares and in public-houses. Mark you, I do not deny that association with the other prisoners, under certain circumstances, would be not only suspicious, but conclusive. But just contrast Drum's behaviour with what Lamie told about the organization to which he belonged,—meetings for drill and for learning the use of the arms with which they were supplied. The whole case against Drum rested on the evidence of Hughes. Now I am not going into any general denunciations of informers. No doubt, they have frequently given true and valuable testimony. But so did persons in the old days under torture. Apart from the inhumanity of the old practice, the objection to both kinds of evidence is very much the same, namely, that the temptation to exaggerate and distort and colour is so tremendous that it is impossible to separate the true from the false. What I ask you to do is, not to disregard Hughes altogether, but only to take him in support and corroboration of an entirely independent case made out on behalf of the Crown. (Mr. Guthrie then took up the points which, according to the Lord Advocate, had been proved against Drum, and argued that every single one of these rested upon the unsupported testimony of Hughes.) Summing up the Lord Advocate's points, the three most important were the scene in the stable, the meetings at the Democratic Hall, and the meetings in Lennox's public-house. In regard to the first, surely the neighbours round about must have been cognizant of the extraordinary proceedings spoken to by Hughes, if any such ever happened. They must at least have seen this large number of men collecting and dispersing. But not a single witness was produced who ever saw or heard anything about it. The same remark applies more strongly to the Democratic Hall. That did not belong to the prisoners. They must have paid money for the use of it; and where was the hall-keeper, to speak of its having been let to them? Don't imagine that the Crown have not tried to find corroboration. Everything that can be accomplished by money and time and talent has been done against these unfortunate prisoners. You may be perfectly sure that where the Crown have failed to produce a witness it has been as in the case of Featherstone and Dalton, and as in the case of the keeper of the Democratic Hall, because he would negative and contradict and disprove their case. Why, again, was Featherstone not shown to M'Ginnes, who spoke to the meetings in Lennox's public-house? Simply because the Crown knew that M'Ginnes would deny ever having seen Featherstone in the prisoners' company in Lennox's public-house. Gentlemen, I have ventured to say to you that Hughes' evidence by itself is not reliable. The Crown now says it is. When did the Crown change its mind? I say it has changed its mind. Observe, Hughes informed the police four or five months before the trial at Liverpool of Featherstone and Dalton. If the evidence of a reliable witness, more valuable evidence against these men than that of Hughes could not have been imagined. The Crown needed all the evidence they could muster, for in some particulars the case at Liverpool was bare enough. Why, then, was not Hughes put into the witness-box at Liverpool? I say to you, and I am entitled to the inference, it was because the Crown did not think him reliable.

The LORD JUSTICE-CLERK.—That may be so; but you would require more proof before you could be certain.

Mr. GUTHRIE.—My Lord, I could not put the Crown authorities into the witness-box on this matter. I had to take the facts as the Crown chose to present them; and my argument is based on their own evidence. The Jury will judge whether my inference is or is not a fair one. It was for the Crown to clear up the matter if it admitted of being cleared up, and they have not done so. Now, gentlemen of the Jury, in conclusion, I do not blame the Crown for having brought this case into Court; you know perfectly well that in Scotland cases are frequently brought forward where, in the public interest, it is desirable that there should be the fullest inquiry—apart altogether from the chance of conviction of the particular prisoners who may be charged with the offence. What I submit to you on behalf of Patrick Drum is that unless you can satisfy yourselves that you have against him evidence reliable in itself, and amply corroborated, you are not entitled to convict him, and I know you will never think of convicting him. You see the peculiarity of this case. You are in this peculiar position, that you are all personally interested in the result of the trial; for you have all the most vital interest to put down such dreadful attempts—fortunately they were not much more—at disturbing public peace and destroying public property, as took place in Glasgow. But I am sure you will not be led away by that. In the indictment you are told that these men are to be punished to deter others from committing the like crimes. That is a consideration which is not for the Jury. It points to a highly desirable result, which would equally follow the conviction of these men, even although they be all innocent. What you have to do is to punish the men who have actually committed the crimes in question. You have simply to say whether the case is proved or not against each or any of these particular men at the bar; and I submit to you on behalf of Patrick Drum, an old, feeble man, worn by humble but honest toil, with everything to lose and nothing to gain by such desperate acts, that the charge against him is one utterly improbable in itself, that it is not supported in one single instance by anything of the nature of real evidence; that if you apply the tests furnished by the Lord Advocate himself the charge utterly fails, and that it would be as much contrary to the plainest instincts of common sense as it would be opposed to a well-known principle of law to convict this prisoner, or indeed any of the prisoners, on the unsupported testimony of an informer. (Applause, which was instantly suppressed.)

FIFTH DAY.—FRIDAY, DECEMBER 21, 1883.

CHARGE TO THE JURY BY THE LORD JUSTICE-CLERK.

Gentlemen of the Jury,—I have, in the first place, to thank you, not only for the attention which you have paid to this very serious case, but for the opportunity which you gave me last night of going over my notes, by so readily acquiescing in the adjournment. Although it was hard to spend another day after our long investigation, you must feel that after hearing the speeches yesterday, and in particular the four most able and instructive speeches consecutively from the counsel for the prisoners, it was as well to bring our minds fresh to the consideration of the result of these four days' investigation, and to the discharge of the duty which now devolves upon me and upon you.

The case itself is one of great moment and great difficulty. Its public aspects you see plainly enough,—I need not enlarge upon them,—and there are private interests of a serious kind. Altogether, I do not think I have ever been engaged in an inquiry which gave me greater anxiety. My first duty is to consider whether there are any questions of law on which I should direct you. As far as the legal aspect of the case is concerned, it will not require me to detain you with any lengthened technical observations. You see by your indictment that it is founded upon the statute 11th and 12th of the Queen, which was passed in the year 1848, technically called the Treason-Felony Act. The main object of that statute was to modify to some extent the law of treason as it then stood; and there was introduced, for this purpose, a certain statutory offence, entitled treason-felony. That statute, which is worded with some technicality of language, sets out various modes of perpetrating the crime which it is the object of the statute to provide for. The first occasion on which that statute came under the consideration of this Court was in the year 1848, in a trial of some celebrity, in which I had some part. It was the trial of the Chartists for words spoken, and acts done contrary to the provisions of that statute.[1] The bearing of the statute was very fully considered and canvassed at the time, and since that there have been cases in England in which it has received a very clear construction. The words are in your indictment, and they bear that "If any person or persons whatsoever, after the passing of this Act, shall, within the United Kingdom or without, compass, imagine, invent, devise, or intend

---

[1] James Cumming and others, High Court, Nov. 7, 1848, in which his lordship appeared as senior counsel for Henry Ranken, one of the panels. See "Reports of Cases in the High Court of Justiciary," by J. Shaw, Advocate. 1848-1852.

to deprive or depose our most gracious lady the Queen, her heirs or successors, from the style, honour, or Royal name of the Imperial Crown of the United Kingdom, or any other of Her Majesty's dominions, or to levy war against Her Majesty, her heirs or successors, within any part of the United Kingdom, in order by force or constraint to compel her or them to change her or their measures or counsels, or in order to put any force or constraint upon or in order to intimidate or overawe both Houses or either House of Parliament, or to move or stir any foreigner or stranger with force to invade the United Kingdom or any other of Her Majesty's dominions or countries under the obeisance of Her Majesty, her heirs or successors; and such compassings, imaginations, inventions, devices, or intentions, or any of them, shall express, utter, or declare, by publishing any printing or writing, or by open and advised speaking, or by any overt act or deed; every person so offending shall be guilty of felony." You observe, at the foot of p. 1 of the indictment, that the things which are struck at by the Act are, to compass or imagine the deprivation or deposition of the Queen, or to levy war against Her Majesty. It has been conclusively ruled, under this statute, that to levy war signifies simply to use—take measures to use—force and violence, to prevent the execution of the law of the land. That is to say, it is the opposition to the authority of the Queen or the Queen's Government by force and violence, which is of the essence of this offence. The definition of the words "levying of war" has been a subject which has been very long and very anxiously considered. I think the definition I have now to give you is sufficient for this case. Resistance to the lawful authority of the Queen and the Queen's Government by force and violence, which indeed is the essence of all civil war, is sufficient to satisfy the expression.

The next question is with regard to the common law charge on p. 7 of the indictment [see p. 3 and p. 7], and it would have required attention, if there had been any difficulty in regard to the statutory charge. The indictment goes on : " Or otherwise, and as alternative to the statutory charge before libelled, you, the said Terence M'Dermott, etc., did wickedly and feloniously conspire to effect an alteration of the laws and constitution of the realm by force and violence, during the period between the month of July 1882 and the month of March 1883, both inclusive, and at or near the places above libelled, or one or more of them, or at some other place or places in or near Glasgow to the prosecutor unknown, the time or times and the place or places being to the prosecutor more particularly unknown, in respect of the secret character and objects of such conspiracy, and more particularly (first) you did"—and then it goes on to allege that the prisoners met and consulted and conspired with each other and with Edmund O'Brien Kennedy, otherwise called Timothy Featherstone, and John Henry O'Connor, otherwise called Henry Dalton, and

John Francis Kearney, "for and concerning the designs and purposes of the said conspiracy, and especially for and concerning the secret purchase or procuring of chemical or other materials to be used in the preparation and manufacture of dynamite, lignin-dynamite, or other explosive substance or substances, and the secret preparation or manufacture of dynamite, lignin-dynamite, or other explosive substance or substances, and for and concerning the clandestine laying or placing and exploding by you, or one or more of you, or by your agents and abettors to the prosecutor unknown, of the said dynamite, lignin-dynamite, or other explosive substance or substances, at or near public buildings, or buildings used for the service of the public, or other buildings or works in or near Glasgow, with the wicked and felonious intent and design of destroying or seriously injuring such buildings or works, and of endangering the lives, persons, and property of the lieges, and with the further wicked and felonious intent and design, by means of such explosions and the terror and alarm to be thereby created in the minds of Her said Majesty and her lieges, to effect an alteration of the laws and constitution of the realm, and more especially of that part thereof called Ireland, by force and violence." These two alternative charges have been found relevant by the judgment of this court on the first day of the trial, the prisoners at the bar having stated no objection to the relevancy. This means that the charge is well laid as regards the crime charged, and that the facts which are specifically alleged, if found proved, are sufficient to sustain a conviction on one or other of these alternative charges.

Having cleared the way so far, I must now make some observations on the facts as they have been proved, and their bearing upon the crime charged in the indictment. You have ten prisoners placed at the bar, and this adds greatly to the gravity and anxiety of this case. You have heard four most able speeches for the prisoners, collectively and individually. The case of each prisoner, of course, is individual and separate, because his liberty is at stake, and it may quite well be that the facts which the public prosecutor has been able to bring out may have a stronger bearing against one or more of the prisoners than against all. All this adds to the labour and the importance of the duty which we have to discharge, though it is quite true, that every member of a conspiracy is responsible for any act which any other member does in pursuance of the objects of the conspiracy of which he is a member. I was asked, however, to say some words on the question of what is an overt act under the statute, and whether a conspiracy is by itself an overt act in terms of the statutory provision. I said I would lay down the law on that subject in terms of a decision in 1868, pronounced by the House of Lords, after consulting the judges of England. [Mulcahy *v.* the Queen, June 29, 30, and July 3, 10, 1868, L. R. 3, Eng.

and Ir. App. p. 306.] The question which was there raised was whether a conspiracy was of itself an overt act under the statute, or whether to constitute an overt act it was necessary that something should be done in order to carry out the conspiracy as a matter of fact, the argument being that mere intention was not sufficient to amount to the crime set out in the statute, unless the intention was carried out into action. Now, in the opinion of the judges, with which the House of Lords unanimously agreed, it is thus laid down:—"A conspiracy consists not merely in the intention of two or more, but in the agreement of two or more to do an unlawful act, or to do a lawful act by unlawful means. So long as such a design rests in intention only, it is not indictable. When two agree to carry it into effect, the very plot is an act in itself, and the act of each of the parties, promise against promise, *actus contra actum*, capable of being enforced if lawful, punishable if for a criminal object or for the use of criminal means." That is the law which I lay down on that matter, that the mere intention to do an unlawful act is not by itself an overt act under the statute, but that when two agree to carry that unlawful object into effect, the very plot is an overt act in itself. I may read to you one sentence in regard to the question of levying war, which brings out very clearly what the foundation of the law in England upon that matter has been. It is a sentence from a well-known work of Mr. Hallam, which is quoted by the judges with entire approbation, and which was also approved of by the House of Lords: "It is as reasonable, therefore, as it is conformable to the usages of every country, to place conspiracies against the sovereign power on the footing of actual rebellion, and to crush those by the penalties of treason who, were the law to wait for their opportunity, might silence or pervert the law itself."[1]

It was said, I think, by the counsel for one of the prisoners, that the indictment did not set out, and the proof did not show what the precise object of the conspiracy libelled here was, because, though it charged the prisoners with a design to overturn the existing Government, it did not say what they proposed to put in its place. I certainly cannot accede to that view. It is quite sufficient that there is here a conspiracy libelled, if it be proved, to overturn or alter the Government of this country by force and violence; but as to what is to be put in its place, it is quite possible that the conspirators have not yet agreed. The essence of the crime is, that there is a combination or conspiracy by force and violence to alter or resist the existing law of the land.

Coming now to the case itself, it presents an aspect of great interest and of considerable novelty in the annals of this court, and raises considerations which go very deep into the social interests of this community. The charge is that this conspiracy

[1] Hallam's "Constitutional History," vol. III. p. 206.

was entered into by the prisoners at the bar, that the object was to resist the lawful authority of the Queen, and that they agreed so to do by acts such as are libelled here. If the question were whether, without any visible or outward action in pursuance of this conspiracy, it was yet in itself an overt act, I should say that if these prisoners were members of a secret society having treasonable objects, and took an oath to be loyal to each other, this would be an agreement of the most solemn kind between the members of that secret association to carry out to each other the purposes for which they were associated, although there were no statement in the rest of the indictment of any further overt act. But we are not obliged to consider the case in so narrow an aspect : for the indictment sets out not merely that the conspirators agreed among themselves, but that they did carry out their conspiracy by overt acts of a very striking and startling kind. I mean to direct your attention shortly to the evidence concerning these three outrages, three attempts to blow up public buildings in the city of Glasgow, by the use of nitro-glycerine or dynamite.

I listened with very great pleasure to the four speeches that were made on behalf of the prisoners. There was only one topic which they touched upon which I thought might have been better omitted, and there was one topic omitted which I thought they might have said a word upon. The prisoners are charged here with having been guilty of these attempts at destroying the public works in question by the use of dynamite. They plead that they are not guilty, that they are innocent ; and that, as I understand, is their sole plea, and a perfectly sufficient plea. We heard something about the wrongs of Ireland, a topic which I was rather surprised to find introduced. There is nothing about the wrongs of Ireland raised under this indictment. This overt act we are considering relates entirely to outrages upon the community of Glasgow. These prisoners say they are not guilty : they are entitled to say, and they do say, as innocent and honest men would say, that they had nothing whatever to do with these outrages ; but how the question of Irish policy can by possibility be brought into such a plea, for my own part I cannot imagine. I do not suppose that the counsel for the prisoners meant to say that if their clients' were guilty of this conspiracy, or were guilty of promoting these explosions, anything connected with public politics in Ireland or elsewhere could form the smallest palliation of so atrocious an offence. I do not think that since I have sat upon the bench I have had to investigate a more abominable and detestable crime. I cannot admit the idea that any one could speak of it, or write of it, except in terms of detestation and abhorrence. No man could palliate such an act on the ground of patriotism or love of liberty, for the act itself is inconsistent with both. I have thought it right to say that, because whatever opinions we may have — and we all have more or less our opinions — upon current policy, I do not think that was a topic which could in any way aid the prisoners at the bar; and I thought it was one which, if carried out to its logical consequence, might tell very strongly in the other direction. I mention it now simply to put aside altogether matters which are truly not involved here, and to ask you to divest your minds entirely of these extrinsic considerations, which, as I have already said, do not appear to me to aid, but, I rather think, injure the case of the ten men at the bar. I should also have liked to have heard from the counsel on the part of the prisoners an expression of the feeling with which every honourable man, every man of humanity, must entertain. For my own part, although a judge's sympathies are not the most important matters with which he has to deal, I have more sympathy with the unfortunate man who, sitting at his own fireside, with his children in bed, was himself with his five children obliged to go to the Infirmary in consequence of the explosion at the gasworks. That was a serious matter, and a matter which, I think, might fairly have been the subject of some sympathetic remark. But while I say that, the very considerations I have now been speaking of render the case of the prisoners a very serious and difficult one. I appreciate their position, and will go on to consider how far the evidence touches them. Doubtless they have the whole power of the Crown arrayed against them. The very secrecy which lies at the root of the allegation against them, tells against them also in the other direction. The Crown had to ferret out the perpetrators of this offence, and it may have been a difficult position for these prisoners to follow the Crown in these intricate and difficult investigations. I do not think, however, that the statement that they were deluded and led on and deceived, is altogether consistent with the plea of innocence which they have urged. I prefer to assume, in the meantime, that what they say to this charge is that it is not true, and that they are absolutely innocent of it. A further topic was insisted on with much greater force, and that was the serious nature of the charge itself and its consequences. You do not need to be told that unless you are quite satisfied of the guilt of each of the prisoners, you cannot and ought not to convict them. I have said some strong words in regard to the crime itself, but the stronger those words were, the more narrowly and scrupulously will you weigh the evidence on which the Lord Advocate asks for your verdict. Every man who is tried here comes here with a presumption of innocence. It is for the public prosecutor to prove him guilty, and the difficulties in the way of the public prosecutor will not diminish his duty in that respect in the slightest degree. Although he alleges a secret crime, he must prove it in broad daylight, as clearly as if the crime were not secret.

Passing from the conspiracy for the present, and leaving over the direct testimony, let us see how far the evidence of surrounding incident aids us in regard to the three alleged overt acts proving the conspiracy and its object. Those three acts form a very remarkable episode in the history of Glasgow. On the night of the 20th and the morning of the 21st of January last three events happened within three hours. At ten o'clock at night an explosion took place in the gaswork at Tradeston on the south side of the Clyde, a work which supplies a large portion of that quarter of Glasgow. The gasometer was blown to pieces. About half-past twelve, on the same night, a party were walking along the Possil Road, a long way from the other place,—I suppose most of you are familiar so far with the localities of Glasgow, as to know that it cannot be much less than two miles between the two places,—and they came to the bridge by which the canal is carried over the road. They found lying on the bridge the tin box which you saw, and which one of the party handled with the result that it exploded and the man was injured. You heard the evidence, and you are quite familiar with the facts. Then at a quarter past one on that morning, in a third quarter of the city of Glasgow, at Townhead, which is at least a mile and a half from the Possil Bridge, a third explosion took place in a disused railway station of the Caledonian Railway. The explosion was exceedingly severe, and knocked the railway station to shivers. It is not said that any injury was done to human life.

Of the perpetrators of these outrages there were no traces obtained for six or seven months afterwards; but there were some matters connected with them from which certain inferences might have been drawn. The first is in regard to the time of these explosions. It may now be reasonable to infer from three such explosions happening within so short a period of each other, that they were the result of a combination,—that is to say, that the same hand which directed one directed all. If they were the result of accident, then that they should all have happened on the same night would be a very singular and improbable coincidence; but if they were designed, I think the necessary conclusion is that they were the result of combination and concert. This conclusion is very much confirmed by the second fact, that the destructive agent was the same in all. Such appeared to be the case at the time, and after this investigation you will now assume it to be the case. The evidence of Colonel Majendie stands entirely uncontradicted and unaffected by anything that has been said in the trial, and so we may take for granted that his conclusions are sound, and that dynamite or nitro-glycerine was the agent in all these three events. He examined the premises immediately after the explosions, and he has embodied his views in a very elaborate report, and this is the result at which he has arrived. In regard to the gas explosion, I do not think it necessary to go through the details of his report. His opinion was clear and explicit. He said that beyond all question the explosion did not come from inside the gaswork, that it came from some force without, and one proof among many which he gave was that a piece of the iron of the gasholder was driven across the gasholder in the inside, and was found sticking in the opposite side. Colonel Majendie's evidence is entirely untouched, and it may be assumed now as all but certain that these outrages were the act of the same persons, whoever they were.

There is a third inference which might be drawn. These were public works. They were works of great importance to the city of Glasgow. Of course the gasholder was a very important piece of property for the owners of the gasworks, the Corporation of Glasgow, to which it belonged, but it was of still greater consequence to the large quarter of Glasgow which was supplied with gas from that tank. I should therefore assume that this was not an act of private malice,—indeed, I do not think that was urged,—but that it had its rise and origin in some feeling relating to public interest. It was no trivial matter for the community to be deprived in a moment of the means of illumination. It was no light matter for the bridge at Possil, the canal being over the road, to be blown down, as it might have been, and was probably intended to be, for in that case Glasgow would have been inundated by the flow of the water from it. The effect of the explosion at the railway might have been a great public inconvenience. From all these things, I do not say one would conclude, but one would suspect that the real origin of these events and the motive which led to them, was not private malice, nor a desire to inflict private injury, but a desire to alarm and terrify the public. Accordingly, the next question the authorities had to inquire into was, Who has done this? who were the people who, from their known views, were likely to have committed, or instigated, or directed these intolerable outrages?

In the circumstances surrounding these events there were still two other elements which might have given a clue to the authors of them. One was this. At the Caledonian Station a man of the name of Kearney had some charge of the works. It came out from the evidence that just at the time of the explosion there, one of the witnesses thought that he saw Kearney give a signal, and the subsequent history of Kearney certainly would strengthen the surmises which his demeanour created. He left the work immediately afterwards. He was found afterward in Hull. He was a great friend of the man Featherstone, of whom you have heard something, and he was also in communication with the man Dalton, of whom you also heard something. He was also, as you will find when I come to another part of the case, an associate of the prisoners at the bar on Glasgow Green, and he was a member of the association of which we have heard so much.

Lastly, on this part of the matter there is a more minute but a very singular fact, which adds to the circumstantial evidence, apart from the parole testimony. There were very few traces left of these explosions, but there were picked up at the gaswork two little bits of brass, one found on the top of the gasometer the day after the explosion, and the other found a couple of days afterwards about three yards from the place [Nos. 4 and 5]. Nobody could make out what these were. Even Colonel Majendie was, at the time they were discovered, at a loss to know what they indicated. At the Possil Bridge, where the explosion took place which injured the artilleryman whom we heard examined, a still more important thing—a brass tube—was found. You saw it. At first Colonel Majendie could make nothing of this brass tube either, excepting that the little brass ring, or cap, was fitted to the end of it. There was a man of the name of Deasey, who was travelling from Dublin to Liverpool, with a box and other things, and I assume in the meantime it was proved, and I think you will agree in that opinion, that Deasey was the agent of the man Featherstone, and that Featherstone had consigned to him certain purchases of sulphuric acid. That Deasey was his agent, I assume. He was apprehended when he arrived at Liverpool, and his box was searched, and in the box were found three other instruments exactly corresponding to that [Nos. 4 and 5],—in the possession of Deasey himself,—and here they are (shows them)—you may have them to look at afterwards when you retire, if you think them important. Now what do these tubes turn out to be? They are implements totally unknown to the scientific or engineering men of this country. Colonel Majendie had never seen one before, neither had Mr. Campbell Brown. But Featherstone was an American, and in the box of his agent implements were found exactly corresponding to the one picked up at Possil Bridge. They are a substitute for the ordinary fuse used in the explosion of dynamite. That is what they are. They work in the way you have heard described, and those two bits of brass which were found at the gaswork were two bits of that instrument. The way in which it was used was this—By wrapping round a part of it a certain amount of paper, through which the acid intended to cause the explosion filtered, according to the number of folds of paper which were put round the instrument, so long was the explosion delayed. In short, they constitute a fuse by which the time of the explosion might be accelerated or protracted, according to the wish of the person using it. Now, gentlemen, you can draw your own conclusions at once. Deasey was the agent of Featherstone. He had these things which no one else had, and this, at once, by a chain of evidence very singular, but very cogent, connects these explosions on the night of the 20th of January 1883 with Deasey, or rather, I should say, with the man whose agent he was—the man Featherstone, whom you saw exhibited at the trial. I have gone over these incidents, which are, after all, only probabilities, stronger or weaker, against the individual prisoners, arising from surrounding fact, apart altogether from the direct evidence which you have had from the witnesses. They raise a very strong presumption, that whatever was the position of Featherstone, he and his associates, whoever they were, were the persons by whom these explosions were planned and executed. I should draw that inference. But of course this presumption remains a good way short of the conclusion which the public prosecutor wishes you to arrive at.

Having laid that foundation, I now go on to inquire, Who was this Featherstone? Was he in Glasgow? What was he doing? Because in his surroundings we find a key to all this mystery. I am now approaching the more delicate and difficult part of this investigation. I express no opinion upon it at all, but will endeavour to bring before you the evidence on which the Crown relies, its strength and its weakness, in regard not only to the prisoners collectively, but in regard to each of the prisoners. It may be that you will come to the conclusion, that whatever the suspicions are, there is no sufficient proof against any of them, or it may be that you may be quite satisfied in your mind of the guilt of some, and not satisfied of the guilt of others, or satisfied of their innocence. Meantime, you should keep your minds entirely free to decide upon that matter for yourselves, and my remarks are not meant to be directed either to one side or the other, but simply to bring before you the evidence as it was laid before you in these four days, and to refresh your memory upon the main points to which the witnesses spoke.

If you are satisfied that Featherstone was connected with these explosions, was there any connection between him and all or any of the prisoners? Having reached this point, that Featherstone, in all probability at least, was connected with these explosions, I now go on to see who his associates were. You have the evidence of the police officer Porter, a very important witness, that he knew all the prisoners at the bar by sight—that they were in the habit of collecting and congregating on Glasgow Green during the year 1882, and he named some of them. He proves that these men used to form a group by themselves on Glasgow Green. That goes for very little, for we all know that Glasgow Green is a resort, and a very fortunate resort, for that large and prosperous and somewhat smoky metropolis of the West, and that many groups go there and discuss many matters on the Saturday afternoon and on the Sunday afternoon, and with the most innocent intentions. There is nothing suspicious in that. It is not necessary to presume an evil intent, or a secret Ribbon Society, because Irishmen meet together, as Scotchmen naturally would, in a foreign land. But Porter says more than that. He says that towards the end of last year, in October, November, and December, his attention was attracted to these groups ; so much so, that after vainly endeavouring to ascertain what it was they were consulting about from one week to another, he took a field-glass in order to see what they were doing. He could only see that they were reading papers. He says that when he passed them they always became silent, and that on the whole matter he was uneasy about them, and did not know what to make of them. And so stands the matter when Featherstone comes upon the field ; and the way in which he came upon the field you have from the witness Hughes, on whose shoulders certainly a great part of the burden of this testimony lies. Some sharp remarks were made against the Crown for not having examined Featherstone and Dalton. They were in the list of witnesses. I do not think there was much to say upon that subject either way. They had been accused and convicted at the Liverpool assizes, and had been sentenced to penal servitude, under an indictment precisely the same as this. The Crown could have called them, and perhaps the curiosity was natural to have heard what these two men had to say, seeing that Featherstone, at all events, knew more about the matter than anybody else. But, on the other hand, there is one view which is manifest,—that if in respect of their evidence a conviction had followed, it might have been said that the evidence of men who were under sentence as convicts had procured it—and thereby it might suggest itself to the Crown officials that the weight and impression of the verdict on this trial, supposing there was to be one, would be lessened. The Crown officers conduct the case of the Crown in the way they think fit, and I am not here to make any observations on the discretion which the Lord Advocate has used. Neither do I say that the fact that the prisoners did not call these men is any reflection upon them. The men were witnesses, and they could have been called by the prisoners beyond doubt, but I do not wonder that they did not call them. I do not believe that any gentleman of the bar acting for prisoners in such a position would have thought of risking the liberties of the accused upon evidence from such a quarter. This matter was entirely in the discretion of the Lord Advocate, whether he thought the ends of justice would or would not be forwarded by calling them. The Lord Advocate has no other object than to further the ends of justice, and perhaps I may without impropriety say that I have heard with great pleasure the moderate, quiet, and dignified tone with which he stated the case for the Crown.

But I am now coming to by far the most important part of this case, viz. the evidence of Hughes, the informer, as he is called. Of course every man who has been more or less participant in a crime charged, and who comes forward in a court of justice to reveal what he knew as an associate of those accused, is open—rightly open—to a great deal of observation; and that observation has not been spared on the part of the accused. I can only participate in what must be the feeling of every man, that the evidence of an informer comes from a quarter not entitled to respect. If a man who has been in that position is against his will put into the witness-box, he must, of course, tell the truth, but few men would wish to be placed in that position, and as regards the evidence of Hughes all I can say is, that the observations which were made were rightly made, and that such evidence is to be received with the greatest caution, if not with suspicion. On the other hand, gentlemen, you are to judge. It is not a matter of law. It is a matter of impression. You heard him and saw him examined, and it is for you to say, taking the whole circumstances together, whether his statement was to your mind truthful or not. It is said he is not corroborated, and that is a matter to which I am now going to speak, and which you will have to consider with the greatest care. If in the general aspect of his evidence he were uncorroborated, it would be difficult to allow it to be the foundation of a conviction; but if in the main he is corroborated, it is not necessary that every minute detail he speaks to should also be spoken to by some other witness. The question which you will have to ask yourselves is, Do you believe him?—Did the aspect of the witness, and his manner of giving his evidence, impress you with its being true, whatever your moral view might be of the man who gave it? In the second place, Do you think in the main that what he said was corroborated by other circumstances in the case? Though I fear you will find it tedious, I must for a few minutes direct your attention to what Hughes says, because probably on the opinion which you form on his evidence will depend to a large extent the result of this case.

Probably the shortest way of reaching the view which I am desirous of illustrating, not merely of showing the general purport of his evidence, but its application to the individual prisoners at the bar, will be shortly to go through the evidence. I shall not read it all in detail, but I shall direct your attention to the more salient points of it. Now Hughes says that he was a member of a society to which the prisoners at the bar also belonged. He says, "They and I belonged to a society. I joined a society about three months before July 1882. The society went under the name of a Ribbon Society. I was asked to join it by Peter Callaghan." And then he goes on to speak of Peter Callaghan as the person who introduced him to the society. He asked what it was like, and Callaghan told him that "the members of the society were to be on friendly terms with all brethren, so if there was anything happened of violence betwixt the Government, or anything of that, we were to take an oath to that effect, so that we would be loyal to our brothers." That is what Hughes says—that if anything of violence happened betwixt the Government, or anything of that, we required to take an oath to that effect that we would be loyal. He is further examined, and he repeats this two or three times over. " Q.—Was anything said about getting into a hobble with the Government? A.—Yes, he said that, and we were to stand by each other if they got into a hobble with the Government." Whether that is enough to prove that these persons belonged to a secret society is another matter, but if it is enough to prove it, then it is clear enough that it was with the Government that they were likely to get into a hobble. It was not a society, to stand by each other not in all circumstances, but in the event of there being a question between the members of the society and the Government. He took an oath, and he says,—"Amongst those whom I knew at that period were Patrick Drum, M'Cabe, Callaghan, Kelly, Casey, and Tom Devany." He says that on the occasion when the oath was administered, in the public-house in the Saltmarket, the prisoners present were Casey, M'Cann, Callaghan, Drum, Devany, and Kelly. He says he held up his hand and repeated the words of the oath, and then he goes on into some detail about money that was given. He speaks to Kearney as being one of them. He says, " Kearney came with Peter Callaghan on the 3rd of July, and said, 'There is some person wanting to see you,' and he went away, and Peter Callaghan and Peter Drum went with him. They went towards the Briggate, and when they came back I made the remark, ' You have been pretty long away,' and they said they were seeing two fine gentlemen who had come from America." Now you observe that is in July ; and, "one night," he says, " I was going across to my own stable, and Peter Callaghan touched me on the shoulder, and said, 'You are the very one I was looking for,'" and what he wanted with him was that he should take some dynamite —vitriol, at any rate—into his stable, and he said he would do it. Then he goes on to say that he did it, and that Patrick Drum, M'Cabe, Casey, Kelly, Kearney, M'Cann, and Callaghan were present, and that one of the gentlemen who had come from America, viz. Johnston, was introduced to him. " They came to my stable, and Kearney took a white powder out of his pocket and spilled some on the floor, and then Johnston took a small bit of stick and poked it into the vitriol, and it made a small puff;" and then he says, " I was told at that time that the gentlemen had come from America for the purpose of learning them"—that is, teaching them —" how to manufacture dynamite. It was the man Johnston who said that first. He was introduced to me on Sunday 9th July, the Sunday before we went into the stable"—and he asked him to give him a hand, and he understood him to mean to manufacture dynamite. Now, the question is, is that corroborated ? It is not corroborated, so far as I see, by any of the persons who are said to have been present. You will consider whether the unquestionable fact of these explosions happening immediately afterwards, along with the fact that straightway after the period referred to by Hughes, not only Featherstone himself, but others of the accused, particularly M'Dermott and M'Culloch, purchased vitriol and glycerine, is or is not a corroboration of the statements here made. He goes on with some details. He says, "I heard the stuff was to be used for blowing up buildings;" and he says that the money which Callaghan got, with the apparently avowed object of supporting some widow, was really to buy stuff to manufacture dynamite, as Featherstone's funds were running out. Then there is a conversation which he gives,—that it would be a very good job to teach the Government a lesson, and all that,—you heard it all, and I do not think it necessary to read it over. That was the kind of conversation which seemed to have gone on. He is introduced to Featherstone, but here is rather a singular passage. He says about Featherstone, "Featherstone was coming about the meetings off and on, for, I daresay, about two or three months. He was there in the months of July, August, and September. It was he who explained what the dynamite was, and he said that by putting some into a tin box and throwing it out of the window of a carriage, wherever it was thrown it would explode and blow up." It is a curious thing that in the pocketbook of Dalton, found on him when he was apprehended in England, to which we were referred, there is a description of a machine of that kind, and a notandum put to it, to the effect that this is the most satisfactory way of setting fire to a building—that if thrown out of a carriage, or thrown in at a window, it will immediately explode. I do not go into details,—they are curious,—but such was the nature of an entry contained in Dalton's pocketbook; and we have this witness—Hughes—describing it exactly as what Featherstone told him. If you believe the following passage, it is very important:—"About two months after Glasgow Fair, Peter Callaghan asked Horan to see if he could get a young man who had neither wife nor family, and no care; so that if any such things as any of these explosions were taking place, he would not leave any trouble behind him." Then you have the quarrel between M'Cann and Hughes, the detail of which you heard, and I have no doubt you have it fresh in your recollection. It is important in this matter, because it brings Porter and Featherstone on the field; for, in the quarrel, M'Cann struck Hughes, and Hughes mentioned to Porter what had happened, and Featherstone came up to Porter and begged him not to make a police case of it, seeing that Hughes was as much to blame as the other—corroboration clearly of the relation that Featherstone had at that time to Hughes, and also to M'Cann. Now we come to a very important matter. Devany is one of the accused, and Hughes says that the day after the explosion Tom

Devany said to him, "'Last night I had a very narrow escape.' I said, 'With what?' He said, 'I threw myself down on the top of the bed to have a sleep, as I was very wearied'"—that is, after the explosion—"'and I heard some one speaking to my wife on the floor. I jumped up, and there I got two detectives talking to her;' and he said, 'If they had made any search I would have blown them into eternity.' I said, 'Why? it would have been very foolish. Had you anything such as that dynamite in the house?' 'Yes,' he said, 'I had; and I had a good case of revolvers.' I said, 'You would be a very foolish man to risk your life for anybody.' He said 'He would have blown them into atoms.' He did not show me the revolvers." Now Devany volunteers an explanation of this in his declaration, and he says he did say those things, but they were a joke—they were said in jest. Hughes says further, "About two months after the Fair, one night in the middle of the week, he came down,"—that is, Johnston, about whom I shall say a few words immediately,—"and Drum, Devany, Callaghan, and the old man, James M'Cabe, were there. I was standing along with them, and he said, 'The neighbours where I am manufacturing the stuff are complaining about the pipes being burned, and we will have to look out for another place, for fear the stuff is got.'" Then he says, "They went to the Townhead. M'Dermott lives up that way. On the occasion when Johnston spoke about the pipes, there were none of the prisoners present except Patrick Drum, Tom Devany, Peter Callaghan, James M'Cabe, and myself. The four others went away along with Johnston, to carry their share of the stuff out of the place." Now, whether that be a true statement of the occurrence or not, you have it proved clearly by witnesses entirely apart from this man, that the pipes were burned. There was another cause suggested which might have produced the same effect, but the corroboration of Hughes, as regards that statement, is that in point of fact, in the lodgings where M'Dermott lived, the pipes were corroded as if by an acid. That this caused public talk, in consequence of which this man Johnston said he must find another place to make the stuff, is, so far, corroboration of what Hughes said. In re-examination Hughes said, "Constable Porter did not speak to me about Featherstone on the night after M'Cann struck me, but afterwards he asked me who the man was that had come and tapped him on the shoulder, and I told him. I said it was Timothy Featherstone, who had come from America for the occasion of manufacturing dynamite." On the conclusion of his evidence, he said in reply to questions from me, "I know all the prisoners. The only ones that were attending the dynamite meetings were Patrick Drum, Devany, and Callaghan. The rest used to meet on the Green, but they never went into the private meetings. There was talk about dynamite in their company, but they appeared not to be sympathizing." Gentlemen, if that evidence is trustworthy, I cannot say to you that it is uncorroborated. It is liable to observation on the first ground I referred to, but I do not think that, in any material fact spoken about by Hughes, he is contradicted, unless it be the alleged conversation with Ward, as to which, no doubt, the two men are at variance. You must judge of it.

But the most important corroboration of Hughes' evidence are the purchases after that date. They were clearly gone over by the Lord Advocate, and no question has been raised about them so far as the facts go. The purchases by Featherstone himself were not questioned on the part of the prisoners. They were made openly, it is said. It is true there was no attempt at concealment, and these carboys of acid were consigned to Deasey, a man who unquestionably had a residence in Dublin under his own name, and was carrying on business there. So far there was nothing suspicious, save the fact of the carboys of vitriol being so consigned. As it turned out, only one of the carboys sent by Messrs. Hope was taken delivery of, and it was taken delivery of by Deasey. The other two were returned. But on that part of the case I think it unnecessary to do more than refer you to the explanation given by the Crown, which was not traversed or denied on the part of the prisoners. The two men at the bar who are said to have purchased material are Terence M'Dermott and James M'Culloch. As to M'Dermott, it is said that he gave a false name and a false purpose to the person from whom he purchased the glycerine. I suppose it can hardly be doubted that he did give a false name, and that there was no man of the name of Bolyn in that district, at least, none known to anybody. But it is some time since. Nearly a year elapsed before any inquiry was made, and no man of that name was to be found by the police. That is a fact which you will take along with you; whether it is conclusive that there was no such man there I do not say. There may have been, but so far as appears, no such person was to be found. The purchase of the vitriol and the glycerine is a very serious matter, and throws a light back upon the evidence which it is impossible to disregard. How came it that these two men were purchasing vitriol and glycerine? For what purpose was it? You have no explanation of any kind, except so far as M'Dermott is concerned; he said that it was for the back of a horse; but if that was the real reason, it admitted of some proof, and there is none. In regard to M'Culloch, the matter stands somewhat differently, and probably I ought, if it does not weary you, in fairness to read the statement which he makes, and indeed volunteers, in his declaration. That he bought the vitriol he does not in the least dispute, but the statement he makes about it—and it is for you to say whether it carries conviction with it—is as follows:—" A man came some time before the New Year to my house. I think it was about a couple of months before the New Year. He gave me his name as Bill afterwards, but not on the occasion I refer to. He also gave me his second name, but he spoke so quick that I did not catch it. He asked me if I was M'Culloch, and then he asked if I was working at the chemical works. I said I did. And then he asked if they made vitriol there, and he said he would require a small sample if he could get it. I said I did not know whether I could get it or not, and he said he understood I could get it, either from the works or from my namesake up the road," referring to a soda-water maker named M'Cullough. And then he does apply to these persons, and they do in the end furnish him with a bottle of vitriol, and that bottle of vitriol this man, whose name he does not know, received. Then he says: "The man called a night or two afterwards. He took the bottle away with him. He came back some time afterwards—I am not sure of the precise time—and said it was not strong enough. Buchanan had told me that if the sample was not strong enough, strong enough could be got. I told the man this, and then he asked me to get a carboy of the strongest vitriol they had. I did go to Buchanan, and asked Buchanan to procure for me a carboy of the strongest vitriol he could get. I gave Buchanan a sovereign, which the man had given me, and I got back from him, I think, about 11s. Buchanan told me that the carboy was left in M'Cullough's yard, and I went along with the man. He emptied the vitriol into two or three jars, which were put into a sack. I carried the sack to about the centre of the street," and there he left the man. Now this might not excite much suspicion, undoubtedly, if it were simply an isolated fact without the surroundings. It is an unfortunate fact for this prisoner. If you believe the statement of Hughes that there were discussions about dynamite at that time among those persons, M'Culloch must have known of it, and that he purchased vitriol afterwards I cannot but think is significant.

That concludes, so far as Hughes is concerned, the substance of his evidence. If Hughes is to be believed, there is no doubt as to the nature of the secret society—none. If you assume that Hughes is speaking the truth, it was simply a Ribbon Society, having for its object matters which might bring the members into collision with the Government, and the oath which was tendered, according to Hughes, was that they should help each other in the event of such a collision taking place. If you think his evidence an entire fiction on the part of Hughes, and that he was speaking from old animosity, or anything of that kind, you can discard it as unworthy of credence. If, on the other hand, you think he is speaking the truth, if, from what you have heard, you are of opinion that in the main the substance of his testimony is correct, then I do not think that any of the observations which have been made will prevent you from giving such effect to it as to your minds may seem just.

There is one point remaining, and that is in regard to the explosions themselves. Are any of these persons individually connected with them, or are there any other circumstances which should tend to bring any of the prisoners into contact with these acts? There are some facts connected with some of the prisoners, at least, that it is my duty to bring under your notice. On the night of the explosion, two of the prisoners were identified by a witness in the box as having been close to the scene of the explosion at or about the time it took place. The witness Lawrie, who was passing along there with his friend Longmuir, at ten minutes to ten, saw a man leaning against the paling close to the gasometer, with his head rather turned away. The little fellow—you saw him—he was about fifteen years of age—was attracted by it, and he looked at the man in the moonlight, and he says that that was Devany. He has no doubt about it. His companion Longmuir, according to their statement, was on the other side, and therefore the boy was between him and Devany, but Lawrie says quite distinctly that Devany was the man, and it is also proved that Longmuir said to his companion that the man seemed to have something on. They stopped, turned, and looked back at him, having been attracted by something in the man's appearance. Then there is the boy Aitken, who some little time afterwards saw two men running out of the lane. One of them, he says, was Devany, and the other, he says, was M'Cann. He pointed out M'Cann in the witness-box. He had said M'Cabe, and it rather appears that he thought the man's name was M'Cabe. He had not known him before. You heard the observations made by counsel about that matter; but evidence of identification is always a matter for the Jury to judge of. So far as Devany is concerned, there does not seem to be any doubt. In regard to M'Cann a good deal was said as to Aitken having identified M'Cabe at the police office, and then identified M'Cann at the bar. Whether that invalidates his testimony about M'Cann you will consider; it is possible the boy had only made a confusion between M'Cann and M'Cabe, and that while he knew the man he mistook his name. The identification of Devany does not end with what I have referred to, because there was a lady, a Miss Smith, who had seen a man rather earlier in the evening, close to the wall of the bridge across the Caledonian Railway branch, and she says that it was Devany. She recognized him, and rather a curious incident happened. Her sister and a detective officer were considering the matter about another of the accused, and this sister was told to go to a window and see a man pass. She did so, but before she spoke the witness Miss Smith came into the room, looked out at the window, and said, "That is not the man my sister saw; that is the man I saw leaning against the bridge." And thus you have the fact of Devany being close to the spot sufficiently proved. The evidence of the boy Aitken as regards M'Cann, coupled with the other matters to which Hughes spoke, indicates that he also was there at the place and locality of the explosion. Then there is the case of Callaghan. Callaghan, according to Hughes' testimony, was a ringleader of this party, and whether he was or was not concerned in this depends mainly on the testimony of Hughes. That he belonged to the ring that met on the Green is quite certain, and if you give any effect to the evidence of Hughes, he belonged to the dynamite inner circle. All that, however, depends on the weight you give to Hughes' testimony. If Hughes is to be believed, Callaghan was at the very head and front of all this. If you do not believe him, I do not recollect any circumstances proved in regard to him which would lead you to the conclusion that Callaghan was engaged in it. Then there is Terence M'Dermott, against whom the case is serious. I have read that passage in regard to the pipes in M'Dermott's lodgings, where it would rather seem that Johnston—whoever he was—said that he was making dynamite, and that he must change his place. I have referred you to the fact that the pipes were corroded, and apparently corroded by acid, though there was another explanation. But M'Dermott bought the glycerine, and bought the glycerine upon a statement that is certainly not proved to be true, and without any evidence whatever that there was a legitimate purpose for the purchase. You will also keep in mind that he accompanied Donnelly, when Donnelly took the cab down to the neighbourhood of the gaswork, and met a man to whom he delivered a parcel, on the Friday of the week before the explosion, and then drove straight back to Ronald Street, where a man named Moorhead lived. You will also keep in mind that apparently he was acquainted with Moorhead, that he had called upon him there, and was seen on the stairs, and that he and Dalton, who had by that time come to Glasgow, were with Moorhead when they all three went away together, saying they were going to London. Then there is the case of M'Culloch, of whom I have already spoken. You will consider it, but I should think that the purchase of vitriol which he made was a very important element in the question whether this man was implicated as Hughes has said. It is a corroboration of the whole indications on that matter, and possibly you may be of opinion that this is sufficient to connect M'Culloch with the whole transaction. In regard to Donnelly, the evidence about him is by no means so distinct, as far as identification is concerned on the scene of the explosion, as that in regard to Devany or M'Cann, but still there is some evidence by Mrs. M'Kersie and her daughter, who both speak to a man whom they saw walking across the railway bridge, and staggering and singing as if he was the worse of liquor, but who when they were past walked perfectly straight, and apparently was not the worse of drink. They both said that Donnelly was very like the man, but they will not swear to him. That, I think, is all the identification in regard to the explosion at the gaswork. There were four men who were seen, and it is for you to say whether that corroborates the account which Hughes gives. Hughes says Donnelly was present, and was one of the party in the stable when the experiment was made with the dynamite materials, and that he got 10s. to buy stuff, and he is also identified by Porter with the others in Jail Square, as one of the party who frequented the place.

With regard to Featherstone himself, of course we have it most amply proved that he was actually in Glasgow, and we have only too strong reason to be certain as to what his objects were. He came to Glasgow in May 1882, and was there off and on till certainly the end of the year. The people he lodged with say so. Hughes says he was there in July, August, September, and October. I think I may assume that in point of fact he was there for the best part of the last eight months of the year 1882. I started by drawing your attention to the fact that there were indications to connect him very closely with these explosions, by the finding of these brass implements at Possil Bridge and at the gasometer, and the evidence which was given to us about Deasey. I assume what the Lord Advocate proved elaborately, that Featherstone sent the vitriol which he purchased in Glasgow to Deasey, that Deasey took delivery as arranged, that he was his agent at the time he travelled to Liverpool, and the things found in his box were truly things belonging to Featherstone. The whole story about Dalton is left in a little doubt. Whether Johnston was Dalton or not is a question which has not been cleared up. I do not know it was necessary that it should be cleared up, as the evidence in regard to Featherstone was so clear. Apparently there is a doubt in the mind of the prosecutor whether that is so or not. If he was not Johnston, then Johnston was a third man of whom we have no clear trace, but Dalton was in Glasgow on the 8th of March 1882, and we know well enough now that he was in communication with Featherstone in regard to this Liverpool offence, for which, in point of fact, he is now suffering penal servitude for life. The story about his acquaintance with the witness Schonmann and their subsequent communications in London, and the apprehension of Dalton under the name of O'Connor, tend in the same direction, and it is not necessary I should detain you by going over them.

I have now said enough upon the evidence in this important case. It is a perplexing case, because it is made up of little bits which must be pieced together, and the question for you is whether, having these pieced together, they establish the charge in the indictment. It is a very important trial in a great many aspects of it—deeply important to the men at the bar, and this you will not forget. You must have evidence against them which satisfies you absolutely of their guilt. On the other hand, there are considerations which may make a distinction between them. Some of the men were directly connected, at least so far as personal presence was concerned, with the scene at least of the first explosion. As to the others, some of them purchased vitriol or purchased glycerine, leaving that without explanation. M'Dermott, again, was certainly in close connection with Dalton, and you will consider whether his purchase of glycerine was an important element against him. As regards the others, Callaghan, I think, is the only one of whom Hughes says he was a ringleader. Patrick Drum was spoken to, but I think the Lord Advocate admitted that except the general evidence of Hughes there was nothing special or specific to connect Drum with the crime. I say the same thing about Casey. As to Donnelly, I have just gone over the evidence applicable to him. He is all but identified by these two women, and if Hughes' evidence is believed, he was one of the principal parties.

With these remarks I have no more to say. I leave the case in your hands with a very deep sense of its importance, but perfectly satisfied that whatever verdict you give in the case of any of the prisoners will be one not only satisfactory to your own minds, but will be substantially in accordance with the evidence.

Mr. KENNEDY.—Will your lordship allow me, on behalf of the prisoner M'Cann, to ask your lordship to refer the Jury to the evidence of the Crown with reference to Inspector Carmichael, who said that the two men whom the witness Aitken identified in the police office in August were not Devany and M'Cann, but Devany and M'Cabe?

THE LORD JUSTICE-CLERK.—I did refer to that, and it is quite right that counsel should refer to it more particularly. Carmichael did say so, but the question still remains whether it was not rather a mistake of the name than of the man. It is for you to consider.

VERDICT.

The Jury returned the following verdict:—" The Jury unanimously find the panel Terence M'Dermott guilty of the statutory charge, as libelled; by a majority find the panels Thomas Devany, Peter Callaghan or Kellochan, Henry M'Cann, and James M'Cullagh or M'Culloch, guilty of the statutory charge as libelled; and by a majority find the panels James Donnelly, James Kelly, Patrick M'Cabe, Patrick Drum, and Denis Casey, guilty of the common law charge as libelled. And in consideration that the Jury are unanimously of opinion that James Donnelly, James Kelly, Patrick M'Cabe, Patrick Drum, and Denis Casey, were not aware of the full extent to which the leaders of the society were carrying them, recommend them to the leniency of the Court."

THE LORD ADVOCATE.—Some of the counsel for the prisoners are desirous the Jury should be asked whether the meaning of the verdict against the second set of prisoners is not rather that the

Jury are of opinion that they were parties to a conspiracy, speaking generally, but without particular knowledge or intention of the purpose,—to blow up the places which are mentioned. It may have an effect upon the sentence.

THE LORD JUSTICE-CLERK (to the Jury).—You find them guilty of conspiracy, and consequently guilty of the explosions which were the result of the conspiracy, but you find that they were not fully aware of the intentions of the leaders. Is that so?

THE FOREMAN OF THE JURY.—Your lordship describes it exactly.

THE LORD ADVOCATE having moved for sentence,

THE LORD JUSTICE-CLERK.—Terence M'Dermott, Thomas Devany, Peter Callaghan, Henry M'Cann, and James M'Cullagh, the Jury have found you guilty under the first charge of this indictment. The duty now devolves upon me—and a very painful one it is—of pronouncing sentence, and there is only one sentence which it is open to me to pronounce under a conviction for the crime charged, and that is, that you be detained in penal servitude for the rest of your natural lives. I greatly regret that you should have brought yourselves into such a position as that in which you now stand, but you must plainly see that the outrages of which the Jury have found you guilty might have terminated in something even more serious than the occurrences that actually took place. In any well-regulated community, such a crime cannot possibly be passed over without the severest sentence, and therefore I announce the sentence of penal servitude which I now have pronounced against you. James Donnelly, James Kelly, Patrick M'Cabe, Patrick Drum, and Denis Casey, I think the Jury have taken a very merciful but a very discriminating view of the circumstances as regards your respective cases. They have found you guilty of the common law charge, and they have added to their verdict a recommendation couched in very strong terms, which the Court are bound to consider with great respect, and which may very fairly modify the sentence which otherwise we might have pronounced. The sentence of the Court is, that you be detained in penal servitude for seven years.

The following is the record of the sentence :—

"The Court sentenced the panels Terence M'Dermott, Thomas Devany, Peter Callaghan or Kellochan, Henry M'Cann, and James M'Cullagh or M'Culloch, to be each kept in penal servitude for the term of his natural life; and sentenced the panels James Donnelly, James Kelly, Patrick M'Cabe, Patrick Drum, and Denis Casey, to penal servitude for seven years each."

www.ingramcontent.com/pod-product-compliance
Lightning Source LLC
Chambersburg PA
CBHW032136230426
43672CB00011B/2354